SALT AND PEPPER SHAKERS

Identification and Price Guide

First Edition

SALT AND PEPPER SHAKERS

Identification and Price Guide

First Edition

GIDEON BOSKER and LENA LENCEK

The **CONFIDENT COLLECTOR** ™

AVON BOOKS ◆ **NEW YORK**

Important Notice: All of the information, including valuations, in this book has been compiled from the most reliable sources, and every effort has been made to eliminate errors and questionable data. Nevertheless, the possibility of error always exists in a work of such scope. The publisher and the author will not be held responsible for losses which may occur in the purchase, sale, or other transaction of property because of information contained herein. Readers who feel they have discovered errors are invited to *write* the author in care of Avon Books so that the errors may be corrected in subsequent editions.

THE CONFIDENT COLLECTOR: SALT AND PEPPER SHAKERS IDENTIFICATION AND PRICE GUIDE (1st edition) is an original publication of Avon Books. This edition has never before appeared in book form.

AVON BOOKS
A division of
The Hearst Corporation
1350 Avenue of the Americas
New York, New York 10019

Copyright © 1994 by Gideon Bosker
Cover photographs courtesy of Gideon Bosker
The Confident Collector and its logo are trademarked properties of Avon Books.
Interior design by Suzanne H. Holt
Inside cover author photo of Lena Lencek by Marv Bondarowicz

Published by arrangement with the author
Library of Congress Catalog Card Number: 93-50201
ISBN: 0-380-76958-1

Library of Congress Cataloging in Publication Data:

Bosker, Gideon.
   The confident collector : salt and pepper shakers : identification
   and price guide / Gideon Bosker and Lena Lencek.
      p.   cm.
1. Salt   and   pepper   shakers—Collectors   and   collecting—United
States—Catalogs.   I. Lencek, Lena.   II. Title.
NK4695.S23B67   1994
730'.075—dc20   93-50201
                                                                           CIP

First Avon Books Trade Printing: July 1994

AVON TRADEMARK REG. U.S. PAT. OFF. AND IN OTHER COUNTRIES, MARCA REGISTRADA, HECHO EN U.S.A.

Printed in the U.S.A.

OPM 10 9 8 7 6 5 4 3 2

to Bianca,
the best little shaker of all!

CONTENTS

SALT AND PEPPER SHAKERS

Identification and Price Guide

First Edition

INTRODUCTION

LET'S SHAKE

I have hundreds of them. And, I confess, on occasion, I even talk to them. They are my saints and my demons, my advisors, and my friends. I think of them as theater in the round packed with an audience that is as quiet as the sound of one grain of salt disappearing into a swirl of mashed potatoes. They fill the walls and every spare nook and cranny in my kitchen. They seem to breed before my very eyes. They are my very own zoo without walls. It's as if I've been invaded by them. I have called them everything from my extended family to my very own private Noah's Ark. They are both my children and they are frozen characters from a silent movie that plays over and over in my imagination.

They are a constant source of fascination. Inexpensive, maniacally colored, endless in their variation, these treasured objects have a capacity for shrinking an intricate web of human activities into a miniature world. More than any other utilitarian novelty designed for the home, their *raison d'être* is best summarized in the phrase "form *ignores* function." By now, you know I am talking about my salt-and-pepper shaker collection.

SHAKE IT UP, BABY!

My love affair with these wildly colored, wacky, whimsical, and wonderful collectibles began with an innocent voyeuristic act about ten years ago. It was a hot summer afternoon in Portland, Oregon. My co-author, Lena Lencek, and I were shooting formal architectural photographs from a rooftop located in a part of town filled with glorious cast-iron buildings from the turn of the century. After finishing the shoot, we made one last diligent sweep of the urban landscape to be sure we hadn't missed any important architectural landmarks. As we surveyed the neighborhood, our eyes came to a screeching halt at a third-floor window across the street. Through the delicate lace curtains, we could make out a wall of shelves packed with several hundred salt-and-pepper shakers.

We'd never seen anything like this before. From a distance, the collection looked like a giant multicolored crystal. We had to see it. So we took note of the building's location, collected our photo gear, and made a beeline for the apartment. We rang the buzzer and within moments, Mattie, a kind, elderly woman, appeared at the door. "We noticed your salt-and-pepper collection from the rooftop across the street," we offered by way of an introduction. "C'mon on in," she said. And the rest—several thousand shakers, one picture book, *Great Shakes*, and this *Confident Collector Guide*, later—is history.

Mattie's small apartment was one seamlessly stitched, wall-to-wall, ceiling-to-floor, salt-and-pepper-shaker emporium. Carefully displayed in thematic groupings that ran the gamut from dinosaurs to spaceships, Mattie's collection covered more square inches in her apartment than did the wallpaper. She picked up a pair of plastic root beer floats and said, "My son gave these to me as a birthday present in 1949, and I've been collecting shakers ever since."

Looking over the hundreds of sets in her collection filled us with the kind of delight and amusement reserved for an art museum or chocolate store. Made of glass, ceramic, chalk, Bakelite®, metal, and porcelain, Mattie's ensemble covered all the bases of contemporary culture—from the Seattle Space Needle to beer bottles and flying saucers. In fact, her collection was so diverse that virtually no aspect of the natural or man-made world was neglected. There were unusual species of tropical fish, jungle birds, people from exotic lands, advertising memorabilia, and cartoon characters galore, all staring at us from walls where shakers were crammed together like sardines.

"Now, let me see," she continued, while highlighting individual sets that brought back memories for her. "I got these ceramic flamingoes in the Everglades in 1968, and I picked up this metal set of

Niagara Falls in 1952 . . . it's very rare. My friend sent me this Canadian Mountie and horse from British Columbia." She knew the vital statistics for every set in her collection. We asked Mattie which pair she used on her kitchen table. "The one over there," she said, pointing to a carton of Morton salt.

The visit with Mattie sparked our obsession with collecting salt-and-peppers. In fact, from that visit on, as Lena and I traveled across America, we made it a point to stop at every flea market, vintage store, collectibles outpost, antique store, and souvenir stand that we thought might yield a shaker that would catch our fancy. Because of our interest in architecture, popular culture, and design, we concentrated on shakers of such architectural landmarks as the World's Fair Trylon and Perisphere, the Empire State Building, the Statue of Liberty, and on a wide range of Art-Deco-inspired shakers made from plastic and Bakelite.®

Eventually, we networked with hundreds of collectors all over the country. We learned of them through word of mouth, through store owners who shared their individual suppliers with us, through newsletters, and friends. Within a year of our visit to Mattie, we had met individuals who boasted collections that were six thousand pairs strong! By this time, every windowsill, bookshelf, and cabinet in our house was overflowing with shakers. We traded shakers the way young kids trade baseball cards. We knew we were hooked. Our residence had turned into a Noah's Ark of pop culture and there seemed to be no end in sight.

The more we collected, the more these shakers got under our skin. This is an experience that virtually all collectors will share. Over time, there was a purely aesthetic quality that drew us to these mysterious objects. We began to admire these wonderful objects for their beauty, for their scale, for the brilliant pigments and hues that adorned their plastic or ceramic skins, and for the way they interpreted, rendered, and represented virtually every dimension of human and animal life. As the shakers began to take on a life of their own, we started organizing our collection around narrative themes—story lines, rituals, and events that make up the dance of life as we know it.

In other words, rather than grouping our shakers according to traditional categories—cows, wedding-cake couples, miniatures, nodders, fish, sports, exotic cultures—we recognized that they could be grouped into ensembles that told a story or recreated scenes from a fictional story or from a time-honored, day-to-day activity. We brought shakers from diverse categories together so they created a cast of characters that would tell theme-oriented stories. To this end, we constructed elaborate dioramas and set up our shakers as if they were actors and actresses in a play. We felt like the Steven Spielbergs of the salt-and-pepper world.

By this time, our love affair with shakers had evolved to the point where, along with photographer Miriam Seger, we were photographically documenting every shaker we saw and had chronicled all the "shaker dioramas" in a studio set up explicitly for this purpose. The result of this romance with shakers was eventually compiled into a picture book called *Great Shakes*, published by Abbeville Press in 1985.

This book helped catapult us to the hub of a salt-and-pepper network that extended from coast to coast. After documenting more than fifty collections and seeing more than fifteen thousand shakers, we thought we'd seen it all. But nothing could be farther from the truth. We learned there is no such thing as a jaded salt-and-pepper-shaker collector. This is a decorative world that's always filled with surprises. To this day, no matter how many shakers we've seen over the years, a set or two always crops up that we've never seen before. Thousands of shakers later, this is still true, and, with the resurgence in making reproductions, we are sure we'll never see our last pair of shakers.

A WHOLE LOT OF SHAKIN' GOIN' ON— STRATEGIES FOR COLLECTING SALT-AND-PEPPER SHAKERS

Acquiring salt-and-pepper shakers is an art in itself. The reason is that unlike many other collectibles, which tend to be distributed through established commercial channels (auctions, stores, dealers, etc.), there are many different ways of amassing a respectable, valuable salt-and-pepper-shaker collection.

It should be stated at the outset that, as collectibles, salt-and-pepper shakers are becoming increasingly valuable. While it may have been possible to purchase a plastic Trylon and Perisphere for around $5 five years ago, today it is well known that such sets are rare and may run as high as $50, depending on where you buy them. It is ironic, in fact, that the price of containers for salt and pepper has outstripped the cost of the seasonings themselves. There was a time when salt was used as a currency and when entire continents depended on the salt trade for their economic well-being. Today, salt and pepper are lack-luster commodities, while the shakers that hold them are becoming increasingly rare and have started to command hefty prices.

Inheriting a Collection

The best way to start a collection is to inherit one. This may sound obvious and farfetched, but it's easier than you think. As mentioned, during the 1940s and 1950s, many American families began collect-ing salt-and-pepper shakers on vacation road trips across the country. People who are now in their seventies and eighties are part of that generation and if you just ask around, you may get lucky and discov-er an aunt, a grandmother, or a cousin who was an avid shaker collec-tor. More often than not, any collection they may have accumulated is no longer on display and has been packed in storage for many years. But that's fine. Chances are that these collections will be in excellent condition and that they will be peppered with valuable, dif-ficult-to-find sets that were readily available forty to fifty years ago. Unfortunately, many collectors who assembled small collections many years ago have given their collections away because they "took up too much space." But it's really worth exploring this angle, because if you find a family member who's kept shakers over the years, and is willing to hand down the collection, you'll be way ahead of the game.

Buying a Collection

Depending on your financial resources, the next best way to start a collection is to take the plunge and and buy a pre-existing collection *en masse*. I've had success with this approach. The usual scenario goes something like this. Talk to your friends who are already avid collec-tors. They may know about someone who has had to move to smaller quarters, or on occasion, even to a retirement center, and who must dispose of the collection for space reasons. The advantage of this approach is that the price will be set according to the number of pairs in the collection, regardless of the quality of the shakers. The usual approach is to offer a fixed price per pair (let's say $2 to $5 per set) and buy the entire collection outright—sometimes, even sight unseen—for a lump sum. If there are three hundred pairs in a collection, you'll find that you might be able to purchase the entire ensemble for $600 to $1,500. Given that the price of most collectible shakers is in the $10 to $25 range, you may be able to pick up a collection worth anywhere from $3,000 to $7,500 for an initial investment of less than $1,000.

Naturally, this approach requires a little bit of luck. First, you've got to find a motivated seller. Ask antique store owners, collectors, and older friends for possible leads. And second, you've got to stumble onto a collection that includes some valuable sets. I expanded my collection a few years ago using this method and I've never been happier. I paid about $2 a set for a collection with 1,400 pairs, and among them were some of the most unusual, delightful, and valuable pieces I'd ever collected.

If you cannot identify an individual who is anxious to part with his collection, you should try talking to local antique dealers and inquire as to whether they have been approached by someone interested in selling an entire shaker collection. These dealers know the local gossip, they keep track of estate sales, and they are more than willing to act as intermediaries for such transactions. As a rule, unless antique/collectible dealers specialize in shakers, they usually are unwilling to risk the outright purchase of a large collection. They simply may not have enough display or storage space at their retail store. However, they may have the contacts. And this is what you're interested in. What is reasonable is for a dealer to broker the sale of a collection at a substantially reduced price, and take a five to fifteen percent commission on the transaction.

Register Yourself

You don't have to be on the road to nuptial bliss to unofficially register yourself as a shaker collector. One of the best ways to collect shakers is to let your friends, family members, and business associates know you are an avid collector. Unlike so many collectibles with princely price tags, shakers can be purchased for as little as a few dollars in almost any city, which makes them ideally suited for gifts. If you have oriented your collection around specific themes—sports, animal kingdom, pigs, advertising premiums—let your friends know this so they can be on the lookout for sets that are of special interest to you. You'll find that your friends will enjoy finding a set that matches your needs and, more often than not, you'll convert many of those individuals purchasing sets for you into bona fide collectors themselves.

Retail Shopping

Without question, the most enjoyable thing about collecting shakers is having the pleasure of choosing, hunting down, or happening upon that special shaker that you've wanted for your collection. That's where shopping retail comes in. Looking for shakers at flea markets, vintage/collectible stores, antique stores, garage sales, Goodwill, and other secondhand stores, offers you the luxury of window shopping, comparing quality, and on occasion, even haggling over price.

Flea Markets

Flea markets and secondhand stores still offer the best values. Although most collections have been picked over by the time they get to these outlets, you still can find very nice sets at reasonable prices if you look hard and long enough. If you don't look carefully, however, you may miss the shakers altogether. Usually, in the setting of flea markets and secondhand stores, the shakers are scattered on tables along with all sorts of other collectibles. So you need a keen eye and plenty of patience to pick up that unusual find. Just stroll through a flea market, scan the shelves and tables, and you'll be rewarded. And it doesn't hurt to ask. Many of the dealers will know of colleagues who specialize in shakers and will refer you to a booth where you'll find more shakers than you know what to do with. Because of the reduced overhead associated with flea market distribution, the prices at these locations tend to be about ten to fifty percent lower than what you can expect at vintage/collectible stores.

Vintage and Collectible Stores

Vintage/collectible stores specializing in shakers tend to offer a wide variety from which to choose, but the prices here also tend to be among the highest you'll encounter. For example, a ceramic set consisting of a horse and rider might fetch $10 at a flea market, $15 at a secondhand store, $20 by mail through the *Salt-and-Pepper Novelty Club Newsletter*, and as much as $35 at an upscale vintage store on Melrose Avenue in Hollywood. Although there are many wonderful vintage/collectible stores specializing in salt-and-pepper shakers— Ruby Montana's in Seattle, The Soap Plant in Los Angeles, Habromania in Portland, Once Upon A Time in San Francisco, and many others—these collectors are skilled at pricing shakers in order to capitalize on prevailing trends in the collectibles market. When icons and images from the Wild West are hot, the shakers will reflect this demand for Western memorabilia, and so it goes for all fashionable trends of the moment.

Although you'll pay strictly retail prices at these stores, you'll have the advantage of picking and choosing among hundreds of highly desirable sets to which you wouldn't otherwise have access. Because you'll probably be collecting shakers oriented around certain themes, you'll find retail shopping an ideal place to pick and choose, mix and match, and selectively add to your collection. If you have the patience to be a discriminating shopper, you'll always find some little gem worth adding to your collection.

Shopping by Mail

One of the most rewarding ways to shop for shakers is to shop through the mail-order options provided by the *Salt and Pepper Novelty Club Newsletter*. If you plan to collect shakers with any degree of seriousness, you must, you absolutely *must* have a subscription to this tell-all, trade-all, share-all, buy-and-sell-all publication. Published quarterly for a subscription price of $20 (which includes a one-year membership in the Salt-and-Pepper Shakers Novelty Club), this fun and folksy publication will instantaneously connect you to America's thousand or so most devoted shaker collectors.

This is the place to shop when you're looking for that off-beat, must-have, quasi-valuable set of shakers that you haven't been able to find anywhere else. Each issue includes black and white photos of shakers being sold by various club members. Entire collections for sale by members and nonmembers are also published as a service to the membership. There is a "Haves" and "Wants" section where free, four-line ads highlight shakers for sale, shakers desired by newsletter readers, and trading options. A membership roster list is published that includes members not only by name, but also indicates their collecting preferences. Members are encouraged to call and correspond with each other in order to trade and/or purchase sets from fellow club members. Salt-and-pepper shakers purchased through the newsletter are priced fairly. And the best news is, if you've paid for something that's not quite what you wanted, merchandise is returnable within five days of the sale.

The newsletter also does an admirable job keeping abreast of the salt-and-pepper collectible market. News feature stories about collectors, trends in shaker collecting, and new resources are often reprinted as a service. Oftentimes, members will share snapshots of themselves alongside their collections and then provide a brief biographical sketch describing how and when their interest in collecting shakers began and an inspirational synopsis of what collecting shakers means to them.

The club also holds an annual convention, which is well publicized in the newsletter. For the salt-and-pepper collector, a trip to this annual convention is a must. This is where collectors who have amassed as many as fourteen thousand pairs travel from all parts of the country to display their wares and sell sets for whatever the market will bear. If you've had a problem finding the set you want, this is the place to unleash your collecting obsession and return with rare and valuable collectibles.

All in all, a subscription to this newsletter is probably the best investment you can make if you've got the salt-and-pepper bug.

SALT-AND-PEPPERS FOR ALL TASTES

This is where the advice stops. If there is one quintessential feature to collecting salt-and-peppers, it's that this hobby-cum-endeavor caters to the pluralistic, democratic, do-your-own-thing—whatever-pleases-you—carve-your-own-niche ethos of collecting. With an estimated forty-five thousand different sets of shakers to choose from, it's impossible for any one person to amass the "complete collection," and it's equally unrealistic to think that any collector will enjoy this pastime by acquiring for quantity's sake alone. Consequently, nearly all collectors survey the shaker landscape and settle upon themes, shaker styles, materials, groupings, or periods on which to concentrate their collecting instincts. There are countless themes from which to choose, and there is enough variety to please even the most eccentric personality.

substances   If you prefer to collect shakers made of one particular thing, you will have the option of choosing among shakers made from celluloid, Bakelite®, plastic, wood, metal (including stainless steel, pewter, silver), glass, Plexiglas, chalk, clay, red clay, bone china, ceramic, leather, magnets, marble, and snowdomes. There are many combinations of these materials, as well as shakers that feature trimming with ribbon, fur, lace, wool, and gold leaf.

size   If size is your thing, you can collect miniatures, which are ideal if you do not have much room for displaying your shakers. Most miniatures are 1 1/2 inches in height or less and are mostly "gowiths," that is, a wedding ring paired with marriage license, album/camera, lamp/bible, thimble/thread. These miniatures, the "Bonsai" of the salt-and-pepper world, are fascinating to collect and many of the finest sets are made by Arcadia Ceramics.

go-withs   Many collectors specialize in go-withs because they explore so many different themes within larger groupings. A go-with is defined as a two-piece shaker set in which the two pieces are totally different from one another, but they do relate, complement, or go-with one another in some way. A lock and key, a football player and helmet, a dog and doghouse, and a state in the shape of Florida and an orange are examples of go-withs.

one-piece sets   One-piece shakers have two chambers, each with its own stopper, and when shaken one way will dispense the salt, and when shaken in the other direction, the pepper. Sometimes you will see S or P printed near the holes. There are countless variations on this theme from accordions and palm-tree islands to nuptial couples and chimpanzees.

huggers   Two shakers, each resting on the ground and hugging each other, are called huggers. They can be different—for example, a donkey hugging a bale of hay, a bear hugging a fish, or they can be two mirror images embracing each other.

squeakers   These shakers are usually made of wood with the majority of the piece housing the squeak and a very small area devoted to salt and pepper. You turn the sets upside down and they say, "Ma-Ma," or something close to that.

movable   These are shakers that move on the ground, such as automobiles, lawn mowers, and bicycles, as well as shakers with movable parts, such as a piano that pops the salt-and-pepper shakers when the keys are pressed.

hangers   Palm trees and other vegetation from which the salt-and-pepper chambers dangle are called hangers. Look for trees with hanging monkeys, fruits, bears, squirrels, and birds. Or you can find elephants with hanging saddle bags and Chinese farmers carrying urns on sticks. Because of their size and complexity, prices are on the high side: $20 to $50 per set.

carriers   A central figure carries salt-and-pepper shakers hooked on the sides. Porters carrying suitcases and cooks carrying milk bottles are popular examples of this category.

swingers   The base shaker is usually U-shaped and the top (swinging) shaker is T-shaped, so when the top is placed on the base, it swings. These are rather pricey, highly desirable, very elaborate, and difficult to find.

nesters   A nester has one piece resting on top of the other, or two pieces resting in a base, but not just on a tray. Nesters include two birds sitting on a branch, two baby kangaroos in their mother's pouch, a bear holding two salmon fish, and countless others.

nodders   This is a highly collectible shaker category and prices can range from $35 to $100. These sets consist of a base with two wells into which a salt-and-pepper-shaker chamber is inserted. The salt-and-pepper chambers have notches and the shakers nod if you give them a little push.

condiment sets   These consist of two shaker chambers and a condiment chamber, usually for mustard, integrated into a thematic grouping.

GREAT SHAKES! WHAT SHOULD YOU COLLECT?

In general, the more complex the shaker set, the more expensive it will be. Nesters, nodders, hangers, and condiment sets are considered top-of-the-line collectibles by most experts. Once you decide whether you want to concentrate on a particular shaker configuration, the next decision you'll have to make is what themes you will want to concentrate on. As far as groupings go, the possibilities are endless, but here's a breakdown that will help bring some of the options into clearer focus.

advertising   Shakers that were used as premium giveaways by major food, beer, and gasoline companies are highly collectible. Light in weight, hospitable to primary colors, and inexpensive to manufacture, plastic was widely used for shakers designed to promote American products from Planter's Peanuts to Lucky Strike Cigarettes. The Fiedler and Fiedler Mold and Die Works of Dayton, OH, manufactured a variety of sets used by such companies as Campbell Soup, General Mills, and R.J. Reynolds. The clearer the product name, the more intact the label—for example, labels on miniature beer bottles and gas pumps—and the less scuffed the plastic is, the more valuable the set will be. Expect many of the better shakers to be sequestered away in private collections, but when you do find sets on the open market, you'll pay $25 and up.

people   This is an expansive category, and includes everything from the well-known Goebel monks to "naughty" sets consisting of topless sunbathers, in which removable breasts have been fashioned into salt-and-pepper-shaker chambers. Building a collection around a "people" theme is not realistic for novice collectors, since the category is so wide open. The better approach is to focus on nationalities, bride-and-groom couples, certain occupations, cowboys, Indians, clowns, babies, Black Americana, and others. Once you've put together a strong group from one of these categories, begin to concentrate on another and build your collection from there.

animals   With thousands of shakers to choose from, the options are staggering. This category can be divided into realistic animals—for example, those that look exactly like the animal they are supposed to be—or comic or dressed animals. Within these larger categories, you can concentrate on cats, pigs, dogs, giraffes, prehistoric animals, birds, fish, forest fauna, frogs, and many other species from the animal kingdom.

food   Name a fruit or vegetable and you can be sure you'll find it as a shaker, from baked potatoes to chocolate sundaes. You can concentrate on natural foods or junk food, on beverages, fish, or fowl.

Fruit heads, in which vegetable or fruit heads sit on human bodies, are especially collectible.

buildings and places   If you're an avid traveler, this category may be for you. There are generic buildings such as windmills, churches, and lighthouses as well as the more prized architectural landmarks—Empire State Building, London Bridge, Hoover Dam.

black americana   This is a highly collectible subject. Racial stereotyping was put to an end in the 1950s. Shakers of Black Americana have not been produced for almost four decades, and because of this, they command premium prices and are extremely difficult to find.

christmas   Options in this category include angels and numerous variations on Santa and Mrs. Claus.

Movers and Shakers—Manufacturers You Should Know

The value of most shakers will vary according to rarity, condition, complexity, and prevailing trends in the collectibles market. Celebrity shakers, Black Americana, advertising salt-and-peppers, and Western motifs are guaranteed to increase in value over time. Collectors should also be aware that there is a brisk market in shaker reproductions. Many vintage shakers have been copied and are now available in gift shops, vintage stores, and card shops across the country. Usually manufactured in the Orient, these shakers command prices in the $25 to $50 range. In general, you're almost always better off with the original collectible shaker set rather than the reproduction, but it's worth keeping in mind that today's reproductions will become tomorrow's collectibles.

Beyond the condition, complexity, trend, and supply-and-demand parameters that affect prices of salt-and-pepper shakers, collectors should know that certain ceramic, die works, and porcelain manufacturers made a name for themselves in the shaker market. Although the vast majority of shakers were made by manufacturers in Japan who can no longer be identified, there are companies for which you should be on the lookout. If the shaker clearly bears the name, logo, or insignia of this manufacturer it will increase the value of your set by about twenty percent.

parksmith company Based in New York, this company designed souvenir snowdomes rigged with chambers that held salt and pepper.

emeloid company This Arlington, NJ, plastic manufacturer designed the slick two-tone plastic shakers of the Trylon and Perisphere for the 1939 World's Fair.

heather house Heather House of Burlington, IA, responded to America's cross-country travel craze with mail-order sales of ceramic shakers consisting of states (the salt shaker) and their respective symbols (the pepper shaker). They were manufactured by Park Craft and available for $1.25 per pair.

national potteries company (NAPCO) Food shakers would be just another bland category if not for the fruit and vegetable people, a deliciously painted family of anthropomorphic shakers with human bodies grafted to stylized fruit and vegetable faces. These sets were designed and manufactured by NAPCO of Cleveland, OH, between 1930 and 1945. These ceramic sets featured a wide range of storybook characters with superb detailing and coloring, including some sets colored with gold-painted lace trim.

lenox china company A premier ceramics manufacturer, Lenox made a wide variety of shakers including the eminently collectible Nipper the Dog, the trademark for the Radio Corporation of America.

burroughs company A Bakelite® manufacturer with many outstanding sets to its credit.

william goebel company Based in Germany and celebrated for its Hummel figurines, William Goebel designed and manufactured animal shakers between 1940 and 1956.

osuga ware A Japanese ceramics maker known for its fine animal bisque pieces manufactured between 1950 and 1952.

ceramic arts studio A Madison, WI, ceramics company that produced hundreds of imaginative animal and Black Americana shakers, both considered among the most collectible shakers.

whapeton pottery company (rosemeade) A North Dakota giant in the shaker making business, this was one of the country's most prolific producers of animal shakers. It gained a reputation for exquisitely painted and delicately crafted salt-and-pepper shakers, many of them glazed with bright pigments faithful to species coloration.

shawnee pottery company Specializing in cookie jars and shakers depicting pigs (a very collectible shaker), this Zanesville, OH, manufacturer made durable and sought-after sets between 1937 and 1961. Adorable humanoid faces, paper labels bearing the company's imprint, and large openings on the bottom of the shakers help identify Shawnee sets, which also feature a distinctive white glossy glaze punctuated by spare detailing in primary colors, usually red, yellow, and blue. Unlike the pigs and cartoon animals made by Shawnee's competitor, the American Pottery Company (A.P.Co.) of Marietta, OH, Shawnee shakers were always painted beneath the glaze, making them especially durable and resistant to chipping. Shawnee shakers trimmed with 22-karat-gold paint are very much in demand.

pearl china company A Cleveland, OH china manufacturer that produced the most imaginative and complete lines of Black salt-and-pepper memorabilia. Many sets featured Black characters who had become symbols for major American food companies— Aunt Jemima for General Mills, Tappan Chefs for Tappan Range, Uncle Rastus for Cream of Wheat, and Luzianne Mammy for the now-defunct Luzianne Coffee Company.

shafford This firm specialized in cats with high-gloss black glazes.

fiedler and fiedler mold and die works This Dayton, OH, company manufactured a number of plastic sets used by such corporate giants as Campbell Soup, R.J. Reynolds, and the Ken-L Ration Pet Food Company. The "F&F Co." logo should be visible on the bottom of the set.

hull china This American company produced a line of fairy tale salt-and-pepper shakers in the late 1930s and early 1940s.

beswick china An English manufacturer who made bone china sets of Laurel and Hardy and Howdy Doody. These sets are rare and fetch premium prices.

edward a. muth & sons, inc. This Buffalo, NY, novelty maker flooded the market with mini-beers representing breweries from more than thirty states. Purchased by breweries and used as premiums or giveaways, the Muth mini-beers all had metal salt-and-pepper caps.

bill's novelty and premium company This Milwaukee, WI, company distributed mini-beers with solid caps.

vallona starr This California manufacturer produced a wide variety of humor-oriented shakers during the 1950s, including a two-piece set available in various colors featuring a Martian piloting a flying saucer.

Shake It Up—How to Display and Care for Your Collection

Seasoned collectors can tell you there is a predictable sequence of events as one evolves from a novice collector to a bona fide, addicted afficionado of salt-and-pepper shakers. In the early stages of collecting, you will acquire a few sets and casually display them on a windowsill, a desk or kitchen counter, or a vanity. Soon the collection begins to grow, insidiously, and almost effortlessly. Usually, you will clear and designate a book or cabinet shelf to store your collection. This works for a while. But as more time passes, you find that these temporary display spaces are quickly being overrun by your shakers and, even worse, because the shelves you've designated are almost invariably deeper than four inches, your shaker collection starts to take on the unruly appearance of an indistinguishable glob of people being crammed together in Times Square on New Year's Eve. In other words, the very reason you started collecting shakers—to display the unique qualities of each set—has been undermined by the crowding techniques pressed into service by your quick-and-dirty display methods.

When things get to this point, it's time to start to take the exhibition aspects of your shaker collection seriously. The devoted collector will tell you there's only one aesthetically acceptable way to exhibit your collection: display thematic groupings of sets, side by side, one shaker set deep, and preferably, display them on glass or Plexiglas shelves with indirect, slant lighting provided by halogen or incandescent spotlights (recessed or track).

Salt-and-pepper shakers are richly colored objects boasting many beautiful glazes reflecting pigments and hues from the entire color spectrum. In this sense, they demand the same approaches used for exhibiting fine art. I prefer to have custom-made Plexiglas shelves. The shelves are about 3½ inches to 4 inches deep and I allow for a 6½ inch height separation between each shelf. This will accommodate about ninety-eight percent of the shakers you will encounter. I use halogen lights (the kind used in stores to make merchandise look more attractive) for illumination in casings that provide "wall-washing" with a wide fan of light. If custom-made glass or Plexiglas shelving is not in your budget, wooden shelves can be constructed very easily. I prefer light-colored or blond woods such as maple, since they tend to provide a neutral background color that helps the shakers pop out. Whenever possible, I still try to use spotlighting to bring out the rich colors of the collection.

When it comes to cleaning your shakers, the "less is more" approach works best. The optimal cleaner is a photographic air-duster used to clean negatives and chromes. Hold the nozzle about six to eight inches away, and you'll get any dust that is still clinging to the shaker. Avoid washing your shakers, except perhaps for one initial cleaning with warm, low-suds soap and water. Thereafter, air-cleaning and light feather dusting is the accepted method for keeping your shakers looking fresh and clean. Never wash chalkware. Plastic shakers can be cleaned initially with any plastic cleaner. Use soft cotton rags to avoid scratching.

SHAKER HEIGHTS—HOW TO USE THIS BOOK

Considering that there are thousands and thousands of figural salt-and-pepper shakers, it would be impossible for any single book to cover every single shaker ever manufactured. It is a truism that no single person has seen every shaker produced. Consequently, any identification and price guide to salt-and-pepper shakers must include the most common, the most collectible, and the most available shakers available on the market today. In this vein, we have drawn upon and surveyed more than one hundred of the country's finest collections—more than thirty-five thousand shakers in all—to produce this guide.

To our knowledge, after examining the available resources and collecting guides devoted to shakers, we are able to conclude that this book provides the most comprehensive listing of shakers ever published. For space reasons, we've been unable to provide a photograph of every shaker mentioned, but the descriptions are detailed enough to permit easy identification.

The book is divided into twenty-three sections (see the Contents). To identify a piece in your collection and to obtain its present market price range, simply turn to the appropriate category (Sports, Fruitheads, On the Road, Miniatures) and scan the section until you find a description of the shaker in your possession or the one you are planning to purchase. Within these sections, thematic groupings are clustered together. For example, in the animal section on Chimpanzees, several different variations on chimpanzee shakers are listed together. If all else fails, simply turn to the alphabetized index and you'll be directed to the pages on which your shakers appear. Photographs of a few hundred shakers have been included as a reference for the more commonly encountered sets. Each has its own caption and pricing.

Pricing is, at best, a soft science. The prices in this book are based on quotations you would expect from retail traders in average-size American cities. They are lower than what you might expect to pay at a vintage/collectibles store in cities like New York, Los Angeles, San Francisco, or Chicago, but slightly higher than values you will find at secondhand stores and flea markets.

Now, good luck. Happy collecting. And remember, variety is the spice of life.

—Gideon Bosker and Lena Lencek

CATS AND DOGS

CATS

Cats and Watering Cans Ceramic. Japan. A pair of yellow and white (salt) and gray and white (pepper) kittens rest their forepaws on white, long-spouted watering cans decorated with a floral motif. $10.00–14.00

Cats in Bows Ceramic. Japan. A matching pair of white, long-lashed cats with brown tails, noses, and ears, look rapturously skyward. Both sport white silk bows around their necks. $8.00–$12.00

Striped Kittens Ceramic. Japan. Early 1910s. A pair of orange, black and white kittens with smiling faces and teardrop eyes. One sits and holds out its paw, the other stands waiting to pounce. $10.00–14.00

Tabby Kittens Ceramic. Japan. Black and white and orange-glazed kittens in red bows in playful kitten "pounce" poses. $12.00–16.00

Siamese Cats Ceramic. Japan. Early 1950s. A pair of butter-cup-yellow Siamese with black tails and markings stretch sinuously as they sit. One is taller. $8.00–12.00

Kitten in Basket Ceramic. Japan. Late 1940s. White, pink, and gray kitten stretches her paws out of a pink ceramic "wicker" basket ornamented with two posies. $20.00–22.00

Flat Cats Ceramic. Japan. Early 1910s. A matching pair of white stretching stylized cats with orange spots, black whiskers, round heads, and curled-back tails. $6.00–10.00

Angora Cats Ceramic. Japan. 1940s. Boy and girl angoras in blue and red collars hold paws. Both are white with orange ears, black and orange spots. $20.00–22.00

Cat Family Ceramic. Japan. 1940s. Orange-glazed mother cat flanked by two orange kittens on a gray base. Mother cat is a sugar bowl. $24.00–30.00

Black Cats Glazed red clay. Shafford. 1950s. Black-glazed matching cats wearing red bows, curled in a sitting position with one outstretched paw. $12.00–16.00

Black Cats Glazed red clay. Shafford. 1950s. Matching black-glazed Siamese cats, sitting on their haunches and stretching up their necks, have red bows and red-tipped ears. $12.00–16.00

Black Cats Glazed red clay. Shafford. 1950s. Matching black-glazed Siamese cats in low-slung, stalking position with tails curled up over backs. $12.00–16.00

Black Cats Glazed red clay. Japan. 1950s. Matching black-glazed Siamese cats sitting on haunches, wearing gold collars have red noses and ears. $12.00–16.00

Black Cats Glazed red clay. Shafford. 1950s. Matching large black-glazed Siamese cats in low-slung, stalking position with tails curled up over backs. Large droopy white eyes and red pointed ears. $20.00–24.00

Black Kittens Glazed red clay. Shafford. 1950s. Matching black Siamese kittens sit like human babies, resting their weight on their hands. Yellow "slit" eyes and red features add touches of color. $22.00–24.00

One-Piece Calico Cats Ceramic. Japan. 1960s. White, yellow, and gray calico cats sit, joined together at the shoulder, and wear red and blue collars. $16.00–22.00

White Kittens Ceramic. Late 1950s–early 1960s. White Siamese-like kittens sit and watch dolefully from round black eyes. They have pink ears, noses, tails, and feet, and lovely gold cross-hatching "spots." $16.00–$22.00

Striped Cat on Shoe Ceramic. Japan. 1940s–early 1950s. Black-and-white-striped cat sits on top of a green shoe with a bee on the laces. $16.00–20.00

Stretching Black Cats Ceramic. Japan. 1950s. Black and gray stylized cats stretch luxuriantly. White whiskers and gray "eyebrows" perk up their round faces. $20.00–24.00

Kitten in Mortarboard on Book Ceramic. Japan. 1960s. A yellow-and-gray-striped kitten wearing a black mortarboard perches atop green book with the words "Salt & Pepper Volume VIII" on its spine. $18.00–24.00

Felix Look-Alike and Umbrella Ceramic. Japan. 1940s. A white and black Felix look-alike pokes its front paws out of a hole in a collapsed white umbrella with red and blue stripe at the edge. $26.00–30.00

Romping Kittens Ceramic. Japan. 1950s. Dark gray kittens in red bows romp in two distinct poses, one crouched low, the other reaching high. $15.00–20.00

Romping Kittens Ceramic. Japan. 1950s. Light gray kittens with pert, upturned tails stand in alert poses. $16.00–18.00

Cat in Tub Ceramic. Japan. Early 1950s. A cat, its head sticking out of the tub, is taking a bath in a white tub. $20.00–24.00

Cat on Pillow Ceramic. Japan. 1940s–1950s. A white cat sits on top of a red pillow with grayish trim. $16.00–18.00

Napping Cat on Pillow Ceramic. Japan. 1950s–early 1960s. A white cat naps on a red pillow. $10.00–15.00

Cat and Book Ceramic. Japan. 1950s. A black-striped cat stands on top of a book. $14.00–16.00

Cat and Fishbowl Ceramic. Late 1950s. A cat is staring at a fishbowl on a base. $22.00–25.00

Cat and Ball of Yarn Ceramic. Early 1960s. A yellow and black cat hugs a ball of blue yarn. $14.00–16.00

Cat and Ball Ceramic. Early 1960s. A black and white cat hugs a yellow ball with a green stripe. $14.00–16.00

Kitten with Yarn Ceramic. Japan. Early 1960s. A fluffy white kitten rests front paws on a ball of pink yarn. $12.00–16.00

Kittens on Pillows Porcelain. 1950s. White romping kittens with curly textured paws and heads romp on white cushions trimmed in gold. $16.00–20.00

Furry Kittens Ceramic and fur. 1960s Cute white kittens with black-tipped tail and ears and huge, long-lashed eyes have tufts of actual fur on head and neck. $16.00–20.00

Yellow Eyed Kittens Ceramic. Japan. 1950s. White, sad-looking kittens have big yellow eyes and blue highlights. $16.00–20.00

Cat in Basket Ceramic. Japan. 1960s. This two-piece set consists of a yellow cat that fits into a blue basket. The cat's back paw hangs out of a side hole. $16.00–20.00

White Polka-Dot Cats Ceramic. Japan. 1950s. Stylized white sitting cats have black paws, polka-dots and ears, green eyes, and huge pink bows. They stand and resemble wine bottles in shape. $15.00–19.00

Gray and Pink Kittens Ceramic. Japan. Late 1940s. Fluffy pink kitten wears yellow bow and posie on head, while gray kitten has pink bow and posie. $16.00–20.00

Calico Cat and Gingham Dog Ceramic. Japan. Late 1940s. Yellow-based "fabric" pets have blue design. The cat is a polka-dotted calico, the dog a checkered gingham. $16.00–20.00

Magnet Cats Painted magnets. 1950s. Stylized black cats with "roll" eyes, gold whiskers, gold collars, and jingle bells have large "S" and "P" emblazoned on their chests. Smaller "P" cat has red eyes and nose. Both are magnets and have gold label reading "Magnetic" affixed to the bottom. $16.00–22.00

Cat with Ball Ceramic. Japan. 1950s. A tan, round cat rests its front paw on a shiny red ball. $16.00–18.00

Sleepy and Alert Kittens Ceramic. Japan. 1940s. Adorable white kittens with black paw prints and pink ears stand on their back paws. One has closed eyes. $20.00–22.00

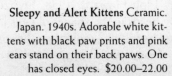

White and Black Siamese in Bows Ceramic. Japan. Late 1950s–early 1960s. Stylized, sitting Siamese cats wear red bows with white dots and have exaggerated eyes. $18.00–22.00

One-Piece Red and Black Ceramic. Japan. 1930s. A fire-engine-red cat is bonded to her black mate at the cheek, chest, and foot. Both have rounded ears, round eyes, and "O"-shaped mouths. $36.00–40.00

Boy and Girl Cat Ceramic. Japan. Coy, butterscotch-yellow cats have pink or blue bows to identify their genders. Boy cat smiles, open-eyed. Girl cat looks demurely away with lowered lashes. $12.00–14.00

Tall NAPCO Cats Ceramic. NAPCO. 1950s. Tall, stylized cats in kingpin shape have rounded heads, green, Siamese eyes, and long collars in a pattern of checks. Salt has blue collar, Pepper has pink collar. both have bluish dots and "S" or "P" on their chests. $14.00–20.00

Abyssinians Bisque. Buff-colored Abyssinian cats with long-lashed eyes have brown-tipped ears, paws, and tails. One stares straight ahead, the other closes its eyes. $16.00–20.00

Holt-Howard Cats Ceramic and metal. Holt-Howard. 1950s. This three-piece set consists of a spring holder for napkins connecting two round stands on wire legs. Into each stand fits a head of a Siamese cat. The female is hatless, the larger male wears a green-and-black plaid cap. $24.00–30.00

Holt-Howard Cats Ceramic. Holt-Howard. 1958. Stylized, round-bodied white cats have heads in the shapes of eggs laid on sideways. Both wear dotted bands, one pink, the other pale blue. Matching cookie jars, creamers, and sugar bowls were available. $12.00–14.00

Cat in Tray Body Ceramic. The head of a pink cat with large, human eyes, "freckles," and smiling lips, fits into a tray shaped like a curled-up feline body with a long black tail.

White Kittens Ceramic. Japan. White, stylized kittens with dour expressions have brown, protruding ears and O-curled tails. $9.00–12.00

Kittens in Boots Ceramic. Japan. 1950s. White kittens with gray paws peek out of black ankle boots with pink lining. $12.00–14.00

Cute Black-and-White Kittens Ceramic. Japan. 1950s. Round-faced kittens with human eyes and pink ears have white faces in black bodies. The one winking sits up on its hind paws. The one with closed eyes smugly curls its tail around its hind quarters. $14.00–16.00

Dotted Siamese Ceramic. Japan. 1950s. Identical, stylized Siamese cats have dotted bodies and neck bows. $12.00–14.00

Teapot Cats Ceramic. Japan. Teapot-shaped cats in brown have round, cartoonish eyes and ears. One has red bow tie, the other, yellow. $10.00–12.00

Teapot Cats Ceramic. Japan. Deeply embossed teapot cats in black and white cross-hatching pattern have realistic feline faces and wear red bows around their necks. $12.00–14.00

White Siamese Ceramic. Japan. Mirror-image white Siamese cats have brown-tipped ears and paws and blue eyes. $10.00–12.00

Cavorting Cats Ceramic. Japan. High-gloss ceramic cats in pale beige with brown overtones are in a playful pose. One piles up its paws as it lies down, the other crouches in a pounce pose. $10.00–12.00

Kittens with Ball Ceramic. Japan. Shiny, tiger-striped kittens sit with curled tails. One plays with a ball. The other sits solemnly. $12.00–14.00

Tiger Kittens Ceramic. Japan. Sitting, identically posed tiger-striped kittens have upturned tails. $10.00–12.00

Cute Kittens with Large Ears Ceramic and plastic wire. White, cute kittens with black-tipped tails and ears have human, baby-doll eyes and plastic wire whiskers. Both crouch, one with lowered, one with raised tail. $10.00–12.00

Playful Kittens Ceramic. Japan. Black and white kittens at play are shown: one on its back, the other sitting and waving its paws. $12.00–14.00

Squeaker Kittens with Whiskers Ceramic, yarn, and plastic wire. White sitting kittens with blue eyes and real plastic wire whiskers hold balls of real yarn in their forepaws. In their bases are hidden squeakers. $12.00–14.00

Flowered Cats on Base Ceramic. Poinsettia Studios, CA. One sitting and one sleeping cat, white with pale blue floral pattern, have a lush overglaze. They sit on an oval rug-detailed tray. $24.00–26.00

Small Gray Kittens Ceramic. Japan. Small gray kittens have white spots and chests, pink ears, and red mouths. One sits, the other lies down. $10.00–12.00

Sleeping Divided Cat Ceramic. Japan. A white sleeping cat with black spots and pink ribbon comes apart into salt and pepper shakers at the middle. $12.00–18.00

Black Kittens Red clay. Black-glazed, red clay kittens are shown grooming themselves. They have white eyes and red bows. $12.00–14.00

Sitting Black Cats Red clay. Shafford. Sitting black cats with red bows have large eyes with painted long eyelashes. $18.00–22.00

Black Cats with Arched Backs Red clay. Small black cats have four legs bunched together into undifferentiated base and sharply upturned tails. They arch their backs and point their red ears. $12.00–16.00

Red-Bowed Shafford Cats Red clay. Shafford. Sitting black cats wear red bows. $12.00–16.00

Black Cats with Tail Handles Red clay. Stylized black kittens with red ears and noses have curled-up tail handles. $10.00–12.00

Calico Cat and Dog Red clay. Simplified black cat and dog with red bows and yellow and white spots cavort. Dog rears up, cat arches its back. $12.00–14.00

Kittens on Piano Keys Ceramic. Japan. White kittens in printed shirts cavort on piano keys. $10.00–12.00

Kittens on Piano Keys Ceramic. Japan. White kittens in pink or blue bows cavort on piano keys. $10.00–12.00

Flowered, Hatted, Bowed Cats Ceramic. Japan. Long, pinkish sitting cats with round heads, black-tipped ears, and very smug expressions wear bright red, oversize bows with white dots and yellow pillbox hats. Their sides are ornamented with flowers and an "S" or a "P" graces their bosoms. $14.00–16.00

Gray Kittens Ceramic. Japan. Realistic gray kittens have pink ears and mewing expressions. One sits, the other stalks. $12.00–14.00

Black Cat with Ball of Yarn Ceramic. Japan. A simplified black cat with green eyes and red circle mouth plays with a large blue ball of yarn. $10.00–12.00

Cats on Telephone Ceramic. Japan. Stylized, cartoonish kittens in butterscotch, with red ears and blue eyes, are shown sitting on 1950s telephones holding the mouthpieces to their ears and deeply involved in their conversation. The open-eyed kitten sits on a phone marked S, the kitten with closed eyes sits on a phone marked with a "P." $12.00–14.00

Pale Yellow Cats Ceramic. Japan. Simplified pale yellow cats have black highlights on paws, ears, eyebrows, eyes, and whiskers. Both sit up. $10.00–12.00

Flowered Bisque Cats Bisque. Matte-finish, stylized cats from the 1950s have exaggerated, pointed eyes, large ears, serpentine tails, and S-shaped bodies. They sit and balance posies on their heads. One set of flowers is white, the other, red. $16.00–20.00

Mother and Daughter Cats Ceramic. Japan. Yellow mother and daughter cats have black eyes, red mouths, and bright red ribbons around their necks. $10.00–12.00

Playing Tiger Cats Ceramic. Japan. Tiger-colored kittens with white bellies either swat at the other or lie back. $12.00–14.00

Cat on Red Cushion Ceramic. Japan. A sleeping, white kitten with pink ears lies on a red cushion edged in black. $10.00–14.00

Stretching Cats Ceramic. Ban Brechner and Co., Inc. Stylized black cats in the shape of a large "S" laid on its side have round heads with white whiskers. $14.00–18.00

Dogs

Dachshunds Ceramic. Japan. Late 1940s. Anatomically correct replicas of dachshunds with black bodies, brown and white bellies. One sits on his haunches, the other struts in a show-dog pose. $16.00–20.00

Divided Dachshund Ceramic. Japan. Late 1940s. Burnt orange, stylized and extremely low-slung dachshund in two pieces with an exaggerated upturned nose, and droopy eyelids. The head holds salt, the tail, pepper. $10.00–18.00

Long Dachshund Ceramic. Japan. Early 1910s. One-piece extremely long-bodied dachshund has a body shading from pale-yellow tummy to black back. The snout is blunt and rounded. $18.00–20.00

Long Dachshund Ceramic. Japan. Late 1940s. One-piece long-bodied dark brown dachshund with only slightly stylized head. $16.00–20.00

Split Dachshund Glazed red clay. Japan. 1940s. Plump, black-glazed dachshund with characteristic anatomical features and perky, upturned tail is divided along the middle into head (salt) and tail (pepper). $16.00–20.00

Split Dachshund Glazed red clay. Japan. Late 1940s. Brown-glazed stylized dachshund has a light brown spot under his S-shaped tail, large oval eyes, and upturned snout topped with a spherical nose. His sagging torso is divided into head (salt) and tail (pepper) sections. $16.00–20.00

Dachshund in Doghouse Ceramic. Japan. Early 1940s. Matching yellow doghouses with slate-blue roofs and pinkish chimneys perforated with salt-and-pepper holes house a dachshund head, curiously peering out of one door, and dachshund behind, disappearing into the other door. $10.00–14.00

Dachshunds Ceramic. Japan. 1950s. Anatomically correct replicas of dachshunds in shiny brown gaze. One squats on its haunches, the other alertly points its nose to sniff the air. $16.00–20.00

Split Dachshund Ceramic. Japan. 1940s. Brown, black, and white dachshund is split down the middle into a head section which delightedly examines the tail section. The dog has round, "Betty Boop" eyes with sweeping eyelashes and bold eyebrows and wears a red, small-brimmed hat and studded collar. The tail is decorated with a pert little red bow. $12.00–16.00

Hot Dog Dachshund Ceramic. Japan. Late 1940s. White stylized dachshund with black ears, eyes, nose, and droopy tail is divided into head (salt) and tail (pepper) sections. His body is made to resemble a white hot-dog bun with a yellow, mustard-slathered center. $18.00–22.00

Puppy in a Basket Ceramic. Japan. Pre-1960s. White puppy with spotted, upturned nose and floppy black ears wriggles out of green wicker basket lined with pink ruffles. One of his paws has ripped through the straw. Two-piece shaker. $12.00–30.00

Beagle Boy Ceramic. Japan. Pre-1960s. White beagle with brown and black ears and spots along the back sits attentively on his haunches as a little boy crouches down next to him in his black pants, green jacket, and yellow cap. The boy holds out his left hand. $20.00–24.00

Boston Terrier in Basket Porcelain. Japan. Pre-1960s. White and black Boston terrier puppy peeks out of green "wicker" basket ornamented with two pink flowers. Two-piece shaker. $20.00–24.00

Dog with Fire Hydrant Ceramic. Japan. Pre-1960s. Yellow dog drops down on his front paws and looks balefully at a yellow and red fire hydrant. $8.00–12.00

Puppy with Slipper Ceramic. Japan. Pre-1960s. This two-piece set features a beige stylized cocker spaniel puppy rolling up his big round, black eyes apprehensively as he stands next to a ravaged slipper (pepper shaker). $12.00–16.00

Sleeping Pekingese Ceramic. Japan. Pre-1960s. Two-piece shaker. White, black-eared Pekingese poses on a red and black cushion. $8.00–12.00

Great Danes Porcelain. Japan. Pre-1960s. "Realistic" russet Great Dane lifts up his head as he wakes up from a nap, while his mate sits up on her haunches with a mournful expression. $20.00–24.00

Bloodhounds Porcelain. Japan. Pre-1960s. "Realistic" white bloodhounds with black and red spots. One sits back on his haunches, while the other trots along, alertly pointing his tail. $16.00–20.00

Border Collies Glazed red clay. Japan. Pre-1960s. Matching pair of "realistic" black-glazed border collies with gold-tipped paws, red ears, and collars. $12.00–16.00

Pugs in Barrels Ceramic. Japan. Pre-1960s. Matching pair of brown pugs with characteristic downturned mouths poke their heads out of black-banded, wood-grained orange barrels. $8.00–12.00

Hugging Canine Couple Ceramic. Japan. 1940s. This two-piece shaker set features a boy puppy dressed in yellow jacket and white trousers, seated on a chair and reaching over front paws to the salt-shaker girl puppy in white, red-dotted dress, sitting primly on her chair. $18.00–24.00

White Poodles Ceramic. Japan. Pre–1960s. Matching pair of stylized white poodles with black polka-dots, pink cheeks, and pink bows pose with tilted heads. $8.00–12.00

Dressed Cocker Spaniels Ceramic. Japan. Late 1950s. Two gray cocker spaniels have adorable red-nosed faces with black, flipped-up ears and colorful caps. Salt has green bow, pepper has red bow. $20.00–24.00

Cocker Spaniel Family on Bike Ceramic. Japan. Pre–1960s. Two pieces. Whimsical cocker spaniel family in matching white with orange markings rides a red motorcycle. "Papa" is in front, of a piece with the black-wheeled motorcycle. "Mama" and "Baby" make up the other piece, and sit in the back. $16.00–20.00

Spotted Dalmatian Heads Ceramic. Rosemeade. 1950s. Two matching heads of Dalmatians are hand-painted with black spots and ears, and yellow eyes. $45.00–50.00

Pluto Ceramic. Japan. Pre–1960s. A pair of Disney Pluto look-alikes play at being waiters. Both are bright orange with black markings, with bright red mouths and scarves, and bat long eyelashes above their round eyes. One sits up holding a spoon in one paw and a fork in the other. The other dog crouches down and balances a red and blue teacup and saucer on his nose. $30.00–36.00

Shih Tzu Pair Ceramic. Japan. Late 1950s. Squat, matching Shih Tzus have gray markings and surly expressions. $16.00–20.00

Spotted Dalmatians Ceramic. Japan. 1960s. One black and white spotted Dalmatian is standing in a "begging" pose, while the other sits on its haunches and reaches out a paw. $16.00–18.00

Droopy Bloodhounds Ceramic. Japan. 1950s. These matching shakers depict white bloodhounds with baleful expressions squatting low to the ground. They have black markings to trace wrinkles. $16.00–24.00

Fox Terriers Ceramic. Japan. 1950s. The white fox terriers sit back on their haunches and hold up their heads alertly. They are white with yellow eye patches and black noses. $16.00–18.00

Sitting Pointers Ceramic. Japan. 1960s. Matching brown-spotted white pointers sit on their haunches and look dolefully out. They have cute faces and yellow paws. $18.00–22.00

Pug with Bone Ceramic. Japan. 1940s–1950s. A brown, fierce-looking pug stands guard next to a long, white bone in this two-piece set. $18.00–24.00

Black and White Scottish Terriers Ceramic. Japan. 1950s–1960s. One white and one black Scottish terrier stand at attention. $16.00–22.00

Floppy-Eared Hounds Ceramic. Japan. 1940s. White, floppy-eared hounds sit on haunches and display red tongues. Their toe nails and ears are detailed in red, their loony eyes outlined in black. $14.00–17.00

Cairn Terriers Ceramic. Japan. 1940s. Cute-faced Cairn terriers in white highlighted with gray are featured in a sitting position, with alert faces. Their tongues are sticking out and tinted pink. $20.00–22.00

Cute Pups Ceramic. Japan. 1940s. Cute, round-headed white pups lie low to the ground and have huge, cartoonlike black-ringed eyes. $18.00–22.00

Beagle Pups Ceramic. Japan. 1950s. Winsome white beagle puppies sit up smartly on their hind legs and roll their big green eyes ringed with black. Both sport collars with heart-shaped name tags, one red, the other black. $18.00–24.00

Great Danes Ceramic. Japan. 1950s. Realistically detailed replicas of adult Great Danes feature one lying down and the other sitting. Brown bodies are highlighted by black feet and snouts. $16.00–20.00

Begging Beagle Pups Ceramic. Japan. 1940s. Cute white beagle pups with cartoon faces and brown and black spots sit up and beg. $16.00–20.00

Yellow Pups in Beanies Ceramic. Japan. 1940s. Yellow puppies in bow ties have large, worried eyes and beanies, one blue and one pink.

Bull Terrier Pups Ceramic. Japan. 1940s. White, grouchy-faced bull terrier pups have brown tails, eyes, and ears. Both are in the classic, resisting-the-tug-of-the-leash position. $14.00–16.00

Toy Poodles in Hairbows Ceramic. Japan. 1940s–1950s. White poodles with black and yellow spots sit with huge, floppy blue bows tied around their heads. In pose and bows these resemble Shawnee Pottery dogs. $19.00–21.00

Pup and Book Ceramic. Japan. 1940s. A gray and white puppy (salt) rests its paws on an open, red-spined book that is trimmed in gold and has the word "Book" on the left cover. $20.00–24.00

White Beagle with Fire Hydrant Ceramic. Japan. 1940s. A white beagle with brown spots sniffs at a white fire hydrant outlined in brown in this two-piece set. $16.00–22.00

White Standing Pugs with Canes Ceramic. Japan. 1940s. Matching white pugs stand on their hind feet saluting with their right paws and clutching a cane with their left. Both wear pale blue bandanas. $22.00–24.00

Golden Labrador Pup in Slipper Ceramic. Japan. 1950s. Two yellow slippers hold, respectively, the back end of a golden Labrador pup (hind paws and tail), and the front end (head and forefeet). $24.00–30.00

Papillon Pups Ceramic. Japan. 1950s. Two Papillon pups in sitting position sport bows, one red, the other green. The red-bowed pup is white with black spots, the green, beige with brown markings. $16.00–20.00

Black Dog and Yellow Hydrant Chalkware. Late 1920s. The matching yellow fire hydrants have red trim and a black dog lifting a leg wrapped around each. $26.00–30.00

Bones Ceramic. Japan. 1950s. Two bones, one shorter than the other, are white with pale brown detailing. $16.00–22.00

Divided Dachshund and Fire Hydrant Ceramic. Japan. 1950s. This three-piece shaker-and-sugar-bowl set features a cute, two-piece dachshund (white and gray with red hat and tail bow) wrapped around a red fire hydrant. $24.00–28.00

Dachshund and Siamese Cat Red clay. 1950s. These long fellows (12") depict a mournful brown and black dachshund and a red-eared, black Siamese cat. $22.00–24.00

Gingham Dog and Calico Cat Ceramic. Japan. 1950s. A brown and green gingham dog is paired with a calico cat in matching colors. $20.00–22.00

Gingham Dog and Calico Cat Ceramic. Japan. 1950s. The yellowish-beige calico cat and gingham dog are marked with periwinkle blue designs and sport bows (red for the cat, blue for the dog). $18.00–24.00

White Dog, Cat, and Tree Ceramic and wood. Japan. 1960s. A comical fat white dog sits on a wooden base staring up at a white cat hanging from the one branch of a radically stylized tree that sprouts from the base. The cat has a cartoon face. $16.00–22.00

Spaniels in Bows Ceramic. Japan. 1940s. Matching spaniels sit with big blue bows tied around their necks. $8.00–12.00

Dog with Picnic Basket Ceramic. Japan. 1940s–1950s. A brown dog carries a picnic basket in his mouth. $21.00–24.00

Dog with Bone Ceramic. Japan. 1950s. A brown, Ken-L-Ration "Fido" look-alike dog is accompanied by his bone. $20.00–22.00

Dog and Doghouse Ceramic. Japan. 1940s. A red-roofed house fits over the long dog shaker of this two-piece set. $24.00–28.00

Dog and Doghouse Ceramic. Japan. 1940s–1950s. Red-roofed doghouse includes the fore section of the dog, whose remaining body forms the second shaker of this two-piece set. $18.00–24.00

Black Dog and Bone Ceramic. Japan. 1950s. A black dog sits, awaiting dinner, and his white bone is alongside him in this two-piece set. $10.00–12.00

Begging Dog and Chair Ceramic. Japan. 1940s. A black dog sits up beside its master's chair, begging. $13.00–15.00

Scottie and Armchair Ceramic. Japan. 1940s–1950s. A Scottie sits in its master's overstuffed armchair. $16.00–20.00

White Poodle and Doghouse Ceramic. Japan. 1940s. A white poodle lies in the doorway of his pinkish-roofed doghouse in this two-piece set. $18.00–24.00

Poodle and Doghouse Ceramic. Japan. 1950s. "Snootie," a black and gray poodle, sits inside his doghouse. $16.00–20.00

Dog and Doghouse Ceramic. Japan. 1940s. A dog lies in the doorway of his white doghouse with brown roof. $12.00–15.00

Weary Dog and Doghouse Ceramic. Japan. 1950s. A weary-looking dog sits in front of his doghouse. $14.00–18.00

Dog in a Basket This two-piece set consists of a basket and a dog who fits into it with his back paw hanging out of a hole in the basket's side. $16.00–20.00

Dog and Pillow Ceramic. Japan. 1940s. A brown and white dog naps on his yellow pillow. $11.00–14.00

Striped Dog and Pillow Ceramic. Japan. 1940s. A white dog with a black stripe lies on his red pillow. $14.00–18.00

Yellow Poodle Carrier Ceramic. Japan. 1940s–early 1950s. Yellow and white sitting poodle has baby poodle twins suspended from each side of her neck. $20.00–24.00

White Poodle Carrier Ceramic. Japan. 1940s–early 1950s. A white, pink-nosed poodle hefts yellow urn-shaped baskets on either side of its back. $20.00–24.00

Black Poodle Carrier Red clay with black glaze. Japan. 1940s–early 1950s. A black-glazed poodle with red detailing has two baskets slung across its back. $16.00–22.00

Man, Dog, and Doghouse Ceramic. Late 1950s. A doghouse has a pair of man's feet sticking out of the door and a separate figurine of Fido looking at him. $26.00–30.00

Bulldog with Baskets Ceramic. 1940s. A yellow-orange bulldog with an orange tie around its neck holds out its paws, from each of which hangs a removable shaker in the shape of a green wicker basket. $12.00–18.00

Gray Hound Dogs Ceramic. Goebel. Crouching, sad-eyed hound dogs are in gray shading into black at their heads. Salt is slightly bigger than pepper. $20.00–28.00

Pekingese on Cushion Ceramic. 1950s. A white Pekingese with black crown and ears sits foul-tempered on a red cushion edged with black. Each component is a shaker. $12.00–14.00

Dog Head in Dog Body Ceramic. A yellow and brown dog's head with floppy ears fits into a curled dog body. $20.00–24.00

Greyhounds Bone china. Beautifully detailed running greyhounds are painted to match in gray with black eyes and noses. $14.00–18.00

Dog Carrying Baskets Ceramic. A white beagle-type dog with orange spots points its snout in the air. Across its back is a "strap" from which hang, on either side, two yellow "wicker" baskets filled with flowers. $10.00–16.00

Friendly Beagles Ceramic. One white beagle with a red bow sits up and begs. The other sits in alert position and shows off its blue collar. Both smile and have one black ear. $12.00–18.00

Dachshunds in Blankets Ceramic. Dark brown dachshunds wear blankets. The larger one has a red blanket trimmed in gold, the smaller one wears a white blanket trimmed in gold. $12.00–18.00

St. Bernards with Barrels Ceramic. Realistically detailed St. Bernards wear barrels around their necks. Barrels are labeled "P" and "S." $15.00–20.00

Sitting Scotties Bisque. Black, realistically detailed Scotties sit up on their haunches and stick out red tongues. $10.00–12.00

Stylized Sitting Hounds Ceramic. Matching glossy black hounds wear red bows and are inscribed, on the chest, with "S" and "P" within a gold diamond. $10.00–12.00

Stylized Poodles Ceramic. 1950s. Curly-textured black poodles with large topknots sit on their haunches and watch attentively with large yellow eyes. $10.00–12.00

Boston Terrier Family Mustard and Shaker Set Ceramic. 1950s. A mother and two-pup family of Boston terriers in black and brown nestle in a yellow "wicker" basket. The mother is the mustard pot, the puppies' heads are the salt-and-pepper shakers. $25.00–30.00

Dog in Blue Bucket Ceramic. A two-part blue bucket comprises the salt-and-pepper shakers. The two parts of the bucket are held together by the head of a perky pup, which is inserted into the wire frame, from which the bucket halves are suspended. $20.00–24.00

One-Piece Deco Dogs Ceramic. Stylized terriers with cylindrical limbs, heads, ears, and tails represent one sitting and one pointing dog attached at mid-body. Salt has holes in the muzzle, pepper has holes in the back of the head. Salt is green and black, pepper is white and orange. $16.00–20.00

Sad Sack Dog in Doghouse Ceramic. A black and white doghouse is ornamented with two signs, "Beware of Dog" and "Sad Sack." Into the door fits a despondent Dalmatian pup. $12.00–18.00

Sad Sack in Basket Ceramic. Sad Sack Dalmatian pup fits into a blue "wicker" basket with yellow liner. The pup's foot protrudes from a hole in the basket. $12.00–16.00

Orange Spaniels Ceramic. 1940s. Bright orange sitting spaniels have black eyes. $10.00–14.00

Orange and Yellow Boxers Ceramic. 1940s. The sitting boxers, one yellow and one orange, have large white eyes with black pupils. $10.00–14.00

Dachshund and Cow Combo Ceramic. A small set of elongated shakers pairs a brown and tan cow with a blue dachshund. $8.00–12.00

Tan Dachshund and Cow Combo Ceramic. Tan, gold, and black dachshund is teamed with a similarly colored cow with curving horns. This pair is very long. $12.00–14.00

Scotties with Tail Handles Ceramic. 1940s. Stylized white Scotties have red ears and collars. White tail handles sprout from their backs and arch to the backs of their collars. $10.00–14.00

Butterscotch Pups Ceramic. 1940s. Adorable soft-looking yellow puppies with flipped ears strike cute puppy poses. $12.00–14.00

Divided Dachshund Ceramic. 1950s. White elongated, stylized dachshund has brown spots and nose and splits down the middle into salt (front) and pepper (back) shakers. $12.00–14.00

English Bulldogs Bone china. Realistically crafted English bulldogs sit in matching poses and glower. Their large ears point straight up. $14.00–18.00

Cartoonish Basset Hounds Plastic. 1960s. Bright orange basset hounds with oversize heads have blue eyes and red tongues. Their various folds and wrinkles are deeply grooved in the plastic. $10.00–12.00

Bulldogs Ceramic. Beautifully detailed, realistic bulldogs in sitting poses are painted in white and deep brown. $10.00–12.00

Dog Family on Motorcycle Ceramic. This three-piece shaker set consists of a spaniel father and a spaniel mother and child that fit into a red and black motorcycle. The dogs are white with yellow trim. $14.00–18.00

Metal Scotties Metal. 1930s. Heavy metal Scotties date from the Deco era. $30.00–40.00

Yale Bulldog Ceramic. The huge head of a white bulldog fits into the small, prone body. Bulldog wears tam on head and is painted in shades of gray on white. $15.00–28.00

Smiling Spaniels Ceramic. Realistically detailed matching spaniels smile and are painted in shades of tan, brown, and gray. $10.00–12.00

White Poodle on Blue Cushion Ceramic. Sarsparilla. 1983. White poodle with black eyes perches gracefully on a blue pillow with black trim. $10.00–12.00

"Choosie" in Doghouse Ceramic. A yellow hound with brown drooping ears squats inside a detachable doghouse with blue "shake" roof. The signs "Choosie" and "Beware of Dog" are attached to the house. $20.00–30.00

Poodle in Bucket and Kitten in Watering Can Ceramic. A gray and white poodle peeks out of a green and white bucket, while a white and black kitten peeks out of a blue and white watering can. $20.00–25.00

"Dreamie" in Doghouse Ceramic. A brown and black beagle squats inside a detachable doghouse with brown "shake" roof and two signs, "Dreamie" and "Beware of Dog." $20.00–30.00

Dachshunds Wrapped Around Stumps Chalkware. 1920s. Yellow shakers depict dachshunds curled around tree stump sniffing their own tails. One has blue bow and writing, the other has brown bow and writing. Wrapped around the top of the stump is the slogan "There's a new dog in town." $10.00–15.00

English Bulldogs Ceramic. Beautifully detailed, realistic English bulldogs are painted in shades of brown, black, and tan. $18.00–30.00

Boston Bull Terriers Ceramic. Black and white Boston bull terriers are depicted in running and in sitting positions. These are realistically detailed. $10.00–16.00

Boston Bull Terriers Being Bad Ceramic. A naughty pair of Boston bull terrier pups in characteristic black and white coloring are caught in the act of chewing a slipper (salt) and mauling a paper-wrapped sausage (pepper). $10.00–16.00

Dachshund-and-Bone Vinegar and Oil Cruet and Shaker Set Ceramic. This complicated set is made up of four parts, cleverly made into various components of the elongated, stylized dachshund holding a bone. The vinegar is contained in the nose part of the dog, with the vinegar stopper in the shape of the dog's red nose. The oil component is housed in the tail end, with the black stopper as the dog's tail. The shakers are a one-piece bone marked

"S" and "P" that hangs from the dog's nose. A black handle is attached to the midsection of the hound. $20.00–30.00

Stylized Yellow Poodles Ceramic. Yellow girl poodles with green bead collars sit up and beg. They have pink kissy lips, long-lashed eyes, and yellow pompom hairdos. $15.00–28.00

"Weary" in Doghouse Ceramic. A gray poodle sits happily inside a detachable doghouse with green "shake" roof and two signs, "Weary" and "Beware of Dog." $20.00–30.00

"Grouchy" in Doghouse Ceramic. A disgruntled-looking dog sits inside a detachable doghouse with green "shake" roof and two signs, "Grouchy" and "Beware of Dog." $20.00–30.00

"Shootie" in Doghouse Ceramic. A hunting hound sits inside a detachable doghouse with rust-colored "shake" roof and two signs, "Shootie" and "Beware of Dog."

Stylized Cat and Dog Ceramic. Japan. 1940s–1950s. White figurines of a stylized sitting cat and a stylized sitting hound are highlighted with orange spots and feet. $10.00–14.00

Stylized Cat and Dog Ceramic. Japan. 1940s–1960s. Stylized white kitten and puppy in sitting position wear blue bows at a rakish angle and have brown dots. $10.00–14.00

Dog in Doghouse Ceramic. Japan. 1940s–1960s. Crouching tan dog with pointed ears fits into a yellow doghouse with an orange roof and a blue framed window. $15.00–20.00

Pastel Pekingese Ceramic. Japan. 1940s–1960s. A pink Pekingese sits atop a white cushion with blue stripes and black trim. A pale blue Pekingese rests on a white cushion with red stripes and trim. $12.00–18.00

Poodle and Kitten in Baskets Porcelain. Japan. 1940s–1960s. A white poodle with gold ears and pink nose and paws peeks out of a white basket that overflows with flowers. The white kitten sits in an identical yellow-tinted basket. $12.00–18.00

Musical Dogs Ceramic. Japan. 1940s. A howling beagle sits atop a miniature grand piano, while another beagle looks confused as he pokes his head through the loop of a French horn. $12.00–18.00

Hound Nester Ceramic. 1940s. A white, slack-jawed hound's head sits atop a sitting canine body with brown spots. $14.00–18.00

Black Lab Pup with Basket Glazed red clay. American. 1950s. An alert black Lab pup holds a detachable "wicker" basket in his open red mouth. The glaze is deep dark brown. $24.00–36.00

Pup in Bucket Nester Ceramic. Japan. 1950s. A gray and white Scottie pup with a pink bow around his neck is inserted into a brown bucket with blue trim. $16.00–22.00

Despondent Dog in Doghouse Ceramic. 1950s. A beige floppy dog lies low in the door of a detachable doghouse with a yellow finish, green roof, and blue trim. $18.00–26.00

White Dog in Doghouse Porcelain. 1950s. A white Dalmatian pup squats at the entrance to his white doghouse with yellow shake roof. The doghouse has a projecting lip at the door on which the pup sits. $20.00–24.00

Yorkie with Hydrant Ceramic. Japan. 1950s. A fluffy Yorkshire terrier sits up in a begging position. His companion piece is a red fire hydrant with a smiling face painted in the midsection. $15.00–20.00

Beagle Raising Leg on Hydrant Ceramic. 1950s. A white stylized beagle with brown markings raises back leg on a white fire hydrant with brown trim. $16.00–20.00

Stylized Hound with Hydrant Ceramic. 1950s. Japan. A brown, long-eared hound squats low on its forelegs next to a black and red fire hydrant from the arms of which a silver chain is suspended. $15.00–24.00

Sitting Bulldogs Ceramic. Japan. 1950s. White matching sitting bulldogs have gray heads and gray and ochre markings. $10.00–14.00

Sitting Setters Ceramic. Japan. 1950s. Realistically detailed golden setters have golden-brown bodies with white noses and underbellies. Both have cheerful, smiling expressions on their faces. $14.00–18.00

Sitting Gray English Setters Ceramic. Japan. 1960s. Shiny gray English setters with black ears have black noses and stylized faces that include finely arched eyebrows. Salt sits up to beg, Pepper plants all four paws squarely on the ground. $12.00–15.00

Cocker Spaniels Ceramic. Japan. 1950s. Realistically crafted cocker spaniels have white bodies and orange eye spots and ears. Pepper sits, Salt stands in alert pose. $14.00–18.00

Spaniels in Green Holder Ceramic. Japan. 1950s. White spaniels in begging poses sit on either side of a green "bush" planted into a green base textured to resemble turf. This is a three-piece set. $20.00–25.00

Black and White Spaniels Ceramic. Japan. 1950s. Cute, cartoonish black and white spaniels have black freckles on their white noses and sit on their back paws. $10.00–14.00

Black and Gold Dachshunds Ceramic. Japan. 1950s. Shiny black dachshunds, realistically detailed, peer curiously from their sitting position. Gold highlights are found on their ears, eyebrows, paws, and tails. $12.00–16.00

Porcelain Greyhounds Porcelain. 1960s. Sleek, realistically detailed greyhounds are depicted in matching running poses. $20.00–25.00

White and Black Terriers Ceramic. 1950s. White terriers with brown markings on faces and black markings on bodies and feet are posed in distinctive ways. Pepper sits on haunches, Salt stands in alert show pose. $15.00–19.00

Bulldog Hugger Ceramic. Japan. 1950s. This two-piece hugger consists of a cartoonish bulldog head (white with gray and ochre markings) inserted into a white squat body with ochre markings. A pink collar is attached to the head. $12.00–18.00

Bulldog Hugger Ceramic. Japan. 1950s. This two-piece hugger consists of a stylized huge bulldog head with white jowls and brown eye spots, and a white, low-slung body with brown tail. $12.00–16.00

Beagle Nester Porcelain. Japan. 1950s. This three-piece nester consists of a one-piece body module that includes the two dogs' bodies, one in white and brown, the other in white and black. The heads come in two pieces. Pepper has large owlish eyes, downcast mouth, and brown markings. Salt has saucer eyes, downturned mouth, and black markings. $20.00–25.00

Great Dane Heads Ceramic. Japan. 1960s. Beautifully detailed heads of Great Danes are tinted in brown with black faces and white throats. $12.00–14.00

Boxer Heads Ceramic. Japan. 1960s. Well-crafted heads of boxers have gray collars, tan necks and heads, and white throats. $12.00–14.00

Collie Heads Ceramic. Japan. 1960s. Finely crafted matching heads of collies have characteristic sharp noses and are colored a golden brown. $12.00–14.00

Small White Pups Ceramic. Japan. 1950s. This small pair of matching shakers features two small white pups with gold detailing on fingernails and name tags that are marked "Salt" and "Pepper." The pups have large, pink-edged ears: one stands up, the other flops over. $10.00–12.00

Small Cartoonish Beagles Ceramic. 1950s. Cartoonish white puppy dogs in a sitting position have white bodies, round black heads with long ears, and round snouts with protruding red tongues. Their most prominent feature is the black whisker dots around the nose. $10.00–12.00

Black/White Poodles Ceramic. 1950s. A black sitting poodle with white collar is matched with a white sitting poodle with red collar and grayish highlights. $10.00–12.00

Small Sitting Puppies Ceramic. Japan. 1950s. A milky-white puppy with floppy ears, big round eyes, and round mouth has a pink flower at its throat. Its mate raises a hind leg to scratch its ear. $10.00–12.00

Begging Spaniels Ceramic. 1950s. Small white spaniels sit up on their haunches. They have brown highlights on back, ears, and tails, and black eyes and noses. $10.00–12.00

Begging Black Labrador Puppies Ceramic. 1950s. Shiny black Labrador puppies sit up and beg. Their matching bodies are entirely black, finished off in a high-gloss glaze. $10.00–12.00

Cartoony Spotted Dalmatians Ceramic. 1950s. Complacent white Dalmatians with prominent scatterings of black dots, black ears, and red collars sit on their haunches. They smile and wink from opposite sides of the face. $10.00–12.00

Cartoony Irish Setters Ceramic. 1950s. White stylized Irish setters with orange ears and markings sit up and beg. $10.00–12.00

"I'm Pep"/"I'm Salt" Puppies Porcelain. 1950s. Beige matching couple of soulful hounds roll their black eyes. The blue ribbons around their necks bear green, heart-shaped tags with the inscriptions "I'm Pep" and "I'm Salt." $10.00–12.00

Begging Baby Boxers Porcelain. 1950s. Cartoony white baby boxers sit up on hind legs and beg with gray-tinted paws. Their cropped ears are black with pink and they have human smiling mouths under their red triangular noses. $10.00–12.00

Healthy and Sick Spotted Dalmatians Ceramic. 1950s–1960s. Comical pink-spotted Dalmatian puppies sit up. Salt winks and flicks his large red tongue over his cheek. Pepper, forepaws crossed across his tummy, shuts his eyes and juts out his tongue. $10.00–12.00

Flirting Poodles Ceramic. 1950s–1960s. Pink stylized poodles sit up and show off their curly-textured bodies. Both have 1950s-style June Allison hairdos with fluffy bangs and flipped up ears. Salt wears a flower at her throat and has large, long-eyelashed eyes. Pepper wears blue flower at throat and closes long-lashed lids. $10.00–12.00

Long-Necked Poodles Ceramic. 1950s. Black and gray sitting poodles have exaggerated long necks clasped by collars with red ornaments. $10.00–12.00

Black Poodles in a Basket Porcelain. 1950s. Long-nosed black poodles with curly textured bodies fit into either side of a black "wicker" porcelain basket with central handle and polka-dotted bow at side. $20.00–24.00

Zebra-Striped Poodles Ceramic. 1950s. White stylized poodles with black zebra stripes have lavish white pom-pom hairdos. Salt sits up to beg, Pepper lies alertly. $10.00–12.00

Wrinkled Chihuahuas Ceramic. 1950s. Small matching shakers depict sitting beige Chihuahuas with extravagant wrinkles and huge blue-and-black bug eyes. $9.00–12.00

Black Handle-Tailed Hounds Ceramic. 1960s. Very shiny black shakers are made in the shape of resting hound dogs with drooping jowls and tails that arch from back to just behind the neck. $10.00–12.00

Yellow Sitting Hounds Ceramic. 1950s. Fat-bellied, stylized yellow hound dogs sit up on their haunches. Both have long black ears that end halfway down their paws and bulbous jowls terminating in a tiny pointed forehead. A sprinkling of black dots under the nose gives them a comical look. Salt wears blue bow, Pepper wears red bow. $10.00–12.00

Stylized Dachshunds Ceramic. 1950s. Stylized brown, high-gloss dachshunds are sculpted as mirror images of each other. Both have very long pointed noses terminating in a black ball, long ears, and eyes with extremely long human eyelashes. $10.00–12.00

Dachshund Mother with Twins Nester Ceramic. 1950s. This white, three-piece set consists of a carrier shaped as the low-slung mother dachshund into whose back are inserted Salt and Pepper pups, who in their yellow highlights, red button noses, and large blue eyes resemble the mother. All have smiling faces. The initials "S" and "P" are embossed on the mother's side beneath the figurines of the pups. $12.00–18.00

Two-Piece Dachshund Ceramic. 1960s. A realistically detailed tan dachshund is split down the middle into a head (Salt) and tail (Pepper) part. $10.00–14.00

Shar-pei Pups Ceramic. Sarsaparilla. 1980s. Identical, heavily wrinkled Shar-pei puppies have black noses and eyes in tan bodies. $10.00–12.00

Dalmatian and Fire Hydrant Ceramic. Sarsaparilla. 1980s. White, stylized Dalmatian with black dots raises hind leg on glossy red fire hydrant. $10.00–12.00

Dobermans Porcelain. 1980s. This beautifully executed pair of Dobermans represent one in a sitting position, the other lying down. Both are black with brown extremities. $10.00–12.00

Poodle with Fire Hydrant Ceramic. Vandor. 1980s. White poodle raises leg on yellow fire hydrant with gray middle. $12.00–15.00

Spaniel with Fire Hydrant Ceramic. Vandor. 1980s. White and black spaniel raises leg on yellow fire hydrant with gray middle. $12.00–15.00

ANIMALS—SAVAGE AND TAME

FARM ANIMALS

Palominos Ceramic. Japan. 1960s. A pair of naturalistic palominos with white fetlocks and manes in a striding pose. $20.00–24.00

Black Broncos Ceramic. Japan. 1960s. A black pair of rearing broncos executed with naturalistic detail. The forelegs are white. $20.00–24.00

Clydesdales Ceramic. Japan. 1960s. A naturalistic pair of roan Clydesdales with white fetlocks and brown tails. $20.00–24.00

Burros Ceramic. Japan. Late 1950s. Comical gray burros have large ears, stocky legs, and wear white, patterned blankets on their backs. $12.00–16.00

Laughing Donkeys Ceramic. Japan. Late 1950s. A matching pair of golden ochre donkeys sit on their haunches wearing black bridles and brown collars. They lay back their ears and laugh big pink laughs. $8.00–12.00

Piebald Donkeys Ceramic. Japan. Late 1950s. Black and white piebald donkeys laugh hysterically. One stands, the other has collapsed on all fours and throws back its pink snout. $12.00–16.00

Tiny Donkeys Ceramic. Japan. 1940s. A matching pair of slate gray, stylized donkeys squat on their haunches. Their ears are laid back and their chins are tucked into their necks. The general effect is late Deco. $6.00–10.00

Hilarious Donkeys Ceramic. Japan. 1940s. A tiny pair of brown stylized donkeys with naughty expressions on their faces. One sits, the other stands. Both have black manes and markings. $6.00–10.00

Grinning Donkeys Ceramic. Japan. 1950s. A tiny pair of beige donkeys with pink, floppy ears and black manes, tails, and markings. One lies down on its side, the other grins raffishly as it hoists itself up on its haunches. $6.00–10.00

Donkeys in Repose Ceramic. Japan. 1950s. A tiny pair of matching beige donkeys with blankets. They wear bridles and tilt their heads in a doelike pose. $6.00–10.00

Curly Lambs Porcelain. Japan. Early 1950s. A matching pair of white curly lambs with blue eyes and pink heart-shaped noses plant their forefeet into a collection of red and blue flowers. $6.00–10.00

Baby Donkeys Ceramic. Japan. 1950s. Tiny brown baby donkeys bat long eyelashes and display perky ears. Both wear red bows beneath their white faces. One is lying down, the other stands. $6.00–10.00

Baby Donkeys Ceramic. Japan. 1950s. Small gray baby donkeys in playful poses have white underbellies and fetlocks. One is getting ready to stand up, the other looks dubiously at his feet. $8.00–12.00

Lambs Ceramic. Japan. 1940s. White and gray lambs have coats textured to resemble wool. Both have pink cheeks and ears. One sits, the other stands. $8.00–12.00

Cow and Calf Ceramic. Japan. Late 1950s. Cutely stylized cow and calf pose their white bodies, yellow "hair," and golden hooves and horns. Mother stands, while daughter sits demurely. $10.00–14.00

"Delft" Cows Ceramic. Japan. 1950s. Matching pair of white, semi-naturalistic cows with tails that curl up like handles wear bells around their necks. On their foreheads and sides they have painted floral patterns in blue reminiscent of Delft. $8.00–12.00

Ruminating Cows Ceramic. Japan. 1950s. This small pair of brown and white cows is blissfully ruminating with closed eyes. One stands, the other lies down. $6.00–10.00

Pink Bull and Cow Ceramic. Japan. 1950s. Pink bull squats down, holding up his black longhorns on either side of red tuft of mane. The pink cow has prominent, angular hipbones, round stomach and udders, and looks amorously at her mate. $10.00–16.00

Heifers Ceramic. Japan. 1950s. A matching pair of naturalistic white heifers with brown and black spots poses alertly, tails horizontal and ears on the alert. Both stand. $20.00–24.00

Beehive Ceramic. Occupied Japan. Late 1940s. White beehives with octagonal texture have one sculpted bee on top and one painted bee on the side. $14.00–20.00

Yellow Beehive Ceramic. Japan. Yellow beehives with horizontal striations and a tiny arched "opening" on the bottom have a sculpted bee form on the side. $12.00–18.00

White Beehive with Clover Ceramic. Occupied Japan. Late 1940s. White beehives with octagonal texture and an overall pattern of clover leaves have two bees, one sculpted at the top, and one painted on the side. $14.00–20.00

Blue and White Cows Ceramic. Japan. 1960s. White cows with blue snouts, horns, hooves, and tail tufts also have a pattern of blue and black tulips scattered across their backs. These matching shakers resemble cow creamers. $12.00–14.00

Pink Cows with Bows Ceramic. Japan. Pink, cartoonish cows sit up on their haunches. They have yellow horns, tails, and hooves, wear blue bows, and smile. The eyes of one are open, the eyes of the other are closed. $10.00–12.00

White Cows with Bells Ceramic. Japan. 1960s. Stylized, geometric cows are white with black spots. Between their pink ears they have bas-relief white and pink flowers. Around their necks they have golden ceramic bells. $12.00–14.00

Cows with Halos Ceramic. Japan. White cartoony cows with yellow bangs have glittery tails, golden hooves, and horns. On the tops of their heads they have golden halos studded with rhinestones and flowers. $12.00–14.00

Brown Cartoony Cows Ceramic. Japan. 1970s. Brown cartoony cows with black dots have long rabbitlike ears that hang down, black bangs, and yellow muzzles and horns. Their mouths point down. One cow wears a lavender bow around her neck. $10.00–12.00

Cow Head Shaker Bells Ceramic. U.S.A. 1960s. Brown "busts" of cows with gray horns and golden bells sculpted around their necks have shaker chamber in the head, and a bell in the neck. The shakers are identical except for the variable distribution of the letter "S" and "P." $14.00–18.00

Lambs Ceramic. Japan. 1950s. White lambs with bodies textured to resemble wool have cute smiling faces and baby-doll eyes. One sits, the other stands. $10.00–12.00

Steer Ceramic. Japan. Beige realistic steer have long horns. $10.00–14.00

Cows with Flowers Ceramic. Japan. 1950s. White cows have cartoonish features consisting of bright pink snouts, pink ears, blue eyes with eyebrows, and brown horns. One sits, the other stands, but both curl their tails in "S" shapes so they cling to their backs. Two yellow daisies are painted on their flanks. $10.00–12.00

Contented Milk Cows Ceramic. Japan. 1960s. Pale yellow cows with white pear-shaped heads have beatific grins on their faces, as though they were admiring their newborn calves. One lies down while the other stands and both have large, yellow bells hanging from their necks. Their pink udders are in evidence. $10.00–14.00

Cow and Horse Heads Ceramic. 1950s. Nicely detailed figurines depict a brown horse head and a white, brown, and black cow head. $12.00–14.00

Cow and Calf Ceramic. Japan. 1960s. A dark brown cow with yellow horn and red tuft wears a red collar with a yellow bell and shimmies down to a clump of green grass. Her brown calf has small yellow horns and a red collar and looks excited. $12.00–14.00

Sitting Cows with Handles Ceramic. Japan. 1960s. Two large-lipped, white-faced cows sit. Their tails form handles. $12.00–14.00

Spotted Cows Ceramic. Japan. 1950s. White cows with black spots have yellow horns and simplified bodies. One crouches down, the other stands taller. Both seem to be complaining about something. $14.00–16.00

Pink Bulls Ceramic. Japan. 1950s. Squat, pink bulls with golden hooves have red halters around their heads. $10.00–14.00

Gray Longhorn Steer Ceramic. Japan. Very realistically detailed and highly glazed replicas of gray, longhorn steer. One sits, the other stands. $12.00–16.00

Gray Longhorns Ceramic. Japan. 1960s. Gray and white cows with pink ears and noses, golden hooves and bells, and have baby-doll eyes. Their long horns are painted gold. $20.00–24.00

Black Spotted Cows Porcelain. 1960s. Small identical, standing cows with brown hooves are white with black spots. There is not much detailing. $10.00–14.00

Yellow Sitting Cows Ceramic. Japan. 1950s. Identical bright yellow cows sit and curl back their tails, which thereby are transformed into handles. Both have devilish, brown horns, brown bow ties, and brown topknots. $10.00–12.00

Milk Cans and Cow Bas-Relief Ceramic. White milk cans with black trim have in the center section a bas-relief, cartoony face of a cow with blue bulging eyes. $12.00–14.00

Brahmin Bulls Ceramic. Japan. Gray Brahmin bulls are realistically sculpted. They wear gray halters. $12.00–14.00

Cow with Nursing Calf Ceramic. Japan. Realistic set depicts a white cow with orange spots and gray horns, turning to look at her calf who reaches out his muzzle to nurse. $20.00–24.00

Buffalo Ceramic. Japan. Beautifully detailed buffalo shakers have a bright glaze over the sepia and black paint. $18.00–24.00

Steer Ceramic. Japan. Realistic matching steer have chunky bodies, squat legs, and brown halters around their white faces. Otherwise they are bright orange to yellow in coloring. $16.00–18.00

Ox with Hay Wagon on Tray Ceramic. Japan. 1950s. The three-piece set consists of a green rectangular tray with an orange realistic ox and a brown and black cart heaped high with yellow hay. $20.00–24.00

Standing Lambs Ceramic. Japan. 1950s. White lambs with knobby bodies and black hooves have floppy pink ears. One paw rests on "hip," the other points for some reason. $12.00–16.00

Stylized Lambs Ceramic. Japan. 1960s. One lamb sits, the other stands, holding its tail high. Both have a scattering of yellowish dots on their bodies, black hooves, and pink ears. $10.00–14.00

Goofy Lambs Ceramic. Japan. 1960s. Identical sitting lambs, with very large heads and gigantic "Walter Keene"-style eyes, have black paws. Their bodies are deeply embossed in a swirling wool pattern. $12.00–14.00

Goat with Cart Ceramic. Japan. 1950s. A gray goat in harness stands in front of a brown cart. $16.00–20.00

Bulls Ceramic. Japan. White-faced bulls with curving horns have textured bodies painted a rich brown. $14.00–20.00

Palominos Ceramic. Japan. Realistically sculpted figurines of walking golden Palominos with white manes, tails, and fetlocks. $14.00–18.00

Percherons Ceramic. Japan. Realistically sculpted figurines of bay Percherons with white stars and fetlocks. One strides, the other stands. $14.00–18.00

Donkeys Ceramic. Japan. Stylized gray donkeys with large ears have red and white baskets sculpted onto their sides. $8.00–10.00

Beige Donkeys Ceramic. Japan. 1950s. Cute beige donkeys have black tails, manes, and hooves. One stands, the other lies down and balances a big red bow on her forelock. $10.00–12.00

Brown and White Donkeys Ceramic. Japan. 1960s. Cartoonish donkeys with a faint resemblance to Bambi have white bosoms and faces, brown backs with a scattering of white dots, and smug expressions on their faces. One sits, the other stands. Their most distinctive characteristic is the deep V-shaped spot of brown extending from their foreheads to their noses. $12.00–14.00

Donkeys Ceramic. Comic-looking yellow donkeys in sitting position have black bridles and red collars around their necks. They lay back their ears and grin stupidly. $8.00–12.00

Donkeys Ceramic. Japan. Black and white donkeys with pink noses and inner ears strike typical donkey poses. One is lying down and braying, its head flung back. The other firmly plants four feet on the ground. $12.00–14.00

Small Gray Horses Ceramic. Japan. 1950s. Small (3½") horses in sitting position have large heads and ears and are stylized in the Deco manner. $8.00–10.00

Donkeys Ceramic. Japan. 1960s. These small figurines in tan, pink, and black are highly glazed. One donkey is curled up, the other stands smiling. $8.00–10.00

Donkeys with Packs Ceramic. Japan. 1960s. Small yellow glazed donkeys crouch into grass-textured bases and have packs sculpted into their backs. $8.00–10.00

Donkeys Ceramic. Japan. 1950s. Cartoonish white-faced, brown-bodied donkeys wear red bows under their chins. One lies down, the other stands. $8.00–10.00

Donkeys Ceramic. Japan. 1950s. High-gloss, finely detailed donkeys in dark brown have white extremities. One sits, the other stands. $8.00–10.00

Deco Horses Ceramic. Japan. 1930s. White stylized horses have red manes and double red line pattern scattered over body. The legs are simplified into solid planes, front and back, and the neck and head curve in the Art Deco style. $10.00–12.00

Donkey with Cart Ceramic. Japan. 1930s–1940s. This three-piece set comprises a base in the shape of a realistic tan donkey harnessed to a wicker cart and standing on a grass-textured base filled with red flowers. On the cart are two square wicker-textured baskets, each holding a yellow chick. These two baskets are the salt-and-pepper shakers. $20.00–25.00

Horses Lying Down Ceramic. Japan. 1950s. Identical tan horses with black tails and noses are in lying position with one leg extended. Both wear red bridles. $10.00–12.00

Donkey Pulling Cart Ceramic. Japan. 1950s. A braying, black and white donkey throws back its head. The body fits between the traces of a Sicilian-style cart. $10.00–12.00

Horse Heads Ceramic. Japan. 1960s. Realistically rendered horse heads are glazed glossy brown. Salt tucks in its head, while Pepper juts its nose forward. $12.00–14.00

Mare and Colt Heads Ceramic. Japan. 1950s. Tan mare and colt with white blaze and black mane rest on gray bases. The mare is roughly double the size of the colt. $12.00–14.00

Black Stallion Heads Ceramic. Rosemeade Pottery. Wahpeton, ND. 1940–1961. High-gloss black horse heads have flowing manes and pink mouths and nostrils. $15.00–20.00

Rearing Horses Bone china. Beautifully detailed identical rearing horses on sloping bases are glazed in contrasting colors. Pepper is black with white blaze, Salt is tan with white blaze. $14.00–16.00

Horse Heads Ceramic. U.S.A. Brown, realistically detailed matching horse heads and necks rest on horseshoe-shaped bases marked "Kentucky." $10.00–12.00

Donkey with Saddlebags and Rider Red clay. Large, brilliantly glazed black donkey plants its feet in a stubborn pose. On his back sits a Mexican boy wearing a yellow sombrero, and a pair of saddle bags (the shakers) hang on either side. Hooves, nostrils, mane, tail, and saddlebags are detailed with gold. $12.00–18.00

Horse with Saddlebags Red clay. Small, brilliantly glazed black horse with gold mane and hooves carries a pair of saddlebags (the shakers) that are suspended from hooks on his back. $12.00–14.00

Saddled Horses Bone china. Identical small white horses with black hooves, manes, and tails are fully tacked in Western saddles outlined in gold. $12.00–14.00

Donkeys with Rhinestones Ceramic. Japan. 1940s. Identical stylized donkeys with huge ears, bug eyes, and vast grins sit back on their haunches. Their bodies are bright pink and white, with black hooves, and their legs resemble the body of the Michelin tire man. Into the gumline above the top teeth are inserted three rhinestones. $10.00–12.00

Donkey with Cart and Jugs Ceramic. 1950s. Terra-cotta-colored stylized donkey forms a single piece with the wood-grained wagon with red-spoked wheels into which he is harnessed. The shakers are two terra-cotta-colored jugs on which the sides are embossed the words "Little Brown Jug." $10.00–14.00

Donkey with Jugs Ceramic. 1950s. This three-piece set consists of a white donkey with black markings and two flowered jugs suspended from hooks on the donkey's back. The jugs are marked "Salt" and "Pepper." $10.00–12.00

Horse in Trough Ceramic. Japan. 1950s–1960s. This two-piece nester set features a tan horse with black mane, tail, and hooves rolling on its back and resting on a brown oval water trough. $15.00–20.00

Apaloosa Horse Heads Ceramic. Japan. 1950s–1960s. Apaloosa heads with brown spots, manes, and tails hold themselves in different positions. Pepper looks straight forward, while Salt tucks in its chin. $12.00–14.00

Black Horse Heads Ceramic. Japan. 1950s. Unusual black sculptured horse heads have S-shaped necks terminating in gracefully curving heads. The manes have a mosaic pattern in white and black. Eyes are large and bejewelled. $12.00–14.00

Mule Heads on Stand Ceramic. Japan. 1960s. A pair of matching tan mule heads and necks rests on a tan, oval ceramic base. Pepper has black horse collar, and Salt has red collar. $8.00–12.00

Small Stylized Horses Ceramic. Japan. 1950s. Small white ceramic horses with black hooves, tails, and ears and long black eyelashes are ornamented with one pink flower each. $8.00–10.00

Stylized Horses Ceramic. Japan. 1950s. White stylized horses with very rudimentary features have brown manes and tails and yellow flowers with brown leaves. $8.00–10.00

Hatted Donkey and Cart Ceramic. Japan. 1950s. A brownish donkey wearing a green hat and red harness is teamed with a white carriage with black wheels and green roof. $14.00–18.00

Smiling Horses Ceramic. Japan. 1960s. White horses with tan backs and black manes either buck or stand quietly. $8.00–10.00

White Horses in Hats Ceramic. Japan. 1950s. Matching crude white horses with brown spots have blue noses and wear yellow hats. $8.00–10.00

Donkey and Cart with Barrels Ceramic. Japan. 1950s. This three-piece set consists of a small blue donkey that is attached to a white and black cart. A large gray barrel and a large brown barrel rest on the cart and hold salt and pepper. $12.00–16.00

Donkeys Ceramic. Japan. 1960s. Cartoonish gray donkeys with pink ears and noses, black hooves and eyes, and white bellies either lie and laugh or sit up and stare sternly. $8.00–10.00

Laughing Horses Ceramic. Japan. 1950s. Matching white stylized horses on bases textured to resemble tall grass lift up forelegs and throw open mouths in wild laughter. $8.00–10.00

Sitting White Horses Ceramic. Japan. 1950s–1960s. Matching white horses with pink mouths, brown manes and hooves, and tails sit on their haunches. Pepper has brown bridle, while Salt has pink bridle. $8.00–10.00

Deco Zebra Red clay. Art-Deco-styled matching zebras in shiny black glaze have pink stripes. $10.00–12.00

Zebras Porcelain. 1940s. Small matching zebras with black stripes and manes are of one piece with the green "grassy" base that fills the space between their legs. $10.00–12.00

Zebras Ceramic. Japan. 1950s. Identical zebras with articulated though simplified bodies have diamond-shaped black pattern on heads. $10.00–12.00

Small Zebras Ceramic. Japan. 1940s. Matching small white zebras have lovely black stripes and ears. $12.00–16.00

Stylized Zebras Ceramic. Japan. 1950s. White zebras cast in curving geometrical shapes have bold black stripes. One rears, while the other plants its feet firmly on the ground. $14.00–18.00

Small Pigs Bone china. Japan. Before 1960. Matching pair of tiny white ceramic pigs in mirror poses, crouch on their forepaws. They shine and sport black dots and pink ears. $8.00–12.00

Small Pigs Ceramic. Japan. Before 1960. Matching pair of small pinkish-white pigs with wide open snouts tinted black. $8.00–12.00

Piggy-Back Pigs Ceramic. Japan. Before 1960. A pair of piggy-back pigs, the "adult" in pink pants, light blue "Eton" jacket with yellow bow, bends over, while the "child" in black jacket and yellow pants straddles his back. $12.00–16.00

Musician Pigs Ceramic. Japan. Before 1960. Small white pigs in baggy pants, detailed with gold lines, play the guitar (salt) and the accordion (pepper). $8.00–12.00

Yellow Pigs Ceramic. Japan. Before 1960. Matching pair of yellow standing pigs with black hooves, dramatically arched black eyebrows, and white snouts. $8.00–12.00

Dancing Pigs Ceramic. Japan. Before 1960. Two white pigs hold out their arms to embrace each other in a waltz. She wears a pink bow and matching ballerina skirt. He is in pink suspendered trousers and pink "porkie-pie" hat. $16.00–20.00

Gold Pigs Ceramic. Japan. Before 1960. A matching pair of sitting, gold-bodied pigs with serene white faces and red lips. Their golden glaze recalls Shawnee shakers, but the "Made in Japan" stamped on the bottom identifies them as otherwise. $12.00–16.00

White Sitting Pigs Ceramic. Japan. Before 1960. A large, matching set of white sitting pigs with golden hooves and naturalistic eyes. Their graceful faces bear friendly smiles, and each coyly flips an ear. $12.00–16.00

Sleeping Pigs Ceramic. Japan. Before 1960. A pair of naturalistic pink-toned sleeping pigs who snuggle up with each other, one laying his beatifically smiling face on his pal's head. $16.00–20.00

Black and White Standing Pigs Ceramic. Japan. Before 1960. A pair of naturalistic black standing pigs with white forelegs. $20.00–24.00

Pink Pigs Ceramic. Japan. Before 1960. A pair of pink pigs whose bodies shade off, on their tummies, into white. One stands on all four legs, while the other rears back. Both have black accents and flirty, long-lashed eyes. $12.00–16.00

Pig Cooks Ceramic. Japan. Before 1960. A pair of white standing pigs in chef's toques grin invitingly. One holds a dish, the other a knife. $12.00–16.00

Mother Pig with Baby Ceramic. Japan. Before 1960. A two-piece shaker featuring a piebald mother pig lying on her side, while a predominantly white baby snuggles up for a sip on her yellow teats. $10.00–14.00

Brown Pigs Ceramic. Japan. Before 1960. A matching pair of brown, long-bodied pigs with round, yellow eyes and smug, utterly porcine expressions on their bulbous faces. $6.00–10.00

Pig Couple Bisque. Before 1960. Mr. and Mrs. Pig step out on the town. She wears a ruffled orange hat and pale green cape on her body. He wears an orange jacket, green bow tie, and brown hat. While she seraphically closes her eyes, he peers over his black pince-nez. $12.00–16.00

Pigs in Hats Ceramic. Japan. Before 1960. A large set of fat, white pigs crouching down on all fours. Both wear hats, one pink, the other blue. Both have flowers painted on their sides. $12.00–16.00

Pigs in Trough Ceramic. Trish Ceramics. Pittsburg, PA. Before 1960. A pair of pink, round pigs nestles in a wood-grained brown trough. The salt pig wears a periwinkle blue bow. $20.00–24.00

Blue Pigs Ceramic. Japan. Before 1960. This pair of blue pigs flashes rhinestone eyes. One stands, the other has just tumbled onto his behind. $10.00–14.00

Pig Couple Ceramic. Japan. 1950s. Round, white Mr. and Mrs. Pig clasp black-hooved paws on their rotund stomachs as they smile complacent, weak-chinned smiles. Mrs. Pig wears a white dress with blue polka-dots, Mr. Pig ties a black ribbon around his neck. $10.00–14.00

Farm Pigs Ceramic. Japan. 1940s. White, round pigs stand up, arms akimbo, and eyes blissfully closed. Salt has a red neckerchief, pepper wears a blue one. $10.00–14.00

Happy Pigs Terra-cotta. Mexico. Before 1960. Matching pair of terra-cotta porkers with beady eyes, black snouts, and smiling red mouths. Each has one black, floppy ear. $8.00–12.00

Baby Pigs in Crate Ceramic. Japan. Before 1960. Matching pink pale piglets peek out of "wood" crate. $12.00–18.00

Buster Brown Pigs Ceramic. Japan. 1940s. Matching pair of white, standing pigs wearing suspendered trousers and blouses with red collars smile contentedly. $12.00–16.00

Digesting Pigs Ceramic. Japan. Before 1960. Naturalistic matching pair of white porkers lie down after a full meal, narrowing their eyes and smiling with pleasure. $12.00–16.00

Big Pink Pigs Ceramic. Japan. Before 1960. Large pair of stylized pink pigs with barely articulated ears and conical snouts. Blue highlights define nostrils, tail, and ears. "P" and "S" are inscribed below holes. $12.00–16.00

Musician Pigs Ceramic. Japan. Before 1960. Matching pair of orange, standing pigs with humanoid faces and large ears play yellow flutes. On their stomachs they bear the slogan "I'm pepper" and "I'm salt." $12.00–16.00

Pigs in Costume Ceramic. Japan. 1950s. Anthropomorphic Mr. and Mrs. Pig wear tiny hats on their bald heads. Mrs. Pig poses in a green dress with red and black trim. Mr. Pig shows off a brown suit over a red vest, white shirt, and yellow bow tie. Both have large, soulful eyes rimmed in soft blue, and rosy, shiny cheeks. $14.00–20.00

Pink Standing Pigs Ceramic. Japan. 1950s. A matching pair of bright red pigs stand, screwing up their eyes with the effort. $12.00–16.00

Small Pig Couple Ceramic. Japan. 1950s. Small white pig couple in aprons and bow ties outlined in kelly green. He wears a green beret. Both have broadly smiling faces highlighted with brown. $12.00–16.00

Green Pigs Ceramic. Japan. 1950s. A matching pair of obese green pigs, sitting on their haunches and clutching in their front paws yellow corn cobs on which they gnaw with rhapsodic concentration. Their eyes are shut tight. Both have red snouts and ears. $12.00–16.00

Dancing Pigs in Green Ceramic. Japan. 1940s. Pink dancing pigs wear pale green outfits. He wears a green sailor cap with a black ribbon, while she is in a kicky green skirt with suspenders and bonnet with black ribbon. Both display black corkscrew tails on their behinds. $12.00–16.00

Sitting Pigs Ceramic. Japan. 1950s. Small pink pigs in identical poses sit up and beg. $10.00–12.00

Pig with Sailboat Ceramic. Japan. 1940s. Pink, spherical pig with black-rimmed ears is teamed with a pink sailboat whose sail is highlighted in salmon. $14.00–20.00

Pigs in Buckets Ceramic. Japan. 1950s. White pigs with large, blue eyes and pink cheeks and ears struggle out of buckets that are either pink or yellow. $12.00–14.00

Sow and Piglets Red clay. A very big, very round sow is accompanied by twin piglets. Glazed in glossy black, this set has red and gold detailing. $14.00–20.00

Hampshire Pigs Porcelain. Realistically detailed Hampshire pigs have black bodies with a white band running directly behind their heads across their shoulders. $30.00–34.00

Hampshire and Pink Pigs Ceramic. Otagiri. 1980s. Realistically detailed set features one Hampshire and one pink pig. $12.00–18.00

Brown Pigs Ceramic. Japan. 1950s. Simplified, identical round pigs with black feet have pink snouts and very disagreeable porcine faces. $12.00–14.00

Metal Pigs Metal. Small gold-plated pigs have very stylized bodies and blue eyes. $12.00–14.00

Pig with Leather Ears Ceramic and leather. Japan. 1960s. These pink pigs have been reduced to the essence of pigness: nearly spherical bodies; vestigial legs; prominent, salmon-colored snouts; and small leather ears. $12.00–14.00

Pigs on a Tray Ceramic. Japan. 1950s. The grass-textured tray has a fencelike handle that separates two pig shakers that are white with pink and black highlights. One pig sits on its hind legs, the other stands on all four and looks up belligerently. $20.00–24.00

Piggy Back Pigs Ceramic and magnets. Japan. 1960s. Simplified pigs in white ceramic with hand-painted floral decorations balance atop each other. The smaller one clings to the larger, lower one by means of a magnet. Both have sleepy blue eyes. $16.00–20.00

Sleeping Pigs Ceramic. Japan. 1960s. Realistic, though simplified, pink pigs snuggle up as they sleep. These are nesters in the sense that one pig is shaped to fit on top of the other one. $14.00–20.00

Pigs on Green Bases Ceramic. German. Realistic, though simplified, pink pigs with floppy ears, fat cheeks, and narrow eyes sit on green circular bases. $24.00–28.00

Kissing Magnet Pigs Ceramic and magnets. U.S.A. Stylized white pigs with bodies in the shape of fat bottles laid on their sides have flat-ended snouts which cling to each other thanks to magnetic attraction. Pigs stand on yellow, tubular legs, have triangular blue ears, and are hand-painted with a brilliant blue and green floral motif. $16.00–24.00

Little White Pigs Ceramic. Japan. Small white pigs with very simplified bodies and prominent pink snouts are decorated with a dot pattern in red, pink, and green. $10.00–12.00

Male Chauvinist Pigs Ceramic. Japan. 1970s. Realistic beige pigs—one sitting, the other standing—wear brown bows and the sign "Male Chauvinist" around the middle. $12.00–14.00

Pink and Black Pigs Ceramic. Japan. 1960s. Very bright pink pigs have black spots, ears, and hooves. Their huge snouts overshadow their complacent smiles. $12.00–16.00

Spherical Small Pigs Ceramic. Japan. 1950s. Very round white pigs on four little feet have large, triangular ears with pink highlights, a squat, button-nose, and round, baby-doll eyes. Their backs are decorated with hand-painted flowers. $10.00–12.00

Rambunctious Pigs Ceramic. Japan. 1960s. Pale pink pigs with bisquelike finish have gray snouts and paws. One pig stands, the other scrunches down on its fours. They can be positioned so the standing one rests on the supine one. $14.00–18.00

Green Pigs Ceramic. Japan. Simplified pale green pigs with pink snouts and ears have a white spiral painted on their backs. $10.00–12.00

Forest Animals

Skunks Ceramic. Japan. 1960s. Cartoony skunks with sleepy, baby-doll eyes and feathery tails seem to be sharing secrets. $12.00–14.00

Skunks Ceramic. Japan. 1950s. Identical, simplified skunks with spatulate tails and rectangular bodies look like cats at first glance. $10.00–14.00

White Skunks Ceramic. Japan. 1950s. White skunks have black stripes and pink cheeks. One sits up, the other creeps along on all fours. $10.00–14.00

Cartoony Skunks Ceramic. Japan. 1960s. Very simplified skunks with S-shaped tails adhering to their bodies have oval, white faces and red noses. They are grinning. $10.00–14.00

Skunks with Turned-Up Noses Ceramic. Japan. 1950s–1960s. Black skunks with white bellies sit up and beg. They have pert, turned-up noses. $10.00–12.00

Brown-Eyed Black Skunks Ceramic. Japan. 1950s–1960s. Black skunks with shiny bodies sit up and hold out their paws to each other as though they were playing a clapping game. Their long S-shaped tails adhere to their heads. Strikingly, their eyes are brown. $12.00–16.00

Skunk Couple Ceramic. Japan. 1950s. A girl skunk sits up, wearing a pink skirt and a green flower in her hair. The boy is "naked," and smiling. $12.00–14.00

Black Skunks Ceramic. Japan. 1950s. Black skunks with sharp profiles sit up tall and stretch out their long tails so that they are level with the ground. A ragged white line runs down the backs of their heads and along their tails. $10.00–14.00

Cute Black Skunks Ceramic. Japan. 1950s. Black skunks with white faces and tummies sit up and press their hands to their chins as they look over their shoulders. Their bushy tails meet their cheeks. They have large, baby-doll eyes. $10.00–14.00

Pink-Cheeked Skunks Ceramic. Japan. Black skunks have long bodies that lie on the ground. Their long tails are pressed flat against their bodies and meet the backs of their heads. Their faces are white with bright pink circles for cheeks. $10.00–14.00

Squirrels Ceramic. Japan. 1950s–1960s. Realistic squirrels have white underbellies and deep brown backs. One lies down, the other sits up. $12.00–16.00

Squirrel with Acorn Ceramic. Japan. 1950s. A small, cute, brown squirrel is teamed with a giant green and brown acorn. $10.00–14.00

Realistic Squirrels Ceramic. Japan. 1960s. Rich brown squirrels with deep embossing sit up and hold an acorn in their forepaws. They are identical. $12.00–14.00

Simplified Squirrels Ceramic. Japan. 1950s. Small, light brown squirrels have fat bodies. One crouches down, the other sits up, hugging its fat tummy. $10.00–12.00

Standing Squirrels Ceramic. Japan. 1950s. Realistic, deeply embossed, brown squirrels stand and stretch out their long tails. $10.00–12.00

Cute Squirrels Ceramic. Japan. 1960s. Cute, yellowish squirrels with fluffy, S-shaped tails that rise along the height of their bodies have big white and black eyes. $12.00–14.00

Brown Squirrels Ceramic. Japan. 1950s. Realistic, very shiny squirrels have deeply embossed bodies and black features. One sits, the other squats down low and curls its tail. $10.00–14.00

Grinning Raccoons Ceramic. Japan. 1950s–1960s. Large-headed raccoons with white pointy ears sit up and sniff the air with sharp noses. They are pale yellow in front, shading into brown on the sides and black in the black. Their eyes are framed by black "masks." $14.00–16.00

Raccoons in Bow Ties Ceramic. Japan. 1950s. Simplified, deep brown raccoons wear red bow ties. Their backs are glossy, their tummies and heads are matte. $12.00–16.00

White Raccoons with Furry Tails Ceramic and fur. Japan. 1950s. White, cute raccoons stand on their hind legs and smile. Their tails are made of real gray and black fur. $12.00–14.00

Smiling Chipmunks Ceramic. Japan. 1950s. Chipmunks with childlike faces and baby-doll eyes stand on their hind feet and wave. Their cheeks are pink, but their bodies are deep tan. $10.00–12.00

Cartoony Chipmunks Ceramic. Japan. 1950s. Small, dark-brown chipmunks sit up and show off tan tummies. They have large, round eyes and prominent incisors. $10.00–12.00

Chipmunks with Swirly Tails Ceramic. Japan. 1950s. Cute chipmunks with reddish-brown bodies and white faces have round, baby-doll eyes and circular ears. One sits up and swirls its large tail so that it meets the ear. The other scrunches down on all fours and looks back at its tail. $10.00–12.00

Chipmunks Ceramic. Japan. 1960s. Cartoonlike chipmunks with large tails and prominent round ears are beige with dark brown backs and tails. They have very big round eyes and two prominent incisors. $10.00–12.00

Foxes Ceramic. Relco. Japan. Realistic, beautifully detailed red foxes skulk along on gray paws. $14.00–18.00

Deer Couple Ceramic. Japan. 1960s. The shiny brown deer have yellow faces and three real jingle bells around their necks. One sits, the other, with horns, stands. These resemble Bambi. $10.00–12.00

Furry Deer Ceramic and fur. Japan. 1950s. These cartoony deer have white bodies that shade off into deep brown speckled with white along the backs. They have yellow horns, pink ears, and tufts of real fur on their tails and crowns. $10.00–12.00

Fawn Ceramic. Occupied Japan. 1940s. Graceful, sitting fawns have white bodies with a yellow glaze and a scattering of white spots. $18.00–24.00

Fawn Ceramic. Japan. 1950s. Sitting, tan fawns with very large, pointed ears that are tinted pink, have black hooves, and sharply pointed noses. $12.00–14.00

Realistic Fawn Ceramic. Japan. 1950s. Realistic though simplified representations of fawns have brown bodies with white dots. One sleeps, the other looks up, big-eyed. $12.00–14.00

Deer Heads Ceramic. Japan. 1950s. Graceful heads of deer are grayish-brown with white necks and faces. $14.00–16.00

Moose Heads Ceramic. Japan. 1960s. Realistic heads of moose with large antlers are brown with white highlights. $12.00–14.00

Mother and Baby Bear Ceramic. Japan. This nester set consists of a yellow pair of bears with pink ears and paw pads. The mother sits up, the baby bear sits in her lap. $14.00–20.00

Mother and Baby Bear Ceramic. Japan. A round, happy mother bear sits and, with one hand, supports her baby, who

also sits up and smiles down at her. This set, in various shades
of brown and yellow, also qualifies as a nester. $14.00–20.00

Mother and Cub Ceramic. Japan. 1940s–1950s. A brown
mother bear sitting on a green log has her arm out to embrace
the cub. The cub, also sitting on a green log, is white with
pink ears and paws. $24.00–28.00

Smiling Panda Bears Ceramic. Taiwan. Mid-1970s. Sitting
panda bears have baby-doll eyes and smiling faces.
$12.00–14.00

Sitting Bears with Yellow Ears Ceramic. Japan. 1960s.
Brown bear cubs with textured bodies have realistic features.
Their ears and snouts are yellow, and the pads on their paws
are pink. $10.00–12.00

White-Faced Bears Ceramic. Japan. 1950s. Deep brown sitting bears have white faces. $10.00–12.00

Grizzly Bears Wood composition. Multi Products. Chicago,
IL. 1948. Brown grizzly bears sit up on their hindquarters.
$12.00–14.00

Bear Cubs with Bottle and Beehive Ceramic. Japan. 1950s.
Black bear cubs cavort. One sits up and sucks from white baby
bottle. The other clings to a gray beehive which has a single
yellow bee sculpted on its side. $12.00–16.00

Mother Bear with Cubs on Tray Ceramic. Japan. 1950s. A
gray and white mother bear is attached to a blue base. On
either side of her sits a gray cub. $18.00–24.00

Cute Bears on Log Ceramic. U.S.A. 1950s. Cute, brown bear
cubs with baby-doll eyes and red tongues lounge, resting their
heads on logs. $10.00–12.00

Gray Bears Ceramic. U.S.A. 1950s. Realistic gray bears have
dark upper bodies and white patches around their eyes. One
stands, the other sits. $10.00–12.00

Bear with Salmon Ceramic. Japan. This three-piece nester
consists of a brown, sitting bear who holds, in each curled arm,
a blue salmon. The salmon are the shakers. $15.00–20.00

White Rabbits Porcelain. Japan. 1950s. Cute, white rabbits
with teardrop-shaped baby-doll eyes have very long ears that
stand straight up. One rabbit sits up on its hind legs, the other
one prances on three. $12.00–16.00

Rabbit Heads in Garden Ceramic. Holt-Howard. Stamford, CT. A green napkin holder fashioned to resemble a stand of grass, holds two pink rabbit heads, which are inserted into the holes. Both cute faces are winking. $15.00–20.00

White Rabbits Ceramic. Japan. Identical white rabbits with simplified bodies have a very reflective glaze. $10.00–12.00

White Rabbits in Baskets Ceramic. Holt-Howard. Stamford, CT. White, floppy-eared rabbits with doe-eyes peer out of small wicker baskets. $15.00–20.00

Yellow Rabbits with Bow Ties Porcelain. Japan. 1940s. Yellow rabbits with kingpin bodies wear blue bow ties and have a cluster of three gold balls for their muzzles. $14.00–18.00

Stylized Rabbits Ceramic. Japan. 1960s. White rabbits with very stylized bodies sit up on hind feet. $12.00–14.00

Sitting White Rabbits with Flowers Ceramic. Japan. 1950s–1960s. White rabbit couple is distinguished by the scattering of pink flowers with brown leaves on the bodies. They have pointy cheeks and ears that stand straight up and meet at the tips. $12.00–14.00

Waving Bunnies Ceramic. Japan. 1950s. Identical gray bunnies with textured bodies and ears perpendicular to their heads stand up and thump with one foot. They wave. Their cheeks have big pouches on either side. $10.00–12.00

Rabbits in Carrots Porcelain. 1950s. Orange carrots lie on their sides. Out of the middle, which is scooped out, emerges a white rabbit with large, floppy ears. $10.00–14.00

Rabbit with Carrot Ceramic. Japan. 1960s. A playful gray rabbit with a fluffy tail and large ears, stands. The orange carrot lies on its side. The rabbit has human eyebrows. $12.00–14.00

Brown Rabbit and Mushroom Ceramic. Japan. 1950s. A sleeping brown rabbit is curled up next to a brown mushroom. $10.00–14.00

Rabbit Mother and Child Nester
Ceramic. Japan. 1950s. A cute mother rabbit, all pink with salmon highlights, nestles in her lap a cute baby rabbit, which raises its "arms" up over its head. Both have floppy ears. $18.00–24.00

Streamlined White Rabbits Porcelain. Japan. 1950s. Matching white rabbits with pink ears and yellow eyes have streamlined bodies sculpted in a running position. $10.00–14.00

Cartoony Mice Ceramic. Japan. 1950s. White mice with large heads and large round ears have big black eyes. Both hold their hands up to their chins and seem to be gossiping. $12.00–14.00

Mice Ceramic. Japan. 1960s. Cute gray mice with long, dark gray tails and gigantic ears are depicted in a standing and a sitting position. $12.00–14.00

Orange Bunnies Ceramic. Japan. 1950s. A mirror-image pair of orange, sitting bunnies with bright red eyes and heart-shaped muzzles. The faces, tummies, and inside of ears shade off into white. $6.00–10.00

White Bunnies Ceramic. Japan. 1950s. A matching pair of stylized white bunnies sits alertly. The pink ears stick straight up and are joined in the middle. Both have patches of yellow on the tummy. $6.00–10.00

Floppy-Eared Bunnies Porcelain. Japan. 1950s. A mirror-image pair of orange bunnies sits up to "beg." One ear sticks straight up, the other flops over. $10.00–14.00

Cavorting Bunnies Ceramic. Japan. 1960s. Two bounding bunnies with hilarious expressions show off huge incisors. Both have floppy ears and round tails. One is up on all fours, the other is stretched out. $8.00–12.00

Pink Squirrels Ceramic. Japan. 1960s. Pink squirrels with baby-doll eyes and eyebrows have bushy tails. One squirrel lies down, the other sits up. $16.00–20.00

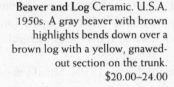

Beaver and Log Ceramic. U.S.A. 1950s. A gray beaver with brown highlights bends down over a brown log with a yellow, gnawed-out section on the trunk. $20.00–24.00

Gray Rabbits Ceramic. Japan. 1950s. These gray rabbits have white underbellies and pink ears. One sits up, holding its paws in the front, with one floppy ear. The other crouches down and looks up, curious. $8.00–12.00

Blue Rabbits Ceramic. Japan. 1940s. A small, stylized pair of blue rabbits highlighted with white markings, pink ears and noses, and black paws and whiskers. The bunnies are identical and sit up in typical rabbit-sniffing posture. $4.00–6.00

Gray Mice Ceramic. Japan. 1950s. A matching pair of stylized gray mice resemble the rodent half of "Tom and Jerry" cartoon characters. They have large, lateral ears that are white, a shock of white "hair," and white highlights on belly and cheeks. Both sit up and bring a paw to the face. $10.00–14.00

Alarmed Mice Ceramic. Japan. 1950s. A matching pair of brown, black, and white mice with very long tails that curl back are sitting up on their haunches and holding up both paws by their face. "O"-shaped mouths express alarm. $12.00–16.00

Goofy Mice Ceramic. Japan. 1960s. Stylized gray mice sit up on their haunches with broad red grins and tongues hanging out of their mouths in looks of utter goofiness. One mouse keeps her eyes open, the other closes them. $8.00–12.00

Blue Mice Ceramic. Japan. 1950s. Two small blue mice with big pink ears sit back on black, curlicue tails. Their faces bear a profusion of whiskers and red eyes with black eyeballs. $8.00–12.00

Orange Mice Ceramic. Japan. 1960s. Bright orange mice celebrate a piece of yellow cheddar cheese. One mouse (pepper) sits up and ogles the cheese, the other (salt) sinks its teeth into the top. $12.00–16.00

White Mice Ceramic. Japan. 1950s. Stylized white mice have a distinct "Chihuahua" look, with huge pink-and-black-rimmed ears, gigantic eyes, and broad grins that showcase two prominent incisors. One mouse sits up and holds on to its long black tail. The other is on all fours and trails its tail behind it. $8.00–12.00

Yellow Mice in Jackets Ceramic. Japan. 1950s. Small yellow stylized mice with big, round, red ears, wear green jackets with white collars and dark green bow ties. One mouse looks back to nibble on its long yellow tail. The other looks on, aghast. Both have round black noses and big round eyes. $10.00–14.00

Mice in Corn Cobs Porcelain. Japan. 1950s. This pair of mirror-image gray mice emerges from teardrop-shaped corn cobs. The yellow cobs are half concealed by green corn husks. The pink-eared mice are waist deep in the kernels. $12.00–16.00

Miniature White Mice Ceramic. Japan. 1940s. This tiny pair of white mice is detailed to reveal long tails curling across the backs. The ears and facial features are outlined in black. $4.00–6.00

Brown Bunnies Ceramic. Japan. 1950s. A matching pair of brown, white-ruffed rabbits peer up from beneath pink, fleshy ears. Their black noses and eyes quiver with alertness. $12.00–16.00

WILD ANIMALS

Sitting Chimps Ceramic. Japan. These brown sitting chimpanzees have tan faces, ears, and paws. They have solemn expressions and hold their paws over their stomachs. $12.00–16.00

Chimp and Palm Tree Ceramic. Japan. The bright brown chimp hangs one-armed from the single-trunked palm tree whose bright orange trunk and green fronds rise from a black base. $16.00–20.00

Sitting Gorillas Ceramic. Japan. This matching pair of russet gorillas sit, long-armed, staring out of black faces. The torsos bear a black cross-pattern. $12.00–16.00

Grooming Chimpanzees Ceramic. Japan. Two naturalistic chimpanzees with bright orange fur sit in typical grooming poses. One scratches his head, the other sucks his thumb. $8.00–12.00

Chimpanzee on Telephone Ceramic. Japan. 1930s. A cheerful golden chimpanzee holds an old-fashioned telephone earpiece to his ear. The stem of the phone, in black, is a separate piece. $16.00–20.00

"Speak No Evil" Chimpanzees Ceramic. Japan. 1930s. These matching black chimps have white faces and hold their paws over their mouths as if to say "Speak No Evil." $24.00–30.00

Chimps Hanging from Trunk Ceramic. Japan. This three-piece shaker set consists of a gnarled tree trunk punctuated by leafy trefoils and a pair of burnt sienna chimps peacefully hanging from each truncated branch. $24.00–30.00

Gray Bears Ceramic. Japan. 1960s. Standing gray bears have realistic bodies. One holds a salmon. $16.00–20.00

Drinking Chimps Ceramic. Japan. Two bright orange chimps, sitting in postures of limp abandon, lean back as they hold black bottles up to their mouths. $12.00–16.00

Pondering Chimps Ceramic. Japan. Small black-bodied chimps in crouching position turn quizzical expressions to each other. One holds up his paws pugilist-style, the other scratches his forehead. $6.00–10.00

Pink Elephants Ceramic. Japan. Two matching pink elephants with upturned, serpentine tusks sit on their haunches and flap their ears. $12.00–16.00

Sitting Elephants Ceramic. Japan. Two sitting elephants with brown bodies, white bodies, and pink feet and ears curl their trunks in expressions of great glee. $12.00–16.00

Realistic Elephants Ceramic. Japan. A pair of brown, naturalistic elephants with upturned trunks is represented in benign poses. One leans back, while the other advances. $16.00–20.00

Tiger Couple Ceramic. Japan. One sitting, one stalking tiger are realistically depicted with yellow bodies and typical, black markings. $20.00–24.00

Hippo Pair Ceramic. Japan. These matching hippos are tiny and gray, with broad red mouths. $16.00–20.00

Leopard Couple Ceramic. Japan. One sitting and one stalking leopard are realistically depicted with yellow bodies and typical, black markings. $20.00–24.00

Zebras Ceramic. Japan. 1940s–1960s. These small black-eared zebras are standing with outspread legs and are boldly painted in black-and-white chevron stripes. $16.00–20.00

Deer Leaping Ceramic. Rosemeade. 1940s. Golden-brown deer in leaping position are attached to a base sculpted to resemble long grass. $35.00–40.00

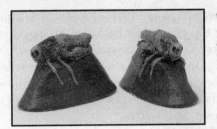

Cicadas Ceramic. Japan. 1940s. A beige cicada clings to a green "rock." $18.00–22.00

Sitting Polar Bears Ceramic. Japan. 1940s–1950s. These beige-tinted polar bears have prominent black nostrils and eyes and sit spread-legged holding their paws to their hairy chests. $8.00–10.00

Geometric Zebras Ceramic. Japan. 1940s–1960s. The stylized zebras have "Mohawk" manes and black, "inverted comma" tails. One rears up, the other poses with arched neck. Their white bodies bear black chevron markings. The eyes are outlined in three sets of lozanges. $16.00–20.00

Embracing Bears Ceramic. Japan. 1940s–1960s. These realistic brown bears stand on their hind paws and embrace, seeming to deposit air kisses on each other's cheeks. $16.00–20.00

Bear Couple Ceramic. Japan. 1940s–1960s. Brown-ochre grizzlies assume different poses: one crawls on all fours, the other stands up in threatening stance. $4.00–12.00

Dancing Bears Ceramic. Japan. 1940s–1960s. Black, white, and brown spotted bears stand on their hind legs and hold on to each other's paws. Tiny corks protrude from the middle of their backs. $16.00–20.00

Panda Bears Ceramic. Japan. 1940s–1960s. An adorable pair of white and black pandas with smiling faces wave with one hand while holding the other on their tummies. $12.00–16.00

Sitting Black Bears Ceramic. Japan. 1940s–1960s. These matching, black-glazed bears sit with their forepaws hanging limply in front of their chests. Both have gold-tipped ears and paws. $8.00–10.00

Small Polar Bears Ceramic. Japan. 1940s–1960s. Small white polar bears with gray tint sit on their back legs, propping up their torsos on their forepaws. Both are realistic. $6.00–10.00

Teddy Bears Ceramic. Japan. 1940s–1960s. Adorable teddy bears with green bows, red lips, button eyes, and yellow-tipped ears, paws, and tummies reach out their orange arms in typical stuffed bear pose. $8.00–10.00

Tiny Pandas Ceramic. Japan. 1940s–1960s. Large-eyed pandas with white faces and torsos and black ears, arms, and legs sit dolefully, dropping their forepaws between their back legs. $6.00–10.00

Crouching Raccoons Ceramic. Japan. 1940s–1960s. Realistically painted raccoons crouch attentively. Their deep brown bodies are highlighted with pale yellow around the eyes, ears, chin, and underbelly. One crouches on all fours, the other rests on his back legs. $16.00–20.00

Tiny Teddy Bears Ceramic. Japan. 1940s–1960s. Enchanting baby teddy bears in bright orange sit on their round, black legs and fumble with their forepaws on their rotund tummies. Their large eyes stare sleepily to the side. $8.00–12.00

Loony Pandas Ceramic. Japan. 1940s–1960s. Loony, large-headed pandas clap their hands in a sitting position. Both have red smiling mouths and pinpoint noses and tear-shaped black-rimmed eyes, plus a naughty forelock dropping over their foreheads. $12.00–16.00

Piggyback Monkeys Ceramic. Japan. Stacking mother and baby monkeys have big, baby-doll eyes and heavy black bangs. Mother sits and curls one arm to her ear. Baby's lower

Koala Bear Mother and Child
Ceramic. Japan. 1950s. A mother-and-child shaker depicts the koala bear holding one of its young on her back. The other youngster is an autonomous shaker. These are realistic-looking figurines in a buff color with black details. $16.00–20.00

Comic Panda Bear Ceramic. Japan. 1960s. White panda bears have bodies shaped like golf balls stacked atop a triangular base. The texture of the bear bodies is pebbled. The comical bears have black ears, black eyebags, and red noses. $12.00–16.00

Naturalistic Panda Bears Ceramic. Japan. 1950s. Realistic pandas have white heads and black stripes. One sits, the other stands on all fours. $16.00–18.00

foot fits into the crook of the mother's arm as he perches on her back. $14.00–18.00

Monkey Hanging from Palm Tree Ceramic. Japan. 1940s. An orange palm tree with Deco-style green fronds stands on a brown base. The Capuchin monkey hangs from one leaf by one arm. $24.00–28.00

Two Monkeys Hanging from Palm Tree Ceramic. Vandor. 1980s. Two monkeys hang from a central palm tree stand. $15.00–20.00

Monkey Resting on Banana Ceramic. Japan. 1940s. A baby monkey with blue, baby-doll eyes reclines on a yellow banana. This is a nester-type set. $14.00–18.00

Monkey Balancing Bowl of Bananas Ceramic. Japan. 1940s. A brown monkey with blue, baby-doll eyes balances a green bowl of bananas. $12.00–14.00

White Monkeys Ceramic. Japan. 1950s. Japanese white monkeys with tan faces stand and hold out their arms. $12.00–14.00

Smiling Cartoon Monkeys Ceramic. Japan. 1950s. Large-headed, big-eared, apple-cheeked monkeys sit. They have brown bodies, white faces, and pink cheeks and ears. $12.00–14.00

Realistic Monkeys Ceramic. Japan. 1950s. Grayish-brown monkeys have white tummies and gray muzzles. One scratches its head, the other holds a piece of food and is eating. $14.00–18.00

Monkey under Palm Tree Ceramic. U.S.A. A tan, smiling monkey, sits under a green palm tree that is stylized to look like a hybrid umbrella. $16.00–20.00

Monkeys in Banana Boats Ceramic. Japan. 1950s. Brown, smiling monkeys ride a banana boat each. $16.00–20.00

Gray Monkeys Porcelain. U.S.A. Gray, smiling monkeys have deeply embossed bodies. Both sit, but only one scratches itself. $14.00–20.00

Brown Monkeys Porcelain. U.S.A. Brown, smiling monkeys have deeply embossed bodies. Both sit. One holds its arms behind its head, the other cradles one arm in the other. $12.00–14.00

Gorillas Ceramic. Japan. White gorillas have comical faces. One waves and grins, displaying a large, pink mouth and a gap-toothed smile. The other frowns. $12.00–14.00

Giraffes Ceramic. Japan. Sitting giraffes look over their shoulders. Their beige bodies are deeply embossed with a giraffe pattern. $12.00–14.00

Black Giraffes Ceramic. Japan. 1950s. Simplified giraffes with red horns have black bodies and yellow polka-dots. $12.00–14.00

Kangaroo Mother and Joey Nester Ceramic. Japan. 1950s. A comical mother and joey set is pale beige with brown highlights. The large ears are pink, as are the cheeks. Both charac-

Pink-Eared Elephants Ceramic. Japan. 1950s. Realistic though prettified gray elephants have very large pink ears and yellow tusks. They raise their trunks and can be positioned in such a way that the trunks appear to intertwine. $20.00–24.00

ters have human eyebrows. The joey sits in the mother's pouch. $14.00–20.00

Kangaroo Mother and Joey Nester Ceramic. Japan. White mother kangaroo has a round, bowl-like pouch in which nestles the white joey. $20.00–24.00

Kangaroo Mother and Joey Twins Nester Ceramic. Japan. This three-piece set consistsof a mother kangaroo with a bowl-like pouch, in which sit identical joeys, which are the shakers. The three are golden yellow with brown highlights and baby-doll eyes. $20.00–24.00

Beige Kangaroo Mother and Joey Nester Ceramic. Japan. 1950s. A beige kangaroo mother and joey have dark brown shading and realistic features. $20.00–24.00

Red Clay Kangaroos Red clay. Japan. 1950s. Each figurine consists of a mother kangaroo with a joey in her pouch. Gold highlights the shiny black glaze. $14.00–18.00

Walrus Ceramic. Japan. Realistically detailed walruses have gray bodies, white underbellies, and red mouths. $12.00–14.00

Bears Lustware. 1940s. Identical, rounded bears have golden ears and golden lines to mark their limbs. $12.00–14.00

Elephants Ceramic. Japan. 1950s. Standing gray elephants have white faces and underbellies. Their cartoony faces are smiling, their eyes are closed, and their little trunks are turned up. $10.00–12.00

Gray Elephants Ceramic. Japan. 1950s. Gray elephants with realistic bodies have large, pink-lined ears and upturned trunks. One stands, the other strides, with green grass visible between his legs. $10.00–12.00

Small Red Clay Elephants Red clay. Japan. 1950s. Small, sitting elephants hold out their forepaws and curl up their trunks. They are glazed in highly reflective black. $10.00–14.00

Pink Elephants Ceramic. Japan. 1950s. Large-headed, cartoonish pink elephants have blue, baby-doll eyes and small, sitting bodies. $10.00–14.00

Elephants with Daisies on their Heads Ceramic. Japan. 1950s. White, stylized elephants with baby-doll eyes have pink daisies plopped down on their heads and stalk with leaves embossed onto their backs. $10.00–14.00

Kneeling Camel Carrier Ceramic. Japan. A beautifully colored kneeling camel has a box on its back which is the mustard container. From either side of this box extend hooks from which two parcels are suspended. These are the shakers. $30.00–40.00

Lion Couple Ceramic. Bright brown lions are realistically rendered. The male paces, the female reclines. $14.00–18.00

Lions with Fur Ceramic and fur. Sitting lion couple with blue, baby-doll eyes have tufts of fur on their tails and manes. The tags around their necks read "From Norcrest Furland" and "May I be your pal." $14.00–18.00

Leopards Ceramic. Yellow, spotted leopards are realistically rendered. The female reclines, the male stalks. $14.00–18.00

Jaguars Red clay. 1950s. Highly glazed black jaguars have red tongues and ears and golden claws. $12.00–14.00

Iguana and Stump Ceramic. Japan. 1950s. A brown and chartreuse stump is teamed with a chartreuse iguana with a brown head and ridged back. $16.00–18.00

"Wrap Around" Giraffes Ceramic. Japan. 1940s. Bright yellow giraffes feature "wrap around" necks and peer over each other's shoulders. Their yellow bodies bear a black stripe along the back and bold black polka-dots. $20.00–24.00

Geometric Zebras Ceramic. Japan. 1930s. These zebras have the stylized geometric patterning that is characteristic of the Art Deco style. $14.00–18.00

FISH and FOWL

MARINE LIFE

Sunfish Ceramic. Japan. 1940–1960s. Lovely silvery, matching sunfish have scale-textured bodies and ride atop bases sculpted to resemble cresting waves. The bodies are tinted light pink, shading into magenta along the bottom. $15.00–24.00

Comical Tropical Fish Ceramic. Japan. 1940s–1960s. Round, white tropical fish with yellow, beaklike mouths that are wide open, have white fins and tail tinted brown at the edges. $12.00–16.00

Comical Bullheads Ceramic. Japan. 1940s. Red bullhead are almost totally spherical. They have mouths turning down at the corners, a wavy crest at the top of the head, and white eyes. $12.00–16.00

Tropical Fish Porcelain. 1930s. White, matching tropical fish with crescent-shaped dorsal fins ride wave-shaped bases that bear the distinct imprint of the Art Deco style. A pale blue wash is more pronounced in one fish. $16.00–24.00

Tuna Ceramic. Japan. 1940s–1960s. Realistically sculpted and hand-painted pair of tuna have yellow tails, bodies gradating from pale lavender through red to black. $18.00–24.00

Grouper Ceramic. Japan. 1940s–1960s. Realistically executed grouper have pink, open mouths, white eyes, and bodies that range from pale to dark green (pepper) and yellow to deep orange (salt). $18.00–24.00

Speckled Sea Horses Ceramic. Japan. 1940s–1960s. Tan, realistic-looking horses are speckled with brown. $12.00–16.00

Pike Ceramic. Japan. 1940s–1960s. Dark tan pike sit on their lower fins. They are hand-painted and detailed in black. $18.00–24.00

Tiger Fish Ceramic. Japan. 1940s–1960s. Delicately executed tiger fish have pale lavender to pink bellies and pale brown bodies striated with darker stripes. $18.00–24.00

Grouper Ceramic. Japan. 1940s–1960s. One gray and one brown grouper have lovely, feathery fins fully extended. $18.00–24.00

Tropical Fish on Tray Ceramic. Japan. 1940s. Red, purple, and yellow tropical fish sit on a scalloped-edged tray, the interior of which is tinted blue. $20.00–24.00

Angelfish Ceramic. Japan. 1940s. White angelfish sit on their lower bellies. Traces of pink are evident on their gills, and their scales are outlined in gold. $12.00–18.00

Comical Tropical Fish Ceramic. Japan. 1950s. Lavender-hued tropical fish with round mouths, bulging eyes, and exaggerated fins have flat bases. $12.00–16.00

Mackerel Ceramic. Japan. 1960s. Very realistic mackerel with pink underbellies and characteristic black markings on the back balance on three caudal fins. $15.00–22.00

Perch Ceramic. Japan. 1940s–1960s. Realistic, bright pink perch have yellow tails and black outlines on tails and fins. $15.00–20.00

Trout Ceramic. Japan. 1940s–1960s. Spotted trout with down-turned mouths curve gracefully from head to toe. They rest on their fins. $15.00–20.00

Comical Walrus Ceramic. Japan. 1950s. Wrinkled walruses have bright yellow snouts with gargantuan white teeth. $16.00–18.00

Swordfish Ceramic. Japan. 1940s–1960s. Realistic swordfish with bodies tinted light gray to black, rest on lower fins. $15.00–20.00

Mud Guppy and Catfish Ceramic. Japan. 1940s–1960s. Red mud guppy with yellow fins is paired with a red catfish with white fins. The fins and tails of both have lovely, lacy quality. $15.00–20.00

Trout Ceramic. Japan. 1940s–1960s. Smallish pink trout have gray faces, yellow underbellies, and black-and-white-striped tails. $15.00–20.00

Tuna Ceramic. Japan. 1940s–1960s. Brown trout, realistically shaped and detailed, have yellow underbellies and markings. $15.00–20.00

Tropical Fish Ceramic. Japan. 1940s–1960s. Feathery tropical fish with black bodies and dark purple fins have whitish tails. $15.00–20.00

Blue Tropical Fish Ceramic. Japan. 1940s–1960s. Generic tropical fish, very stylized, attached to wave-patterned bases. The fish are blue with lavender tails, and the bases are white with blue wave lines. $15.00–20.00

Black Sunfish Ceramic. Japan. 1940s–1960s. Black, stylized sunfish sit atop simplified and enlarged bottom fin that is red in the front and black on the side to match the shiny black body. Upper fin is sharklike in dimension. White, red, and gold markings fill the body and a white and black border runs along the edge of the fish. $18.00–24.00

Sunfish Ceramic. Japan. 1940s–1960s. Very realistic sunfish have yellow eyes and striped bodies. $15.00–20.00

Orca Whale Ceramic. Japan. 1960s. Black Orca or killer whales with white underbellies have eye-shaped spots on sides. $15.00–20.00

Pink Perch Ceramic. Japan. 1940s–1960s. Pink perch with straight, black mouths have pale blue eyes and gray vertical stripes. $15.00–20.00

Comic Goldfish Ceramic. Japan. 1950s. White comical goldfish with downturned mouths have big yellow eyes and brown fins and tails. $15.00–20.00

Black Tetras Ceramic. Japan. 1940s–1960s. Simplified, though realistic, black tetras have feathery fins and tail terminating in pale blue and yellow. $15.00–20.00

Bluefish Ceramic. Japan. 1940s–1960s. Bluefish with little anatomical detail have black eyes, gray stripes, and pink edging on fins. $15.00–20.00

Yellow and Green Goldfish Ceramic. 1940s–1960s. Sculptural goldfish ride atop substantial belly fins and have flourishing dorsal fins and tails. One is yellow with green fins, the other blue with yellow fins. $15.00–20.00

Sunfish Ceramic. Japan. 1940s–1960s. Cute white goldfish with "kissy" mouths have gray stripes and yellow splotches. They sit on tiny bases sculpted to resemble lacy waves. $15.00–20.00

Red Guppies Ceramic. Japan. 1940s–1960s. Red guppies rest on very full, fanlike tails that are white on the inside, bright red on the outside. Touches of lavender appear on the fins and tail. $15.00–20.00

Fish and Fishing Creel
Ceramic. U.S.A. 1950s.
The pink fish rises out
of a cresting wave base.
The fishing creel is
done in green "wicker."
$20.00–24.00

Tiger Fish on Tray
Ceramic. U.S.A. 1940s.
Yellow, white, and
black tiger fish sits on a
scalloped tray.
$14.00–18.00

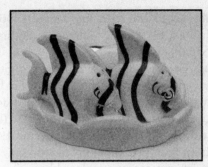

Dolphin Ceramic. Japan. 1940s–1960s. Smiling dolphin have shimmery, silvery-gray bodies. $15.00–20.00

Sturgeon Ceramic. Japan. 1940s–1960s. Anatomically accurate gray sturgeon have pink underbellies and formidable fins. $15.00–20.00

Flying Fish Ceramic. Japan. 1940s–1960s. Simplified flying fish have fully opened gill fins and disgusted expressions on their faces. They are pink with yellow fins and tails. $15.00–20.00

Trout Ceramic. Japan. 1940s–1960s. Brown, realistically detailed trout have yellow fins with black spots. $15.00–20.00

Gray Trout Ceramic. Japan. 1940s–1960s. Bluish-gray trout with simplified bodies have dark blue spots and pink streaks. $15.00–20.00

Brown Trout Ceramic. Japan. 1940s–1960s. Brown trout with yellow fins have dark purple stripes and subtle dots. $15.00–20.00

Cod Ceramic. Japan. 1940s–1960s. Realistic, silvery cod with pink and blue highlights have sharp tails. $15.00–20.00

Stylized Cod Ceramic. Japan. 1940s–1960s. Stylized yellow cod have ill-tempered expressions on their faces. Red dorsal lines are cross-hatched with blue-green diagonals. $15.00–20.00

Stylized Goldfish Ceramic. Japan. 1940s–1960s. Pink goldfish balances on its fins and has a curly upper fin. Green goldfish balances on its tummy. $15.00–20.00

Grouper Ceramic. Japan. 1940s–1960s. Bright orange grouper with pale pink underbelly balances on its chin. $15.00–20.00

White Goldfish Ceramic. Japan. 1940s. Stylized white goldfish with large fins outlined in red, have red "Bulls-eye" eyes. $15.00–20.00

Trout Ceramic. Japan. 1940s–1960s. Stylized trout with three yellow bottom fins has a shiny blue body tapering into pink and yellow and lovely black polka-dots. The mouth is open to reveal a pink tongue. $15.00–20.00

Standing Trout Ceramic. Japan. 1940s–1960s. Simplified trout with pale pink, green, and gray bodies balance on tails rising out of wave-sculpted bases inscribed "Rainbow Trout." $15.00–20.00

Leaping Swordfish Ceramic. Japan. 1940s. Simplified swordfish rise out of a base representing a large, cresting wave. Base is pale brown, fish is yellow with lavender back and fins. $15.00–20.00

Sailfish on Base Ceramic. Japan. 1940s. Pinkish sailfish, simplified and stylized in the manner of the Art Deco style, fit into a oval base sculpted to resemble geometric waves. $20.00–24.00

Big-Mouth Bass Ceramic. Japan. 1940s. Stylized big-mouth bass stand on their tails. Their finely sculpted bodies, littered with scales, are pink in front, grayish-blue in back. Large open mouths have holes for dispensing salt and pepper. $18.00–24.00

Sunfish Ceramic. Japan. 1940s–1950s. Simplified sunfish with yellow to brown bodies have touches of pink on their lower tummies. $15.00–20.00

Deep-Sea Diver and Starfish Ceramic. U.S.A. 1940s. Deep-sea diver in a pink helmet, gray suit, and brown weight belt straddles seaweed. The starfish is greenish-blue with a red border. $16.00–18.00

"Fiesta" Goldfish Ceramic. Japan. 1940s. Stylized goldfish with lavish fins and small, down-curving tails sit atop hexagonal bases tinted deep green. The fish are in "Fiesta" pottery colors. One is orange, white, and green; the other is blue, orange, and pale blue. $18.00–24.00

Fish with Top Hats Ceramic. Japan. 1940s. White, stylized fish rear up, wearing black top hats. $15.00–20.00

Whales on Beach Balls Ceramic. Japan. 1960s. Shiny gray and smiling whales balance on black, white, red, and yellow beach balls. $15.00–20.00

Puff Fish Ceramic. Japan. 1940s. Simplified white puff fish have flirtatious eyelashes and black markings. They purse their lips in the middle of puffy cheeks. $15.00–20.00

Laughing Whales Ceramic. Japan. 1950s–1960s. Shiny, stylized whales laugh and flip their giant tails. $12.00–14.00

Bluefish Bone china. Stylized bluefish on a very simple wave. $10.00–12.00

Whales with Mobile Eyes Ceramic. Japan. 1960s. Very stylized whales have movable eyes. Bodies are yellow and brown. $12.00–14.00

White and Black Whales Ceramic. Japan. 1960s. Stylized, small whales have open, red mouths. $10.00–12.00

Sitting Lobsters Ceramic. Japan. 1940s–1960s. Simplified red lobsters sit on their turned-under tails. Their sculpted features are picked out in black paint. $12.00–14.00

Lobsters with Spring Claws Ceramic. Japan. 1940s–1960s. Stylized red lobsters balance on semispherical green mounds textured to resemble seaweed. They hold up claws that are attached to the body by means of springs. $28.00–32.00

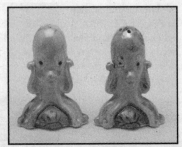

Comical Octopus Ceramic. Japan. 1950s. Matching octopi have giant yellow eyes and clasp a clam shell with six legs, waving two in the air. $14.00–18.00

Lobster Couple Ceramic. Japan. 1940s–1960s. Cute, stylized lobster couple consists of a long-skirted "Pepper" and bow-tied "Salt." Heavy horizontal stripes mark their bodies. Salt holds claws akimbo. The yellow base of each is marked with "Pepper" and "Salt." $18.00–24.00

Stylized Lobster Ceramic. Almost shrimp in shape, these stylized lobster shakers have characteristic large claws and balance on tails. In profile, they assume a flattened S-curve. $15.00–20.00

Lobsters Ceramic. Japan. 1940s–1960s. Red, simplified lobsters are flat on their bellies. $12.00–16.00

Crabs Ceramic. Japan. 1940s–1960s. Red, simplified crabs are flat on their white bellies. They have yellow highlights on face and claws. $15.00–18.00

Metal Sea Horses Metal. Stylized, sinuous sea horses sit on squat bases. $16.00–20.00

Green Sea Horses Ceramic. Japan. 1950s. Shiny green sea horses with smooth bodies and coiled tails rise from circular bases. $10.00–12.00

Sea Horse and Coral Ceramic. Ceramic Arts Studio. Beautifully detailed, yellow sea horse with coiled tail and "bull's-eye" eye nestles into a piece of brown coral. $26.00–34.00

Comical Alligators Ceramic. Japan. 1940s–1960s. Gray comical alligators with very long snouts and dragonlike bodies balance on their tails. $12.00–14.00

Alligators Ceramic. Japan. 1940s–1960s. Gray alligators with truncated bodies stand up on their tails and show each other a mouth full of sharp teeth. $10.00–15.00

Lobster and Scallop
Ceramic. U.S.A. 1950s. A bright yellow scallop shell serves as a base for a red lobster that nestles atop it. $14.00–15.00

Smiling Alligators Ceramic. Japan. 1950s. Comical alligators crawl along, one turning his head back, the other continuing benignly forward. They have brown bodies that turn pale along the underbelly. $10.00–12.00

Yellow Alligators Ceramic. Japan. 1940s. Small, stylized alligators with cross-hatching on their bodies have smiling expressions on their faces and short tails. $10.00–12.00

Octopus Ceramic. Japan. A comical, orange octopus with big yellow eyes and pursed lips curls two tentacles to its cheeks and clutches a stone with its remaining "legs." $12.00–14.00

Large Clam Shells Ceramic. Japan. 1950s. Large, realistic clam shells are painted gray with white highlights. $10.00–12.00

Small Clam Shells Ceramic. Japan. Small clam shells have realistic fold marks detailed in dark gray. $10.00–12.00

Starfish and Olive Shell Ceramic. Japan. 1960s. Very realistic starfish is teamed with olive shell. The starfish is pink on the bottom, blue on top, while the olive shades from brown to yellow to pink with a white lip. $12.00–14.00

Nautilus Shell on Coral Ceramic. Japan. 1950s. Lovely white Nautilus shell rests on a base of brown-painted coral. $12.00–14.00

Whelk Shells Ceramic. Japan. 1950s. Very realistic whelks are white and brown. $10.00–12.00

Cowrie Shells Ceramic. Japan. 1950s–1960s. Very realistic cowrie shells are white with pale blue wash, dark gray spots, and black zig-zag "lip." $12.00–14.00

Scallop Shells Ceramic. Japan. 1950s–1960s. Realistic scallop shells are standing on their hinges. Pepper is tinted blue, salt is entirely white. $10.00–12.00

Abalone Shell Ceramic. Japan. 1950s–1960s. Realistic abalone shells are pale blue, pink, and gray, with yellow highlights. $10.00–12.00

Razor Clam Shells Ceramic. Japan. 1940s–1950s. Slightly rounded razor clam shells are pale brown with lavender markings. $12.00–14.00

Spikey Shells Ceramic. Japan. 1940s–1960s. White, spikey whelks have beautiful, nacreous luster. $12.00–14.00

Generic Shells Ceramic. Japan. 1940s–1960s. Beige, corkscrew shells have brown rings and pink lips. $10.00–12.00

Whelk with Creature Ceramic. Japan. 1940s–1960s. A brown, simplified whelk shell shows its inhabitant protruding from the front. $10.00–12.00

Turtles Ceramic. Japan. 1940s–1960s. Yellow turtles with white underbellies carry large, well-articulated shells in white shading into dark gray. $10.00–14.00

Comical Turtles Ceramic. Japan. 1940s–1950s. Cartoonish turtles stand on their hind feet and show off their yellow, striped bellies. One salutes, while the other smiles. $20.00–26.00

Sitting and Lying Turtles Ceramic. Japan. 1940s–1960s. One beige, stylized turtle sits and "begs" while the other lies on its brown shell. Both have the "feel" of cartoon characters. $20.00–24.00

Yellow Turtles Ceramic. Japan. 1940s–1960s. Cartoonish, simplified yellow turtles with squat shells have green highlights and black outlining. $10.00–12.00

Snails Ceramic. Japan. 1940s–1960s. Realistic brown snails emerge from their shells and show their horns. $14.00–18.00

Frog and Water Lily on a Lily Pad Tray Ceramic. Japan. 1950s. This three-piece set consists of a green lily-pad-shaped tray with a split bamboo handle. On it sits the shakers: a frog and a blue water lily. $24.00–28.00

Fish and Worm on Hook Ceramic. U.S.A. 1940s. A yellow fish with gold highlights purses its mouth at a green worm that is twisted around a golden hook. $20.00–24.00

Starfish Ceramic. Japan. 1950s. These starfish have brown bodies and blue centers. $10.00–14.00

Snails Ceramic. Japan. 1940s–1960s. Simplified snails feature spiral-shaped shell to which adheres the wormlike body of the creature, capped by knoblike antennae. $14.00–18.00

Snails Ceramic. Japan. 1940s–1960s. Cartoonish snails, rather small, rise up on small bases and display humanoid faces devoid of antennae. One has brown body, white shell, and yellow base; the other has green body, white shell, and yellow base. $14.00–18.00

Snail Shell Ceramic. Japan. 1940s–1960s. Realistic, empty snail shell is brown with pink interior. $10.00–14.00

Sea Lions Ceramic. Japan. 1960s. Realistic sea lions (a larger male and a smaller female) have actual hair whiskers. $14.00–20.00

Penguins Ceramic. Stylized penguin has spiral-detailed body with black wings and knobby head and yellow conical beak. $12.00–16.00

Frogs on Base Ceramic. Japan. 1940s. Green realistic tree frogs with yellow markings fit into a base textured to look like grass. $20.00–25.00

Comical Frog in Lily Flower Ceramic. Sears, Roebuck & Company. 1977. Green comical frog with saucer eyes fits into yellow water lilly. $16.00–18.00

Frog and Mushroom on Base Ceramic. Japan. 1940s–1970s. Green frog with yellow underbelly faces a yellow mushroom with green cap. Both fit on base textured to resemble leaves. $22.00–28.00

Comical Frogs Ceramic. Japan. 1940s–1970s. Mother and child frogs have free-standing saucer eyes, large grinning faces, and bright green bodies. $10.00–12.00

Frog on Red Water Lily Ceramic. Japan. 1940s. Dark green frog with red mouth and blue capelet sits atop a red, apple-shaped water lily. $24.00–30.00

Frog and Toadstool Ceramic. Japan. 1940s–1950s. Dark green realistic frog is teamed with a brown toadstool which is twice the frog's size. Conceivably, the frog may sit atop the toadstool. $12.00–18.00

Frogs in Tray Ceramic. Japan. 1940s–1950s. Cartoonish, sitting frogs with large, antennaelike eyes sit side by side in a water-lilly-shaped leaf that is white on the outside and green on the inside. One frog is green, the other brown. $20.00–24.00

Little Frogs Ceramic. Japan. 1950s. Small frogs have simplified bodies painted yellow and deep green. One opens a red mouth, the other keeps its mouth shut. $12.00–14.00

Frogs Ceramic. Japan. 1940s–1950s. Identical green frogs have yellow tummies, red mouths, and white eyes. Both sit. $12.00–14.00

Toads Ceramic. Japan. 1940s–1960s. Smiling, simplified, green toads have brown spots all over their bodies. $12.00–18.00

White Bullfrogs Ceramic. Japan. 1950s. White bullfrogs with bulging cheeks have grayish backs. Both sit and frown. $12.00–14.00

Comical Frogs Ceramic. Japan. 1960s. Comical frogs with bulging cheeks have human hands. One sits, clasping its ·hands on its round tummy, the other reclines on one elbow. $16.00–24.00

Comical Frogs Ceramic. Japan. 1950s. Sitting, comical frogs eye each other. One has pink tummy and holds its arms in conversational position. The other has green tummy and folds its paws over its tummy. $16.00–20.00

Comical Frogs Ceramic. Japan. 1950s. Green, sitting frogs with comic expressions have large eyes atop their heads. One crouches with all four feet on ground, the other sits up. $16.00–20.00

Frogs, Water Lily, and Bug Set Ceramic. Japan. 1940s. This four-piece set consists of a handled tray made to resemble a water-lily-covered pond; a central yellow mustard pot on which detachable leaf reclines a black-winged, pink-hat-

ted bug; and, on either side, a pale green frog sitting on a
brown bump. $50.00–60.00

Mermaids on Nautilus Shells Ceramic. Japan. 1950s.
Identical little mermaids with green fishtails and red hair
perch on white nautilus shells. $14.00–20.00

Mermaid Children Ceramic. Japan. 1940s–1950s. Mermaid
girls with large heads, ponytails, and green tails have pink
cheeks, large eyes, and gold highlights. $16.00–20.00

Deep-Sea Diver Ceramic. Japan. 1960s. One white and one
gray deep-sea diver look up, holding one arm up to their ears,
the other to their belts. $12.00–18.00

Pink Fish with Handle Tails Ceramic. Japan. Totally stylized fish with white, oversize heads, long black eyelashes
cast down in repose, have pink fins and tails that curl up and
over to meet the dorsal fin, making a carrying handle.
$10.00–14.00

Creel of Fish Ceramic. Portugal. An open, basket-textured
creel holds two gaping, purplish fish. $14.00–18.00

Fish Hanging from Coral Ceramic. Japan. A smiling pink C-
shaped fish hangs from a ring of green coral attached to a
white scallop base. $14.00–18.00

Starfish Ceramic. Japan. Yellow starfish have green tops and
red centers. $10.00–14.00

Tropical Fish Ceramic. Japan. Cute, stylized tropical fish
come in a variety of colors, usually with salt the lighter shade
and pepper the darker. They tend to have simplified bodies,
with just a hint of scales in the body pattern. $10.00–14.00

Tropical Rainbow Fish Ceramic.
Japan. 1950s. These tropical fish
are remarkable for their intense and
nuanced coloring. Bright pink fins
flutter atop bodies that shade from
pale blue to ultramarine and are
striated with maroon. The tails are
white and green and the bottom
fins are yellow. $12.00–16.00

Clown Fish Ceramic. Vandor. 1980s. Clown fish, beautifully painted and embossed, are green with pink, yellow, and blue details; or yellow with pink, black, and blue details. $12.00–14.00

Tiger Fish Ceramic. Vandor. 1980s. Tiger fish are black with yellow stripes or yellow with blue stripes. $10.00–12.00

Real Clam Shakers Clam shells. A closed clam shell is attached to half a shell base. The words "Salt" and "Pepper" are written on the top. $10.00–14.00

Razor Clams on Clam Bases Ceramic. Japan. Realistic razor clams with the animal protruding from either end sit on speckled white and black shell bases. $10.00–14.00

Whelk Ceramic. Japan. Flattened whelks with eight spines are tinted brown, beige, and rose. $10.00–12.00

Red Tropical Fish Ceramic. Japan. Red fish with copious blue fins have blue stripes. $12.00–14.00

Rainbow Trout Ceramic. Japan. Pouty rainbow trout in realistic color have pink fins and tails. $12.00–14.00

Swordfish Ceramic. Japan. Stylized with simplified swordfish with white bodies tinted blue, yellow beaks, and blue, white, and yellow tails and fin have the words "San Diego, Calif." written on their sides. $12.00–14.00

Laughing Hippopotamuses Ceramic. Japan. Gray, laughing hippopotamuses have pink nostrils and ears and gaping, red mouths. Their folds are shaded in gray. One stands, the other lies down. $14.00–18.00

Pink Laughing Hippopotamuses Ceramic. Japan. Pink hippopotamuses in identical poses laugh uproariously. Their tongues are pink, and the folds on their skin are outlined in brown. $14.00–18.00

Gray Smiling Hippopotamuses Ceramic. Japan. Identical gray hippopotamuses with white faces have red nostrils and smiling mouths. $14.00–18.00

Brown Nesting Hippopotamuses Ceramic. Japan. 1950s. Brown hippopotamuses with tan faces stack up on top of each other so that the lower one lies down and the upper one rests its forepaws on the lower one's back. $12.00–14.00

Hippopotamus with Ball
Ceramic. Japan. 1950s. A gray, laughing hippopotamus contemplates a ball that resembles a melting ice cream sundae. $14.00–18.00

Sitting Brown Hippopotamuses Ceramic. Japan. 1950s. Goofy-looking tan hippopotamuses sit in human poses and ogle each other. Their most distinctive features are the nostrils, which are drawn as spirals. $12.00–14.00

White Hippopotamuses Ceramic. Japan. 1960s. White hippopotamuses have very simplified bodies and pink cheeks. One is larger than the other. They are remarkable for the large folds around the necks. $12.00–14.00

Seals Ceramic. Matching seals, rendered in realistic detail, have gray bodies, white bosoms, and red mouths. $12.00–16.00

Comical Crocodiles Ceramic. Japan. White, comical crocodiles with uplifted tails have green eyes and mouths and a charming green cross-hatching pattern on body and tail, interspersed with red dots. $16.00–20.00

One-Piece Alligator Ceramic. This one-piece, simplified alligator has a yellow underbelly and a brown top, as well as unusual blue eyes. The mouth is one shaker, the tail the other. $16.00–20.00

Walrus Ceramic. Japan. Beautifully detailed pair of walrus in deep brown feature a female and a male with tremendous white tusks. $16.00–20.00

Small Frog Ceramic. Japan. Crudely fashioned kelly green frogs have black smears for mouths. $8.00–10.00

Giant Toad Shakers Ceramic. Japan. Smiling green toads with red mouths, bug-eyes, and very large bodies are covered with wartlike excrescences. $16.00–20.00

Frog on Crocodile Ceramic. "Sigma." A green and white frog sits in a human pose on the rounded tail of a pensive, yellow-bellied crocodile with grinning mouth. $45.00–60.00

Deep-Sea Diver, Fish and Base Porcelain. Japan. 1930s–1940s. This spectacular set consists of a gray base with embossed and hand-painted deep-sea life (starfish, shells, seaweed) from the middle of which rises a deep-sea diver in a red helmet. On either side of this stand shiny gray sharks with black stripes. $40.00–50.00

Lobster and Trap Goebel. 1954. Schumann. The lobster, as salt, has three holes, while the lobster trap, with two holes, is the pepper shaker. $25.00–30.00

Big and Little Fish Nesters Goebel. 1939. Arthur Möller. White rotund fish with orange trim nestle so that the large one cradles the small in its fin. $25.00–30.00

Clams Bone china. Matching white clam shells stand upright on the small base of scalloped rock tinted brown. The base may also be white. The letters "S" and "P" are embossed on the corner of each clam. $10.00–14.00

Birds

Chicken and Rooster Ceramic. Japan. Pre–1960. Black and white eating hen and crowing rooster with red combs and yellow feet. $20.00–24.00

Chicken and Rooster Ceramic. Japan. Pre–1960. White rooster and hen with brilliant red combs and yellow beaks, and white feet—touched with yellow—straddling black bases. $20.00–24.00

Chicken and Rooster Ceramic. Japan. Pre-1960. White and black sitting hen and standing rooster, both with ruby-red combs and red-rimmed eyes. Yellow beaks and claws. $16.00–20.00

Chicken and Rooster in Basket Ceramic. Japan. Early 1930s. Polychrome hen and rooster nesting in white and blue "wicker" basket filled with varicolored flowers. $24.00–30.00

Chicken and Rooster on "Lawn" Ceramic. Japan. Early 1930s. Polychrome hen and rooster grazing on flowered green "lawn" base. $30.00–36.00

Chickens in Basket Ceramic. Japan. Early 1930s. A pair of predominantly yellow hens, one roosting, the other pecking

Green Parrots Bisque. Beautifully detailed, anatomically correct green parrots with pin bosoms sit on brown stumps. $16.00–20.00

White-Ringed Ducks Ceramic. Rosemeade. 1940s–1960s. Realistically painted mallards have green heads, beige bodies, white neck rings, and stand on bases resembling rocks. $26.00–30.00

at the "hay" in a blue "wicker" basket lined with green leaves. $24.00–30.00

Black Hens Glazed red clay. Black-glazed hens with brilliant red combs and golden beaks. Claws resemble paws. $6.00–10.00

Chicks in Shells Ceramic. Japan. Pre-1960s. Matching pair of round yellow chicks on green bases flanked by eggshell halves, all resting on a pale green base. $16.00–20.00

Roosters Ceramic. Japan. Pre-1960s. Matching pair of white crowing roosters with red combs, yellow beaks, and smears of orange glaze on the belly. $6.00–10.00

Ducks Ceramic. Czechoslovakia. Round white ducks with orange and navy bills, black dot eyes, and wings outlined in black brushstrokes. $10.00–14.00

Ducks Hand-painted ceramic. Japan. Pre-1960s. Matching pair of ducks, hand-painted with navy beaks and feet, red heads, brown chests, and white bellies. Each duck stands on a "log." $12.00–16.00

Ducks Hand-painted ceramic. Japan. Pre–1960s. Matching pair of ducks, hand-painted with navy beaks and feet, orange bodies highlighted with brown. Each duck stands on leaves. $10.00–14.00

Swans Bone china. Japan. Pre-1960s. Large set of white swans with S-curving necks, graceful, upswept wings, and orange beaks. Pepper has one hole in neck, while salt has three. $12.00–16.00

Turkeys Ceramic. Rosemeade Pottery. Wahpeton, ND. Laura Taylor. 1940–1961. The realistically detailed turkeys are 3" high. $12.00–16.00

Pheasants Ceramic. Rosemeade Pottery. Wahpeton, ND. Laura Taylor. 1940–1961. Lifelike pheasants are 3" high. $14.00–18.00

Cardinals on Branch Ceramic. Japan. 1930s. Bright red cardinals, each a shaker, nestle on a three-twigged branch with leaves. Birds and branch are realistic. $20.00–24.00

Canaries on Branch Ceramic. Japan. 1930s–1950s. Bright yellow canaries, each a shaker, sit on a two-pronged branch with a flat base and a cluster of flowers at the fork. $14.00–20.00

Mother Bird and Nest on Branch Ceramic. Japan. 1930s–1950s. A yellow-bellied, red-headed mother bird perches on a stump and looks down at yellow nest, filled with eggs, that sits on lower stump. The bird and the nest are shakers, the branching stumps are the base. This set appears in several colors variations, among them one with a grayish stump and nest and green bird. $18.00–24.00

Pink Birds on Branch Ceramic. Japan. 1940s. Pink birds, the male with outstretched wings, the female at rest, nestle on a branch set diagonally into a stump. $14.00–18.00

White Birds on Tray Ceramic. Japan. 1930s–1950s. White birds and brownish feathers on top nestle on a base textured to resemble a log. One bird has red-tipped wings, the other, blue-tipped wings. $12.00–14.00

Blackbird on Nest and Babies Ceramic. Japan. 1930s–1950s. A black, red-throated mother bird is attached to an orange nest in which sit two babies (the shakers) with deep green backs, white bellies, and red, open mouths. $18.00–24.00

Pink Birds Hanging from Branch Ceramic. Japan. 1930s–1960s. Two pink birds hook swirling tails around the arms of a T-shaped branch. The birds are shakers. The branch rises from a grass-shaped base. $14.00–20.00

Birdcage with Cat Ceramic. Japan. 1930s–1940s. A white and black cat (a shaker) raises its paw at a white birdcage (a shaker) hanging from a branch sprouting out a stump which forms the base. $12.00–16.00

Birdcage with Cat Ceramic. Japan. 1930s–1940s. A tabby cat sits at the base of a tree trunk, bedecked with flowers, and raises a paw menacingly. From the trunk hangs a birdcage with the picture of a bird painted on its side. $20.00–22.00

Canaries on Stylized Perch Ceramic. Japan. 1930s. Simplified canaries sit on a faintly Japanese-inspired perch that looks like a self-supporting swing. The letters "S" and "P" are on the birds' bosoms. The birds fit into the crossbar of the perch. $12.00–18.00

Birds on Stumps with Handle Ceramic. Japan. 1940s. A pair of yellow birds, one with outspread wings, the other at rest, fit into the two levels of a brown stump with flowers. The taller of the two stumps sprouts a handle that connects it to the base. $14.00–18.00

Birds on Stumps with Handle Ceramic. Japan. 1940s. Pink birds, very simplified, perch on a brown, double-stump base with handle on one side. $12.00–18.00

Spotted Birds on Perch Ceramic. Japan. 1940s. Yellow birds with brown and gray spots nestle atop a perch that resembles an anvil with a cut-out central arch. $12.00–14.00

Parrots Ceramic. Japan. 1940s. Crudely fashioned parrots sit on green bases. One has orange head and yellow body, the other has yellow head and orange body. $12.00–16.00

Canaries in a Basket Hanging from Metal Stand
Ceramic and metal. Japan. 1950s. A white and gold checked basket hangs from a metal stand. On each side of the basket perches a singing bird (the shakers). $18.00–22.00

Pink Flamingos Ceramic. Japan. 1950s. The flamingos have bright pink upper bodies, white lower bodies with black spots on wings, and stand on ornamental bases that merge with their spindly legs. One bends its head down, the other looks straight ahead $20.00–24.00

Pink Flamingos Ceramic. Japan. 1930s. Beautiful, light pink flamingos with yellow beaks fan their wings. Their long, pink legs are surrounded by grayish, Deco-inspired foliage. $20.00–24.00

Pink Flamingos Ceramic. Japan. 1950s. S-shaped necks of these deep pink flamingos terminate in pointed heads with small beaks. The long legs are straight and are flanked by columnar foliage in green. $18.00–22.00

Cardinals Ceramic. Japan. 1950s. Bright red cardinals sit each on its own branch-with-feather cluster. One cardinal fans its wings, the other looks quietly forward. The detailing is realistic. $10.00–14.00

Orange Birds Ceramic. Japan. 1940s. Bright orange underbellies contrast with blue, yellow, and black wings of these two birds on simulated branch bases. One crouches, the other sits tall. $10.00–14.00

White Birds with Black Wings Ceramic. Japan. 1940s. White birds with black wings have red and yellow eyes. One looks up, the other opens its wings. $10.00–14.00

White Turtle Doves Ceramic. Japan. 1950s. Stylized white turtle doves have gold trim. The bases are painted, in gold, in a design of laurel leaves. $10.00–14.00

White Seagulls Ceramic. Japan. 1940s. White seagulls with yellow beaks stand on black bases. $14.00–18.00

White Birds with Red Heads Bone china. 1940s. White birds with deeply textured bodies preen. They have red heads and backs and stand on yellow bases. $10.00–12.00

Long-Beaked Birds Ceramic. Japan. Brown and white long-beaked birds with red spots on their heads perch on simulated branch bases. $10.00–12.00

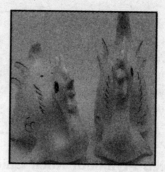

Stylized Chicken and Rooster Ceramic. Japan. 1950s. White hen and rooster have roughly S-shaped bodies with scalloped tail feathers. Hen's beak is open, the rooster's is closed. $14.00–20.00

Owls Ceramic. Japan. 1950s. Stylized owls are cast with deep feather details. One extends its wings, the other keeps them close to its body. $12.00–14.00

Stylized Birds Ceramic. Japan. 1940s. Stylized sparrowlike birds have blue upper bodies and bright pink underbellies. One crouches down, the other sits up. $10.00–12.00

Birds in Twig Nest Ceramic and twigs. Dark brown bird couple with red heads and yellow beaks sits side by side in a twig nest. $12.00–14.00

Doves Ceramic. Japan. White, round, stylized doves with fat bosoms have pale blue wings and tails, and orange spots on the front. One looks up, the other looks straight ahead. $12.00–14.00

Flying Blue Jays Ceramic. Japan. Blue jays with outstretched wings in flying position have grayish upper bodies. Their feet are shown clutching a twig rising from a cluster of leaves. $12.00–14.00

American Bald Eagle Ceramic. Japan. Sepia-colored bald eagles have white heads and bosoms, and stand on simulated branch bases. One fans its wings, the other sits at rest. $14.00–18.00

Yellow Birds Ceramic. Japan. A pair of plump, bright yellow birds with white bosoms and black rings around their beaks are supported by pedestal bases. $10.00–14.00

Rooster and Hen Ceramic. Japan. White rooster and hen with chartreuse bosoms, black wing and tail feathers and lavender backs have bright red combs. Hen pecks, rooster looks around. $10.00–12.00

Luster Toucans Luster. Japan. 1930s. Long-billed toucanlike birds were available in a variety of color combinations. $20.00–25.00

Barred Plymouth Rock Chickens Ceramic. Japan. 1970s. A large rooster and a smaller hen have the characteristic black and white stripes of the Barred Plymouth Rock species. Both stand on green bases. $14.00–18.00

White Chickens Ceramic. Japan. Very ordinary white chickens with very simplified bodies set on flattened bases. They have red combs. $10.00–14.00

Rooster and Hen Ceramic. Japan. Fat-footed rooster and hen have deeply textured bodies. Rooster towers over hen with his fanned tail and large crest. The birds are white with a yellow, gray, and pink wash. $10.00–12.00

Rooster and Hen Ceramic. Japan. Black-and-white speckled hen and rooster have solid black wings and tails and yellow feet painted onto rectangular bases of green "grass." Rooster is one-third taller than the hen. $10.00–12.00

Rooster and Hen Ceramic. Japan. White rooster and hen with moderately detailed bodies have pink tail tips and bases, bright combs, and black beaks. Rooster is larger than hen. $10.00–12.00

Black Rooster and Hen Ceramic. Japan. Stylized rooster and hen come in a modified kingpin shape with brilliant red combs, yellow beaks, and white "S" and "P" on the chest. $10.00–12.00

Chicken Holding Eggs Ceramic. Japan. A buff, deeply textured chicken with bright red comb and typically beady chicken eyes holds in its prehensile hands two brown eggs, which are shakers. $14.00–20.00

Rooster and Hen Ceramic. Japan. Deep green chicken and rooster have fluffy, yellow-feathered necks, red combs, and white throats. Tall rooster raises one leg from the green base, while shorter hen squats down on her green base and opens her beak to squawk. $12.00–16.00

White Hen and Rooster Ceramic. Japan. Crudely detailed rooster and hen are entirely white except for the combs (red) and beaks (yellow). In this instance, it is the hen that towers over the rooster. $10.00–12.00

Chickens in Wire Stand Ceramic and metal wire. Italy. Whtie, stylized hens with red combs sit in a red wire stand that comprises of double sets of circles attached to a central carrier. $10.00–12.00

Cartoonish Chickens Ceramic. Japan. White, cartoonish chickens in elongated egg shapes have black beaks, red combs, and rounded drawings of wings, "sunburst" eyes, and bosom feathers. The juncture between neck and chest is scalloped and the tails protrude almost like small handles. $10.00–12.00

Rooster and Hen Egg Cup Shakers Ceramic. Japan. Deeply textured rooster and hen come apart at the juncture of neck with chest to reveal egg cups. They have gracefully arched tails, flamboyant combs. Hen's mouth is open. $10.00–12.00

Rooster Hen Black clay. Brightly glazed sitting rooster and standing hen have red combs. $10.00–12.00

Cartoonish Chicks in a Basket Carrier Ceramic. Japan. Busts of white chicks with large, baby-doll eyes, orange mouths, and red crests are placed on either side of the handle of an orange "wicker" basket with red bow. $10.00–12.00

Chicks with Floral Pattern Ceramic. Japan. Very simplified chicks, whose form has been reduced to three spherical shapes, have yellow, double-triangular beaks and red flower design. $9.00–12.00

Turkey and Hen Ceramic. Japan. Crude though realistic turkey cock and hen have gray and white bodies, red combs, and stand on trapezoidal bases. $10.00–12.00

Hugging Geese Ceramic. Japan. 1970s. White geese with stylized bodies and orange beaks and feet interlock necks and wings. $12.00–16.00

Ducks Ceramic. Japan. Unusual lavender ducks and pale green wings, dark green heads, and yellow beaks have simplified bodies. $14.00–16.00

Duck Couple Ceramic. Japan. A green-headed male with yellow beak and dark brown body is teamed with a rust-colored female with yellow beak. $10.00–12.00

Brown Ducks Bisque. Lovely brown ducks with loonlike faces and beaks have realistically detailed bodies and stand on simulated rocks. $16.00–20.00

Duck Couple Ceramic. Japan. A black-headed, white-breasted duck preens on a green base. The brown-headed duck is identically posed, differing only in coloration. $10.00–16.00

Mallard Ducks Ceramic. Japan. Classical mallards with green heads, deep-red breasts, and white underbellies are realistically detailed. They stand on marshlike bases. One duck preens itself, the other looks about attentively. $14.00–18.00

Clay Ducks Clay. Mexico. Crudely shaped orange clay ducks nudge their beaks under their wings, which are pale blue and yellow. $12.00–14.00

Ducks Ceramic. Japan. White ceramic ducks with simplified bodies that show a touch of embossing on the back and wings, have striated orange feet grasping the sides of a round base tinted with green. The ducks have green heads, orange beaks, brown bodies, and black, red, white and green wings. $12.00–14.00

Yellow Ducks Ceramic. Japan. Yellow-bosomed ducks with black heads, dark green rings, and exaggerated yellow beaks have orange smears of paint for feet on dull green bases. $12.00–14.00

Red-headed Ducks Ceramic. Japan. Matte-finish red-headed ducks in identical positions have gray beaks and feet, brown bodies, and brown, mud-simulating bases. $12.00–14.00

Scolding Ducks Ceramic. Japan. Yellow ducks with brown-speckled bodies, green wings, wave-patterned tails, and large, flat orange feet have green heads and reptilian eyes. Both have open yellow beaks with orange interiors and appear to be scolding. Male is larger than female. $14.00–20.00

Toucans Clay. Mexico. One beige and one black toucan have huge beaks and crude bodies. $10.00–14.00

Peacocks Ceramic. Japan. 1950s. Black-headed peacocks with pastel-colored body feathers perch on tan rocks. $15.00–18.00

Toucans Ceramic. Japan. Simplified, squat toucans have slicked back, brightly colored head feathers, large, flat beaks, rounded bodies, and flat feet. They come in a variety of bright color combinations, and all have round eyes with prominent black pupils. $12.00–18.00

Toucans Ceramic. Japan. Rounded toucans have huge yellow beaks, red heads, and bluish wings. Their large eyes are outlined in black. $10.00–14.00

Large, Red Toucans Ceramic. Large red toucans with gray bills and white eyes have little gray claws clutching a brown twig terminating in three green leaves. Salt is larger then pepper. $10.00–14.00

Fancy Cartoonish Birds Ceramic. Staffordshire, England. Cartoonish birds on yellow pedestal feet have orange bodies, green heads and tails, and yellow, smiling beaks. Tails are attached to corks. $18.00–20.00

Baltimore Orioles Ceramic. Japan. Realistic, yellow-bellied, black-backed Baltimore orioles have blue beaks and sit on bases simulating twigs on ground. $14.00–20.00

Comic Woodpeckers Ceramic. Japan. Long, yellow-billed wookpeckers with stylized bodies stand on brown bases and have black "topknots" that resemble bellhops' caps. $12.00–16.00

Blue Jays Ceramic. Japan. Identical blue jays with black backs stand on bases simulating tree stumps. $14.00–20.00

Pink Blue Jays Ceramic. Japan. Very unusual, pink blue jays have gold-trimmed bodies. They stand on very delicate pink feet. $10.00–14.00

Chicks in a Basket Ceramic. Japan. Yellow, round chicks sit in broken eggshells which nestle into a green, wickerlike basket stuffed with ceramic flowers. $16.00–20.00

Pink Flamingos Ceramic. Japan. 1930s. Entirely pink flamingos stand on green bases textured to resemble reeds rendered in the Art Deco manner. One flamingo preens its back feathers, the other picks at its foot. $20.00–24.00

Pink Flamingos on One Leg Ceramic. Japan. 1930s. Pale pink flamingos with black beaks stand on one foot in identical poses. Their claws are yellow. The pink, rectangular bases effloresce into Deco-stylized foliage. The word "Florida" appears on the base. $20.00–24.00

Salmon-Colored Flamingos Ceramic. Japan. 1930s. Salmon-colored flamingos stand on smokey bases, on which, in gold, is scrawled the word "Florida." One flamingo preens its back, the other pecks at the grass. The details, in Deco-sinuous lines, are rather crudely handled. $16.00–20.00

One-Legged Pink Flamingos Ceramic. Japan. 1940s. Beady-eyed, pink flamingos have prominent yellow beaks terminating in black. Their wings are opened, they stand on one leg in a clumb of Deco-dictated foliage. The embossing is very deep and stylized. $16.00–20.00

Squat Pink and Gray Flamingos Ceramic. Japan. 1930s. Pink flamingos have golden, very sharp beaks and legs, and stand in gray, Deco-inspired foliage. One bends down to pick at its one outstretched wing, the other swivels its head to root out a flea from its back feathers. $18.00–22.00

Flamingos with Outspread Wings Ceramic. Japan. 1930s. Pink flamingos with white underbellies and orange legs spread out both wings. They stand on pedestal bases embossed with fern design painted green. $16.00–18.00

Flamingo With Palm Tree Ceramic. Japan. A pink flamingo with black tail rises from Deco-inspired foliage. The mate to this shaker is a graceful, triple-trunked palm tree. $20.00–24.00

Blue and White Penguins Ceramic. Japan. Small white stylized penguins have blue beaks, wings, feet, and eyes. $10.00–12.00

Black, White, and Orange Penguins Ceramic. Japan. White penguins with simplified bodies stand on hexagonal orange feet and have very long and pointed orange bills. The backs of their bodies are black. $12.00–16.00

Penguin Pals Plastic and swirled glass. Stylized penguins have bodies made of white swirled glass with black wings and heads made of plastic. Labels on the bodies read "San Juan." $12.00–16.00

Plastic Penguins Plastic. Matching, stylized penguins stand on white bases that resemble a twelve-petaled flower. $10.00–14.00

Tiny Penguins in Hats Ceramic. Japan. Tiny penguins with long, outstretched wings and pink feet wear white boaters and natty, dotted bow ties. $12.00–14.00

Yellow Penguins Ceramic. Japan. Squat, rounded, yellow penguins have black heads and red beaks. Two yellow stripes run the length of the head. $10.00–14.00

Penguin Chefs Ceramic. Japan. Cartoonish penguins in bow ties (one yellow, one red) wear chef's toques. $12.00–14.00

Yellow and White Penguins Ceramic. Japan. Identically posed penguins on "ice floe" bases have yellow bellies, black heads, wings, and feet, and white underbellies. $12.00–14.00

Gold-footed Penguins Ceramic. Japan. Stylized round penguins on round bases have white dots for eyes, rounded wingtips, and gold, pointed feet. $12.00–14.00

Penguins in Formal Wear Ceramic. Japan. Distinguished-looking penguins in formal wear have white eyes, black bodies. One wears bow tie and black vest. $12.00–14.00

Gray Stylized Penguins Ceramic. Highly glazed, stylized standing penguins with wings molded into the body have

Deco Birds Ceramic. U.S.A. 1930s. Bizarre, stylized birds in a deep, cobalt blue have spherical bodies and heads and a peculiar, zig-zag comb that betrays the influence of Art Deco. $20.00–24.00

rhinestone eyes and the letters "S" and "P" on their bellies. $10.00–12.00

Pelicans Ceramic. Japan. White, identically posed pelicans have long yellow beaks and feet on a blue, water-simulating base that may or may not carry the inscription "Florida." $12.00–16.00

Cockatoos Ceramic. Vandor. 1985. Beautiful reproductions of Art Deco set show white cockatoos standing on green tiered pedestals. $22.00–24.00

Ostrich and Baby Ceramic. Japan. A comical-looking mother ostrich with a brown body, moony eyes, and long, yellow legs in a green base is flanked by a white baby emerging from a yellow egg. $24.00–28.00

Cartoony Ostriches Ceramic. Japan. Goofy-looking ostriches with black bodies, hot-pink necks, and yellow bills stare googly-eyed at each other. Their scrawny yellow legs rise amid cacti. $12.00–14.00

Owls on Tree Trunks Ceramic. Japan. Tiny gray owls with colorful wings balance on a green, ornate base resembling two moss-covered tree trunks. $10.00–12.00

Yellow and Red Owls Ceramic. Japan. Yellow owls with very simplified bodies and anxious expressioins on their faces stand on brown bases. The heads and backs are red. $12.00–14.00

Owls on a Tray Ceramic. Squat, yellow owls with white and brown feet have brown "ears," yellow "sunflower" eyes, and blue topknots. They nestle on an oval, yellow tray textured to resemble bark. $10.00–14.00

Bobwhite Quail Ceramic. Rosemeade. 1940s–1960s. Realistically sculptured and painted bobwhite quail— male and female—stand on green bases. $20.00–25.00

Comical Owls Ceramic. Japan. 1960s. Yellow, crude, owls with brown-outlined embossing simulating feathers and wings have orange, beaklike noses. The female with blue eye shadow sleeps. The male looks at her, bug-eyed. $10.00–12.00

Owls on Green Bases Ceramic. Japan. 1960s. Ugly horned owls with protruding eyes have tiger-striped bosoms and sit on green, bark-shaped arches. One owl has blue eyes, the other, beige. $10.00–12.00

Luster Owls Lusterware. Simplified, squat owls with no detailing, round red and black eyes, and oval black beaks have yellow, spectacle-shaped eye areas. $10.00–12.00

Cartoony Owls Ceramic. Japan. 1970s. A couple of flirting, brown owls have red and white eyes, a nosegay of yellow flowers, and white bosoms with brown and black sides and backs. Their bodies are deeply embossed with feather pattern. Girl stands in a demure pose with closed eyes. Boy towers over her. $10.00–12.00

Green Owls Ceramic. Japan. 1970s. Green owls with overall braiding pattern have red feline ears, white googly eyes, and triangular red beaks. A sticker at their base reads "Grand Junction, Oregon," $10.0–12.00

Pigeons Ceramic. Germany. Realistic, pastel-colored pigeons stand on pale green, grass-shaped bases. Pepper bird is dove gray, salt bird is yellow. $12.00–16.00

Fawn-colored Birds Ceramic. Japan. Small, fawn-colored birds crouch on pale green bases. The beaks of the simplified birds are black, the tops of their heads, orange. $10.00–12.00

Luster Doves Lusterware. Pale gray doves with fantails and yellow beaks stand on yellow bases. Gold trim highlights their eyes and feet. $12.00–14.00

Doves in Red Ceramic. Japan. Very stylized mother and child doves have elongated tails and S-shaped bodies. No wing or feet details distract from the smooth, modern lines. Both are bright red with black highlights on tail and head. $10.00–12.00

Red Cardinals Bisque. Realistic. Identically posed cardinals sit on beige stumps. $16.00–20.00

Swans Ceramic. Japan. A male and a female swan pose on bases simulating water and reeds. The male has a long, serpentine neck gathered into a loop. The female stands tall. Both have golden beaks. $12.00–14.00

Luster Swans: Shakers and Sugar Bowl Lusterware. Mother swan (sugar bowl) with two swanlings (salt-and-pepepr shakers) have wings in blue, red, and dark blue, and red beaks capped by green. $35.00–40.00

Road Runners Ceramic. Japan. Brown, realistic road runners stand on greenish bases. One holds up its tail, the other drops it. $12.00–14.00

Finches Ceramic. Japan. Yellow-headed finches, one large, the other small, sit on round bases textured to resemble leaves on ground. The finches have either blue or green wings and tails, and a red wedge on the head. $12.00–14.00

Doves on Branch Ceramic. Japan. White doves in different positions have pale blue or pale lavender wash. The branch on which they sit is also white ceramic, though with a dusky wash, and is L-shaped. $10.00–12.00

Peacocks Ceramic. Russia. Ornamented, stylized peacocks have white bodies and red, blue, and gold ornamentation. $20.00–24.00

Brown Partridges Ceramic. Japan. Brown partridges sit on brown bases. One lowers its head to peck at food, the other sits up. $15.00–17.00

Pheasants Ceramic. Japan. Small brown pheasants with green-ish tails have prominent white rings around their necks, blue heads, and red, donut eyes. Each is cast in a different pose. $10.00–12.00

Pheasants Ceramic. Japan. Brown realistic pheasants with green heads, narrow white rings around their necks, and red eyes, stand on brownish-white bases sculpted to resemble swirling grass. One pheasant extends its wings, the other stands at attention. $10.00–12.00

Pheasants in a Basket Ceramic. Green pheasants with yellow tails nestle in a blue "wicker" basket filled with berries and flowers. One pheasant has yellow and red wings, the other has yellow and blue wings. $15.00–20.00

Large Swans Ceramic. Japan. Large swans (5½" x 4½") are white with deep red bills. They arch their necks in "S" curves. $15.00–18.00

Baltimore Orioles Ceramic. Japan. 1950s. Red-headed, blue-bodied orioles perch on bases fashioned to resemble leafy branches. $16.00–20.00

Small Swans Bone china. Small white swans have black bills and eyes. $10.00–12.00

Powder Puff Pigeons Ceramic. White powder-puff pigeons with orange and black bills have black eyes. $10.00–14.00

Cartoony Chicks on Stands Ceramic. Japan. Chicks with oversize heads, baby-doll eyes, and scalloped tails stand on hassocklike bases. One is pink with yellow bosom, the other is pale blue with yellow bosom. $14.00–18.00

Toucans Ceramic. Simplified and stylized black toucans have tremendous yellow beaks and white throats. Each holds out one wing. One tucks its beak under its wing, the other looks over its shoulder. $14.00–28.00

Flamingo with Sunflower Ceramic. Japan. Deep pink flamingo with green-tipped outstretched wings arises out of an Art-Deco-inspired foliage base. From each side of the flamingo's neck protrude small hooks from which two yellow sunflowers are suspended, the salt-and-pepper shakers. $20.00–24.00

FAUNA IN COSTUME

Kissing Mice Ceramic. Japan. Late 1930s. A tiny pair of kneeling, kissing mice, beige with brown highlights. The girl wears a conical straw hat, yellow skirt, and red blouse. The boy wears gray trousers. $6.00–10.00

Kissing Mice Ceramic. Japan. Late 1930s. Standing pair of shiny white mice with black-tipped ears and black sashes draped across lower body. The boy wears a tie, the girl wears a hat. $10.00–14.00

Flirting Mice Ceramic. Japan. Late 1930s. Standing pair of white mice with pink-edged ears, large "kewpie doll" eyes, and smiling lips. She wears pink frock over gray body, he wears black vest with pink and white bandana. $12.00–16.00

Sherlock Holmes and Dr. Watson Birds Ceramic. Japan. Late 1930s. Small pair of generic birds rigged up in Sherlock Holmes (red hat, brown jacket, blue shoes, and black pipe) and Dr. Watson (black bowler and jacket, brown monocle) costumes. $10.00–14.00

Fireman and Doctor Chipmunks Ceramic. Japan. Mid–1940s. Yellow fireman chipmunk and gray doctor chipmunk holding doctor bag in his mouth. $8.00–12.00

Birds in Hats Ceramic. Japan. Mid-1940s. Blue and yellow canaries perched on yellow leaf clusters and wearing daisy hats, one yellow and one pink. $8.00–12.00

Mr. and Mrs. Blackbird Ceramic. Japan. Early 1930s. Mr. Blackbird with red ruff, yellow beak, and checkered vest, with a black top hat and bow tie, preens before yellow-bellied Mrs. Blackbird, in red shawl and yellow bonnet. $12.00–16.00

Birds in Bonnets Ceramic. Japan. Early 1930s. Blue-bodied bluebirds perch on leafy twigs in large-rimmed yellow straw bonnets secured under the "chin" by broad sashes, one red, one black. $12.00–16.00

Mr. and Mrs. Stork Ceramic. Japan. Mid–1940s. Yellow Mr. and Mrs. Stork nuzzle up to each other from a sitting position, their cheeks touching. He is wearing a black top hat, she is in a red kerchief. Yellow bodies with orange wings are inscribed "P" and "S." $8.00–12.00

Dressed Ducks Ceramic. Japan. Mid–1940s. One sitting and one standing duck with white bodies, russet necks, yellow beaks, and wings painted blue, green, and black. Mr. Duck holds an open blue and white umbrella. Mrs. Duck is in a yellow bonnet with green trim. $10.00–12.00

Monsieur and Madame Duck Ceramic. Japan. Late 1930s. White crouching ducks with yellow bellies, feet, bills, and brown wings. Monsieur Duck wears black beret and red neckerchief. Madame Duck wears red-and-white-checkered scarf. $10.00–14.00

Graduating Ducks Ceramic. Japan. Early 1940s. Pale yellow, standing ducks in black graduation hats cheerfully wave one wing. Boy duck wears red necktie, girl duck wears blue tie and brown handbag. $10.00–14.00

Musician Ducks Hand-painted ceramic. Japan. Mid–1930s. A pair of musician ducks featuring yellow bodies with orange beaks and sailor blouses. The accordion player has blue pants and red cap. The fiddler wears blue cap and red trousers. $12.00–16.00

Dancing Turtles Ceramic. Japan. 1940s. Black-bodied, white-shelled girl turtle holds pink parasol. White-bodied, yellow-shelled boy turtle wears red cap and holds out his arms. $10.00–14.00

Strolling Squirrels Ceramic. Japan. Late 1930s. Brown-bodied girl squirrel wears a red bow on her white front and holds down her large-brimmed black hat festooned with yellow ribbon. Her beau carries a black cane, wears a black bowler hat, and red bow tie. Both feature prominent incisors. $12.00–16.00

Turtle Tramps Ceramic. Japan. Mid–1930s. Green boy and girl turtle tramps with brown shells, red hats, and red and white polka-dot bundles. Boy wears white shirt and slings his stick over his shoulder, while the girl, in a green dress, holds her stick in one hand, the bundle in the other. $12.00–16.00

Ballroom Pigs Ceramic. Japan. Late 1930s. White pig couple in formal dress. He wears brown tails over black and white pin-striped trousers and holds a black top hat under his arm. She is in a shell-pink gown with a gold necklace and pale blue sash draped across her "bosom." She holds a floral bouquet in one arm. $16.00–20.00

Donkey Couple Ceramic. Japan. Early 1950s. Boy and girl donkey in brown with dark gray highlights are wearing bridles and are ready for a "hoedown". She is in a pink frock with a black bodice. He is in a yellow shirt, blue pants, and holds a walking stick in one hand. $12.00–16.00

Yellow Bunnies Ceramic. Japan. Early 1930s. Sunshine yellow boy and girl bunny with childlike faces and tall, upstanding ears. The boy wears black overalls, the girl bunny is in a short red suspendered skirt with matching red shoes. $6.00–10.00

Rabbits in Rockers Ceramic. Japan. 1930s. White bunnies in flowered bathrobes and glasses sit on rockers. The pink rabbit wears a red and yellow polka-dotted apron and knits a sock as she rocks in her black rocker. The blue rabbit reads a

Boy and Girl Pigs Ceramic. Ceramic Art Studio. Madison, WI. Pale pink piglets with black locks, pink ears, snouts, cheeks, hooves, and belly buttons wear green suspendered shorts (boy) or skirt (girl) and matching green caps. $20.00–24.00

newspaper in his brown rocker. His ears are twisted on top of his head. $24.00–30.00

Donkeys in Hats Ceramic. Japan. 1940s. Brown donkeys sit on their haunches, relaxing. The one in the yellow hat crosses his "arms" on his chest and opens his mouth wide in a laugh. The donkey in the blue feathered hat leans back on his "arm" and smiles. $10.00–14.00

Monkey in Car Ceramic. Japan. 1940s. A monkey in a green hat drives an old-fashioned automobile. $28.00–32.00

Dog in Car Ceramic. Japan. 1940s. A dog wearing a black coat drives a roadster. $20.00–24.00

Dressed Dog on Ball Ceramic. Japan. 1940s. A dressed dog stands on top of a circus ball with a juggling pin in its mouth. $28.00–32.00

Monkey on Circus Drum Ceramic. Japan. 1940s. A monkey stands on its hands atop a flat circus drum. $28.00–32.00

Cat and Beach Ball Ceramic. Japan. 1940s. Cat in green pants rests its paws on a beach ball with a bee on the side. $18.00–22.00

Worm in Apple Ceramic. Japan. 1940s–1950s. Adorable pink worm with long eyelashes pops out of the top of apple "house." $20.00–24.00

Goat Fiddler Ceramic. Japan. 1940s–1950s. An old white goat in striped trousers plays a violin while sitting in "shaker" chair. $20.00–25.00

Barber and Pig Ceramic. Japan. 1940s–1950s. A black-frocked barber strops his razor while white, lathered pig leans back in barber chair. $24.00–28.00

Mr. and Mrs. Cat Ceramic. Japan. 1940s. A brown, black, and white female cat with huge semicircular eyes wears a blue with green polka-dotted skirt and halter top. She holds one hand on hip, and holds out the other. Her mate, in matching fur, wears a yellow turtleneck sweater and cap and holds a green fish in one hand. He winks with one eye. $16.00–24.00

Cat Fisherman and Wife Ceramic. Japan. 1940s. This three-piece set consists of two feline shakers on a green "river-bank" base ornamented with flowers. The male cat wears a green turtleneck and red bowler hat, and holds a red fish. The female cat wears a strapless green gown and green bow. $16.00–24.00

White Cats in Long Dresses Ceramic. Japan. 1940s. Stylized white cats have pink noses, ears, and fingernails. They wear pale yellow dresses trimmed with pale blue buttons and scallop collars. $10.00–14.00

Kittens in Oversize Bonnets Ceramic. Japan. 1940s. Tiny white and black ceramic kittens wear oversize bonnets. Red-trimmed bonnet has blue bow, yellow-trimmed bonnet has green bow. $10.00–14.00

Cats in Trousers Ceramic. Japan. 1940s. Brown standing cats wear trousers, sailor-striped undershirts, and short jackets. One is in blue trousers, yellow and blue jersey, and brown jacket; the other is in brown trousers, beige and blue jersey, and yellow jacket. Both stand on green bases. $12.00–14.00

Father and Baby Kangaroo in Tails Ceramic. This pair of nesting shakers features a beautifully detailed papa kangaroo in white shirt, cravat, and black tails, raising his top hat. The baby, in matching outfit but with hat still on head, holds a bouquet and sits cozily in the father's capacious waist. Gold trim picks up the details of the shirt, vest, and belt buckle. $45.00–55.00

Formally Attired Pig Couple Ceramic. 1940s. Cross-looking pink-faced bald pigs wear formal attire. She has a green necklace, purple sash, red sleeves, and green pleat lines on her skirt. He has green stripes on trousers, yellow vest, blue frock coat, and red bow tie. $12.00–14.00

Yellow Dressed Pig Couple Ceramic. 1940s. Bright yellow, fat walking pigs stand on green bases textured to look like grassy mounds. She wears a bright red dress, and carries a blue handbag coordinated with her hat. He wears a pale blue jacket with red bow tie and cap and carries a black cane. $12.00–14.00

Mr. and Mrs. Shawnee Pigs Ceramic. Shawnee Pottery. Zanesville, OH. 1937–1961. White shiny pigs with closed, long-lashed eyes have rotund, smooth bodies. He wears a red bandana around his neck, has two green buttons in overall button position, and holds a red flower. She wears a white cap with a green sprig, a green collar, and pink buttons on her coat. $24.00–30.00

Pig Musicians Ceramic. 1940s. Tiny white porcelain pigs play musical instruments. The girl, in a yellow, floor-length skirt and brown jacket, holds a guitar and sings. The boy, in brown trousers and yellow shirt, plays a yellow and black accordion. $10.00–14.00

Fiddler Goat Ceramic. 1940s. An aged, white goat with black spectacles sits in a brown, yellow, and green rocking chair, which is also a shaker. The goat, in brown, green, and white striped trousers and green jacket, holds a fiddle. $20.00–24.00

Girl Pigs in Polka-Dotted Dresses Ceramic. 1940s. Fat white girl pigs with long-lashed downcast eyes are dressed in short smocks with red frills and red, green, yellow, and blue dots. Each has several yellow parallel lines for bangs. $12.00–14.00

Urbane Monkey Couple Ceramic. Pink-faced chimps are dressed for the city. Mrs. Chimp wears a yellow hat, brown jacket, and long red skirt. She demurely looks down and purses her-lipsticked lips. Mr. Chimp wears yellow trousers, black cutaway, and bow tie and raises his black bowler hat. A walking stick is in the other hand. $14.00–20.00

Mother Mouse with Child Ceramic. A white mother mouse with huge eyes, brown hair tucked under a yellow and red polka-dotted cap, and lavender jacket cradles baby mouse in pink trousers and lavender jacket. The faces of both have pink highlights. $12.00–14.00

Mr. and Mrs. Elephant Ceramic. 1940s. White ceramic elephants with upturned trunks are dressed for a stroll in the city. Mrs. Elephant is in a pink dress, yellow shoes, and yellow handbag. Mr. Elephant wears yellow trousers, black jacket, and red cap. $12.00–18.00

Beetle Musicians Ceramic. 1940s–1950s. Beige and black winged beetles with human faces represent a pair of musicians. The one in the white cap and wings holds sheets of music. The one in the black tophat and wings holds a white lute. $14.00–18.00

Dressed Brown Bears Ceramic. Germany. 1960s. Brown bears with realistic though oversize eyes hook their thumbs into the pockets in their white and black dotted vests. These round-bellied bears wear red bowties, green frock coats, and white trousers. $14.00–18.00

Dressed Bears on Bicycle Built for Two Ceramic and metal. White-faced black bears sit behind each other on a brass wire bicycle built for two. The boy, in front, wears a plaid shirt with yellow trousers. The girl is in a red dress and yellow shoes. $14.00–18.00

Operatic Pigs Ceramic. Small white pigs in evening attire open their mouths wide in operatic performance. The "diva" wears a gold necklace, pale green gown with blue sash, and holds flowers. The male singer has a blue jacket, striped trousers, and black top hat in hand. $14.00–18.00

Colonial Girl Mice Ceramic. 1960s. Cute, gray-faced mice with pink ears wear colonial costumes. The one in the red dress has an orange bonnet and stirs something in a large, earthenware pot. The one in orange wears a red bonnet and holds a yellow mug. Both sport white aprons. $12.00–14.00

Rabbits with Purse and Umbrella Ceramic. 1950s. Dainty white-fronted rabbits with pink ears and black backs cavort with a handbag (salt) and pink umbrella (pepper). $12.00–14.00

Ducks in Blue Fezzes Ceramic. 1940s. Yellow stylized ducks with brilliant orange bills have green feet. They wear high-

Bear Baby in Kiddie Car Ceramic. 1940s–1950s. A cute yellow bear with brown ears, pink shirt, and red bow fits into a green kiddie car with orange wheels and yellow bumper. There is an entire series on the theme of animals driving cars. The steering wheel is always part of the animal. Among the animals are a rabbit, cow, pig, mouse, and horse. $12.00–16.00

collared blue coats and fezzes of a matching color. $12.00–14.00

Ducks in Vests Ceramic. 1950s. Pale yellow ducks with bright brown bills and wings stand on celadon blue bases. Both wear orange bow ties and pale green vests and have bright red "topknots." $12.00–14.00

Dressed Ducks Ceramic. White ducks with yellow feet and bills stand on a leaf-shaped, green tray. She wears a yellow bonnet with a pink ribbon, he wears a red cap and blue necktie. $12.00–14.00

Terrier Musicians Porcelain. 1950s. These small shakers (3½") feature white porcelain figurines of terriers playing musical instruments. Pepper sits up and holds a green and brown accordion, while Salt sits and beats a yellow drum between its legs. $12.00–14.00

Cairn Terriers in Berets Ceramic. 1950s. Black and white Cairn terriers in matching poses sit on their haunches and wear orange berets. They have doleful expressions on their faces. $12.00–14.00

Golden Retrievers in Bonnets Ceramic. 1950s. Matching golden retrievers sit with paws demurely together. Salt has red bonnet with blue bow, Pepper has blue bonnet with red bow. $12.00–14.00

Beagles in Bowlers Ceramic. 1950s. Small (3½") white beagles with black spots sit, wag their tongues, and show off brown bowler hats and red bow ties. The shakers match. $12.00–14.00

Beagle and Boxer with Rhinestone Monocles Ceramic. Japan. 1950s–1960s. Cartoonish beagle and boxer wear tattersall vests with rhinestone buttons. Both sport rhinestone monocles in their eyes and hold canes. $14.00–16.00

Chihuahua Couple with Rhinestone Eyepieces Ceramic. Japan. 1950s–1960s. Pinkish Chihuahuas have rhinestone eyepieces and buttons. The male, in tattersall vest and yellow bow tie, holds a pipe and supports a monocle. The female, in eyeglasses, wears striped vest and clutches a yellow handbag. $14.00–16.00

Cat Couple Ceramic. Japan. 1950s. Yellow cat couple comprises a male cat in green turtleneck and pink cap holding a pink fish, and a female in a green, floor-length skirt and brassiere, both ornamented with black dots. Both fit into an oval tray embossed with a grass/flower/log design. $14.00–1800

Formal Boxer and Poodle Couple with Rhinestone Eyepieces Ceramic. Japan. 1950s–1960s. A beige boxer in evening attire wears a low black tophat and a rhinestone monocle. His "date," in a lemon-yellow ball gown and daisy in her hair, holds a black-rimmed rhinestone lorgnette to her eyes. $16.00–24.00

Dishevelled Terriers with Head Bows Porcelain. 1960s. White porcelain terriers with black and brown markings are in identical sitting positions. Pepper has a red scarf tied about his throat and running up to the top of his head where it is tied into a floppy bow. Salt wears a green bow around his neck and has a red floppy cap on his head. $14.00–18.00

Dad and Junior Ducks in Caps Ceramic. Japan. 1940s. Pale yellow Dad and Junior ducks (Dad is twice as large as Junior) wear identical white caps with blue trim. Webs are outlined in black on their yellow feet. Dad wears red necktie, Junior has blue bow tie. $12.00–14.00

Mother Duck and Chic Chick Ceramic. Japan. 1940s. White mother duck with long yellow beak is dressed in a blue outfit with matching blue "pillbox" hat. Yellow chick, identical in size to the mother, is naked except for blue wings and orange cap. Both have green feet. $12.00–14.00

Mr. and Mrs. Duck in White Ceramic. Japan. 1940s. Round-bodied Mr. and Mrs. Duck have white faces, deep orange triangular beaks, and beady black eyes. Mr. Duck is in a white suit and blue shawl. Mrs. Duck is in a long white dress and pink head scarf. All folds on clothing are delineated with gold highlights. $12.00–14.00

Geese in Bows Ceramic. Japan. 1940s. Matching white geese with bright orange beaks, yellow feet, tails, and wings, wear pale green "vests" and red bows. Both stand on deep blue bases. $12.00–14.00

Pig Musicians Ceramic. Japan. 1950s–1960s. White ceramic pigs with protruding pink ears have big black eyes. Pepper plays a yellow and brown accordion, and wears a squat black bowler that matches his black pants. Salt wears a pink stocking cap, gray jacket, beige pants, and strums a guitar. $12.00–14.00

Gophers in 18th Century Costume Ceramic. Japan. 1950s. Small, beautifully tinted figurines represent a grinning male gopher in yellow doublet, orange jacket, and white tights, and his serious spouse in white and blue flounced skirt, orange jacket with yellow trim. Both are in a sitting position. $12.00–16.00

Mr. and Mrs. Skunk Ceramic. Japan. 1950s. Small white skunks with black markings and upturned black noses have red smiling mouths. Both wear blue jackets. Mr. Skunk is short and round with a yellow cap. Mrs. Skunk is slimmer in her blue jacket with yellow bow and carries a small handbag. $12.00–14.00

Mr. and Mrs. Squirrel Ceramic. Japan. 1950s–1960s. This small set features bushy-tailed sitting squirrels in shades of orange, brown, and white. Mrs. Squirrel wears a yellow cap with black dot pattern, and a pink bow. Mr. Squirrel wears a black beret and black monocle. $12.00–14.00

"Sammy and Samantha" Squirrels Ceramic. Late 1970s. White figurines of squirrel couple outfitted for tennis are tinted in shades of brown. Samantha is in a yellow tennis dress and green sunshade and carries a tennis racket. Sammy wears a green sweatshirt and carries a tennis racket. These are part of a series of alliteratively-named costumed animals. $12.00–14.00

"Oliver and Olivia" Owls Ceramic. Late 1970s. Brown and yellow tinted owls with gigantic eyes, wearing identical frilly caps secured with a green bow perch on brown, branch-shaped bases. Oliver holds black frying pan with the letter

"P" embossed on the bottom. Olivia holds yellow spoon and teacup with the letter "S" embossed on its side. These are part of a series of alliteratively named costumed animals. $12.00–14.00

"Burt and Bertha" Birds Ceramic. Late 1970s. Brown and yellow tinted birds with owlish faces represent Burt in a brown outfit with blue apron wielding a yellow oar, and a white-pantalooned, blue-dressed Bertha in white cap clasping her hands in mock distress. These are part of a series of alliteratively named costumed animals. $12.00–14.00

"Fernando and Francine" Frogs Ceramic. Late 1970s. Pale green figurines represent a flirting frog couple. Fernando, in yellow boater and bow tie and brown pants, grins at Francine, who strikes a flamencoesque pose in her pink slinky gown and red shoes, hiding her smile behind a yellow fan. These are part of a series of alliteratively named costumed animals. $12.00–14.00

"Rocky and Raquel" Bears Ceramic. Late 1970s. Tan and white tinted figurines represent a boy bear in blue overalls presenting a white fish with a red ribbon to Raquel, in red dress and bow, who clasps her hands appreciatively under her chin. These are part of a series of alliteratively named costumed animals. $12.00–14.00

Blue Jay Couple with Rhinestones Ceramic. Japan. 1940s. A stylized pair of birds with outstretched wings rests on white bases painted with bird feet. The male, in shades of blue and

Monkey Couple Ceramic. Japan. 1960s. Brown sitting monkey couple have large round eyes and smiling faces. He wears a red suit, yellow shirt, and blue bow tie that matches his top hat. She wears a blue bonnet with yellow ties. They nestle in a pale blue-green ceramic basket edged with flowers. $12.00–16.00

yellow, wears a black top hat and has rhinestone eyes. The female, in darker blue with lavender, wears a yellow bonnet and red bow and has rhinestone eyes. $16.00–20.00

Cat Doctors with Rhinestones Ceramic. Japan. 1940s. Brown standing cats with white faces, pink cheeks, and black square eyeglasses wear white doctor's smocks and yellow and blue stethoscopes. Both have old-fashioned doctor's lights with rhinestone bulbs affixed to their foreheads, and strike mirror-image poses of one hand on hip, other upraised to point to head. $16.00–20.00

Glitter and Rhinestone Pussy Cats Ceramic. Japan. 1940s. Sweet little cats in sitting position are bedecked with "pearls" (on bows), and rhinestones (on bonnets), and glitter (on bonnets, bows, and toes). Pepper is gray with pink bow and yellow bonnet, while salt is pink with blue bow and yellow bonnet. $16.00–20.00

Cat Boxers Ceramic. Japan. 1950s. Tan kittens with black highlights are depicted in boxing gloves and boxing poses. Pepper, in brown gloves, delivers a blow to Salt's chin. Salt wears yellow gloves and white trunks. $10.00–12.00

Cats in Eton Jackets Ceramic. Japan. 1950s. White standing kittens with pink ears are highlighted in yellow, pink, and dark gray. Salt, in a standing pose, wears yellow cap and yellow jacket, while Pepper, in a running pose, has gray cap and gray jacket. Both stand on white bases. $12.00–14.00

Cat Family on Bicycle Ceramic. Japan. 1950s. This two-piece shaker consists of a yellow bicycle with father piece and mother with child piece. The cats are white with yellow hair-textured backs and blue eyes. $12.00–16.00

Roaring Twenties Singing Cats Ceramic. Japan. 1950s. White-faced brownish cats stand on their hind paws and wave their forepaws in Charleston moves. He wears a yellow fedora with black band, black vest, and pink neckerchief. She has blue frock with bow and white headband. $12.00–14.00

Cats in Hats and Double Bows Ceramic. Japan. 1960s. White sitting kittens with pink ears, pink noses, and pale blue eyes wear small black hats, pink bows under their chins, and green and yellow bows behind their necks. $8.00–12.00

Monocled Cats Ceramic. Japan. 1940s. A pair of stylized Siamese cats in mirror-image poses holds one paw up to rhinestone-monocled eye. Female cat is white with yellow bow, checkered vest with two rhinestone buttons. Male cat is gray with checkered vest, rhinestone buttons, and bow tie. $14.00–18.00

Angora Cats in Apron and Hat Ceramic. Japan. 1960s. Gray angora cats stand with opposite arms akimbo. Both have white faces and pink highlights. Female cat wears pink chin bow and white apron. Male cat wears white top hat, secured at the chin with a big bow, and white striped shorts. $12.00–14.00

Siamese Couple with Fur and Bells Ceramic, fur, and bells. Japan. 1960s. White Siamese cats with pink ears sit on three paws and lick their lips. Each has a tuft of white fur sprouting from the head and a black metal bell suspended from the collar. He wears green plaid cap, she wears yellow bonnet. $12.00–18.00

Sheep Couple Ceramic. Japan. 1950s–1960s. A large white male sheep with brown hooves, pink ears, green eyes, and black bow tie is teamed with a smaller ewe with brown hooves, pink ears and bow, and downcast eyes. Both are textured to simulate curly wool. $10.00–15.00

Bovine Bride and Groom China. 1960s. Gray stylized bull in black top hat and black-and-white-striped bow tie arches his back and flips his tail up and over his haunches. The white bride wears a wreath of white daisies on her head and a yellow necklace. Gold highlights the horns and hooves of both figurines. $12.00–14.00

Pig Waiters Ceramic. Japan. 1950s. Identical white pigs in waiter jackets and aprons wear red bow ties with red buttons to match their red ears. With arms akimbo, they strike the characteristically supercilious poses of snobby maîtres d'. $14.00–18.00

Squeaking Pig Chefs Ceramic. Japan. 1960s. Cartoonish pale pink standing pigs in tiny white chefs hats wear white aprons. Salt holds yellow spoon, pepper holds red open cookbook. The lower halves of the bodies hold squeakers, while the hollow heads hold the condiments. $12.00–16.00

Penguin Couple Ceramic. Japan. 1950s. Yellow-footed penguins with white bodies and black faces and wings turn yellow-beaked faces toward each other. She has a yellow scarf with black dots on her head and carries a red umbrella. He tips a red top hat to her. $14.00–18.00

Ballerina Pigs Ceramic. Japan. 1960s. White cartoonish girl pigs with bow-shaped ears wear pink tutus and ballerina slippers. They sit and point their legs in pin-up poses. Both wear blue eyeshadow. $16.00–20.00

Miss America Pigs Ceramic. Taiwan. 1960s. Shiny white standing pigs are shown with their noses in the air, closed eyes and hands gracefully supporting a wreath of flowers. The hooves and flowers are touched with gold. $12.00–14.00

Pig Clarinetists Ceramic. Japan. 1960s. Peach-colored standing pigs with humanoid faces hold yellow clarinets to their lips with their brown-hooved paws. $10.00–12.00

Horses in Bandannas Ceramic. Japan. 1960s. Stylized matching horses wear red bandannas with white dots around their necks. Pepper is gray with black dots, while salt is white with black cross-hatching pattern. $10.00–14.00

Turtles in Vests and Caps Ceramic. Japan. 1940s. Green, standing turtles with gray tails look upwards in open-mouthed wonder. The shorter turtle wears a red striped vest and white cap, while the taller one wears a yellow vest and pink cap. $14.00–18.00

Crows in Victorian Garb Ceramic. Japan. 1940s. Black crows plant their black feet into white ceramic bases. She wears green cap, yellow shawl, and pink skirt ornamented with red dots. He wears brown top hat, green waistcoat, red vest, yellow bow tie, and striped trousers. $14.00–18.00

Donkeys in Vests Ceramic. Japan. 1950s. Sitting brown donkeys in identical poses throw back their heads in huge laughs that expose their large white teeth and pink throats. Pepper wears blue striped vest, while Salt has red striped vest. $10.00–14.00

Chickens in Scarves Ceramic. Japan. 1940s. White chickens with gray tails and outspread wings stand on pale green bases. Both wear red scarves from which their red combs protrude. $12.00–14.00

Gentlemen Bears Porcelain. Germany. 1950s. Matching rotund brown bears with white snouts hold their fat tummies. Both are in white trousers, gray vests with lavender dots, red bow ties, and green cutaways. $28.00–32.00

Gray Frogs in Frock Coats Porcelain. 1950s. Matching gray frogs sit cross-legged in green jackets with lilly-pad leaf jabots. Their gaping mouths are red. $16.00–20.00

Chipmunks on Ice Skates Ceramic. Japan. 1940s. Hilarious white chipmunks are shown on black ice skates. Pepper wears a blue cap, green jacket, and brown pants. Salt, in yellow one-piece suit with blue bow, takes a spill and lies on back with legs up in air. $14.00–18.00

Monkeys in Tails Ceramic. Japan. 1950s. White ceramic monkeys in black-and-white-striped trousers, blue-and-white-striped shirts, and black jackets and top hats reach for their hats. Both have pointed snouts. $12.00–16.00

Ducks on Books Ceramic. Japan. 1950s. White ducks with bright yellow beaks stand on black books. One wears flat yellow hat, the other a blue hat. $10.00–14.00

Shopping Duck Couple Ceramic. Japan. 1960s. Round-headed white ducks with yellow beaks opening to reveal red interior pose with their "arms" at waist level. He sports a black jacket, brown pants, white vest, and yellow bow tie. She wears a red kerchief, black top, green skirt, and holds a basket in one arm. $14.00–18.00

Musician Cats Ceramic. Japan. 1960s. Standing tan cats with belly buttons play musical instruments. Pepper, in black top hat and exuberant side whiskers, holds a yellow accordion. She, with bow in hair, blows into a piccolo. $12.00–14.00

Cats in Trousers Ceramic. Japan. 1960s. Rotund, white cats with black heads wear striped shirts, and reach their hands into the pockets of their suspendered trousers. Pepper has red trouser creases and blue suspenders and shirt stripes, while Salt has blue trouser creases and suspenders and red shirt stripes. $12.00–14.00

Graduating Mice Ceramic. Japan. 1950s. Cute little white mice with oversize heads and round ears smile and roll up their large eyes. They wear flat black mortarboards with yellow tassels over the right ear. $10.00–12.00

Hares with Shoes and Jewels Ceramic. Japan. 1950s. White standing hares with upstanding large ears are painted by hand. Salt has pink ears, yellow gloves, and blue shoes. Pepper has pink ears, blue gloves, and yellow shoes. Both wear heart-shaped pendants suspended from "gold" chains. $12.00–14.00

Yellow Rabbits with Bows Porcelain. 1940s. Stylized rabbits with limbless, bulbous bodies and round heads have black bases and bright blue bow ties around their necks. Their floppy flat ears are touched with gold on the underside, as are their round noses. $14.00–18.00

Bear Weightlifters Ceramic. Japan. 1950s. Largish black bears in blue shoes and white exercise outfits emblazoned with a black "P" and "S" hold black and yellow dumbbells to their chins. Both stand on white bases that bear the inscriptions "Salt" and "Pepper" on the top. $15.00–20.00

Teddy Bears in Blue Overalls Ceramic. Japan. 1950s. Largish tan teddy bears with pink ears, round eyes, and black noses wave with one hand and hitch the other into the front of their blue overalls. $12.00–18.00

Mouse Couple Ceramic. Japan. 1950s. Round, gray mice with pink ears are smiling. He wears gray pants, checkered shirt, and green neckerchief. She wears a yellow dress and a white, flowered apron. $14.00–18.00

Grandma and Grandpa Bears Ceramic. Japan. 1950s. Hand-painted yellow bears are given an unusual matte finish. Grandma is in a red dress, green shoes, and blue collar and consults a book on her lap. Grandpa, in blue bow tie and brown vest, rests one paw on a black cane. Both wear half-moon eyeglasses. $14.00–18.00

Baby Elephants Ceramic. Japan. 1950s. Smallish white elephants in sitting poses with upturned trunks are dressed in children's outfits. Salt sports pink bow and a blue skirt with black dots, while Pepper wears blue trunks with black dots. $10.00–12.00

Blue Elephants in Hats Ceramic. Japan. 1950s. Pale blue dancing elephants have pink upturned trunks and large, pink-lined ears. He wears black top hat, she wears pale green hat. $10.00–12.00

Elephants with Blankets Ceramic. Japan. 1950s. This pair of elephants wears brightly flowered blankets on the backs. Dark gray Pepper rears up and fully extends its trunk. Pale gray Salt stands on all fours and curls back its trunk. $16.00–22.00

Elephants in Blue Overalls and Red Bandannas Ceramic. Japan. 1950s. Identical standing elephants have gray and white faces with pink cheeks and upturned trunks. Both wear black caps, bright orange shirts, red bandannas, and blue overalls. $14.00–18.00

Elephant Couple Heads Porcelain. 1950s. White female elephant head with long-lashed eyes and down-curling trunk has green scarf wrapped around her pink bust. The male elephant head, in deep gray, curls up his trunk and rests on a blue collar and black bust. $14.00–18.00

Elephant Bride and Groom Ceramic. Japan. 1950s. White standing elephants with a faint pink blush turn up their trunks. The larger groom wears a black top hat, the smaller bride has white headdress. $14.00–18.00

Monkey Shoe Shiners Ceramic. Japan. 1950s–early 1960s. Matching white-bodied monkeys on white bases ringed with a gold line hold a brush in the left hand, a shoe in the right, and stand next to a brown box labelled "Shine. 5¢". Salt wears

Mouse Playing Piano
Ceramic. Japan. 1950s. A gray mouse with a sharp nose and a pink polka-dotted bow on her head sits on a piano bench. The piano is painted in a convincing, wood-grain finish. $14.00–18.00

green overalls, brown T-shirt, and yellow cap. Pepper wears blue overalls, green shirt, and brown cap. $20.00–24.00

Monkey Couple on Bicycle Built For Two Ceramic and metal. Japan. 1950s–early 1960s. Two brown monkeys with black highlights are inserted in a metal stand in the shape of a bicycle with two seats. Girl monkey wears white dress with red and green checks. Boy monkey is in a red, yellow, and blue striped turtleneck. $24.00–30.00

Victorian Lady and Gent Monkey Couple Ceramic. Japan. Early 1960s. Gentleman monkey with brown hair and white face holds aloft a black bowler hat. He wears a black cutaway, white shirt, and green trousers. Lady monkey with rouged cheeks wears a yellow hat, pink dress, and carries a black purse. $20.00–24.00

Monkey Heads with Caps Ceramic. Japan. 1950s. Tan heads of chimps with brown and black fur and ears furrow their brows and make alarmed faces. Salt, with downturned mouth, balances green cap on head. Pepper, with open mouth, has brown hat on head. $16.00–20.00

Monkey Couple Ceramic. Japan. 1950s. Pink-faced squatting monkeys with black bodies and white tummies feature a gentleman in black top hat and white bow tie smoking a black pipe, and a pink-faced lady. $12.00–14.00

White Giraffes in Gold Bows Porcelain. 1960s. Matching smallish white porcelain giraffes with pink eyes wear gold bows at the tops of their long necks and have golden pom-poms on their forepaws and tails. $10.00–14.00

Giraffes in Suits Ceramic. Japan. 1950s. Matching white giraffes with orange spots are dressed in blue jackets, black slacks, brown shoes, and red ties. They carry brown briefcases under their left arms and their heads point toward the right. $14.00–18.00

Chicks in Hats Ceramic. U.S.A. 1940s. Small yellow chicks with open beaks wear blue hats: bonnet on girl, and cap on boy. Beaks, webbed feet, wings, throats, and buttons are painted in gold. $8.00–12.00

Goose Couple Ceramic. Japan 1950s. White geese on gray pedestal-type bases have black beaks with red linings and black circle eyes. Their wings are tinted pale brown. Boy goose wears black top hat, girl goose wears black hat with red bow. $8.00–12.00

Hen with Chicks Mustard and Shaker Set Porcelain. This four-piece set consists of a tray depicting the bodies of a central mother hen flanked by her two chicks, a pink-collared girl and a blue-collared boy. The chick heads are the shakers. They are fish-shaped with a prominent orange comb running across the top, yellow opened beaks, and round, bulging eyes. Between them sits the mustard-pot mother with tightly compressed beak. The top of her head is the lid. $50.00–56.00

Duck Couple Ceramic. Japan. 1940s. Yellow-bodied ducks with red, green, and blue wings and tails rest their green feet on pedestal bases textured to resemble leaves. The male

Donkey Couple Ceramic. U.S.A. 1950s. Standing upright, this tan donkey couple is dressed for a stroll in town. He wears blue pants, short yellow jacket, and carries a cane. She is in a pink dress and carries a handbag. Both wear bridles. $20.00–24.00

wears a red scarf and red top hat. The female wears a red neck bow and hat. $12.00–16.00

Canary Couple on Tray Ceramic. Japan. 1930s. Tiny yellow canary couple sits on a green, leaf-shaped tray. He wears blue hat, she wears green bow. $12.00–14.00

Black Crow Couple on Ear of Corn Tray Ceramic. Poinsettia Studios, CA. Small, glossy crow couple stands on tray fashioned to resemble a flattened-out ear of corn flanked by greens and terminating in a nobby stem. Mr. Crow wears brown hat and white tie with blue dots. Mrs. Crow wears green bonnet. $24.00–30.00

Cats with Sunglasses and Beach Umbrellas Ceramic. Japan. 1940s. Matching white cats with pointed ears and black spots on backs and tails wear red sunglasses and dive their front paws into folded white umbrellas with borders of double red stripes and yellow handles. $12.00–14.00

Monkey in Car Ceramic. Japan. 1950s. A gray monkey with white chest wears a yellow vest and green top hat which it lifts with one hand. The monkey fits into a very small green jalopy. $18.00–24.00

Long-Haired Kittens with Bows Ceramic. Japan. 1960s. Matching white kittens, textured to mimic long hair, sit and roll their round, long-lashed eyes. Pepper wears green bow around neck and in hair, while Salt wears yellow bows. $10.00–12.00

Flirting Cartoonish Cats Ceramic. Japan. 1960s. Bright orange stylized cats with bat ears and human eyes represent flirting couple. She downcasts her blue-shadowed eyes, bows down her red-bowed head, and clasps her hands to her yellow bib. He winks and tilts his yellow-hatted head in her direction. $10.00–12.00

Gray Mouse Family Ceramic. Japan. 1960s. A cartoonish mouse couple in deep gray has round, pink-lined ears. Mother mouse clutches naked baby to her tummy. She wears a pink dress and bow. Papa mouse shuts his eyes. He wears a pale gray top hat and has wrapped a white scarf around his neck. $14.00–20.00

Donkey Golfers Ceramic. Japan. 1960s. Glossy gray donkeys with pink noses, red mouths, and black eyes wear white booties and pink panties. Pepper raises black club over one shoulder, while Salt leans on club. $12.00–15.00

Blue Hare in Orange Go-Cart Ceramic. Sarsaparilla. 1981. Blue-tinted hare with backward flopping ears, red bow tie, and green jacket fits into a bullet-shaped go-cart with orange body, blue nose, and red wheels. $8.00–10.00

Rabbit in Go-Cart Ceramic. Sarsaparilla. 1981. White rabbit with pink lips and nose and pink jacket fits into a bullet-shaped yellow go-cart with green nose and black wheels. $8.00–10.00

Yellow Bear in Go-Cart Ceramic. Sarsaparilla. 1981. Yellow bear in pink shirt with red bow fits into a red bullet-shaped green go-cart with yellow nose and red wheels. $8.00–10.00

Mother Cow with Baby Ceramic. Japan. Late 1960s. A brown-faced mother cow with yellow horns, black bangs, and pink nostrils wears a pink dress with blue collar. In her arms she cradles a small figurine in the shape of a brown-faced calf in white pants and blue top. $24.00–30.00

Baseball Elephant and Monkey Ceramic. Japan. 1950s. A white elephant with upturned trunk crouches in catcher pose holding a white ball in his brown glove. A white monkey on green turf-textured base raises yellow bat to his shoulder. $20.00–24.00

Cats on Couch Ceramic. Japan. 1960s. This three-piece set consists of a pink couch on which sit two white cats with pink and blue spots. Salt cat wears yellow skirt and green top. Pepper cat wears red dress with black ribbon belt. $12.00–16.00

Gentlemen Foxes Ceramic. Japan. 1950s. Matching bright-orange foxes with lush tails wrapped around their hind legs rest their front paws on black walking sticks. They scowl, wear tall black top hats, and white vests. $14.00–18.00

Elephant Trainman and Chambermaid Ceramic. Japan. 1950s. White elephants with upturned trunks, pink cheeks, and large, long-lashed eyes are dressed as trainman and chambermaid. He has blue cap, red bandanna, and blue overalls. She wears a red bonnet, white apron, and black skirt. $14.00–18.00

Frog with Accordion Ceramic. Japan. 1930s. Crouching green frog with bug eyes and gaping red mouth holds detachable accordion with blue bellows and red sides. $18.00–24.00

Frog Holding Tray with Tomatoes Ceramic. Japan. 1950s. A sitting, green-headed, red-mouthed frog in a blue jacket, red bow tie, and red trousers sits and supports on its knees a double leaf-shaped tray on which rest two bright red tomatoes, the shakers with green leaves. $60.00–75.00

Monkey Playing Bass Fiddle Ceramic. 1940s. A brown-faced monkey in an orange top hat, blue jacket, and green trousers sits cross-legged and cradles in its arms a detachable brown bass fiddle that is as tall as the monkey. $20.00–24.00

Pigs Playing Accordion Ceramic. 1950s. Small white pigs with round pink snouts and pointed ears wear dark green beanies, light green tops, blue pants, and black shoes. Identical, they hold accordions with yellow bellows and brown ends. $10.00–12.00

Leap-frogging Pig Kids Ceramic. 1960s. Tiny pink pigs play leap-frog with one pig resting atop another. Bottom pig wears pink pants, blue shirt, and yellow bow. Top pig wears yellow pants, green jacket, and yellow bow. $12.00–14.00

Pig Nodder Couple Ceramic. This three-piece nodder set consists of a base depicting the bodies of a pig couple, and the detachable heads of the couple which are inserted into the neck holes. The girl wears a green skirt, blue top, and car-

Cute Blue Birds Ceramic. Japan. 1940s. Cute little blue birds with huge "Betty Boop" eyes raise their wings. Pink flowers are sculpted on their heads. One wears a pink bow, the other wears a blue bow tie. $14.00–18.00

ries a bouquet of flowers. The boy wears yellow trousers, brown jacket, and white shirt. Their arms are intertwined. The yellow heads have golden snouts. $55.00–60.00

One-Piece Pig Couple Ceramic. Signed: C. Miller. Regal China Company. This one-piece shaker in pale beige with color highlights depicts a smiling girl pig, a weeping boy pig, both anchored to a base simulating grass. The girl's colors are blue, yellow, and red, the boy's, blue and black. $30.00–45.00

One-Piece Fish Couple Ceramic. Signed: C. Miller. Regal China Company. This one-piece shaker in pale beige is beautifully textured to mimic waves in the base and fish scales in the animal's bodies. A jowly Madame Carp in green hat and brown lips rises out of the waves and rests a fin on Monsieur Carp's upturned fin. He wears a black bowler and brown tie. Dark green ornaments the fins. $30.00–45.00

One-Piece Pig-in-a-Blanket Ceramic. 1950s. A long white pig with pink blush spots on cheeks and buttocks is wrapped into a yellow blanket with green fringe, blue bow tie, and brown ribbon around the middle. The head end dispenses the salt, the back, the pepper. $15.00–20.00

Hedgehog Cooks Ceramic. 1970s. Furry-faced hedgehogs represent cooks. Salt, in a long white skirt and bonnet and red checkered blouse, holds a yellow spoon. Pepper, in dark blue shirt, light blue pants, white apron, and chef's toque, holds black spoon. $12.00–15.00

Dressed Cat and Dog Ceramic. 1950s. A beige cat in blue bow tie and red and blue cap stands with arms akimbo. He is paired with a beige hound dog in a yellow cap, yellow and brown patterned trousers, and light blue dotted shirt, who folds his arms across his chest. $12.00–14.00

Baby Penguins on Skates Ceramic. 1960s. Black-faced, glossy baby penguins with yellow beaks and feet wear old-fashioned ice skates. Boy wears yellow pom-pommed cap and yellow muffler. Girl wears white cap and polka-dotted muffler. $16.00–18.00

Canaries with Bows Ceramic. 1950s. Kissy-beaked yellow canaries with blue crests, wings, and tails have bottle-shaped bodies. Around their necks they wear ribbons, green for pepper and red for salt. Both have large round eyes and feathery eyelashes. $10.00–12.00

Boy and Girl Birds Ceramic. Japan. 1950s. Small (3½") pinkish birds with stylized bodies have yellow outflung wings and downcast, long-lashed eyes. Both have pink and yellow daisies on their chests. Boy wears pink beanie, girl wears pink flower on head. $8.00–10.00

Duckling Musicians Ceramic. Japan. 1950s. Small (3½") white ducks on round bases play musical instruments. Pepper, in blue cap and brown jacket, holds an accordion. Salt, in red cap and blue jacket, plays a red fiddle. $8.00–10.00

Monkey Family on Motorcycle Ceramic. This two-piece set consists of a father monkey astride a blue-bodied motorcycle and the mother-and-child piece that fits behind him. The monkeys have tawny, hair-textured bodies and pink faces. $14.00–20.00

Pig Couple in Basket Bisque and straw. 1970s. White cartoonish pigs with round cheeks have pale pink highlights. He wears striped overalls and matching cap. She wears striped pinafore with flower in brown hair. Both fit into a real straw basket. $12.00–14.00

Frog Musicians Ceramic. 1970s. Pale green frogs with lily-pad leaf hats and green bodies have bulging yellow eyes. One plays a blue tuba, the other accompanies him on a pale blue and pink accordion. $8.00–10.00

Yellow Mice in Green Jackets Ceramic. Japan. 1940s. Cute, bright yellow mice with large pink ears, round black eyes, and black noses cavort in green jackets. $10.00–12.00

Dressed Turtles Ceramic. Japan. 1940s–1950s. A yellow turtle wearing a striped vest stands on its hind feet. A green turtle plods along on all fours, carrying its domed brown shell. $10.00–12.00

Cat's Pajamas Ceramic. Fitz and Floyd. 1985. Stylized fat cat couple in pajamas feature a green "Papa" in pink pajama bottoms with blue and white polka-dots and a blue "Mama" in the pajama top. $15.00

Mother Rabbit with Baby Ceramic. Fitz and Floyd. 1983. A fat white mother rabbit in a pink dress and blue and white apron sits and cradles on her lap a white bunny who is asleep sucking her thumb. $15.00

Penguins in Yellow Caps Ceramic. 1980s. Standing penguins with outstretched wings wear bright yellow caps and yellow straps. $10.00–15.00

Cruising Cat Ceramic. Vandor. 1980s. The upper half of a white cat in blue 1950s sunglasses, red dress, white fur throw, and yellow cap fits into a white convertible with blue trim. $12.00–15.00

Cruising Poodle Ceramic. Vandor. 1980s. The upper half of a white poodle in aqua goggles fits into an aqua roadster with silver trim. $12.00–15.00

Shopping Cat Ceramic. 1980s. A white cat in blue shoes, black-and-white-striped shirt, yellow collar and hat, blue sunglasses, and red purse stands next to a blue shopping bag crammed full of parcels and marked with "Cats Fifth Avenue" in the "Saks Fifth Avenue" calligraphy. $12.00–15.00

Poodle on Recliner Ceramic. 1980s. White poodle in blue sunglasses sits in a black and white zebra-striped lounge chair with metal legs. $12.00–15.00

Surfer Cow Ceramic. Vandor. 1980s. A white cow with red square sunglasses, yellow trunks with palm tree design, pink tummy and black spots stands on two legs next to a blue, white, and red surfboard. $15.00

Cow in Beach Tube Ceramic. Vandor 1980s. A black and white cow in red sunglasses and blue bikini reclines in a red-and-white-striped beach tube. $15.00

Horse Musician and Dog Diva Ceramic. Japan. 1950s. Wearing similar pink flounced gowns, a horse and a dog are teamed in an unlikely musical combination. The horse plays a saxophone, the dog, holding an umbrella, might be preparing to sing. These two pieces may not go with each other. $16.00–20.00

Cow and Beach Ball Ceramic. Vandor. 1980s. A black and white cow in red sunglasses sits next to a red, yellow, blue, and white beach ball. $15.00

Frog Drummer Ceramic. U.S.A. 1940s. A green and yellow frog holds red drumsticks to a brown and blue drum in this two-piece set. $24.00–30.00

Frog Tuba Player Ceramic. Sarsaparilla. 1980s. A green yellow-bellied frog is accompanied by a yellow tuba. $12.00–14.00

Doctor Owls Ceramic. Japan. 1940s. Brown owls in square eyeglasses and forehead lights wear white jackets and black and yellow stethoscopes. $14.00–20.00

Owl Academics Ceramic. Japan. 1940s. Brown owls in sequined eyeglasses wear black mortarboards and carry either a rolled diploma or a book. $14.00–20.00

Walrus in Top Hat Ceramic. Japan. 1940s. Identical, stylized black walrus in formal attire wear golden top hats and bow ties. $14.00–20.00

Cat Graduate and Book Ceramic. Japan. 1950s. A yellow, green-eyed pussy cat in a black mortarboard goes with a green book with the words "Salt & Pepper. Volume VII" on the spine. $14.00–20.00

Bookworm Ceramic. Japan. 1950s. Two books, their spines inscribed either with "Book" or "Worm," have each one half of a bookish worm emerging from its sides. One has a pink tail, the other a round, button-nosed, bespectacled head with a black cap. $20.00–24.00

Cows in Overalls Ceramic. Japan. 1950s. Identical cows with totally pear-shaped, oversize heads, sit in white overalls and clasp their little arms to their little throats. Their ears are as pink as their nostrils, and they roll their large baby-doll eyes heavenward. $14.00–18.00

Cow Postman and Doctor Goat Ceramic. Japan. 1940s. A white cow with brown spots wears green trousers, pink top and green hat, and carries a yellow bag. In one hand it holds an envelope. The goat doctor, all in white, holds on to a black stethoscope. $20.00–28.00

Yellow Pig Housewives Ceramic. Japan. 1950s. High-gloss yellow ceramic pigs stand up. They have pale orange ears, nostrils, mouths, and hooves. Both wear aprons that are merely outlined in green and wink. $12.00–18.00

Girl Pig on Scale Ceramic. Vandor. 1980s. A cute girl pig in a pink polka-dotted dress with a blue coin purse perches on a black scale. $14.00–18.00

Pig Gothic Ceramic. Clay art. 1980s. The pig couple parodies Grant Wood's "American Gothic" couple. $16.00–18.00

Patient and Doctor Beetles Ceramic. U.S.A. Green beetles with white faces are dressed as a physician in black top hat and medical bag and patient in nightcap and hot water bottle. $20.00–24.00

Doctor Beetle and Broken-Hearted Patient Ceramic. U.S.A. Dark green beetles with black wings wear black top hats and white spats. One beetle carries a black bag marked "Doctor." The other beetle holds a large pink heart which is torn down the middle. $20.00–24.00

Mouse Couple Ceramic. Japan. 1960s. Cute gray mice with pink cheeks and ears, have huge, protruding incisors. He wears a brown fedora, yellow shirt with red tie flapping in the breeze, and blue trousers. She wears a pert white hat, a pink dress, and carries a red purse. Both are shown taking large strides. $14.00–20.00

Monkey on a Circus Ball Ceramic. Shafford. Japan. 1940s. A monkey in gray pants balances on its hands and holds a red ball in its feet. It is resting on the upper quarter of a sphere, which is the detachable lid for a spherical shaker. The monkey and the lower portion of the sphere are each a shaker. The sphere is painted in bands of yellow, white, and red. $24.00–28.00

Monkey Playing Cello Ceramic. Japan. 1940s. A monkey in a red top hat, dark green jacket, and pale green pants cradles what appears to be either a cello or an oversize guitar. $20.00–24.00

Lamb Couple Ceramic. Japan. 1950s. Cartoony yellow lambs with orange polka-dots prance on bases embossed with a tall

Puppies in Beanies Ceramic. Japan. 1930s. Cute little puppies in yellow or buff wear beanies. Yellow puppy with saucer eyes wears a blue beanie and a scarf to match. Buff puppy snoozes in its pink beanie and blue bow. $18.00–20.00

grass design. She wears a blue hat and a pink bow. He wears a black hat. $14.00–20.00

Hugging Dogs Ceramic. Japan. 1940s. Brown dogs with white faces, baby-doll eyes, and red mouths embrace on a brown seat. This two-piece shaker consists of a boy dog in white pants and yellow jacket, and a seat to which the girl, in her white flowered dress, is attached. $14.00–18.00

Turtle with Umbrella Ceramic. Japan. 1950s. A gray turtle with a beige shell carries a pink umbrella. Its mate has a yellow shell and beige body and wears a pink bonnet. $12.00–14.00

Shawnee Cat in Hat Ceramic. Shawnee. White sitting cats wear pink bows, hats with blue bows, and blue anklets. $12.00–18.00

Shawnee Pig Couple Ceramic. Shawnee. Farmer pig wears a red bandanna, green-buttoned suspenders, and brown shoes. Mrs. Pig wears hat with green bow that matches the collar of her white dress with its three brown buttons. $12.00–18.00

Shawnee Farmer Pig Ceramic. Shawnee. Identical white pigs wear hats with blue bands, blue bandannas, and brown shoes. Each holds a shovel in the left hand. $12.00–18.00

Pig Couple Ceramic. Taiwan. 1960s. White, Shawnee-like pigs have baby-doll eyes with spikey eyelashes. Pink highlights their cheeks and noses. The girl wears a yellow overall dress, the boy, green overalls. Their most prominent feature is one erect and one floppy ear. $14.00–18.00

Pigs with Flowers Ceramic. Japan. 1960s. White identical pigs on all fours have huge round ears and backs filled with pink, sculpted flowers. $14.00–18.00

Penguin Couple in Cars Ceramic. Japan. A black cartoony penguin with a pink scarf drives a pink and white convertible. Behiind him a girl penguin in a pink bow and pink scarf looks out of the window of the lavender trailer. $15.00–20.00

Penguins in Hats Ceramic. 1980s. Penguins with outspread, pointy wings have yellow sailor caps. $12.00–14.00

Dapper Duck Couple Ceramic. Japan. 1930s. Stylized ducks are painted in shades of brown, green, yellow, and gray. One wears a cloche, the other, a beanie. Both have ribbons around their necks. Their eyes are their most striking feature: they are circled with long eyelashes. $14.00–20.00

FLORA: NATURAL, FANCIFUL, AND FICTIONAL

PLANTS

Potted Crocuses and Primroses Porcelain. 1950s. White, fanciful pots hold, on the one hand, multicolored crocuses and, on the other, pastel-colored primroses. $16.00–20.00

Pink Rosebuds Ceramic. U.S.A. 1940s. A single pink rosebud rises from a leafy base. $16.00–20.00

Tulip Heads Ceramic. U.S.A. 1940s. A single red tulip rises from a dark green leaf. $10.00–14.00

Water Lily on Base Porcelain. 1940s. Small, white water lily is attached to a green leaf which, in turn, is attached to a broad white base. $10.00–12.00

White Porcelain Basket with Roses Porcelain. 1950s. A graceful white "wicker" basket holds, on either side, a white bouquet of roses. $16.00–20.00

Comical Worms Ceramic. U.S.A. 1940s. Blue-headed grinning worms have S-shaped bodies marked in light blue, dark blue, and red spots. $10.00–14.00

Ladybugs Ceramic. U.S.A. 1940s. Simplified, large red ladybugs have black markings. $10.00–14.00

Butterflies on Pansies Ceramic. U.S.A. 1940s. Fragile-looking pink butterflies perch on two yellow pansies. $24.00–30.00

Green Crickets Ceramic. U.S.A. 1950s. Large-eyed green crickets have low-slung bodies. $10.00–14.00

Plastic Rosebuds Plastic. U.S.A. 1930s. Stylized roses form the tops of white, cylindrical bases. The roses are either red or blue. $12.00–18.00

Cornucopia of Flowers Ceramic. Japan. 1950s. Silver cornucopia holds a flood of green foliage with a scattering of pink and blue flowers. $12.00–18.00

Arbor and Well Miniatures Ceramic. U.S.A. Arcadia Ceramics. This extraordinary set by Arcadia features an arbor overgrown with climbing roses and a wishing well. $16.00–24.00

Plastic Roses Plastic. U.S.A. 1950s. These yellow and red plastic roses are usually seen as part of a tableau, such as a plastic arbor napkin holder-cum-shakers, or flowerpot-sugar bowl-cum-shakers. $10.00–14.00

Gerbera Daisies Ceramic. U.S.A. 1040s. Pink gerbera daisies with yellow centers sit atop a cylindrical bowl with four leaves as its sides. Salt has dark green leaves on a pale green background, pepper reverses the color combination. $14.00–18.00

Pink Rosebuds Ceramic. Japan. 1930s. Heavy ceramic rosebuds have pink flower in an aqua blue leaf. $12.00–16.00

Palm Trees Ceramic. 1930s. The intertwining trunks of several palm trees form the base from which a tangle of fronds explodes. A Deco influence is perceptible in the geometric stacking of fronds. $14.00–18.00

Fruitheads

Pumpkin Man and Cart Carrier Ceramic. Japan. Early 1950s. Pumpkin-headed man with round eyes, button nose, and red smiling mouth wears a pale blue "straw" hat, orange shirt and shoes, navy pants, and beige bandana. As he holds on to the traces of a yellow wooden wagon, he grins smugly at the two robust cabbages (salt-and-pepper shakers) in the cart. $20.00–24.00

Turnip Twins Porcelain. Japan. 1930s and early 1940s. Matched pair of white turnips nestled in lace trim. The turnip faces feature round tiny eyes and dot lips. Greens make up the hair. $16.00–20.00

Hubbard Squash Tots Porcelain. Japan. 1930s and early 1940s. Orange hubbard squash toddlers straddle the floor in pale blue shirts and green trousers. They smile and screw up their tiny round eyes, snuggling their chins on a collar of lace trim. $16.00–20.00

Radish Heads Porcelain. Japan. 1930s and early 1940s. Matching bright red radish heads with green tufts for "hair," triangular smiling lips, and blue toddler suits edged in gold and lace trim around the collar. The radish heads are crawling on all fours. $16.00–20.00

Tomato Babies Porcelain. Japan. 1930s and early 1940s. Matching bright red tomato babies sit with outstretched feet in bright green jumpsuits trimmed with white lace ruffles. $16.00–20.00

Carrot Bunnies Ceramic. Japan. Early 1940s. Matching horizontal carrots are scooped out in the middle from which emerge white, floppy-eared bunnies, waving rakishly with their right paws. $16.00–20.00

Pink Beet Ladies Ceramic. Japan. Early 1940s. Matching pair of beet ladies in green dresses, red shoes, and white collars wave their arms. The beet ladies' heads shade from bright red at the top to white at the bottom and are capped with tiny, flowered hats. Their eyebrows are quizzically pointed. $12.00–16.00

Corn Cobs Ceramic. Japan. Early 1940s. Matching pair of yellow corncobs with a tuft of silk for hair and green arms and body shaped from the foilage. A row of buttons ornaments the vest, on either side of which tiny black feet and shoes protrude. $12.00–16.00

Pink Radishes Ceramic. Japan. Early 1940s. Matching pair of blushing beets with circular mouths and slightly distressed expressions in their eyes. Both wear brown trousers and shoes, pale blue jackets over white shirts, and red ties. They raise their right hands as they sit. $12.00–16.00

Savoy Cabbage Ceramic. Japan. Early 1940s. Matching shakers depicting white and green heads of savoy cabbage that have toppled over on their side, crushing beneath them a pair of tiny, red-headed lads in blue trousers and black boots who had evidently been trying to uproot them. $12.00–16.00

Mushrooms Ceramic. Japan. Early 1940s. A pair of mushrooms of contrasting personalities. The chanterelle with her upswept orange crown and black collar smiles benignly, while the poisonous browncap in a pale blue bow tie sheds tears. $12.00–16.00

Yellow Squashes Ceramic. Japan. Early 1940s. A matching pair of bulbous, yellow squashes, entirely without torso or limbs, with pronounced oval eyes, black rotund lips, and magnificently lush black eyebrows. $12.00–16.00

Lettuce Heads Ceramic. Japan. Early 1940s. A matching pair of cheerful, green-faced lettuce heads with asymmetrical hairstyles wearing white dresses under yellow jackets and red shoes. Both clutch their left hands to heart and wave exuberantly with the right. $12.00–16.00

Roman Beauties Ceramic. Japan. Early 1940s. A matching pair of Roman beauty apples sit with black hands demurely folded on green-and-black-striped skirts edged with white aprons. The stem side of the apples furnishes the face—a white circle rimmed with speckled red. $12.00–16.00

Watermelon Heads Ceramic. Japan. Early 1940s. A matching pair of rotund, light and dark green watermelon heads sits atop figures sitting with their knees drawn up. The red skirts contrast with the black arms. The watermelon heads have large, eyelash-rimmed eyes, round white noses, and petulant round mouths consisting of a yellow circle rimming a red center. Their expression is fierce. $12.00–16.00

Pensive Pineapples Ceramic. Japan. Late 1930s. A matching pair of bright yellow pineapple heads rests heavily on tiny, sitting bodies dressed in dark green suits, pale green vests, and red bow ties. The pineapple stems resemble caps. The pineapple characters are wearily supporting their heads on their right hands while pointing into the distance with their left

Eggplants Ceramic. Japan. Early 1940s. A matching pair of retiring plump purple eggplants tilt their bulbous heads on tiny bodies clad in red skirts and yellow jackets. A rustic hat is contrived from the eggplant's stem. $12.00–16.00

hands. Their round eyes stare directly ahead with an expression of metaphysical boredom. $12.00–16.00

Turnips Ceramic. Japan. Late 1930s. This matching pair of white turnips looks up flirtatiusly from beneath long eyelashes. With white faces shading into pink at the crown, the coy turnips are dressed in blue overalls ornamented with red and white gingham bows, and hold their arms akimbo. $12.00–14.00

Peach Kids Ceramic. Japan. Late 1930s. A matching pair of white-faced peach boys in black pants and green shirts stares stonily ahead, while raising left hands from their laps to point to the distance. Their heads are cleft at the top and shaded, in the "hair" area, with red fading off into yellow. $12.00–16.00

Strawberry Brats Ceramic. Japan. Late 1930s. A matching pair of red-faced strawberries in black jackets and white trousers stares googlie-eyed and open-mouthed. $12.00–16.00

Pineapple and Banana Bunch Ceramic. Japan. Late 1930s. A yellow pineapple boy in black trousers and red shoes converses with Miss Banana, whose face is made of a bunch of yellow bananas. She is dressed in teal blue with red accents. $12.00–16.00

Bartlett Pears Ceramic. Japan. Early 1940s. These matching red plump pears puff out their cheeks and purse their lips while their rotund white eyes seem to pop out of their heads. These shakers consist entirely of heads. $12.00–16.00

Cantaloupe and Watermelon Ceramic. Japan. Early 1940s. A bright-red wedge of watermelon beams a winsome smile as she sits, her hands in white gloves folded on her knees. She is dressed in dark green as is her companion, a chubby cantaloupe head with puffy cheeks. $12.00–16.00

Bananas Ceramic. Japan. Early 1940s. A matching pair of banana heads dressed in green suits and red ties reclines languorously, supporting their banana-bunch heads on one elbow. $12.00–16.00

Cantaloupe and Watermelon Tennis Players Ceramic. Hand-painted. Japan. Early 1950s. A yellow-headed cantaloupe (pepper) in tennis whites waves and holds a black tennis racket. His charming opponent, in a white skirt banded in red, holds her brown racket up to her large green watermelon face, painted so that the distinctive markings of the watermelon rind resemble a pageboy haircut. $16.00–20.00

Dancing Fork and Spoon Ceramic. Japan. Late 1940s. A friendly pink fork and spoon each hold up one arm. They wear matching yellow aprons trimmed in black. $22.00–30.00

Creamer and Sugar Bowl Ceramic. Hand-painted. Japan. Late 1940s. A dancing pitcher head tugs at a corner of her ultrashort green dress in a knock-kneed pose as she holds one arm up to her handle. Her sugar-bowl partner, equally white with pink cheeks, also stands knock-kneed with arms akimbo on a short dress that shades from white to deep rose. $12.00–16.00

Tomato and Pepper Baseball Players Ceramic. Japan. Late 1940s. The tomato-headed pitcher (salt) in gray-and-white-striped uniform prepares to pitch to the green pepper-headed batter who winds up his bat. $16.00–20.00

Carrot and Onion Housewives Ceramic. Japan. 1940s. Orange carrot head in yellow skirt (pepper) holds a broom to her white apron, while yellow onion head (salt) in a green dress and white apron gossips, holding one arm akimbo and supporting a basket of groceries in the other. $16.00–20.00

Bell Pepper and Tomato Musicians Ceramic. Japan. 1940s. Wearing a yellow dress with black, vertical stripes, green-faced bell pepper (pepper) sings, consulting a songbook she holds before her. Tomato face (salt) accompanies her on the guitar, which she presses to the white and red dotted apron that keeps her green dress neat and clean. $16.00–20.00

Lemon and Orange Artists Ceramic. Japan. 1940s. Yellow lemon head (pepper) in long green dress with black stripes holds up a framed painting of two red flowers, while her yellow-dressed colleague, the orange head, dourly exhibits a palette and brush. $16.00–20.00

Orange Dandies Ceramic. Japan. 1950s. Two yellow oranges with pink faces, "Betty Boop" eyes, and button noses, smile cheerfully. The orange heads are pitted like orange skin, rest on mauve "collars," and wear matching bowler hats at a rakish angle. The white hat is salt, the black, pepper. $12.00–16.00

Pineapple Heads Ceramic. Japan. 1950s. Matching pineapple heads with broad, U-shaped smiles, have round eyes in faces

Banana and Strawberry Musicians Ceramic. Japan. 1940s. Banana head (pepper) in a long, green gown striped with dark green holds up a pair of tambourines. Strawberry head (salt) saws on a fiddle and is dressed in a long rose dress with black stripes. $16.00–20.00

shading from deep orange at the top (stem part) to yellow at the center, and sepia at the base. $12.00–16.00

Grape Cluster Heads Ceramic. Japan. 1950s. Matching pair of purple grape clusters roll their round eyes skywards as they smile narrow U-shaped smiles. The purple clusters shade off into dark green grapes. $12.00–16.00

Peanut People Ceramic. Japan. Late 1940s. Mr. and Mrs. Peanuts' rubicund faces emerge from the top half of matching brown and black peanut shells. Mrs. Peanut wears a green hat with pink ribbon, and shapes her mouth into a "comma." Mr. Peanut, in black bowler hat, peers over his black spectacles and shapes his mouth into a "comma," mirroring his wife's. $12.00–16.00

Egg People Ceramic. Japan. Mid 1940s. Pink-shelled Mr. and Mrs. Egg eye each other flirtatiously. With flaming cheeks, their heads emerge from egg-cup bases, his black with a white, stand-up collar, hers red with a white ruffle. Her black bow inclines coyly in the direction of his rakish top hat. $12.00–16.00

Coconut Heads Ceramic. Japan. Early 1940s. Matching pair of brown, elliptical coconuts with black "topknots," crossed eyes, and thick red lips. Across their foreheads the matching heads are emblazoned "FLORIDA." $12.00–16.00

Corn Heads Ceramic. Japan. Early 1950s. A nearly matching pair of heads-of-corn misses whose smooth, round, apple-cheeked faces peer out of yellow, corn-cob hairdos which terminate in pompadour swirls of corn silk. Their collars are formed of beige-tinted "leaves" gracefully draped around their chins. $12.00–16.00

Tomato Heads Ceramic. Japan. Early 1940s. A matching pair of red, jovial tomato heads with round cheeks and noses, bulging white eyes with black eyeballs, and huge, toothy smiles. On their heads they wear bright green hats. $12.00–16.00

Green Grape Heads Ceramic. Japan. Early 1940s. Matching pair of green grape clusters forms the heads of pensive misses who are lying down and supporting their heavy chins on white arms. They wear pink tops, green pants. The grape clusters form gigantic, elaborate hairdos. $12.00–16.00

Cucumber Babies Porcelain. Japan. 1930s. A matching pair of pale green cucumber babies emerges from lace collars. They wear blue pants and brown shoes, and their long heads are topped with a cucumber leaf and yellow blossom. "O"-shaped mouths and eyes give them an expression of distress. $16.00–20.00

Tomato Heads Ceramic. Japan. Late 1940s. Bright red tomatoes, one round, the other oblong, eye each other in alarm, eyes bulging, mouths rounded in silent appeal. Their hairdos are fashioned from swirling green leaves. $12.00–16.00

Winking Bartlett Pears Ceramic. Japan. Early 1940s. Matching pair of yellow Bartlett pears with lavish pink lips opened in sexy smiles wink playfully. $12.00–16.00

Yellow Squash Babies Ceramic. Japan. Early 1940s. Matching pair of round, yellow squash heads with green

Peach and Watermelon Ladies Ceramic. Japan. Late 1940s. Red peach head sits atop a long-skirted body, sliding one yellow arm into her white apron pocket, and, with the other, hugging her head. She wears a pale blue skirt with royal blue polka-dots. Her friend sits in a long, yellow dress with green polka-dots, resting her huge watermelon head on her chin. Both have roll eyes. $14.00–17.00

markings sits atop sitting toddler bodies dressed in yellow rompers and red booties. $12.00–16.00

Apple Heads Ceramic. Japan. Late 1940s. Charming pair of apple heads, one red, the other yellow, in blue, rakishly tilted berets with a coy leaf peeking from the corner. Both smile with lush lips, showing off perfect white teeth. $12.00–16.00

Eggplant People Ceramic. Japan. Late 1940s. The "bodies" of this pair of eggplant people are entirely purple. $12.00–16.00

Yellow Pumpkin Kids Ceramic. Japan. 1930s–1940s. Pale green pumpkin heads with painted-on, dark green "puddin' bowl" hairdoes, are planted on the sitting bodies of skirted girls. The pumpkins wear yellow dresses trimmed in red and hold out their little arms on each side. $16.00–20.00

Mushroom Pals Ceramic. Japan. 1930s. Red-capped mushrooms with yellow undersides top beige stems that rise from pale blue "collars" with dark blue bow ties. The boy face (judging from the lips) is cheery, the girl face, with drooping eyebrows, seems perplexed. $16.00–20.00

Red Pepper Toddlers Ceramic. Japan. 1940s. Red bell-pepper faces with toddler features are attached to small bodies in white rompers that are crawling on all fours. Gold trim adorns the collar. Green stems substitute for hair. $16.00–20.00

Peanut Babies Ceramic. Japan. 1940s. Pale beige peanuts form the heads of these cute little toddlers who have just landed on their round bottoms, judging from the fact that their hands and feet are up in the air. Shoes are brown, pants are pale green, and gold trims the ruffled collar. $16.00–20.00

Orange Head in Hat Nester Ceramic. Japan. A winking, male orange head is topped by a detachable brown fedora. The fedora carries the label "Souvenir of Pennsylvania Turnpike." Mr. Orange's leaf forms the rakish hairdo, and a blue bow tie gives dash to the dark gray suit. $14.00–20.00

Corn People Ceramic. Japan. Five-inch-tall corn people stand on black shoes. Their faces are painted on to the corn-cob body, which is shrouded in husks. $18.00–22.00

Cabbage Girls Ceramic. Japan. 1940s–1950s. A realistic girl's head in a cabbage-leaf bonnet pops out of each cabbage head. $14.00–20.00

Mr. Pea Pod Ceramic and metal. Japan. 1950s. This unusual shaker features one hatted pea pod with big eyes and one bare-headed pod with smiling lips. The hatted pod is marked "P" and is inserted into a wire frame with two wire arms ending in stylized hands and wire legs ending in flattened loops. When assembled, the Pepper pod is inserted into the frame so that the hands clutch his middle, and the Salt pod is laid at the base. $20.00–24.00

Grinning Pineapple Heads Ceramic. Japan. 1940s. Nearly spherical pineapples with green tufts and embossing simulating pineapple skin have laughing mouths and round eyes. In coloring they shade from dark brown to beige to dark brown. $12.00–18.00

Tomato Head Couple Ceramic. Japan. 1940s–1950s. Happy, bright red tomato heads on tiny feet have leaves arranged to represent, for the female, a bandanna knotted on the top, and for the male, a ragged sunhat. $12.00–18.00

Turnip Heads Ceramic. Japan. 1940s. Pale pink turnip heads have identical laughing expressions with closed eyes. Both have pink cheeks and tiny, protruding button noses. $12.00–18.00

Pearl Onion Heads on Tray Ceramic. Japan. 1940s. White, smiling pearl onion heads with black eyes nestle into a green, leaf-shaped tray. $18.00–22.00

Four Peas in a Pod Ceramic. Japan. 1940s–1950s. Four dark green peas nestle in a pod tray. The two outside peas are smaller, the two inside ones have faces. $18.00–22.00

Boxing Banana and Pineapple Ceramic. Japan. 1940s. A banana boxer with a black eye, lowered arms, and red shorts marked "P" is teamed with a pineapple boxer with uplifted arms and green shorts marked "S." The fruits form the heads, the bodies are normal human bodies. $20.00–24.00

Carrot and Pea Housekeepers Ceramic. Japan. 1940s. A carrot-headed housekeeper in a green shirtwaist with white apron wields a broom. A pea-headed housekeeper in a white shirtwaist with yellow-banded apron carries a marketing basket. $20.00–24.00

White Radish and Pea Pod Housekeepers Ceramic. Japan. 1940s. A white radish-headed housekeeper in a blue pinafore, umbrella, and handbag, is teamed with a pea-headed housedeeper who wears a blue dress and white apron and carries a basket for provisions. $20.00–24.00

Romaine Lettuce Kids Ceramic. Japan. 1940s. Sad Romaine lettuce-headed toddlers are on all fours. They wear red tops and yellow bottoms. $15.00–20.00

Celery Tots Ceramic. Japan. 1940s. Happy celery-headed boys wear yellow tops and brown bottoms. They hold on to their shoes in typical toddler poses. $15.00–20.00

Celery and Carrot Kids Ceramic. Japan. 1940s. Sad lettuce-headed and carrot-headed kids flail around on the floor in temper-tantrum poses. $15.00–20.00

Googly-Eyed Watermelon Couple Ceramic. Japan. 1940s. Courting watermelon-headed couple consists of a girl in a yellow skirt with green dots and red-outlined blouse, sitting and smiling, and a hatted, bewildered looking cavalier covering his mouth with his hand, as though he had just committed a gaffe. Both have round movable eyes. $16.00–20.00

Peach Couple Ceramic. Japan. 1940s. Very pale peach couple with "Xs" for lips and round, movable eyes, are trying to communicate. She, in pink skirt with red dots and green top, holds her hands up to her mouth to shout. He, in blue jacket and yellow trousers, cups a hand to his ear. $16.00–20.00

Purple Pepper Men Ceramic. Japan. 1940s. Purple bell pepper heads on orange bow tie bases have round eyes and upturned eyebrows. Their round mouths are twisted to the side.

Carmen Miranda Banana Dancers Ceramic. Clay Art. 1980s. Banana ladies with Carmen Miranda faces and tutti-frutti headdresses wear lavender skirts with red sashes. Pepper holds green maracas. $15.00–18.00

Orange Heads Ceramic. Japan. 1940s. Pebble-skinned orange heads sit in pale-pink, Edwardian collars. Both are

Bee on Flower Ceramic. Japan. Late 1940s. The delightful nester combines a bee with a "Betty Boop"-type face and a yellow flower. $14.00–18.00

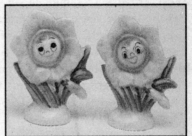

Daffodils with Faces Ceramic. Japan. Late 1940s. These smiling daffodils could be straight out of Alice in Wonderland. At the center of the yellow petals are white faces with bright red lips, blue eyes, and blond hair. $20.00–24.00

grinning and have protruding, tiny button noses. Salt wears white hat, Pepper wears black hat, both at a rakish angle. $12.00–20.00

Mushroom Heads Ceramic. Japan. 1950s. Small brown mushrooms with white dots sit atop yellow stem faces. One is sleeping, the other is awake. $12.00–14.00

Pumpkin Heads Ceramic. Japan. 1960s. One elongated and one round pumpkin are carved into jack-o-lanterns of very different expressions. $12.00–14.00

Reclining Onion Kids Ceramic. Japan. 1950s. Pink-headed onion people with smiling lips and eyes craftily truned toward each other and have bright green "cow-lick" stems. They wear blue shirts and white pants and are lying down with their legs crossed. $15.00–20.00

Apple Heads Ceramic. Japan. 1940s. Bright red Roma apples with yellow bottoms are set on their sides atop small, stylized bodies of girls in long green skirts and black bodices. The bottom dimple of the apple serves as a mouth. $18.00–22.00

Pineapple and Corn Kids Ceramic. Japan. 1950s. Very small, very stylized bodies of tots support large pineapple or corn cob. The pineapple sits atop a blue body, the corn atop a red body. $10.00–14.00

Pineapple and Apple Chefs Ceramic. Japan. 1940s. Stylized, human bodies support large pineapple or apple. The apple wears chef's toque, green uniform with blue bow tie, and white apron, and holds up a plate of food. The pineapple, in a yellow uniform with red bow tie, holds a plate in front of him. $16.00–20.00

Peach Heads Ceramic. Japan. 1940s. Jovial peach heads, without any necks, have green leaves at sides of cheeks, simulating high collars. Their cone heads are tinted orange and they have lush, red lips. $12.00–16.00

Blue Grapes Reclining Ceramic. Japan. 1940s. Pale blue clusters of grapes with tiny faces are attached to pink, reclining bodies. $12.00–16.00

NATIONALITIES

Chinese Peasant Couple Ceramic. Japan. 1940s. Plump-faced Chinese woman in yellow sampan, red jacket, and white toursers is teamed up with a man wearing a red cap, blue shirt, and green trousers. $10.00–14.00

Chinese Couple Ceramic. Japan. 1940s. Bare-headed woman in green dress and white fan goes with man in yellow robe and brown hat. $10.00–14.00

Chinese Kowtowing Couple Ceramic. Japan. 1950s. Kowtowing couple bring their hands up to their noses. She is bare-headed and has long braid cascading down her back. He wears red peaked hat. Both are in orange jackets with green sleeve lining, blue trousers with white cross-hatching. $10.00–14.00

Oriental Heads Ceramic. Japan. 1950s. White figurines of male and female heads in white conical hats have semi-spherical bases. Hers is red, his is green. $12.00–16.00

Pagodas Ceramic. Japan. 1950s. Five-tiered pagodas have golden steeples, red-trimmed stories, and pale green roofs. $10.00–14.00

Chinese Girl with Tea House Ceramic. Japan. 1950s. A red-trousered, white-jacketed girl holds a white fan with gold trim. She is flanked by a small red tea house with a green roof that stands on a rectangular pedestal base, thus being reminiscent of a garden ornamental sculpture. $12.00–14.00

Japanese Couple Ceramic. Japan. 1950s. A Japanese geisha in a yellow kimono holds a white fan. She is accompanied by a man in a dark green coat and yellow hat. $10.00–14.00

Geisha Busts Ceramic. Japan. 1950s. Beautiful geishas, with traditional features and finely-detailed hairdos and costumes drawn from traditional Japanese woodblock prints, hold fans. $14.00–20.00

Japanese Stylized Couple Procelain. Japan. Stylized figurines in the shape of two balls stacked atop each other represent a geisha with black topknot and a Japanese warrior. They have traditional Japanese faces and lovely detailing of costume. $14.00–20.00

Japanese Babies Porcelain. Japan. Very round, bare-limbed babies are depicted in sitting position. The girl has large, black and pink smock. The boy is bald and wears green suspenderd pants. $14.00–20.00

Chinese Driver with Rickshaw Ceramic. Japan. A green rickshaw holds the separate figurine of a driver in a black hat, pink jacket, and yellow trousers. $12.00–14.00

Chinese Couple in Conversation Ceramic. Japan. A Chinese boy in a yellow hat, black coat, and white trousers leans forward to listen to a pigtailed girl in a pink jacket and yellow trousers who leans forward with inclined head and closed eyes. $10.00–14.00

Chinese Couple Heads Ceramic. Japan. Round, tan heads of Chinese couple with pink cheeks and smiling mouths wear matching olive green caps with gold knobs and sit on semi-spherical bases in the same olive green color. $10.00–14.00

Chinese Seer with Scroll Ceramic. Japan. 1950s. Identical figurines of an ancient Chinese sage with a long, white beard holding a white scroll bear the inscription, "One Laugh is Worth a Hundrd Sighs." $10.00–14.00

Chinese Reading Couple Ceramic. Japan. Chinese woman in red sits on a pile of baskets reading a red book. The man, in black, sits on a pile of black baskets and reads a black book. $10.00–14.00

Chinese Boy and Girl Ceramic. Japan. 1950s. A black-haired girl in a yellow hat and pink pajamas holds her folded hands next to her cheek. The boy in an identical hat and brown pajamas holds his arms folded across his chest. $10.00–14.00

Chinese Couple on Base with Pagoda Ceramic. Japan. 1950s. A white, green, and red pagoda rises from a pale green, rectangular base with an embossed scroll design. On either side of the pagoda sits a shaker. One is in the shape of a girl in a yellow smock and red overskirt, the other represents a bald boy with a topknot in a green sock with black overskirt. $18.00–24.00

Chinese Couple Ceramic. Ceramic Arts Studio, WI. Chinese couple wears identical outfits consisting of a bright yellow smock trimmed in pale blue and white trousers. He wears a white hat with a blue brim, she wears blue ribbons with red dots. These shakers come in two sizes. $24.00–34.00

Japanese Scholars Ceramic. Japan. 1950s. Lavender-robed figurines of moon-faced Japanese scholars wear shiny black pagoda-shaped hats. $12.00–14.00

Oriental Boy Porter Ceramic. Japan. 1950s. A red-trousered, blue-jacketed boy in a green hat carries a pair of shakers shaped like rectangular parcels on his back. $12.00–14.00

Oriental Boy and Pagoda on Boat Tray Ceramic. Japan. 1950s. This three-piece set consists of a waving Oriental boy in brown vest and yellow shift, standing next to a white pagoda with green roof. Both are balanced on a graceful, buff-colored boat with an upturned prow. $18.00–24.00

Ho Toi God of Luck Ceramic. Japan. Matching white figurines depict "Ho Toi," the Oriental God of Luck. According to legend, when you rub his tummy, you will have health and happiness. $12.00–16.00

Artistic Chinese Couple Ceramic. Japan. 1950s. Chinese man sits on barrel chair playing a stringed instrument. His wife also sits and holds a fan. This set is available in various colors, from black, white and gold to red, yellow, black, and green. $14.00–18.00

Metal Watercarrier with Bakelite "Buckets" Metal and Bakelite. A leggy, black metal water carrier on a round case wears a copper-colored hat and balances a yoke across his shoulders. From each end of the yoke is suspended a "bucket" of bakelite in the shape of a large acorn. $30.00–40.00

Small Chinese Couple Ceramic. Japan. 1940s. Small shakers (under 3 1/2") depict a finely featured Chinese lady in green with a red jacket, and her spouse in yellow straw hat, blue jacket, and orange pants. $10.00–14.00

Japanese Fan Dancer and Spouse Ceramic. Japan. 1940s. An S-shaped Japanese fan dancer weras pink kimono and holds lavender fan to her hair. Her mate wears orange hat, green jacket, blue trousers, and orange pants. $10.00–14.00

Green-Faced Aliens Ceramic. Japan. 1960s. Blobby white Martians stand on white oval bases that are inscribed "I'm so bashful when you shake me" and "Watch it! I'm full of pep." Their original tags read " I just arrived from Mars" and "Hi Ho I'm a LiLiLo." $14.00–16.00

Japanese Couple Reading and Playing Koto
Ceramic. Japan. 1940s. Identically dressed couple in red
jacket, black pants, and black hat, sit cross-legged. He
strums a koto, she reads from a book. $10.00–14.00

Siamese Boys Ceramic. Japan. 1950s. Bulbous-bottomed
Siamese boys in green shirts, yellow scarves, and conical
hats painted with red and white spirals have delicately featured faces. Their yellow, pointed slippers meet in front.
Their trousers look like the cheeks of a fat peach.
$10.00–14.00

Japanese Couple Kissing on Bench Ceramic and
wood. Japan. 1950s. Bald Japanese boy in blue and black
purses his lips to a black-haired Japanese girl in red and
pink who purses her lips right back. They sit on a real
wood bench. $12.00–14.00

Hindu Boys Ceramic. Japan. Identical boys in ballooning
white trousers, narrow orange jackets, and white, oversize
turbans have babyish faces. $14.00–18.00

Hindu Boy and Girl Ceramic. Japan. 1950s. Child-faced
Hindu boy and girl are 3½" tall. She weare white trousers,
blue sash, and red top, he wears red trousers, blue sash,
and white top. $10.00–14.00

Hindu Boy on Elephant Ceramic. Japan. This two-part
shaker is a nester, consisting of a white-clad, white-tur-
boned boy atop a white elephant with orange trim.
$12.00–16.00

Hindu Lady with Mosque Ceramic. Japan. 1940s. A
Hindu lady in a white veil, pink dress, and red caste mark

Kissing Dutch Couple
Ceramic. Japan. 1950. A blond
Dutch girl in a white bonnet
and blue dress holds a bouquet
of red flowers behind her back
as she purses her lips to kiss
the Dutch boy in blue pants,
white shirt, and red cap, holding a model boat behind his
back. $14.00–18.00

Oriental Man with Baskets
Ceramic. Occupied Japan.
1945–1952. An Oriental water
carrier in black pants and maroon
top holds a yoke across his shoulders. A bucket is suspended from
each end of the yoke. A white
goose pecks at his trouser leg.
$16.00–20.00

is flanked by a white mosque with a red and green onion dome. $12.00–16.00

Hindu Man on Pillow Ceramic. Japan. 1940s. A bearded Hindu in a red turban, green jacket, and yellow pantaloons sits cross-legged on a pink pillow trimmed in green. The Hindu and the pillow are each a shaker. $12.00–16.00

Scottish Piper and Lassie Ceramic. Japan. 1930s. Scottish lassie in yellow kilt, blue jacket, and blue cap on her strawberry blond bob is teamed up with a red-capped boy in a red kilt blowing on bagpipes. Shakers are 3½" tall. $10.00–14.00

Scottish Couple Ceramic. Japan. 1950s. Large Scottish couple (6½") have simplified bodies that consist of a long, kilted bottom, a torso, and an egg-shaped head. Both have red hair, large eyes with spidery eyelashes, and green caps. $14.00–18.00

Small Scottish Couple Ceramic. Japan. Small Scottish couple (3") wear red, white, and blue kilts, black tops, and shoes. Little boy plays yellow bagpipes. $10.00–14.00

Scottish Piper and Lassie Ceramic. Japan. 1950s. This small, 3½" couple features very stylized, simplified figurines. The braided, blond lassie wears a blue cap and top over a white and blue kilt. The boy, in blue cap and top over red and blue kilt, plays yellow bagpipes. $10.00–14.00

Kissing Scottish Couple Ceramic. Japan. 1960s. Orange-kilted, black-hatted, brown-haired Scottish boy and girl stand with arms akimbo and purse their lips, which meet when they are made to stand toe to toe. $12.00–16.00

Scottish Couple Heavy ceramic. Heavily embossed figurines of a Scottish couple are rendered in muted colors
with heavy, dark brown outlining. She has red scarf, he
wears blue jacket and cap. $16.00–18.00

Eskimo Couple Kissing on Beach Ceramic and wood.
Eskimo couple in green outfits trimmed in white and with
yellow goves sit on a wooden bench and turn their faces
toward each other. $14.00–18.00

Eskimo Couple Ceramic. Japan. 1950s. Eskimo girl in red
coat and hood, trimmed in white fur, holds a yellow basket. Eskimo boy in black jacket and pants set trimmed in
white fur holds large green fish. Label on bottom reads
"1959 Alaska." $18.00–22.00

Cartoonish Eskimo Couple Ceramic. 1960s. Ruddy
Eskimos hold brown harpoons as they stand on oval blue
bases inscribed "Canada." The one in blue has wide-open
eyes and a huge grin. The one in green has closed eyes
and mouth. $12.00–14.00

Eskimo Couple Porcelain. Japan. 1950s. Eskimo girl in white
with brown boots holds up hand to long, black hair. Boy in
yellow coat holds on to white Huskie. $12.00–14.00

Eskimo Couple Kissing Ceramic. Japan. 1950s. Eskimo
girl in pink coat, hood, and mittens, lowers her eyes and
extends her nose to rub the nose of her boyfriend in pale
blue coat and pink hood. Their outstretched arms grasp
each other. $14.00–18.00

Eskimo Couple in Canoe Ceramic. Japan. 1950s. This
three-piece set consists of an original tray made in the

Scowling Chinese Children
Ceramic. Occupied Japan.
1945–1952. Chinese girl
holds a parrot, while the boy
holds a kite. $16.00–20.00

shape of a brown canoe, complete with ornamental markings. In it sits an Eskimo couple, she in a red coat, he in a blue one. $20.00–24.00

Spanish Señorita and Señor Ceramic. Japan. 1950s. The yellow-skirted, red-haired señorita is flanked by a blue-boleroed, black-hatted señor. The set is just 3½" tall. $10.00–14.00

British Couple Ceramic. Japan. 1950s. This small set (3½") is comprised of a blond girl in red cap, white skirt, blue jacket, and yellow blouse in white stockings. Her mate wears long white coat, yellow breeches, white stockings, and black shoes. $10.00–14.00

British 18th Century Couple Ceramic. Japan. Small (3½") couple consists of an elderly gentleman in a black tricorn hat, green jacket, white trousers, and a lady in a green bonnet, blue shawl, and ruffled skirt with yellow and red pattern. $10.00–14.00

British Farmer Ceramic. Japan. Small (31/2") figurines depict a red-cheeked, beefy man in a blue jacket, white waistcoat, brown breeches, and yellow conical hat. $10.00–14.00

Irish Couple Kissing on Bench Ceramic and wood. Boy and girl in Irish green sit on a wooden bench and turn their faces toward each other. Their eyes are closed. $12.00–16.00

Southern Belle and Dandy Ceramic. Japan. 1950s. This small set (3½") features a blond southern belle in a yellow bonnet and a multitiered skirt, paired with a dandy in white with pale pink top hat and black walking stick. $10.00–14.00

Hillbilly Couple Ceramic. Japan. 1950s. This small (3½") sitting couple shows a bearded, deeply tanned old man sitting and cradling a large, black rifle. The old woman wears her gray hair in a topknot, and peers across her half-moon glasses. $10.00–14.00

Amish Couple Ceramic. Japan. 1950s. Amish couple (6") wears black clothing over pale blue underclothing. Both stand on round green bases. $10.00–14.00

Oriental Couple Reading Ceramic. Ceramic Arts Studio. 1941–1955. An Oriental boy and girl sit holding books on their laps and reading. She wears a pink dress, he wears a blue jacket with blue trousers. $20.00–25.00

Chinese Boys with Baskets Ceramic. Japan. Chinese boys cling to the sides of oversize baskets. One boy wears yellow and green, the other wears green and black. $14.00–16.00

Kissing Mexican Couple Ceramic. Japan. 1950s. Red-dressed Mexican señorita bends at the waist, holding her hands behind her back, to plant a kiss on the lips of her boyfriend, who also bends from the waist and rests his hands on his knees. He wears yellow shirt, red serape, and black trousers. $16.00–18.00

Folkloric Milkmaids Ceramic. Japan. 1950s. Braided, bonneted, peasant girls in dirndl costumes have flouncy skirts, balloon sleeves, and flowered aprons. $10.00–14.00

Old Peasant Woman and Peasant Boy Ceramic. Japan. 1950s. Old peasant woman wears yellow headscarf and apron, white dress with blue buttons and sleeve linings. She stands in a disapproving, arms akimbo pose. The peasant boy wears red cap, yellow jacket, and striped wide pants. These could be a Russian grandmother and her grandson.$10.00–14.00

Tyrolean Boy and Girl Busts Ceramic. Japan. 1940s. Busts of Tyrolean-hatted blond boy and girl have white shirts. Girl wears blue scarf, boy wears red tie. $16.00–20.00

Hula Dancers Ceramic. Japan. 1950s. Graceful hula girls in yellow, swirling grass skirts have black hair in 1950s hairdos. One plays the ukulele, the other dances. $14.00–18.00

Hula Dancer and Ukulele Player Ceramic. Japan. 1950s. Sitting, male ukulele player in red and blue lei is teamed with a dancing girl in a green to yellow skirt. $15.00–18.00

White Martians Ceramic. Japan. 1960s. Blobby white Martians stand on white oval bases that are inscribed "I'm so bashful when you shake me" and "Watch it! I'm full of pep." Their original tags read "I just arrived from Mars" and "Hi Ho I'm a Li Li Lo." $14.00–16.00

Calypso Singer Busts Ceramic. Clay Art. 1980s. Charming, smiling Caribbean girls with scarves on their heads, large-collared decolletage dresses are sculpted from the bosom up. One wears pink gown trimmed in black, the other a black gown with yellow dots. $15.00–18.00

Dutch Couple Ceramic. Japan. 1940s–1950s. White-faced Dutch couple has bright yellow hair. She stands, arms crossed over her white apron. He shoves his hands into his voluminous blue trousers. They have baby-doll faces. $14.00–18.00

Kissing Delft Couple Delftware. Holland. Blue and white Delftware Dutch boy and girl incline from the waist and purse their lips for a kiss. $20.00–22.00

Dancing Dutch Couple Ceramic. Japan. 1940s. Yellow-haired Dutch couple dances. She wears blue dress, white blouse and apron, and large, yellow clogs. He wears deep blue vest, pale

Hindu Couple Ceramic. Occupied Japan. 1945–1952. A Hindu couple sits. One plays a sitar, the other listens. $16.00–20.00

Spanish Couple Ceramic. Japan. 1950s. Señor, in a black Spanish hat, strums a guitar. Señorita, in a red shawl, listens, waving her fan. $14.00–18.00

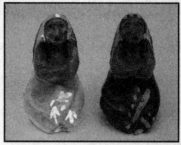

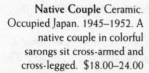

Native Couple Ceramic. Occupied Japan. 1945–1952. A native couple in colorful sarongs sit cross-armed and cross-legged. $18.00–24.00

blue cap and pants, and oversize yellow clogs. They bow to each other. $12.00–14.00

Dutch Couple on Green Ceramic Bench Ceramic. Japan. 1950s. This three-piece set consists of a green ceramic bench, on which sits a Dutch couple with crudely executed bodies. She wears a red dress and green cap; he wears a red caps, yellow shirt, and blue pants. $18.00–24.00

Kissing Dutch Couple Ceramic. Japan. 1940s. Dutch boy and girl each sit on white clog ornamented with blue imitation Delft flowers, and stretch out their faces to each other. Their lips actually meet. They are dressed in typical blue skirts, black vests, and white shirts. $10.00–14.00

Delft Couple Delftware. Holland. Stylized Dutch boy and girl in typical Delft colors have cartoonish faces. $14.00–18.00

Delft Couple Delftware. Holland. Realistic Dutch couple has white skirt or trousers shaded in blue. The figurines are otherwise rendered in shades of blue. $14.00–18.00

Colorful Dutch Couple Ceramic. Japan. 1940s. Dutch girl in pink blouse, yellow scarf, and blue skirt looks up coyly from under her bonnet. The boy, in pink shirt, yellow scarf, and blue pants smiles at her. $10.00–14.00

Eskimo Couple Ceramic. Japan. 1950s. Smiling Eskimo couple are dressed in furs. $14.00–18.00

Yellow Dutch Couple Ceramic. Simplified figurines of Dutch couple are yellow. Details of clothing are picked out in green lines and hair, basket, and flowers are painted deep yellow. $10.00–12.00

Round Dutch Couple Ceramic. Japan. 1940s. Round-bodied Dutch girl and boy have stick arms and round heads. The girl wears yellow top, blue bottom, the boy wears pink top, white pants. $10.00–14.00

Sitting Dutch Couple Ceramic. Japan. 1950s. Baby-faced Dutch couple is depicted in sitting pose. The girl in blue scarf, black skirt, and green underskirt is teamed with a boy in red cap and shoes, blue trousers, and green jacket. $12.00–14.00

Dutch Couple Ceramic. Japan. 1940s. A white-faced childish Dutch couple consists of a girl in a yellow bonnet, red scarf, and blue skirt, and boy in red cap, blue shirt, and yellow trousers. $12.00–14.00

Sitting Imitation-Delft Dutch Couple Ceramic. Japan. 1950s. A pale-blue Dutch boy with a white face sits by the side of a Dutch girl in a blue bonnet and dress with a large white apron with pink dots. $10.00–12.00

Red Dutch Couple Ceramic. Goebel. Germany. Round-bodied Dutch boy and girl wear red clothing. She has white bonnet with a yellow line, he has a yellow cap. Both have black, painted clogs peeking from under their round tummies. $24.00–28.00

Delft Windmills Delftware. Holland. Identical white windmills with handles have blue blades, roofs, and detailing. $12.00–14.00

Dutch Couple Ceramic. Germany. Boy in brown cap with black visor wears red shirt and round, pale blue trousers that resemble the cheeks of a fat peach. The girl in the white bonnet wears a dark blue blouse, pale blue skirt, and white apron with a double red stripe along the bottom. $14.00–16.00

Dutch Couple Kissing on a Bench Ceramic and wood. Japan. Dutch couple in red and white costumes sits on a wooden bench, holding bunches of yellow flowers. $12.00–14.00

Colorful Dutch Couple Ceramic. Japan. 1960s. A white-faced Dutch couple features a boy in pale yellow pants with wonderfully soft-looking creases, blue shirt, and beige hat. The girl in a green dress and red bonnet has a yellow apron with red dots. $12.00–14.00

White, Yellow, and Blue Dutch Couple Ceramic. Ceramic Art Studio, WI. Beautifully rendered Dutch couple depicts a girl with bright yellow hair, deep blue apron, and white dress. The boy, in white suit, yellow buttons, and blue scarf, resembles the Dutch Boy Paint mascot. $18.00–22.00

Dutch Couple with Landscape Aprons Ceramic. Japan. Imitation-Delft figurines depict yellow-haired Dutch couple with windmill-in-landscape motifs on their trousers or skirt. $12.00–14.00

Large Dutch Couple with Landscape Aprons Ceramic. Japan. Imitation-Delft figurines are 6" tall and depict yellow-haired Dutch couple with windmill-in-landscape motifs on trousers or skirt. $14.00–16.00

Tyrolean Couple Ceramic. Japan. 1940s. Boy in green cap and lederhosen is teamed with a girl in a hat and a long skirt. $14.00–20.00

Kissing Dutch Couple Ceramic. Japan. 1950s. Child-faced Dutch couple in wooden clogs holds hands behind their backs and bends forward from the waist to present their lips to each other. This set comes in various colors, among them red outfits with white dots, black outfits with white dots, and blue outfits with white dots. The shakers are 6" tall. $18.00–24.00

Colorful Dutch Couple Ceramic. Crudely detailed Dutch couple is painted in bright colors. The girl wears a blue bonnet and a purple apron. The boy wears a red cap, blue scarf, and orange pants. $12.00–14.00

Chinese Couple Ceramic. Japan. 1940s. Ornately dressed Chinese couple features man in red cap, yellow jacket, and black trousers, and woman in black cap, red buns, dark green coat, and yellow dress. $10.00–14.00

Thai Nodders Ceramic and metal. These large nodders (6") have shaker bodies and large heads that sit atop tightly coiled gold springs. Girl wears red dress and carries gold and black fan. Boy wears black rose decorated with gold. $14.00–18.00

Japanese Couple Ceramic. Ceramic Arts Studio, WI. This large (4½") set of shakers depicts a Japanese couple in white with gold trim. Girl has gold ribbons over her black hair, boy wears gold hat. $18.00–24.00

Japanese Couple Ceramic. Japan. 1940s. Japanese girl in blue kimono and red fan is flanked by boy in blue cap, red shirt, and green trousers. $10.00–14.00

Hula Dancer and Ukulele Player Ceramic. Japan. 1950s. Sitting male ukulele player is teamed with a dancing girl in a yellowish skirt. $16.00–20.00

PROFESSIONS

One-piece Bellhop Ceramic. Japan. 1950s. This one-piece shaker features a green-painted bellhop holding two suitcases, one on his shoulder, the other in the opposite hand. The condiment holes are in the suitcases. The bellhop stands on an octagonal white base. $14.00–18.00

Redcap with Cart Ceramic. Japan. A redcap with bulging eyes, handlebar moustache, and protruding ears wears a short gray jacket, blue pants, and huge, black shoes. He pushes a cart loaded down with suitcases. Two of the suitcases are removable as salt and pepper shakers. The redcap and cart are one piece. $20.00–24.00

Red Bellhop and Suitcase Ceramic. 1980s. A child-faced bellhop in red holds a tan suitcase and stands on a white base. He is flanked by a larger tan suitcase which is the other shaker. $15.00–18.00

One-piece Bellhop Ceramic. Japan. 1950s. A boy-faced bellhop with blond curly hair and pillbox hat carries a suitcase in each hand. The salt holes are in the front of one suitcase, the pepper holes are in the back of the other suitcase. This shaker comes in a variety of colors such as green jacket and shoes with blue pants or white jacket with red trim, blue pants, and red shoes or yellow jacket with blue trim, red pants, and brown shoes. $20.00–24.00

Bellhop in Three Pieces Ceramic. Japan. 1940s. A large-footed bellhop in a red cap with a black visor holds a white (salt) and a green (pepper) suitcase in each hand. The suitcases are detachable. Bellhop's face is white with a red clown nose, and big, black eyes. His uniform is brown with two rows of red buttons. $18.00–24.00

Bellhop in Three Pieces Ceramic. Japan. 1950s. A small white ceramic bellhop has a red cap, orange hair, a little-boy doll face, and a bright blue jacket. His arms curve out from the shoulders. He carries a yellow suitcase, suspended from each hand, and wears black shoes. The yellow suitcases are the salt-and-pepper shakers. $16.00–18.00

Butler and Maid Ceramic. 1940s. A bald butler in a white waiter's jacket, black pants, and boutonniere is teamed with a sassy-looking maid in short black dress, white apron, and cap. $14.00–18.00

Organ Grinder with Monkey Ceramic. A smiling, red-haired organ grinder in a blue vest with large pink bow tie and black boater grinds his yellow organ. The brown monkey wears a pink cap, a blue jacket, and holds out a blue cup. $14.00–20.00

Organ Grinder with Monkey Ceramic. A black-moustachioed organ grinder presses one hand to his heart as he belts out a song. His brown monkey scratches its head as it sits atop a wheeled, yellow hurdy-gurdy. The organ grinder wears a red jacket, black hat, and yellow pants. $12.00–18.00

Ship's Captains Ceramic. Japan. Smiling ship's captains in blue suits, black ties, and red shoes pose in typical captain poses. One raises his hand to wave, the other raises his hand to salute. Both wear large white hats, inscribed "Capt. Bob-Lo." $15.00–17.00

Maid and Bellhop China. Japan. 1950s. Adorable, child-faced couple are dressed as European bellhop in a red cap and short, green jacket, and as a maid in a black dress, white apron, and white cap. $14.00–18.00

Shopgirl Ceramic. Occupied Japan. 1945–1952. A white ceramic figurine of a shopgirl in a flowered dress and pert hat is attached to a brown base. In each upturned hand, the shopgirl holds a white ceramic "hatbox" by the strap. $20.00–24.00

Fishermen with Fish Ceramic. Japan. Fishermen in yellow mackintoshes with yellow hats are smoking brown pipes and standing, in their black boots, on brown bases. Under one arm each carries a fishing rod, from the end of which is suspended a blue fish. $14.00–16.00

Old Salty and Cap'n Pepper Ceramic. Hand-painted. Tall shakers (6") represent Old Salty in an orange mackintosh and black boots, smoking a brown pipe as he stands with his hands in his pockets, on a black base inscribed with the words "Old Salty." Cap'n Pepper, in a black pea jacket and white pants, stands on an identical base, though inscribed "Cap'n Pepper," and smokes a black pipe. Both have jovial faces and white beards. $20.00–24.00

Cap'n Pepper Ceramic. Matching figurines represent Cap'n Pepper in white pants, black pea jacket, and black shoes standing on a brown base. $10.00–12.00

Sailor and Fish Wood. Hand-painted sailor with a round body, round head, and round base smokes a pipe and wears light blue cap and jacket over white-and-red-striped shirt. The fish has a green and blue body and also wears a cap, though this one is white. $9.00–12.00

Sailors Ceramic. A first mate in a tan jacket, brown pants, and gray turtleneck, wears a white captain's cap and smokes a black pipe. The sailor is in a yellow mackintosh with brown boots and brown pipe. Both stand on brown bases and are made of chalklike composition. $10.00–12.00

Sailor and Mate Heads Ceramic. The busts of a sailor and a first mate stand on brown bases. The sailor wears a yellow mackintosh and hat, the mate wears a blue turtleneck, yellow jacket, and white cap. Both smoke pipes. $10.00–12.00

Sea Captains Ceramic. Germany. These matching shakers have movable glass eyes. They depict a well-detailed head, grinning, bearded, and wearing a black cap, sitting on a squat, featureless body composed of a red coat, blue tie, and tiny black legs-cum-feet. $12.00–14.00

Gloucester Fisherman Ceramic. Matching shakers depict a cantankerous old fisherman in a yellow mackintosh and black boots standing on a red base on which is inscribed "Cape Cod." On the sailor's shoulder perches a red parrot. $10.00–12.00

Sailor Boy and Girl on Bench Ceramic. Blond sailor boy and girl in matching outfits (white pants, sailor shirts, and caps with blue trim) sit on a wooden bench. The eyes of both are closed. She presses her hands together, he holds his behind his back. $14.00–18.00

Mate Heads Ceramic. Golden-bearded first mates wear white caps with black visors, smoke black pipes, and smile. The heads sit on tapering bases painted white with blue or white with red stripes. $10.00–12.00

Ship's Captains Ceramic. Identically detailed figurines of old sea captains of generous girth have gold detailing on the caps. Both captains stand with arms stiffly at the sides of the pea jackets, and feet encased in geometrically flaring white trousers. One wears black jacket, the other white. $20.00–24.00

White Chefs with Yellow Bow Tie Ceramic. Japan. 1940s. Fat, round chefs with yellow bow ties and pink cheeks, black moustaches, and black shoes are highlighted with gold. $18.00–24.00

Native Chefs in Grass Skirts
Ceramic. Japan. 1940s. Bare-chested black boy and girl wear tall toques and hold bowls filled with fruit in one hand. $14.00–18.00

Captain and Mate Ceramic. A black-bearded captain wears a blue pea jacket with yellow buttons. The mate wears a brown jacket over a blue turtleneck. Both have black beards, black shoes, and have shoved their hands into their pockets. $14.00–18.00

Sailors with Binoculars Ceramic. Cartoony sailors with egg heads and rounded bodies wear white sailor uniforms with pale blue trim, hold white signal flags, and have black binoculars suspended around their necks. $12.00–14.00

Pirate with Chest Ceramic. A very glossy figurine of a one-eyed pirate with a yellow kerchief, white shirt, green pants, and black boots is teamed with a brown, closed treasure chest. The pirate wears an eye patch. $12.00–14.00

Pirate with Chest Ceramic. A boy-faced pirate in a black hat with a skull and crossbones wears a red-and-white-striped jersey, aqua pants, and black boots. He is teamed with a brown chest that is slightly ajar, revealing a gold, glistening interior. $12.00–14.00

Pirates Ceramic. One pirate has a peg leg and eye patch and wears a black jacket over a red shirt. The other pirate, in blue stocking cap and jacket, has a black beard. $14.00–16.00

Street Cleaner Ceramic. U.S.A. 1950s. A dejected-looking street cleaner in uniform holds a broom over his shoulder. He is teamed with a garbage can on wheels. This set is white with very minimal detailing done in black line. $12.00–14.00

Cartoony Policemen Ceramic. 1960s. White ceramic figurines of police have very simplified bodies that include egg-shaped heads without hair, round hands, and winglike arms that are outstretched. The French-style police hats are green, the uniform buttons are pink, and the belts and shoes are black. The policemen hold brown clubs in one hand. $10.00–12.00

Policeman and Policewoman Ceramic. Heather House. Burlington, IA. Child-faced police couple in pale blue uniforms with black shoes features a trousered policewoman and her identically clad male counterpart. These are part of a series that includes a mail carrier set and firefighter set. $12.00–16.00

British Bobby and Palace Guard Ceramic. Japan. A typical British bobby in black with white shirt and blue tie has a gray moustache and bristling gray eyebrows. The palace guard in red and black uniform smiles. The faces and bodies are cartoony. $12.00–14.00

Bahamas Police Ceramic. One Caucasian and one Black policeman in the white-jacketed uniforms of Nassau police have the letters "S" (Caucasian) and "P" (Black) on their helmets. $12.00–14.00

Royal Canadian Mounted Police with Horse Ceramic. A red-jacketed, jodhpur-trousered RCMP stands, arms behind his back, on a base emblazoned with the letters RCMP. He is teamed up with a saddled horse. $15.00–20.00

Royal Canadian Mounted Police Ceramic. Matching figurines of standing RCMP on pale green bases are marked "S" and "P." Both wear yellow hats, red jackets, blue jodhpurs, and brown boots. $12.00–14.00

Royal Canadian Mounted Police Wood. Wooden, kingpin-shaped figurines of "Mounties" have red jackets, black pants and hats, and the letters "RCMP" in yellow on the hats. $10.00–12.00

Policeman and Thug Ceramic. 1930s. A policeman in the blue uniform of the 1920s with a tall, domed hat emblazoned with a gold star is teamed with a heavy-set, large-shouldered thug in a red turtleneck sweater and gray cap. $14.00–18.00

Cartoony Policemen Ceramic. Matching, blue policemen with fat, kingpin-type bodies have tall blue hats. $10.00–12.00

English Bobby Busts Ceramic. Matching English bobbies wear black uniforms and helmets with silver medallions emblazoned with "S" or "P." The busts are cut off at the third button. $18.00–22.00

Graduates Ceramic. Blond girl and boy wear matching black academicals and carry, in opposite hands, a scrolled diploma, and a pile of books. $14.00–18.00

Fat Chefs Ceramic. Fitz and Floyd. Extremely fat chefs in white stand on black round bases and have tiny heads capped with towering toques. One stirs a bowl, the other holds a spoon and fork and holds hand to nose. $25.00–30.00

Fireman Couple Ceramic. A winsome boy and girl fireman couple wears red hats, black boots, and white raincoats. The girl's hat is marked with a "1," the boy's with a "2." The girl holds a bunny, the boy holds an axe. $16.00–20.00

Fireman Hats Ceramic. White firemen hats are made of pottery and have a shield on each emblazoned with "S" or "P." $12.00–14.00

Driver in Green Car Ceramic. 1940s. A beige driver figurine with tan hair and moustache holds on to his bowler hat. He nestles in an undersize green car. This set is part of a "professionals" series. $14.00–20.00

Sailor in Lavender Boat Ceramic. 1940s. A beige sailor figurine with a little boy face sits pensively. The sailor figurine nestles in a lavender, undersize boat. This set is part of a "professionals" series. $14.00–20.00

Cook with Gray Table Ceramic. 1940s. A beige chef figurine with yellow hair holds a rolling pin to the top of a detachable table textured with an ornate, Spanish baroque design. This set is part of a "professionals" series. $14.00–20.00

Friars in a Basket Ceramic. Twin Winton. Rotund friars nestle in white, "wicker" work basket. Salt friar is bigger than pepper. $35.00–40.00

Fireman with Red Engine Ceramic. 1940s. A beige figurine of a fireman nestles in a red, undersize, old-fashioned fire engine. This set is part of a "professionals" series. $14.00–20.00

Shoemaker Ceramic. Identical, cartoonish shoemakers in white spectacles, brown hair, brown shirts, green pants, and white aprons hold a hammer in one hand, a shoe in the other. $12.00–14.00

Surgeons Ceramic. Matching, cartoonish figurines of surgeons in blue scrubs with white face masks and tool pouches around their waists are armed with pliers and saw. $12.00–14.00

Hippies Ceramic. 1960s. Squat, cartoonish figurines feature a girl hippie with hyperbolic brown hair, blue shift, and white "granny" glasses pushed up into her hair. She wears a white peace sign. He has long black hair, white "granny" glasses, and plays with his bare feet. $10.00–12.00

Friars Ceramic. Twin Winton. U.S.A. Identical Franciscan friars in brown robes with bald heads and jovial expressions on their pudgy faces have "S" or "P" on their habits. These came with a matching cookie jar on the bottom of which was written "Thou shalt not steal!" $22.00–24.00

Fuzzy Friars Ceramic and fur. Matching, roly-poly, small friars in brown habits and white cord belts are barefooted. They smile and close their eyes. Their bald pates are surrounded by real fur. $12.00–14.00

Nun and Monk Ceramic. This small set of shakers features a kindly faced nun in pre-reform habit and a rotund, bald monk holding his hands on his ample paunch. $20.00–24.00

Praying Nuns Ceramic. Japan. Small nuns in black habits have bulbous noses and smiling faces. The one with open eyes holds up her hands in prayer. The one with closed eyes clasps her hands. $10.00–12.00

Praying Nuns with Prayer Books Ceramic. Japan. Small, comical nuns with baby-doll faces wear black habits and hold opened prayer books in their hands. $10.00–12.00

Singing Nuns Ceramic. Japan. Small, round-faced nuns in black habits hold arms at sides and round their mouths. $10.00–12.00

Friar Condiment Set Ceramic. NAPCO. This four-piece set consists of a tray made up of three contiguous circles on

Jailbirds Ceramic. Japan. 1950s. Two mean-looking jailbird heads sit atop pedestals marked "7734 Alcatraz." Pepper wears white cap, salt wears black cap. $14.00–18.00

Astronaut and Rocket Ceramic. Japan. 1970s. The astronaut boy in blue salutes as he stands next to his blue, yellow, and red rocket inscribed "To . . . From." $16.00–20.00

which rest two shaker friars and one mustard pot friar. The friars are in identical poses and costumes. They are all black, wear black habits with white belts, and hold red prayer books in their right hands. $24.00–28.00

Friar and Nun Ceramic. Small nun in brown habit and delicate features is teamed with a blond friar in black habit with brown cord. Both are rather sloppily painted. $10.00–12.00

Milkman and Cow Ceramic. 1940s. An energetic milkman in blue jacket, red pants, and black shoes is holding a carrier of milk bottles as he takes a giant stride. His feet are attached to a green base. He is teamed with a brown, malicious-looking cow. $30.00–34.00

Photographer with Camera Ceramic. Japan. A boyish photographer in striped pants, yellow vest, and red bow tie is teamed with an old-fashioned bellows camera on a brown tripod. $14.00–18.00

Mail Carrier Couple Ceramic. Japan. This childish couple depicts mail carriers in white jackets, black ties, and gray pants and caps. The boy waves, the girl pulls a letter out of her brown shoulder bag, which is marked "U.S. Mail." $18.00–24.00

Hunter and Rabbit Ceramic. Japan. A brown hunter holds a dark brown blunderbuss. The small white rabbit sits quietly and flattens its ears. $14.00–16.00

Hunter and Bear Ceramic. Japan. A pink-faced, cartoony hunter in gray pants, red vest and hat, and striped shirt throws up his arms. In one hand he holds a rifle. He is teamed with a serene brown bear, standing on his hind legs, his arms akimbo, and smiling. $12.00–14.00

Brewmaster with Three Barrels Condiment Set Ceramic. A bald, bulbous-nosed brewmaster in a red shirt and black overalls holds out a foaming stein. He is attached to a fancy ceramic base embossed with a design of grapes and grape leaves. On the base are nestled three brown barrels inscribed with "Salt" or "Pepper" or, in the case of mustard, nothing at all. $24.00–26.00

Brewmaster with Barrels Ceramic. Japan. A bald brewmaster in blue overalls with white, red-bordered towel over one arm stands holding a dark brown mug in one hand. He is attached to a blue-gray base, on which stand two brown barrels, the shakers. $18.00–24.00

UPS Driver to Mars Ceramic. A pink, thumb-shaped driver with spotted bow tie and space alien features is teamed with a gray rocket marked "UPS." The driver's base also carries the inscription "UPS." $20.00–24.00

Railroad Workers Ceramic. Yardman and station master figurines stand on oval bases on which the name of a particular railroad line or station are usually inscribed (e.g., Steamtown, U.S.A., Bellows Falls, VT., Strasburg Rail Road). The station master wears a uniform in some shade of gray and carries a black lantern. The yardman is in white with gray jacket and red bandanna and consults his pocket watch. $14.00–20.00

Gas Station Attendant and Pump Ceramic. 1980s. A reproduction of an orange, old-fashioned gas pump with decal advertising gas at twenty-six cents per gallon is teamed with an attendant in pale blue saluting smartly. $18.00–20.00

Policeman with Parking Meter Ceramic. Reproduction of vintage shaker depicts a blue-uniformed policeman writing out a ticket and a gray parking meter. $15.00–18.00

Nun Musicians Ceramic with bisque finish. This series of nuns playing musical instruments has six shakers that are 6" tall. The nuns wear black habits with gold crosses, and have lovely, almost baby-doll faces. They play the following instruments: accordion, bongo drum, banjo, trumpet, guitar, and saxophone. $30.00–45.00

Nun Sports Players Ceramic, with bisque finish. This series of nuns playing various sports has six shakers that are 6" tall. The nuns wear black habits with gold crosses, and each is in a pose appropriate to the sport she is playing. The following sports are represented: baseball, soccer, tennis, golf, ping-pong, and basketball. $30.00–45.00

Chef Heads Ceramic. Japan. 1940s–1960s. Caucasian chef's heads in white toques, white collars, and black bow ties have heavy black brows and moustaches, pink cheeks, and red lips. They have a decidedly Gallic flavor. $12.00–16.00

Stoneware Chefs Stoneware. Geometrical, very stylized chef couple features him in a heavy brown moustache, brown bow tie, and trapezoidal apron with a white toque. She has bangs, toque, and oval apron with scalloping. $16.00–20.00

Chef Heads with Utensils Ceramic. Japan. Ruddy chef's faces with black eyes and moustaches peer out from beneath large chef hats with the words "Pepper" and "Salt" in large red block

Martian and Flying Saucer Ceramic. Japan. 1970s. A green Martian with red eyes stands next to his yellow flying saucer. $16.00–20.00

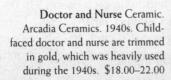

Doctor and Nurse Ceramic. Arcadia Ceramics. 1940s. Child-faced doctor and nurse are trimmed in gold, which was heavily used during the 1940s. $18.00–22.00

Royal Canadian Mounted Policeman on Horse Ceramic. Japan. 1950s. This two-piece set consists of a yellow horse, into whose back fits the figurine of a boy-faced policeman in a red jacket and blue trousers. The RCMP's torso balances on the horse's saddle. $14.00–20.00

letters, and a fork or spoon running from ear to mid-toque. $10.00–14.00

Caucasian Chef and Cook Ceramic. Japan. A Caucasian, winking chef in white costume with three buttons holds a spoon. The round-faced cook in blue dress and white apron holds a brown spoon. $12.00–14.00

Winking Caucasian Chef and Cook Ceramic. Japan. A Caucasian, winking chef in pink costume with yellow apron and three black buttons holds a brown spoon. The cook in pink dress and yellow apron holds a brown spoon. $12.00–14.00

"Kingpin" Chef's Heads Ceramic. Japan. 1950s. Kingpin-shaped chef's heads have white toques edged in gray, red, curly bangs, semispherical bases in dotted pattern with bow ties, and white faces with pink cheeks, round eyes, and articulate lips. $10.00–12.00

Comical Chefs Ceramic. Japan. 1940s. Kingpin-shaped, full-figured chefs in identical poses have round, baby-doll eyes, flaring black moustache, and "X" patterned bow tie, four buttons, and green trousers over brown shoes. The words "Salt" and "Pepper" appear in gold on their white aprons. $12.00–14.00

Cute Chef Busts Ceramic. Japan. 1950s. Pink-faced, black-haired, and moustachioed chefs in white bow ties have squat, white toques and a black button on each chest. $10.00–12.00

Fat, Ruddy Chef Faces Ceramic. Japan. 1960s. Very florid complexioned, shiny, pig-snouted chefs have black eyebrows and goatees and mushroom-shaped toques with the initials "S" or "P." $12.00–14.00

Big Boop and Betty Boop Chefs Ceramic. Japan. Red-skirt-ed and scarved, Betty Boop with a very round figure, stands arms akimbo, balancing a "popover"-shaped toque on her head. Big Boop, in black pants, scarf, and hair, eyes her from the side. $20.00–24.00

Pig Chefs Ceramic. Japan. A red-jacketed, pink-faced chef in white toque holds a white spoon. The blue-clad, blue-toqued cook holds a white spoon too. $13.00–16.00

Cow Chefs Ceramic. Japan. Brown cows in long dresses and white aprons are equipped for gastronomic experimentation, armed with rolling pin. $16.00–24.00

Cook and Chef Ceramic. Japan. 1930s. Small, pink-faced chef and cook in toque or scarf hold spoons. Their white aprons are edged in gold, as are their toques. $16.00–20.00

Chef and Cook Ceramic. Japan. 1930s. Tiny, pink-faced chef with blond hair and red shoes holds a brown spoon. Brown-haired cook with white scarf wears blue shirt, white skirt, white ruffled apron, and holds a black frying pan. $16.00–20.00

Dutch Girl and Boy Cooks Ceramic. Pink-faced, white ceramic Dutch girl and boy wear aprons decorated with gold flowers. $12.00–16.00

Fat Cook and Chef with Rabbit Ceramic. Japan. Tiny, very fat, pink-faced chef holds up a pink rabbit by the ears. The red-haired, blue-dressed, fat cook in dotted apron holds up a huge yellow spoon. $14.00–20.00

Chef and Dutch Girl Ceramic. 1930s. Pink-faced boy in tow-ering white toque with gold trim is flanked by a girl in a Dutch cap and white, gold-trimmed apron. $12.00–16.00

Royal Canadian Mounted Policeman and Horse Ceramic. Japan. 1960s. The RCMP stands at attention and salutes. His horse is sad-dled and stands alertly. $16.00–20.00

Cook and Chef Couple Ceramic. Japan. 1930s. A blue-dressed, red-haired cook hides her hands under her large, white apron. The stout cook, in blue trousers and black shoes, contentedly puffs out his stomach. $12.00–16.00

Chef and Ice Box Ceramic. Japan. Smug chef in yellow costume with white apron, socks, and black shoes poses next to a white, old-fashioned ice chest with gold trim. $20.00–22.00

Fat and Skinny Chefs Ceramic. Japan. A bald, brown-moustachioed fat chef, holds up white finger of one hand. The skinny, brown-whiskered chef in a toque gesticulates with fingers of one hand pursed together. The gestures are typically French, but the inscription on the toque reads "Beacon, N.J." $20.00–24.00

Chef and Toque Nester Ceramic. Japan. A yellowish-faced chef with orange hair and whiskers and gigantic bow tie with green collar balances a large toque on his head. Each piece is a shaker. $14.00–20.00

Chefs with Cat and Chicken Shafford china. China. A grinning, red-haired chef holds a black cat. A tearful, black-haired chef holds up a plucked chicken. Both stand on orange bases. $20.00–24.00

Chef and Ice Box Ceramic pottery. Pink-faced chef in white with gold trim stands next to an old-fashioned ice box with gold trim. $20.00–22.00

Chef Tray with Shakers Plastic. 1950s. A white plastic tray with a chef for part of the handle holds two boxy red shakers on either side. $10.00–12.00

Plastic Chefs Under Awning Holder Plastic and metal. 1950s. White, kingpin-shaped plastic shakers depict chefs. Drawn on their bodies are a pair of hands holding forks, a blue scarf, and rudimentary facial features. Each sits in a metal double ring, connected to a perpendicular carrying handle, from the top of which extends a red-and-white-striped "awning." $12.00–14.00

Plastic Chef with Shakers Plastic. 1950s. A devilish-looking chef with black goatee, arched eyebrows, and pink cheeks clasps white buckets to his belly. Each contains a red-capped shaker. The chef's feet are two circles. $14.00–20.00

Mailman with Box
Ceramic. Japan. A small,
boy-faced mailman in
navy blue reaches his
hand into his red mail
pouch. He is teamed
with a white, rural-type
mailbox on a green base
with "U.S. Mail" on the
door. $20.00–24.00

Short-Order Cooks Ceramic. Japan. 1950s. Cute boy cooks in tall toques, white outfits, and dotted scarves are energetically manipulating either rolling pin or frying pan and spatula. Salt wears blue scarf, pepper wears red scarf. $15.00–20.00

Chef Busts Ceramic. Porcine-faced chefs, in white ceramic with pink cheeks and lips, wear pink-banded toques and pink overalls and green bow ties. The letters "S" and "P" appear on their toques. $10.00–12.00

Lee Chefs Ceramic. White ceramic figurines of chefs in toques and plaid aprons stand on green bases with the word "Lee." One chef holds a stack of logs, the other a tray including a pepper shaker with the initial "P." $12.00–16.00

Cook Condiment Set Ceramic. This four-piece set contains a tray on which are standing two matching shakers flanking a mustard pot that is squatter. The figurines are identical otherwise, depicting fat women cooks in red-flowered dresses, holding one golden spoon to their left temple. $16.00–20.00

Maid and Cook Ceramic. A small set depicts a brown-haired maid in a blue blouse and white apron with 1920s-style facial features. The chef holds a blue spoon and wears red shoes with his white uniform and apron. $10.00–12.00

JUST PLAIN FOLK

Girls in Earphones Goebel. 1920s. Little girls sit with hands on their laps and old-fashioned radio earphones on their ears. $30.00–35.00

Girls in Bonnets Ceramic. Occupied Japan. 1945–1952. Identical girls in flounced pink and white dresses wear oversize yellow bonnets. $14.00–18.00

Boy and Dog in Earphones Goebel. 1920s. A little boy wearing earphones and his dog sit and listen to old-fashioned radio. $30.00–35.00

Boy and Girl Genies Goebel. 1927. M. Möller. Round-bottomed girl and boy genies wear fancy turbans. $30.00–35.00

Boy and Girl Skiing Goebel. 1940–1956. Bare-headed girl in red pants and blue scarf skis with boy in red scarf and blue pants who wears a red cap. $30.00–35.00

"Dick and Jane"-type Children Ceramic. Japan. 1950s. A boy and girl dressed in 1950s fashion resemble Dick and Jane. She wears a white dress with pink roses. He wears blue shorts and a white T-shirt with yellow stripes. The figurines are imitation Hummel. $14.00–18.00

Child Musicians Ceramic. Occupied Japan. 1945–1952. This nester set consists of two children sitting on a base that sculpts their bodies from the knees down. One child plays the accordion, the other sings. $14.00–20.00

Kissing Children on Bench Ceramic and wood. Japan. 1950s–1960s. These "Hummel"-type children in Tyrolean

Children on the Potty
Ceramic. Occupied Japan.
1945–1952. Blond child sits
on a "potty," reading.
$24.00–30.00

costumes are beautifully hand-painted in muted tones. They are shown kissing. The boy holds a large, brown umbrella, the girl holds a basket of berries. $16.00–20.00

Reading Children on Bench Ceramic and wood. Japan. 1950s–1960s. "Hummel"-type children sit on a wooden bench, engrossed in their reading. The girl has brown pigtails, the boy has a brown cowlick. They both hold open books in their laps. $16.00–20.00

Child Musicians on Bench Ceramic and wood. Japan. 1950s–1960s. A brown-haired boy and girl sit side by side on a wooden bench and have their lips pursed as though in song. The boy holds an accordion on his green trousers. The girl wears a short red skirt. $12.00–16.00

Scarecrow Children Kissing on Bench Ceramic and wood. Japan. 1950s. Boy and girl scarecrows in faded, blue clothing that is patched wear yellow straw hats with gold trim and kiss as they sit on the wooden bench. $16.00–20.00

Boy Playing Flute Ceramic. Japan. 1950s. Identical figurines depict a yellow-haired boy with a blue cap, jacket, and shoes, playing a brown flute. His trousers, face, and hands are white. $12.00–16.00

Running Children Ceramic. Japan. 1950s. Imitation Hummel figurines show a running child couple. The little boy's hair is windswept. His pink tie flutters across his shoulder. He wears pale blue trousers. The little girl wears a long-skirted, yellow dress and black ballerina slippers. $12.00–14.00

Farmer Children Ceramic. Japan. 1940s. This reclining couple depicts a boy in yellow pants resting his head on his hand as he snoozes. The girl lies on her tummy and supports her head with her hand. She wears blue. Both are nicely highlighted in gold. $24.00–28.00

Hillbilly Lady with Mountain Juice Ceramic. U.S.A. 1960s. Long-haired brunette in tattered clothes reclines next to a huge jug of "Mountain Juice." $12.00–16.00

Farmer Children Ceramic. Japan. 1950s. This boy and girl are copies of a Hummel set which depicts the girl in an orange scarf, black bodice, green skirt, and white apron, carrying a sheaf of wheat. The boy wears brown overalls and carries wood. $16.00–20.00

Children on a Hike Ceramic. Japan. 1950s. The Hummel-type girl and boy stand on white bases. She wears a blue dress with a yellow apron, and carries a green basket. He wears blue shorts and a green jacket and holds a walking stick. $16.00–20.00

Gardening Children Ceramic. Japan. 1940s. A girl in a pink dress with gold trim holds a red berry in her hand. The boy, dressed in blue overalls, wears a straw hat and brandishes a trowel. Both are decorated with gold glitter. $14.00–18.00

Umbrella Children Ceramic. Japan. A boy and a girl each sit under a tan umbrella. The girl wears a pink coat that matches her pigtail ribbons. A white duck is by her side. The boy wears a blue jacket and has a gray rabbit by his side. $34.00–36.00

Red Umbrella Children Ceramic. Japan. 1940s. A boy and a girl sit beneath large red umbrellas. The girl wears a red cape, the boy wears a blue cape. $22.00–26.00

Winter Children Ceramic. Japan. 1960s. A girl in a red cap and coat wears green gloves and leans to the side with her eyes closed as though preparing to kiss the boy. The boy leans toward her and opens one eye. He wears a pale blue coat over black trousers. $12.00–16.00

Flower Girl Series Ceramic. NAPCO. Little girls in long dresses decorated with flowers wear matching flower hats. NAPCO made a series of twelve of these sets, with a distinctive flower and color matched to each month. $14.00–20.00

Graduating Children Ceramic. U.S.A. 1950s. The blond girl in braids wears a white robe over her gray pleated skirt and a black mortarboard. The boy is identically dressed and also carries a white, scrolled diploma. $12.00–16.00

Babies in Pajamas Bisque. Holt-Howard. Pink-cheeked toddlers sit straddle-legged, holding their hands in front of them. One wears a pink pajama with black dots, the other wears a blue pajama with black dots. Their eyes are closed and their lips are rounded. $24.00–28.00

Babies in Pajamas Bisque. Holt-Howard. Pink-cheeked toddlers sit straddle-legged, holding their hands behind their backs. One wears a pink pajama, the other, a blue one. Both purse their lips and close their eyes. $24.00–28.00

Babies in Diapers Bisque. 1930s. Pale, beige babies with yellow hair, large eyes, and baby-doll faces reach out their hands. They are dressed in white diapers. $24.00–28.00

Confederate Babies Ceramic. Japan. Smiling, cute babies wear diapers in colors to match their uniform hats, which are either blue or gray and blue. $12.00–14.00

Kewpie Babies Ceramic. Kewpie-doll look-alikes support their large heads on small, plump hands as they lie naked and kick up their heels. $40.00–45.00

Children Ceramic. Occupied Japan. 1945–1952. These imitation Hummel figurines represent a boy holding a toy horse and a girl with a basket holding a flower. $24.00–30.00

Sitting Children with Sun Hats Ceramic. Japan. 1930s. Children in gigantic red sun hats sit and daydream. $20.00–30.00

Crying Kewpie Babies Bisque. Naked Kewpies sit up and cry. $40.00–45.00

Flower Babies Ceramic. Japan. 1930s. Kewpie-faced pink babies are entirely naked except for the daisy hats they balance on their heads and the green shoes on their feet. "P" sits on a flower. "S" stands on a pink flower. $14.00–20.00

Baby Nodder and Baby Ceramic. Sarsaparilla, 1980s. This three-piece set consists of two diapered babies. The black-haired one lies on its back. The blond one sits up. The head is a nodder that sits inside the sitting body. $16.00–20.00

Prince and Princess Ceramic. Japan. 1960s. Children with simplified faces reminiscent of the Cabbage Patch Dolls have brown hair and black dots for eyes. The boy wears a pink prince outfit. The girl wears a long white gown with a pink cape and a white crown. $12.00–16.00

Lady and Gentleman in Formal Attire Goebel. Late 1920s. Incised Crown Mark. Gentleman in top hat accompanies lady in long coat and 1920s hairstyle. $30.00–35.00

Betty Boop-like Heads Ceramic. 1930s. Spherical shakers are embossed and hand-painted with faces resembling cartoon character Betty Boop. $24.00–30.00

Busts of Colonial Couple Ceramic. Occupied Japan. 1945–1952. Finely painted busts of a lady and a gentleman from the Colonial period show a lady with yellow hair, rosebud lips, and pink bonnet, and a gentleman in a black, cockaded tricorne, a gold-detailed jabot, and a lavender coat. $24.00–28.00

Boxing Boys Ceramic. Japan. 1940s. Little boys in overalls face off. Their boxing gloves are deep brown. There are very many sets depicting children playing various sports. $16.00–20.00

Elderly Couple in Trouble Ceramic. Japan. 1950s. An elderly man in blue is flanked by his elderly, pregnant wife. On her pink dress, directly over her stomach, is inscribed, "You and Your Once More for Old Times Sake!!!" $16.00–20.00

Elderly Couple on Bench Ceramic and wood. Japan. 1950s–1960s. An elderly man and woman sit next to each other on a wooden bench. She wears her pale, yellow hair in a topknot. He is bald. She wears a green dress with a white apron, while he wears brown trousers, white shirt, and brown vest. $12.00–16.00

Traveller and Suitcase on Bench Ceramic and wood. Japan. 1950s–1960s. A male traveller in a black jacket and white trousers with black stripes reclines, covering his face with a newspaper. A yellow duffle bag sits next to him on the bench. $14.00–18.00

Drunk and Jug on Bench Ceramic and wood. Japan. 1950s–1960s. A red-faced, black-bearded drunk in bare feet sits on a wooden bench, leaning one elbow on a large jug. $12.00–16.00

Ladies in Brown Shakers and Dinner Bell Ceramic. Japan. 1950s. Girl-faced ladies in 19th century dresses wear bonnets and carry muffs on one arm. They have red hair and brown gowns. One of the ladies is a dinner bell. The tray on which they all stand is a white oblong with gold trim. $20.00–22.00

Busts of Ladies in Bonnets Ceramic. Japan. 1950s. Ladies with downcast eyes and red rosebud lips wear flouncy white bonnets and lacy collars. $12.00–18.00

Couple in Roadster Lusterware. Japan. 1920s–1930s. This three-piece set consists of a red, black, and yellow open roadster into which are inserted the driver and, behind her, the passenger. The lady driver wears pink and the steering wheel is attached to her hand. The gentleman wears a blue jacket. $50.00–55.00

Deco Ladies Sugar and Shaker Set Lusterware. Japan. 1920s–1930s. This three-piece set consists of a large figurine of a lady in a bell-shaped skirt wearing a cloche and carrying a bouquet of flowers painted in the Deco style. She is flanked by two figurines a third her size which are the shakers. The figurines were available in peach, blue, green, and orange variants. $75.00–100.00

Hostess and Captain Ceramic. Japan. 1960s. A lady in a long white gown and frilly bonnet holds a basket of purple fruit. Her shoe trim and ribbon are all gold. She wears black sculpted glasses. The captain has a childish face trimmed with a yellow beard and wears a sailor costume detailed in gold. He smokes a black sculpted pipe. $20.00–24.00

Hostess and Captain Busts Ceramic. Japan. 1960s. A lady in brown sculpted glasses wears a white scarf tied around her head rabbit-ear style. Her mate is a sea captain in a white hat, yellow beard, and smokes a black sculpted pipe. $14.00–18.00

Farmer and Farmer's Wife Ceramic. Japan. 1950s. This comical, rotund couple have "folksy" faces with protruding, pointed noses. She wears a red dress with a white apron. He wears a white top with red dots and blue trousers. Their poses mimic the black Mammy and Chef sets. $16.00–20.00

Gentleman and Lady Shaker–Egg Cup Busts Ceramic. Japan. 1950s. This unusual set belongs to a genre that combines shakers with egg cups. The shakers, in this instance, are the hats of the lady and gentleman. The couple's faces are painted on the sides of the egg cups, which rest on saucers. $24.00–28.00

Teenage Girls with Poodles Ceramic. Japan. 1950s. Two variations of the teenager with poodle were available. The girl was one set, the poodle, the other. One girl with orange hair wears a red T-shirt and striped pedal pushers. She sits on a suitcase and holds the leash of her black poodle. The other girl wears a blue top over black pedal pushers and stands next to her white suitcase. Her poodle is white. $18.00–24.00

Woman with Rolling Pin, Husband in Doghouse Ceramic. Vallona Starr. Vallona, CA. 1950s. An angry woman in a white dress sits holding a rolling pin. Her husband is scrunched up inside a red-roofed doghouse. $20.00–24.00

Kissing Couples, "Sweethearts of All Nations" Ceramic. NAPCO. 1956–1957. Kissing, standing couple in national costume incline toward each other from the waist up. This international set drew on a number of nationalities for its sweethearts: Sweden, Spain, Switzerland, Germany, Holland, Italy, Scotland, India, Alaska, U.S.A., American Indian, China, Ireland, Poland, France, Japan, Mexico, and Russia. $16.00–20.00

"What's Hers is Hers" Couple Ceramic. Japan. 1950s. Towel-wrapped husband and wife wear red shoes and stand on bases that read "What's Hers is Hers" and "What's His is Hers." His towel is marked "Hers," while her towel is marked "His." $22.00–26.00

"Is It Fun?" "You Bet" Couple Ceramic. Japan. 1950s. The man's and the women's heads and feet emerge from either end of a striped shower curtain. The man's shaker is inscribed "And is/You bet" with "Shower" on the base. The woman's shaker is inscribed "It Fun?/It is!" with "Bath" on the base. $22.00–26.00

Bathing Beauties Ceramic. U.S.A. 1940s. Identical figurines of bathing beauties in green and red one-piece swimsuits have yellow bobbed hair and red sandals. $18.00–24.00

Bikini Sunbathers Ceramic. Japan. 1960s. Girls in bikinis lie on their backs with their arms behind their heads. The one in the red bikini wears a colorful, flat straw hat. The one in the blue bikini wears a sombrero. $14.00–18.00

Ballroom Couple Turnabout Ceramic. U.S.A. 1950s. A smiling man in a black jacket and red tie holds out one arm. His hand is part of the woman shaker. The woman frowns. She

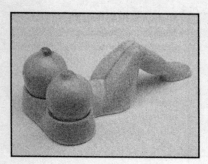

Reclining Nudes with Breast Shakers Nesters Ceramic. U.S.A. 1950s–1970s. Reclining nudes are available in several variations. They may lack arms and heads, consisting only of a torso and legs, and have two mammoth breasts as shakers. Some wear panties. Some have heads and are patterned on the Vargus pin-ups. $10.00–18.00

wears a red skirt with a yellow brassiere top. The back side of the woman shaker reveals her skirt up over her fanny and the man's hand holding up the hem. $20.00–24.00

Nudes on Barrels Ceramic. U.S.A. 1950s. Blond nudes sit on yellow, wood-grained barrels. They wear pearls around their necks. $12.00–14.00

Nudes Clinging to Barrels Ceramic. U.S.A. 1950s. Red-haired nudes in shoes cling to the sides of black-banded barrels and hold aloft their derrieres. $10.00–12.00

Happy/Angry Couple Turnabouts Ceramic. Japan. 1950s. On one side, a middle-aged couple looks happy. She wears a pink, long dress, he is in blue, suspendered trousers. On the other side, the woman frowns, and the man scowls. $20.00–28.00

Elderly Couple on Bench Ceramic. Japan. 1950s. This elderly couple is not in the best of moods. The man, in glasses, scratches his head. The woman in bifocals and gray hair wears a pink dress over her bulging stomach which is inscribed, "You and Your Once More for Old Times Sake!!!" This set was also made of a standing couple, without the bench. $16.00–20.00

Standing Grandparents Ceramic. Japan. 1960s. Bald grandpa wears a green bathrobe and smokes a pipe. Plump grandma wears a nightcap and purple nightshirt and knits a green sock. $10.00–16.00

Grandfather on Rocker Ceramic. 1950s. A bespectacled, pipe-smoking old man sits in a rocking chair, wearing a yellow blanket on his knees. The rocker is a shaker and the figure is another shaker. $16.00–20.00

Grandmother on Rocker Ceramic. 1950s. An old lady in white with red piece of knitting sits in a brown rocking chair. She is a shaker, as is the chair. $16.00–20.00

Smiling Matron Ceramic. Japan. 1960s. A kingpin-shaped matron with yellow, marcelled hair wears a green dress with blue spirals and carries a red handbag. $12.00–16.00

Dancing Couple Ceramic. Vandor. 1980s. The red-haired man holds a blond lady in a long blue gown. This is a nester set, consisting of the couple from the waist down (one shaker) and from the waist up (one shaker). $16.00–18.00

Joggers Ceramic. Japan. 1970s. Comical, overweight joggers are swathed from head to toe in running sweats. Only the bulbous noses protrude. One is red, the other is blue. $16.00–20.00

Couple Doing Push-Ups Ceramic. Japan. 1970s. Comical couple is grossly overweight. They are shown prone, supporting their ample weight on their arms. He wears red and blue, she wears green and red. $25.00–28.00

Dearie is Weary Ceramic. Japan. 1960s. The proverbial tired housewife wears a yellow dress and head scarf and white apron on which is written "Dearie is Weary." $14.00–18.00

Quarreling Couple Ceramic. Japan. 1960s. This gray and red couple have obviously been married a long time. The elderly husband thumbs his nose, while his wife turns her back on him. $18.00–20.00

Hillbillies in Barrels Ceramic. Japan. 1960s. Hillbilly with a long black beard and unkempt black hair peers out of a brown barrel. His blond wife peeks out of the other barrel. $12.00–14.00

Hillbilly Couple in Barrels Ceramic. Japan. 1960s. A gray-bearded, straw-hatted hillbilly peers out of his "Salt" barrel. His blond smiling wife pops out of her "Pepper" barrel, holding a broom in one hand. $16.00–18.00

Sleeping Hillbilly Ceramic. Japan. 1960s. Identical bearded hillbillies lie on their backs, sleeping. $12.00–18.00

Hoboes Ceramic. Japan. 1960s. Short, squat hoboes wear black bowler hats, red neckties, and have red patches on their yellow clothing. $10.00–12.00

Fanciful Beings

Gnomes with Animals Ceramic. Uneboek. 1979. This series of shakers depicts sitting gnomes with red, conical hats, white beards, blue shirts, and orange trousers tucked into high brown boots. The second half of the pair is some sort of forest or field creature. $20.00–24.00

Dwarfs in Brown Ceramic. Japan. 1950s. A waving dwarf in brown stands. The other dwarf lies down and waves. Both have white beards and smiling faces. $14.00–18.00

Elves in Clown Costumes Ceramic. Japan. 1940s. Elves with Betty Boop eyes, huge ears, and pink, pointed noses sit. One wears a blue clown suit with white dots and pink ruff. The other wears a pink clown suit with red dots and a green ruff. $12.00–18.00

Pixies Playing Instruments Ceramic. Japan. Early 1940s. Large-eared pixies sit on drums decorated with a staff, some notes, and the letters "S" or "P." The pixie pairs come in red, blue, orange, green, and yellow, and play various instruments. They are lavishly detailed in gold. There is a conductor who is teamed with a music stand (the pepper shaker) on which the words "The Pixy Band" are inscribed. $12.00–18.00

Pink Pixies on Logs Ceramic. Japan. 1940s. Each of the identical shakers depicts a pink pixy straddling a yellow stump. The caps are a deeper shade of pink, and the collars are a lime green color. $10.00–12.00

Pixies on Mushrooms Ceramic. Japan. 1950s. Pixies in green caps and jackets and yellow tights sit on brown toadstools that are marked "S" or "P." $12.00–14.00

Pixie Heads Ceramic. Japan. 1950s. Kissy-lipped, baby-doll-faced pixie heads emerge from a double layer of flower petals. $12.00–14.00

Musical Angels Porcelain. Japan. 1940s. White porcelain angels with little girl faces, blond hair, and rich, gold detailing play various musical instruments. The musician or singer is teamed with an angel holding the music score. Some of these angels do not cooperate, holding their scores over their heads, for example. $12.00–14.00

Holt-Howard Angels Holt-Howard. 1950s. Candy-cane-striped girl angels have little wings, blond hair, and blue eyes. Their heads resemble eggs laid on their side, their bodies are truncated cones. $16.00–20.00

Angels with Rose Hair Ceramic. Japan. 1950s. White angels with children's faces wear long robes that are trimmed in pink rose blossoms. Their wings are tipped with the same shade of pink. Instead of hair, they have a ball of rose blossoms. $12.00–14.00

Dancing Big Heads Ceramic. Japan. 1950s. This middle-aged couple really knows how to live it up! These shakers have huge heads with unique expressions and small, colorful bodies. $24.00–28.00

Devil Children Ceramic and metal. Japan. 1950s. Cute, boy-faced little devils are dressed entirely in red with matching caps. They hold metal pitchforks and have black horns. $14.00–18.00

Kitchen Witch Ceramic. Taiwan. 1970s. Both kitchen witches are dressed in blue with red head scarves. One wears a white apron and carries an actual straw switch in her hand. $14.00–18.00

Nude on Armchair Ceramic. U.S.A. 1950s. A nude blond kneels on a green armchair. This is a nester set. $18.00–24.00

BLACK AMERICANA

Mammy and Chef Ceramic. Japan. 1920–1955. 4". Black "Mammy" in white bandanna and dress holds yellow wooden spoon in one hand, and holds the other arm akimbo. Her dress has red detailing to indicate apron and shawl. Black "Chef" wears cook's toque and holds yellow spoon. His apron is outlined in red on white. $36.00–44.00

Mammy and Chef Ceramic. Japan. 1920–1955. 5". Black "Mammy" wears red bandanna and white sleeveless apron over black dress. She holds a red wooden spoon and has "New Orleans, LA." inscribed across the bottom of her apron. "Chef" wears a white cook's toque and big white apron identically inscribed and has a red wooden spoon in his left hand. $24.00–30.00

Mammy and Chef Ceramic. Japan. 1920–1955. 4". Black "Mammy" and "Chef" wear white outfits highlighted with black to pick out the aprons and Mammy's shawl. Both hold yellow wooden spoons. Mammy has white scarf on head. $36.00–44.00

Mammy and Chef Ceramic. Japan. 1920–1955. 4". Black Mammy and Chef wear white and hold yellow wooden spoons in opposite hands. Mammy's white scarf is knotted on the top of her head. Chef wears a toque. Aprons are outlined in gold. $40.00–50.00

Mammy and Chef Ceramic. Japan. 1920–1955. 4". Black Mammy and Chef wear green outfits under white aprons and

Mammy and Chef Ceramic. Japan. 1920s–1955. Black Mammy and Chef wear white aprons and hold red spoons. Mammy's kerchief and Chef's toque are red, but they are available in other colors as well. Their shiny black outfits match their faces. $40.00–44.00

hold red wooden spoons. Mammy's kerchief is red, Chef's toque is white. $40.00–50.00

Mammy and Chef Ceramic. Japan. 1920–1955. 4". Black Mammy and Chef wear white outfits outlined in red to indicate aprons. Both hold red wooden spoons. Mammy's kerchief is white with red knot. $40.00–50.00

Mammy and Chef Ceramic. Japan. 1920–1955. 5". Black Mammy and Chef wear bright yellow aprons over black outfits and hold red wooden spoons. Chef's toque is yellow as is Mammy's kerchief. Both have inscribed across the bottom of the aprons: "Pittsburg, PA." $50.00–56.00

Mammy and Chef Ceramic. Pearl China Company of Ohio. 1920–1955. Black Mammy wears yellow dress and red kerchief, and holds both her arms, ending in black hands, akimbo. "Peppy" is inscribed across her waist and a black stripe runs across the bottom of her dress. Chef sports a yellow toque and holds a red spoon in his left hand. He has a black bow tie, black shoes and hands, and, in red, the motto "Salty" across the bib of his apron. $56.00–60.00

Mammy and Chef Ceramic. Japan. 1920–1955. Shiny black Mammy and Chef wear white aprons, kerchiefs, and toques, and hold red spoons. Mammy holds left arm akimbo. $50.00–56.00

Mammy and Chef Ceramic. Japan. 1920–1955. 3". Black Mammy and Chef look to their left, each holding a red spoon. She stands with arms akimbo on her white apron, with a red kerchief knotted atop her head. He sports a white toque and matching apron. $40.00–44.00

Mammy and Chef Ceramic. Japan. 1920–1955. 3". Dark brown Mammy and Chef look to their left, each holding a red spoon. She stands with arms akimbo on her white apron trimmed with red and wears a white kerchief with a red bow knotted atop her head. He sports a white toque and matching apron with red neck trim. Across the bottom of their aprons is written "Ocean View, VA." $44.00–50.00

Mammy and Chef Ceramic. Japan. 1920–1955. 5". Black Mammy and Chef wear yellow outfits with black line highlighting aprons. She wears a red kerchief knotted atop her head and stands, holding a red spoon in her right hand, with her left arm akimbo. He holds a red spoon across his apron. $50.00–60.00

Mammy and Chef Ceramic. Japan. 1920–1955. 5". Black Mammy and Chef wear white outfits with gold tracing the line of the aprons. Both hold gold spoons and have black shoes. Across the bottom of their aprons is inscribed "Souvenir of Pittsburgh, PA." $50.00–60.00

Mammy and Chef Ceramic. Japan. 1920–1955. 5". Black Mammy and Chef wear yellow outfits and headgear (toque and kerchief) with gold tracing the line of the aprons. He wears black shoes. $50.00–60.00

Mammy and Chef Ceramic with black glaze. Japan. 1920–1955. 5". Mammy and Chef in black glaze trimmed with gold feature bright red, O-shaped mouths and, on him, red shoes. He presses a plate to his apron, she holds a spoon to her high-waisted dress. Both look up toward the right and have "P" (Chef) and "S" (Mammy) inscribed on the bottoms of their aprons. $50.00–60.00

Mammy and Chef Ceramic with brown glaze. Occupied Japan. 4½". Mammy and Chef in a rich, dark brown glaze without highlighting stare off into the distance on the right. He wears a gray toque, she has a flat head scarf without bow. Both have bright red lips and white eyes. $50.00–60.00

Mammy and Chef Ceramic. Japan. 1920–1955. 4½". Brown-faced Mammy and Chef roll large, round white eyes and purse their red lips into "O" shapes. Mammy holds her arms akimbo, Chef holds a gold spoon. Their white outfits are outlined in gold and ornamented with tiny gold flowers. $46.00–50.00

Mammy and Chef Ceramic. Japan. 1920–1955. 4". Multicolor, brown-faced Mammy and Chef feature astonished expressions. Mammy wears a white dress, pink apron with blue swirl pattern, green and yellow shawl, and green kerchief. Chef wears white apron striped with red and blue squiggles, black trousers, and gray toque. Both hold yellow spoons. $46.00–50.00

Mammy and Chef Ceramic. Japan. 1920–1955. 4½". Black-faced Mammy and Chef wear white outfits with red highlights delineating apron and hat-band (Chef) and shawl and kerchief (Mammy). Mammy stands on black base and holds red spoon. Chef holds gold spoon. $46.00–50.00

Blue Mammy and Chef Ceramic. Japan. 1920–1955. 5". Black-faced Mammy and Chef wear turquoise outfits highlighted in gold. The tips of his black shoes protrude from beneath his trousers. $50.00–56.00

Tappan Chefs Ceramic. Japan. 1920–1955. 4". Black-faced Chefs in white jacket-and-trouser combos wear red shoes and white toques with the word "Tappan" inscribed across the front of the headband. One holds his hands in a clapping gesture, the other places one hand gracefully on his stomach, the other behind his back. $46.00–50.00

Yellow Chef and Mammy Ceramic. Japan. 1920–1955. 5". Black-faced Chef and Mammy wear pale yellow outfits and hold red spoons. His yellow toque has a red stripe across the band, and his apron has black highlights. Her red scarf is knotted in the front and her shawl and apron are detailed with red lines. $50.00–56.00

Mammy and Butler Ceramic. Japan. 1920–1955. Brown-faced Butler and Mammy smile graciously and hold their folded hands at waist height. Mammy is wearing a brown, back-tied scarf on her head, and a long white dress with horizontal red stripes and black and red polka-dots on the sleeves. The Butler is bald, slightly shorter than Mammy, and wears a black frock coat over his white shirt and trousers. $60.00–70.00

Watermelon Slice and Woman's Head Ceramic. Japan. 1940s. A black woman's head with bright red lips and kerchief is teamed up with a slice of watermelon. Originally, the two rested on a tray. $44.00–50.00

Valentine Couple Ceramic. Japan. 1920–1955. Brown-faced Valentine couple hold up their left hands to wave and smile welcomingly. A pair of blue and red ribbons anchor her curly hair. Her pale green dress is covered by a crisp white pinafore, secured at the waist by a red ribbon. He is in a pale green, tight-fitting "Eton" jacket, white trousers, and shirt. In his right hand he holds card with bright red heart. $70.00–76.00

Mammy and Chef Ceramic. Japan. 1920–1955. 4½". Brown-skinned Mammy and Chef hold yellow spoons and wear white aprons. The Chef has a gray shirt and red trousers. Mammy wears a red dress and a white and gray polka-dotted kerchief. $50.00–56.00

Colorful Boy and Girl Ceramic. Japan. 1920–1955. 5". Brown-skinned boy and girl pose unsmilingly. She has on a red scarf, yellow, short-sleeved blouse emblazoned with "S" on her chest, a white skirt, and a white apron ornamented with red straps and yellow, blue, and black stripes and red dots. The boy is wearing a red chef's hat and a white, black-patched turtleneck ending in a pink collar. His black suspenders hold up a pair of orange trousers. $50.00–56.00

Fat Mammy and Chef Ceramic. Japan. 1920–1955. 4½". Hand-painted fat cooks are light brown-skinned and feature big smiles. Mammy wears a white dress and apron, both ornamented with trim in an alternating black "X" and red dot pattern. His chef's uniform is outlined in periwinkle. $70.00–80.00

Elderly Mammy and Chef Ceramic. Japan. 1920–1955. 4". Black-skinned Mammy and Chef have long, narrow faces, large white eyes, and alligatorlike red mouths. Mammy wears a white dress with red and white trimmed collar over her trim figure. Chef holds a blue spoon and wears a red bow around his neck. $56.00–60.00

Large Chef and Mammy Ceramic. Japan. 8". Brown-faced Chef and Mammy hold arms akimbo and wooden spoons in outside hands. She is in a red dress with a white apron and white bandanna. He is in a white chef's toque and apron, red trousers, and blue shirt. $70.00–80.00

Yellow Chef and Mammy Ceramic. Pearl China Company. 7½". Yellow-dressed Mammy and Chef have black faces, hands and feet, as well as black trim on yellow clothing. She wears a red bandanna which matches her red lips. He holds a red cooking spoon. The words "SALTY" (chef) and "PEPPY" (Mammy) are inscribed on their aprons. $80.00–90.00

Yellow Chef and Mammy Ceramic. Japan. 7". Yellow dressed Chef and Mammy have black faces, round white eyes, and bright red lips which match Mammy's bandanna. Red trim accents the costumes which feature gold gothic "S" (Chef) and "P" (Mammy). She holds red rolling pin, he holds red wooden spoon. $60.00–70.00

Mammy and Chef Ceramic. Japan. 6½". Brown-faced Chef and Mammy hold arms akimbo and wooden spoons in outside hands. She is in a red dress with a white apron and white bandanna with black dots. He is in a white chef's toque and apron, red trousers, and blue shirt. $60.00–70.00

Round Mammy and Chef Ceramic. Japan. 5½". Black-faced Mammy and Chef have large round eyes and smallish red lips that match Mammy's bandanna. Their white clothing is trimmed in red and a large Gothic "P" (Chef) and "S" (Mammy) are emblazoned on the centers of their aprons. She holds a gold rolling pin, he holds a gold spoon. $56.00–60.00

Mammy and Chef Stove Set Ceramic. U.S.A. 1940s. 5" stove, 4" shakers. Black-topped rectangular stove in a variety of colors (among them green, pink, and yellow) which match the clothing of Mammy, and Chef is trimmed in gold and served either as sugar bowl or bacon-drippings container. Mammy and Chef assume their characteristic one-arm akimbo poses, holding gold-trimmed wooden spoons in one hand. $70.00–80.00

Black Family: Salt, Pepper, Vinegar, Oil on Metal Rack Ceramic. Japan. 1940s. Shakers 4", vinegar and oil 5". Colorful brown-faced family of two shakers and two cruets (oil and vinegar) nestles in a rectangular wire rack with ornamental side swirl and vertical handle at the middle. Mother and daughter (cruet and shaker) wear yellow turtlenecks, white aprons with black, red, blue stripes and dot design, and red bandannas with white dots. Father and son (cruet and shaker) wear brown trousers held up by black suspenders, white turtlenecks with pink collars and red berets. $80.00–90.00

Colorful Mammy and Chef Ceramic. Japan. 1940s. 6". Unusual black-faced Mammy and Chef wear colorful outfits: she in pink, blue, and yellow with a blue bandanna over yellow hair. He is in a gray and white apron with a pink wooden spoon and yellow and blue toque. Mammy holds a white plate to her bosom emblazoned with "Salt." Chef holds a gigantic wooden spoon labeled "Pepper." $70.00–80.00

Wooden Bellhop Wood. 5½". Colorful wooden bellhop in a red cap, green jacket, and red trousers holds cylindrical, beige hatboxes in each outstretched arm. $24.00–30.00

Mammy With Barrels Ceramic. Avon. 5". A four-piece set consisting of three barrels (S and P and Mustard) and blue and white floral base to which figure of Mammy is attached. Clearly labeled barrels are brown wood grained with black hoops. Mammy wears a white dress detailed in blue and a white bandanna. In one hand she wields a knife, in the other she holds up a piece of bread. $60.00–70.00

Wood/Wire Bongo Man Wood, wire, straw, and ceramic. U.S.A. 1950s. 6". A wooden-headed bongo man is made of wire to resemble a musician sitting with outstretched legs and supporting pink and blue bongo drums under each arm. The ceramic drums (pink for salt, blue for pepper) have yellow bodies. A straw skirt is gathered fanlike around the waist. $16.00–20.00

Chalkware Chef and Mammy Chalkware. Japan. Early 1930s. 1½". Fat, squat Mammy and Chef show off their broad girth. He wears red pants under a white shirt and apron. She is in a red dress with a white apron, and has a red bandanna on her head. $36.00–40.00

Baby-Faced Chef and Mammy Ceramic. Japan. Early 1930s. 3". Unusual baby-faced Chef and Mammy in a slimmed-down version have ochre faces and charming, infantile expressions. Their white outfits are trimmed in gold and each holds a red wooden spoon. $40.00–44.00

Mammy and Chef Ceramic. Japan. Early 1930s through 1950s. 3". Squat, black-faced Mammy and Chef wear white aprons labeled "Pepper" (she) and "Salt" (he). She wears a red dress under her white apron, he wears a blue shirt and red trousers under his white apron. Both hold red wooden spoons. $36.00–40.00

Fat Chef and Mammy Ceramic. Japan. Early 1930s through 1950s. 2". Very fat and squat Mammy and Chef have burnt sienna faces, white outfits. She wears a yellow apron, he has yellow trousers and a double row of red buttons. Mammy does not wear a bandanna on her black braids. $32.00–40.00

White Flowered Mammy and Chef Ceramic. Japan. Early 1930s through 1950s. 3½". Elongated, brown-faced Mammy and Chef stand on short pedestal bases. Their white outfits are trimmed in gold and ornamented with tiny gold daisies. Mammy's bandanna is topped with a red bow. $40.00–44.00

"Albino" Mammy and Chef Ceramic. Japan. Early 1940s. 4". Rare "Albino" Mammy and Chef have cherubic white-skinned, pink-cheeked faces with Negroid features. Their white outfits are trimmed in gold and blue. She wears a red bandanna and red shoes. $40.00–44.00

Chef Carvers Ceramic. Japan. Early 1930s through 1950s. 3". Matching brown-faced fat chefs in yellow outfits with black bow ties wield carving forks and knives. Their pudgy cheeks and raised eyebrows give their faces a cherubic expression. $36.00–40.00

Cotton Pickers Ceramic. U.S.A. Early 1930s through 1950s. 3½". Black-faced husband and wife cotton pickers wear red and blue outfits with red patches. He holds a white sack. She wears a red bandanna. The shakers have "New Orleans" stamped on the bottom. $56.00–60.00

Pudgy Mammy and Chef Ceramic. Japan. Early 1930s through 1950s. 3" Brown-faced Mammy and Chef are dressed in white and hold yellow spoons. They have childish faces with round features. $16.00–40.00

Colorful Mammy and Chef Ceramic. Hand-painted. Japan. Early 1930s through 1950s. 3½". Very unusual, seemingly mismatched pair showing a thin, "realistic" looking small-headed Mammy in a white dress with a checkered red and blue apron. Chef has a very large, grinning face and wears a green shirt, white bib, and striped apron. $44.00–50.00

"Dressy" Mammy and Chef Ceramic. Japan. Early 1930s through 1950s. 3". Prim, brown-faced Mammy and Chef without their cooking regalia. She wears a blue dress, a white apron, and a lace cap on her short-cropped black hair. He is in a white chef's uniform. $40.00–44.00

Redcap Ceramic. Japan. Early 1930s through 1950s. 4½". Laughing redcap in a blue Eton jacket, red pants, white shirt, and black bow tie holds a yellow suitcase in each outstretched hand. He stands on a white oval base. $60.00–70.00

Boy on Toilet Ceramic. Japan. Early 1930s through 1950s. 3½". A grinning, half-naked boy (salt) perches on an open toilet (pepper) and holds on to his white underpants. The white toilet has yellow and black trim. $60.00–70.00

Sitting Boy with Watermelon Ceramic. Japan. Early 1930s–1950s. This two-piece shaker set consists of a sitting black boy in green trousers and red beret, holding a watermelon slice in his lap. $55.00–60.00

Boy on Cotton Bale Ceramic. Japan. Early 1930s through 1950s. 4½". A pensive boy in white shirt and blue overalls perches atop a white and yellow cotton bale. $60.00–70.00

Black Clown on Drum Ceramic. Japan. Early 1930s through 1950s. 3½". A grinning black clown (salt) in red jacket, yellow shirt, and blue pants tips his green hat as he stands atop a large brown drum (pepper). $60.00–70.00

Minstrel with Hands Ceramic. Japan. Early 1930s through 1950s. 2". A black minstrel's head (salt) with a red, singing mouth peers over a pair of white gloved hands (pepper) joined at the center and fanning outward to resemble a dove in flight. $44.00–50.00

Boxy Mammy and Chef Ceramic. Japan. Early 1930s through 1950s. 3". Book-shaped shakers have Mammy and Chef on their "spines." The figures are dressed in white with black faces and hands, holding a spoon (Chef) and rolling pin (Mammy). "I'm Salt" (Chef) and "I'm Pepper" (Mammy) are inscribed across the bottoms of the aprons. $30.00–40.00

Mammy and Chef Heads Red clay. Japan. Early 1930s through 1950s. 2½". Busts of Mammy and Chef are made of red clay and glazed in glossy black with red (Mammy) and gray (Chef) trim. $44.00–50.00

Sitting Mammy and Chef Ceramic. Japan. Early 1930s through 1950s. Dressed in white, Mammy and Chef sit on the ground, their knees drawn up to their chests. She is wearing a white bandanna and has red polka-dots on her dress. He is bald. Costume coloring and decorations vary on these sets. $40.00–44.00

Piggy-Back Black Babies Ceramic. Japan. Early 1930s through 1950s. Two little black babies in striped diapers sit atop each other, piggyback style. $40.00–44.00

Watermelon Slice and Boy's Head Ceramic. Japan. Early 1930s through 1950s. A black boy's head with bright red lips and beret hat is matched up with a watermelon slice. $44.00–50.00

Boy and Girl Eating Watermelon Chalkware. Japan. Early 1930s through 1950s. A black boy and girl each hold up a slice of watermelon to their chins. Both are depicted from the

elbows up. She wears a red dress and red bow. He is in black.
$50.00–56.00

Watermelon Slice and Girl's Head Ceramic. Japan. Early
1930s through 1950s. A brown girl's head in yellow bandanna is teamed up with a watermelon slice. The girl is grinning
and offers up a well-endowed double chin for contemplation.
$44.00–50.00

Black Boys Riding Corn Cobs Ceramic. Japan. Early 1930s
through 1950s. A matching pair of shakers depicts tiny black
boys in red trunks lying atop half-peeled ears of corn.
$44.00–50.00

Black Boys Riding Lettuce Ceramic. Japan. Early 1930s
through 1950s. A matching pair of shakers depicts tiny black
boys in red trunks lying atop green and white elongated
heads of lettuce. $44.00–50.00

Black Boys Riding Carrots Ceramic. Japan. Early 1930s
through 1950s. A matching pair of shakers depicts tiny black
boys in red trunks sitting astride huge orange carrots.
$44.00–50.00

Gray-Haired Nodder with Watermelon Ceramic. Japan.
Early 1930s through 1950s. This unusual two-piece shaker
features a gray-haired nodder sitting cross-legged and holding a slide of watermelon on her lap. When the slice is
removed, a very busty bare chest is revealed. $80.00–85.00

Sitting Child with Watermelon Ceramic. Japan. Early
1930s through 1950s. This two-piece shaker set is composed
of a black child, sitting cross-legged, and holding a piece of

Boy and Girl in Yellow Basket
Ceramic. Japan. 1940s. A black boy
in blue rompers and a little girl in
white rompers with yellow jacket
and red booties sit at opposite sides
of a yellow basket, bisected by a
white hand. A big red bow decorates
the side. The children resemble characters from "The Little Rascals."
$70.00–75.00

watermelon on its lap. The child's mouth is open and tinted bright pink. $56.00–60.00

Boy and Girl with Ear of Corn Ceramic. Japan. Early 1930s through 1950s. This black boy and girl couple seems based on the characters from "The Little Rascals." She is in a red short dress with red hairbows and holds a piece of corn between her hands. He is in a pair of red and white checkered trousers over a blue shirt and hoists a corn cob over his left shoulder. $44.00–50.00

Singing Boys Ceramic. Japan. Early 1930s through 1950s. A matching pair of little black boys in white outfits with red bow ties and cute little red berets perched precariously on the right sides of their heads. Both have round lips outlined in white and recall characters from "The Little Rascals." $40.00–44.00

African Couple Ceramic. Japan. Early 1930s through 1950s. This set features the busts of a brown-skinned African couple. He holds a brown ceramic bowl on his head, while she sports a black topknot pierced by a gold "bone." $36.00–44.00

African Mother and Child Ceramic. Japan. Early 1930s through 1950s. This nester is composed of a black African mother in a yellow and blue skirt who stands and balances a removable naked black baby on her back. Both have white lips and eyes. $50.00–60.00

African Mother and Child Ceramic. Japan. Early 1930s through 1950s. This nester shaker consists of a sitting, brown African mother who holds her detachable baby in her lap. The baby has a red bow on her hair. Both mother and baby are naked except for a brown grass skirt. $50.00–60.00

Native Boy on Alligator Ceramic. Japan. Early 1930s through 1950s. A brown Pakistani boy in a yellow and black polka-dotted turban and yellow loincloth straddles a green alligator. The shakers are detachable. $40.00–44.00

African Boy and Palm Tree Ceramic. Japan. Early 1930s through 1950s. This two-piece set features a very black African boy, naked except for a strategically placed fig leaf, who scratched his head while looking up at the palm tree. The palm tree has bright green fronds and grass, a pair of yellow trunks, and black coconuts. $40.00–44.00

Black Matador Ceramic. Japan. 1940s. The black matador in a white, yellow, and red costume, trimmed with gold pirouettes around a red cape, is teamed with a brown, white-horned bull. $44.00–50.00

African Boy on Alligator Ceramic. Japan. Early 1930s through 1950s. A brown African boy strums a banjo astride a blue-eyed, brown alligator. The pieces are detachable. $40.00–44.00

Kissing African Couple Ceramic. Japan. Early 1930s through 1950s. A brown-skinned African couple dressed only in grass skirts (his is yellow and white, hers is pink, green, and yellow) purse their lips for a kiss and lean their torsos toward each other. $40.00–44.00

African Chief on Drum Ceramic. Japan. Early 1930s through 1950s. A black African chief in yellow straw skirt and leggings, white shield, and black, white-tipped spear, grins malevolently as he stands atop a gigantic beige and black drum. $40.00–44.00

Native Boy with Ukelele under Palm Tree Ceramic. Japan. Early 1930s through 1950s. A brown-skinned Pakistani boy in white long trousers and white turban strums a white ukelele as he sits under a pair of green-fronded palm trees. $36.00–40.00

Turbaned Native Boys Ceramic. Japan. Early 1930s through 1950s. A very colorful pair of black boys clutch their rotund tummies. They are dressed identically, but their coloration differs. Pepper sports a white turban with a red feather, red shirt, green trousers, and a blue sash. Salt wears a white turban with a blue feather, a green shirt, yellow trousers, and red sash. Both have turned-up shoes. Pepper bears the inscription "Mammy's Pepper," and salt, "Mammy's Salt." $44.00–50.00

Wooden Native Couple Wooden. Japan. Early 1930s through 1950s. This charming black native couple is made of hand-painted wood. The round "clothespin" figurines have round, stylized features, grass skirts painted in shades of yellow and white, and real pearl earrings. $16.00–20.00

African Basket Bearers Ceramic. Japan. Early 1930s through 1950s. This very black couple is dressed identically in billowing, white floor-length skirts banded, at the waist, with red. Both are bare-chested. He steadies a white, pear-shaped basket on his head with his hands. She balances her white trapezoidal basket on her head and holds her arms akimbo. $40.00–44.00

Stylized African Heads Ceramic. Japan. Early 1930s through 1950s. This tribal couple is represented from the neck up. The male is bald with brilliant red lips. The female gathers her hair in a gold-banded topknot and wears a wide gold neckband. $40.00–44.00

Ethiopian Guards Ceramic. Ceramic Art Studios, WI. A pair of handsome Ethiopian guards in traditional white costume and turbans ornamented with red scrollwork and, on the turbans, a stylized red "P" and "S." Pepper clasps his hands in front of his stomach, while Salt folds his arms on his chest. $44.00–50.00

Black Calypso Women Ceramic. Japan. Busts of laughing black Calypso women in fruit headdresses. The pepper wears a pink and green gown with an off-shoulder collar and watermelon slice headdress. The salt wears a black dress with yellow dots and yellow off-shoulder collar and bandanna headdress. $14.00–16.00

Black Jazz Singer and Sax Player Ceramic. Japan. White saxophone player, with slicked back, center-parted hair, wears a black tuxedo and plays a sax. The black singer holds a microphone. She is in a white, long-sleeved, evening gown and wears a white flower in her hair, which is styled into a twenties spit curl. $19.00–21.00

"Someone's Kitchen" Mammies Ceramic. Japan. 1940s. Black Mammy shakers represent two cooks in white dresses. Salt is bending over to pick up a bowl of dough. She wears a red and white polka-dot apron. Pepper stands, mixing batter in a bowl, and wearing a yellow and red polka-dot bandanna. $19.00–21.00

Rio Rita Carnival Dancing Couple Ceramic. Japan. 1950s. A plump pair of black Carnival dancers dressed in colorful costumes features a hatted man in yellow and green, and a woman in a red and white dress with a fruit hat. $22.00–25.00

Aged Mammy and Chef Painted bisque. Japan. Early 1930s. Mammy and Chef in an aged version wear red, yellow and white outfits. She mixes batter in a bowl, he holds a top hat in his hands. $13.00–20.00

Mandy Black Children Ceramic. Japan. Early 1930s through 1950s. This pair of colorfully dressed black babies features a boy in a blue jumper, sitting and clutching a basket of apples between his legs. The girl child wears a red and yellow dress and holds a bunch of yellow flowers between her legs. $19.00–22.00

Small Native Children Ceramic. Japan. Early 1930s through 1950s. Small, brown-skinned African children sit in a kneeling position behind large shields, his blue, hers pink, and hold spears. $17.50–19.00

Mammy Pair Ceramic. Memories of Mama Creations. U.S.A. Mosaic Tile reproduction. 5″. This matching pair of fat, black Mammies in white aprons is available in medium blue, forest green, or red dresses with white dot pattern. $45.00–55.00

Mammy Pair Ceramic. Memories of Mama Creations. U.S.A. McCoy Reproduction. 4½″. This matching pair of fat black

Cannibal with Hut Ceramic. Japan. Early 1950s. This two-piece shaker set features a brown cannibal in a grass skirt clutching a huge cauldron. He wears a white bone through his topknot. The "grass" hut sits on stilts and has a cylindrical roof. $30.00–40.00

Mammies in white-cuffed and white-collared dresses is available in medium blue, forest green, or red with white polkadots. $42.00–52.00

Black Girls Japan. 1930s through 1950s. These black, large-headed girls sit cross-legged in charming dresses and matching bows. $10.00–12.00

Chef Pierre and Chef Pete Ceramic. Japan. 1930s through 1950s. Two chefs, one Black, the other French, are featured from their necks up in white toques. $35.00–55.00

Mammy and Pappy Heads Ceramic. Rick Wisecarver, OH. Black Mammy and Pappy busts are dressed in Sunday best, with blue or pink costumed Mammy in a lace collar and cuffs and gray-suited Pappy in burgundy and white dotted bow tie. $29.00–34.00

"Gone With the Wind" Belle and Mammy Ceramic. Rick Wisecarver, OH. Southern belle in antebellum costume holds her beribboned hat in one hand as she poses next to black Mammy in apron and lace shawl. Both stand on an oval tray with a plantation background consisting of weeping willow trees and white plantation mansion. $39.00–44.00

Cotton Pickers Ceramic. Rick Wisecarver, OH. One older and one younger Mammy dressed in blue and pink antebellum fieldworker costumes empty cotton from their aprons into a sack which stands between them. The sack is part of a stacking of bales, the uppermost of which is the lid for a sugar or mustard jar. $39.00–44.00

Black Children Ceramic. Rick Wisecarver. OH. Big-eyed boy and girl children gaze up with solemn expressions. The boy is standing and wearing overalls over his white T-shirt. The girl squats in a long aproned dress. $29.00–34.00

Black Christmas Elves Ceramic. Rick Wisecarver, OH. Black Christmas elves in pointed caps, and seasonal colors are depicted resting after their labors, reclining on one elbow. $29.00–35.00

Black Angels Ceramic. Rick Wisecarver, OH. Black angels in flowing gowns with tiny wings are depicted in a kneeling position. $29.00–35.00

Relaxing Native Boys Ceramic. Japan. Early 1930s. Two ebony black native boys in pink grass skirts and brown curly hair loll on the shelf. One is lying on his tummy and kicks his legs in the air, the other is resting on one elbow on his back with one leg crossed over the other. $40.00–45.00

Wooden Natives on Kegs Wood. Japan. 1940s. Tiny wooden natives sit atop wooden beer barrels marked "Beer S" and "Beer P." The tops of the barrels swivel to reveal the salt-and-pepper holes. The natives are fashioned of two stacked beads and have real pearl earrings. $20.00–25.00

Black Chefs Ceramic. Japan. Early 1940s. Dark brown chefs in crisp, white toques are naked from the waist up, but wear aprons (yellow or red) over white baggy trousers. Under one arm each carries a bowl of fruit and they eye each other with suspicion. $35.00–40.00

Ethiopian Guards Ceramic. Ceramic Art Studios, WI. Sitting Ethiopian guards in traditional white costume with white turban and red, black, and yellow ornamented vest fold their arms on their chests. $44.00–50.00

Gray-Haired Black Woman Nodder Ceramic. Japan. 1930s. A gray-haired, bare-bosomed black woman sits cross-legged and holds a slice of watermelon on her lap. Her shaker head nods and the watermelon shaker, when removed, leaves exposed a bare bosom. $50.00–60.00

Tap Dancers Ceramic. Japan. 1920s. Boy-faced minstrels in white shirts and hats, black Eton jackets, and red pants hold canes in one hand and purse their white lips in song. $30.00–34.00

Sitting Boys with Watermelons Ceramic. Japan. 1920s–1940s. Black boys in green pants, yellow shirts, and red caps hold big slices of watermelon. $25.00–28.00

Chubby Boy and Watermelon Slice Ceramic. Japan. 1920s–1940s. A chubby little boy in a yellow top and blue pants is sitting and eating a piece of watermelon. Another huge piece of watermelon is the other shaker. $30.00–35.00

Black Couple Ceramic. Japan. 1920s–1940s. A well-dressed Black girl, in blue and gold plaid dress with white pinafore, leans argumentatively into her natty boyfriend. $25.00–30.00

Sitting Boy with Watermelon Ceramic. Japan. 1920s–1940s. A very shiny Black boy in white trousers and top and red cap is holding a huge piece of watermelon which is colored in successive bands of dark green, red, and pale pink. $32.00–36.00

Black Boy on Camel Ceramic. Japan. 1920s–1940s. A brown boy in a white, yellow, and black turban and green top with white pants nestles atop a recumbent yellow camel. $28.00–32.00

Chef With Watermelon Slices on Trays Ceramic. Japan. 1920s–1940s. This three-piece shaker consists of a black chef in chef's toque attached to a flowered base and holding, in his hands, two trays. On the trays repose two giant slices of watermelon. These are the shakers. $30.00–40.00

Black Boys Riding Eggplants Ceramic. Japan. 1930s. Half-naked black boys recline on giant eggplants. $44.00–50.00

Black Boys Riding Pea Pods Ceramic. Japan. 1930s. Half-naked black boys are riding a pair of giant pea pods. $44.00–50.00

Black Boy Riding Whale Ceramic. Japan. 1930s. A dark-brown, half-naked boy fits atop a black whale with menacing ""zig-zag" teeth and huge "bull's-eye" eyes. $35.00–40.00

Black Boy Hugging Puppy Ceramic. Van Tellingen "Hugger." A black boy in white rompers is hugging a gray and white puppy. $30.00–40.00

Black Boys Shooting Dice on Tray Ceramic. Japan. 1930s. Two very pale Black boys in shorts stand on a rectangular tray to which are attached a pair of dice. The boy in blue shorts kneels. The one in green shorts stands. $35.00–40.00

Wooden Porter Wood. This wooden figurine is made up of a semispherical base, two balls (for body) attached to the base by means of a spindle, and two spindle arms. From the hook hands hang the salt-and-pepper-shaker suitcases. $25.00–30.00

African Chieftain and his Lady Ceramic. Japan. 1940s. Dark brown African chieftain in a towering headdress and yellow collar is matched with his lady in a yellow headdress and orange collar. These are busts. $22.00–26.00

Golliwog Ceramic. England. 1970s. The British storybook character is depicted in a simplified, cartoonish fashion on a white stylized shape reminiscent of a gingerbread boy body. $22.00–25.00

Caribbean Women with Baskets Ceramic. Japan. 1940s. Three-quarter figures of Caribbean women in red dress and white shoulder scarves carrying large baskets of fruit on their heads. Each basket is marked with either "S" or "P." $24.00–28.00

African Tribal Couple Ceramic. Japan. 1940s. Childlike African tribal couple stands behind ornamented shields and clutch lances. Her shield is pink, his is blue. $24.00–30.00

Childish Cook and Chef Ceramic. Japan. 1940s. Brown-faced girl cook in white and boy cook in toque hold orange spoons. Outlines of clothing are traced in gold. $28.00–32.00

Wooden Chef with Salt and Pepper Pots Wood. U.S.A. A wooden chef, composed of rudimentary geometric forms, has metal loops for arms. Wooden shakers fit inside these loops. $20.00–24.00

African Tribal Couple Chalkware. U.S.A. 1940s. Stylized native couple with broad red lips, very black skin, and long, gold tribal necklaces are depicted from the neck up. He is totally bald. She has a topknot on her head and gold hoop earrings. $20.00–24.00

Dancing Waiter Mustard and Shaker Set Ceramic. Japan. 1940s. A four-leaf clover-shaped tray holds a dancing black waiter in blue jacket and white pants. Three barrels marked "Salt," "Pepper," and "Mustard" fit into indentations on tray. $55.00–60.00

Chef's Heads on Tray Ceramic. 1940s–1950s. One white and one black chef's head in towering toques and white, starched collars fit into a white tray. Both chefs are grinning. $45.00–50.00

Chef and Cook Kids Ceramic. 1940s–1950s. Flattened busts of a girl and boy chef have very black shiny faces with bright red lips, rotund eyes. The girl, in blue dress and yellow bandanna, makes eyes at the boy in white toque and shirt. $50.00–60.00

Three-Piece Boy in Sailor Suit China. A chubby, standing boy in a blue sailor suit with white collar and white sailor cap is made up of three, standing pieces: the trousers, which form the mustard pot; the mid-chest, which forms the pepper shaker; and the bust, which forms the salt shaker. $60.00–65.00

Girls Eating Watermelons Bisque. Japan. 1940s–1950s. Very black, realistic girls in white dresses munch on watermelon slices. $40.00–45.00

Busts of Girls Ceramic. Japan. 1940s–1950s. Busts of pale Black girls with "O" shaped lips have one pixie hairdo and one feathered bangs hairdo. $35.00–38.00

Children's Heads on Tray Ceramic. 1940s–1950s. Adorable, deep black children's heads with red bows have large white eyes. $40.00–45.00

Boy and Girl Busts Ceramic. Japan. 1940s–1950s. Charming little girl in yellow straw hat and striped dress has pink bows on her braids. She eyes a bald little black boy with blue suspenders. $50.00–55.00

Fighting Mammy and Chef Heads Ceramic. 1940s–1950s. The heads of Mammy and Chef, he grimacing, she shouting, are deep brown. $40.00–45.00

Tribal Couple Ceramic. 1940s–1950s. Busts of brown tribal couple depict a grinning man with a cone-shaped head and a smiling woman with a ring through her nose and bone necklace around her throat. $30.00–35.00

"Fruitheads"—fruits and vegetables with human features—are among the most popular shakers. These are ceramic from Japan and date from the 1930s through the early 1950s.

The assortment of pigs in this sty draws on all the conceits of the porcine subgenre of farmyard animals. There are realistic pigs in porcelain, Shawnee's Porky Pigs, musicians, loving couples, and the inevitable gluttons.

Thumbelina's garden is bursting with flowers in bone china, porcelain, plastic, and ceramic. Thumbelina on her pink rose is from the 1940s Hull series depicting characters from nursery rhymes and fairy tales.

The "Wild West" exercised a powerful pull on the American imagination. Everything from Conestoga wagons to cowboys, rattlesnakes to vultures, Totem poles to teepees appeared as shakers in materials as diverse as wood, chalkware, and even fine bone china.

Dinosaurs were relative latecomers to the world of shakers. With the exception of Sinclair Gasoline's "Dino the Dinosaur," the motley crew of antediluvian reptiles pictured here dates from the 1970s.

Heavenly shakes are an especially intriguing genre for collectors. They offer a broad range of interpretations that include the serious and the comical. While there are hundreds of angel and devil shakers around, we have not found any of actual saints.

Those with a hedonistic streak will particularly enjoy collecting the various "on the beach" and "in the boudoir" shakers. Pink flamingos were among the most desirable birds from the 1920s through the 1950s, and during the Art Deco years, received some very elegant treatments.

Everybody likes a good time, and when it comes to having fun, the shakers really shake it up! All varieties of dance, music, and merriment are enshrined in shakers that include the world of humans, animals, and even inanimate objects.

What could be more perfect than a functional souvenir that could fit in your pocket and not break the bank? While the most popular tourist attractions had their worn shakers, hole-in-the-walls were not left out. All an enterprising roadside vendor had to do was put in a supply of blank cylinders and stick local stickers on them. Presto-chango: a local souvenir!

Bakelite shakers are the elegant distillation of the modern love for combining simple, geometric forms with pure function. The various push-button versions show the era's fascination with mechanical innovation.

The genre of shakers called the "longfellows" were low on utility, but high on humor. The cat and dog pictured here are made of red clay.

America's love for the mechanized home was mirrored in the proliferation of miniature appliances and household gadgets in everything from plastic to ceramic. The small Waring blender or the mixer are perfect for the Barbie doll set.

One could never have enough cows. The car pulling an Airstream trailer on the lower right is an unusual set dating from the 1940s.

Only a connoisseur of tropical fish could identify the many species that were rendered in porcelain, ceramic, and plastic. Among some of the finest were those made by Rosemeade.

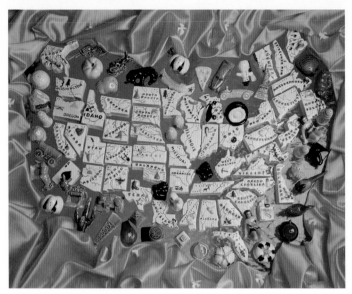

In 1957 and 1968 Parkcraft issued sets of the States of the Union that have become extremely collectible.

Bride and groom couples afforded opportunities for displaying some raunchy humor, as in the turnabout sets with "before" and "after" sides that show the "before" bridal pair in a conventional state of grace, followed up by some scandalous "after" such as pregnancy or old age.

Girl Head with Watermelon Slice Ceramic. 1940s–1950s. A girl's head, supported on two hands, is teamed with a slice of watermelon. $30.00–35.00

Genies China. Germany. 1950s. Matching figurines of black-faced genies have white turbans and pantaloons and red jackets. $45.00–50.00

Boy on Elephant Ceramic. 1940s–1950s. A boy in white turban and clothes crouches atop a white elephant with upraised trunk. The elephant's fittings are outlined in gold. $40.00–45.00

Sultan and Sultanness Ceramic. Japan. 1940s–1950s. Sultan and his First Lady have childlike faces. They have pear-shaped bodies and large, oblong turbans. She is in blue dress with white turban, he is in red charivari with yellow-and-white turban. $35.00–40.00

Valentine Boy and Girl Ceramic. Japan. 1940s. Café-au-lait-colored boy and girl with charming faces and short-cropped black hair enact a Valentine's Day scenario. The boy offers a red, lace-trimmed heart, the girl keeps her hands behind her back. $60.00–65.00

Mammy and Waiter Lightweight composition. U.S.A. Unusual for their use of material, these shakers depict Mammy and Waiter. Mammy wears white dress with red dots at bosom and hem, and red kerchief with white dots. Waiter is in black pants, white jacket, with white napkin draped over one arm. $40.00–45.00

Mammy and Chef Red clay. Arms akimbo, Mammy confronts Chef who stands meekly, with hands behind back. With the

Fat, Short Chef and Mammy Ceramic. Occupied Japan. 1945–1952. Quasi-spherical Chef and Mammy (31/2") are dressed in white. Their black faces have red lips and white eyes. $22.00–24.00

exception of the head coverings (kerchief, toque), lips, and eyes, the figurines are glazed with brilliant black glaze. $45.00–50.00

"Chief Coffee Maker" Ceramic. Japan. 1940s. This three-piece set comprises a chef in pink pants, yellow shirt, and white apron inscribed with the slogan, "Chief Coffee Maker." He holds across his shoulders a yoke from the ends of which are suspended two pink coffeepot shakers. Both are ornamented with flowers and marked with either an "S" or a "P." $50.00–55.00

Old Cowpoke and Old Lady Ceramic. Brayton Laguna Pottery. Laguna Beach, CA. 1951. Unusually dressed, elderly couple have golden-brown faces. The old lady wears a white kerchief, a brown dress with a print of yellow daisies, and a lavish apron. The old cowpoke wears a squat yellow boater, white shirt, bolero and chaps, both painted with the same floral print found on the lady's costume. $70.00–75.00

Southern Housekeepers Ceramic. U.S.A. 1940s. Pale, round-faced women in long dresses, aprons, and shoulder scarves, hold one arm akimbo. Both have green shawls and hair bows, but one has a yellow skirt, while the other has a blue one. From the tops of their heads sprout bits of real tulle. $32.00–38.00

Chef and Mammy Cooking Chicken. Ceramics. Japan. 1940s. Chef with brown chicken over his shoulder holds a black frying pan. Mammy, wearing a yellow kerchief and striped shawl, holds her cheek in horror. $55.00–60.00

Chef and Mammy Ceramic. Japan. 1940s–1950s. Finely detailed Chef and Mammy have white costumes. His white apron has red fold lines, her white dress has red collar. $40.00–45.00

Sitting Girl with Watermelon Ceramic. Japan. 1940s–1950s. A chocolate-brown girl, hair in a ponytail, sits on a chair and holds a slice of watermelon on her lap. The watermelon is a separate shaker. $50.00–55.00

Sitting Boy with Watermelon Ceramic. Japan. 1940s–1950s. A chocolate-brown boy, head in yellow cap, sits on a chair and holds a slice of watermelon in his lap. The watermelon is a separate shaker. $50.00–55.00

Sitting Boy with Plates Holding Watermelons Ceramic. Japan. 1940s–1950s. Brown boy in white shirt, red pants, and blue cap, sits, balancing two plates on his knees. On each plate is a slice of watermelon. $55.00–60.00

Tribal Couple Bisque. Germany. Black tribal girl in yellow skirt, necklace, and earring stands next to boy in white shorts and red cap playing a ukelele. $40.00–44.00

Chef and Mammy Ceramic. Japan. 1940s. Small set of Chef and Mammy figurines are unusual in that Mammy is taller than Chef. Her clothing is outlined in gold, his in blue. $25.00–30.00

Chef and Mammy Ceramic. Japan. 1940s–1950s. Small set of Chef and Mammy figurines shows Chef in short white apron and two-tiered pants. An "S" marks his apron, a "P" hers. Chef wears pale blue shirt. $25.00–30.00

Chef and Mammy Plastic One-Piece Plastic. U.S.A. See-through Chef and Mammy with opaque, brown faces and hands, black hair, and colored headpieces (white toque, yellow hat) are attached to a pale green, inverted T-shaped stand emblazoned with the words "New Orleans." Two buttons on top of the cross piece are used to dispense salt and pepper. $20.00–26.00

Quarreling Chef and Mammy Heads Ceramic. Japan. 1940s–1950s. Brown-faced Chef and Mammy heads on white collars with yellow bow ties, are in the thick of a quarrel. She shouts, he scowls. $40.00–45.00

Solemn Chef and Mammy Heads Ceramic. Japan. 1940s–1950s. Beautifully shaded heads of Chef and Mammy have serious expressions. Chef's toque is white with pink border and he wears a pink bow tie. Mammy has pink cap and yellow collar. Both have delicately worked large eyes. $40.00–42.00

Tall-Toqued Chefs Ceramic. Japan. 1940s–1960s. Busts of brown-faced chefs in exceedingly tall toque show either yellow or blue shirts beneath white apron straps. $35.00–40.00

Tropical Policemen Ceramic. Japan. 1940s–1950s. Tropical policemen in white pith helmets, white jackets, black trousers, and belts stand with arms behind their backs. Set is labeled "Nassau." $30.00–35.00

Boy with Harmonica, Girl Listens Ceramic. Japan. 1940s. Black boy in green and white pants sits and holds a harmonica to his lips. The girl sits holding her knees. She is dressed in a white, polka-dotted dress. Both are lavishly ornamented with gold highlights. $24.00–28.00

Granny in Rocker Ceramic. Japan. 1940s–1950s. A very dark granny in dark green dress, shawl, and cap sits in a brown rocker. Each component is a shaker. $45.00–50.00

Fat Mammy in Plaid Apron Ceramic. 1930s. Identical figurines of deeply wrinkled, brown-faced Mammy in a red kerchief are in the shape of a squat kingpin. Mammy folds hands over stomach. She wears a blue and red dotted white dress under a red-and-white-checked apron. $50.00–55.00

Chef and Mammy as Hosts Ceramic. 1930s. Mammy wears a white dress trimmed in yellow and black. Chef wears white, long-jacketed suit, black bow tie, yellow shoes, and holds a yellow-banded white top hat in his hands. He has prominent white eyebrows. $42.00–50.00

Chef Children Ceramic. Japan. 1940s–1950s. Bare-chested chef children in very large white toques, wear blue shoes and hold plates of food in one hand. She wears a yellow skirt, he wears brown shorts. This set is under 3½" tall. $35.00–40.00

Kissing Couple Ceramic. Japan. 1940s–1950s. A kissing couple with Negroid facial features comes in pale pink or pale blue. He has black hair, she has blond hair, and both have large, floppy ceramic bows on their chests which they thrust toward each other as they bend down on their knees and purse their lips. This set is under 3½" tall. $30.00–34.00

Mammy Bisque, Taiwan. Finely detailed Mammy from Taiwan wears red dress with matching kerchief, white apron with the words "New Orleans" across the hem, and stirs a yellow bowl. This set is 3½" tall. $24.00–30.00

Metal Chef and Mammy Metal. Very short (under 3½"), very round Chef and Mammy have few details other than red lips, white and black eyes, and black hands. Mammy wears blue apron. $40.00–45.00

Chef and Mammy Waving Ceramic. Japan. 1940s. Short and squat (under 3½") Chef and Mammy are very pale and wave with opposite hands. Chef's apron is tied in front with a red bow, Mammy's apron covers a yellow dress. This set also comes in blackface. $30.00–32.00

Dark Chef and Mammy Waving Ceramic. Japan. 1940s. Short and squat (under 3½") Chef and Mammy with very dark faces wave with opposite hands. Chef's hat has dark band, and Mammy's apron covers a deep blue dress that contrasts with her red kerchief. $30.00–32.00

Sitting Chef and Mammy Ceramic. Japan. 1940s. Very short (considerably under 3½") Mammy and Chef with very black faces and red lips are sculpted in a sitting position. The figurines are crude with simple details such as buttons and folds painted in black. $30.00–32.00

Mammy Nudging Chef Ceramic. Japan. 1940s. This small set (under 3½") shows a brown-faced Mammy in a blue dress, white shawl, apron, and kerchief nudging Chef with her elbow (provided the shakers are placed in close proximity). Chef is shorter and is dressed entirely in white. Both have cute, childish faces. $28.00–32.00

Chef with Spoon, Mammy with Fork Ceramic. Japan. 1940s. Small (3½") Chef and Mammy have coal-black faces, hands, and feet. Their bodies are crudely formed and rough red lines indicate folds, trim, and utensils. $35.00–40.00

Fat, Short Chef and Mammy Ceramic. Japan. 1940s–1950s. Chef and Mammy are so short and so fat that they are nearly spherical in shape. They have jet black faces and well articulated hands, round eyes, and a smear of red lips. Mammy holds arms akimbo. Chef clutches his formidable belly. $25.00–30.00

Fat, Short Chef and Mammy Ceramic. Japan. 1940s–1950s. Quasispherical Chef and Mammy (3½") are crudely formed, although Chef's hands are finely drawn. They have bulbous black faces that show no other color. Details of costume are traced in gold. Mammy holds arms akimbo, Chef clutches his stomach. $25.00–28.00

Rastus and Liza Wood. Wood cutouts of black couple bear simple, line painting of each character on the silhouette shakers. Faces are painted black with red lips and, for Liza, white scarf. The names "Rastus" and "Liza" are written on the front of each. $22.00–24.00

Mammy Ceramic. Elbee Art. Cleveland, OH. 1940s–1950s. Crudely formed matching figurines of Mammy (3½") have white, full-skirted dresses and red head scarves. Mammy's face, feet, and hands, clasped in the front, are black. Her dress has appeared in white with red "folds," pink with red and blue dot border on apron, white with red and blue dot border on apron. $24.00–30.00

Wooden Tribal Boys Wood. 1940s. Matching shakers are formed from two black balls stacked on top of each other atop a small round base and capped with a cake-shaped "hat". White and red grinning mouths and round eyes are painted on the faces. A simple white grass skirt is painted on the bottom. The caps have slanted red, yellow, and green lines. $20.00–22.00

Tribal Men on Elephant Wood. This three-piece set consists of a large wooden elephant whose rump is hollowed out to hold toothpicks and two black "kingpin"-shaped shakers that fit into the elephant's back. They are surrounded by holes into which hors d'oeuvres speared onto toothpicks were presumably inserted. The shakers have round eyes and mouths, a large "S" or "P" on chest, and painted on grass skirts in yellow and green or yellow and red. $40.00–42.00

Sitting Boys, One Eating Watermelon Ceramic. Japan. 1940s–1950s. This large set depicts two brown boys with African features. The one eating a slice of watermelon sits cross-legged in his yellow trunks. The other one relaxes with tilted head, resting one hand on knee. He wears green trunks. $32.00–34.00

Two Natives with Hut Ceramic. Japan. 1940s–1950s. This four-piece set consists of a gray, hut-shaped mustard pot, and

Bisque Black Children Bisque. Japan. Early 1930s. This charming pair of black children consists of a little boy in blue shorts, white shirt and socks, and ochre shoes, and a little girl in a pageboy haircut, wearing a red-and-blue-striped dress with a green collar, white socks, and ochre shoes. Both have a rope topknot sprouting from the tops of their heads. $35.00–40.00

two naked natives in sitting position. The three figurines fit on the tray with the natives flanking the mustard pot. $55.00–60.00

Native with Drum Ceramic. Japan. 1940s–1950s. A grass-skirted native girl in earrings and ankle ornaments holds one hand to ear. The yellow drum has brown detailing. $30.00–32.00

Native Boys Resting Ceramic. Japan. 1940s–1950s. One boy lies on his tummy, supporting his head in his hands and kicking up his legs. The other boy sits up and scratches his head. Both have white lips, red trunks. Supine boys wear green ankle bracelet, sitting boy wears red ankle bracelet. $30.00–32.00

Tribal Men with Clubs Ceramic. Japan. 1940s–1950s. Grinning tribal men in yellow grass skirts, beads, and ankle ornaments hold a yellow club in one hand. $30.00–32.00

Chef-Book Spice Rack Ceramic and wood. A wooden rack holds five spice jars in the shape of books, the spines of which are flattened images of Chef in white toque, brown face, white apron, yellow pants, and black shoes. The eyes of all look to the right. The words "Salt," and "Pepper," "Cinnamon," "Clove," "Nutmeg," and "Allspice" appear on the stomachs. $40.00–45.00

WILD WEST

Cowboy Boots Ceramic. Japan. 1940s–1950s. Tan cowboy boots with black soles have black "S" and "P" painted into a white circle in the front. $10.00–12.00

Horse Heads and Saddle Ceramic. Japan. 1970s. This three-piece set consists of a green rectangular base from the center of which rises a tan saddletree holding a russet saddle with gold stirrups. The saddle has a hole in the middle to hold toothpicks. On either side stand shaker horseheads rising from squat necks. Pepper is black with yellow bridle; salt is tan with yellow bridle. $16.00–24.00

Cartoony Cowboys Ceramic. Large-eared, grinning cowboys in bow-legged poses have colorful costumes. Salt wears yellow stetson, red shirt, blue chaps. Pepper wears red stetson, blue jacket, and yellow chaps. $10.00–12.00

Seguaro Cactus and Skull Ceramic. Vandor. 1980s. A white skull with gray horns is teamed with a two-armed Seguaro cactus on a circular, sand-colored base. $15.00

Prickly Pear Cactus and Vulture Ceramic. Vandor. 1980s. A prickly pear cactus in an oval, sand-colored base is teamed with a black vulture with pink head sitting on a round, sand-colored base. $15.00

Cacti in Pots on Tray Ceramic. Vandor. 1980s. Small cacti (Seguaro and barrel) in clay pots are set into a tray made to resemble stones. $15.00

Cowboy and Hat Ceramic. 1980s. Bust of white, winking cowboy with black, bushy eyebrows and hair has black dots on his shirt. A red cigarette dangles from his lips. The beat-up Stetson is detachable. $12.00–14.00

Cowboy on Rearing Horse Ceramic. Rossware by H.L. Ross. 1942. A child-faced cowboy in pink hat and shirt and blue trousers is astride a rearing palomino, whose legs rise out of a base painted to resemble grass and flowers. This is a nester. $25.00–30.00

Gun and Holster Ceramic. Vandor. 1980s. A gray Colt with "S" on the handle slips into an orange holster, textured to look like tooled leather and bullet cartridges. A large "P" is "branded" into the holster. $15.00

Chili Pepper in Sombrero Ceramic. Vandor. 1980s. A grinning red chili pepper with movable eyes wears a detachable pink sombrero with black trim and turquoise hatband. $15.00

Cowboy and Hat Ceramic. Vandor. 1980s. Bust of smiling, handsome cowboy, beautifully painted in smoky, earth tones, has detachable Stetson. A red silk cord is threaded through two holes in the brim and knotted at the cowboy's chin. $15.00

Señor and Señorita Clay. Mexico. 1940s–1980s. Hand-painted in earth tones, a señor in brown sombrero sits next to a señorita in orange veil. $14.00–18.00

Señor and Señorita Clay. Mexico. 1940s–1980s. Hand-painted set features a sitting señor in a yellow sombrero and a black-haired, pink-skirted señorita holding a black and orange sombrero. $12.00–14.00

Mexican Peasants Clay. Mexico. 1940s–1980s. This hand-painted set depicts a sitting peasant in a black sombrero hiding his face in his arms. He wears a brown shirt and white trousers. His companion, in yellow sombrero, green shirt, and white pants looks up as though just awakened. $12.00–14.00

Prickly Pear Cactus Clay. Mexico. 1940s–1980s. Matching, hand-painted prickly pear cacti are beautifully detailed in shades of green, ochre, and brown. $10.00–12.00

Barrel Cactus in Pots Clay. Mexico. 1940s–1980s. Hand-painted barrel cactus in terra-cotta pots which are themselves painted with cacti and casita scenes. One cactus is yellow, the other, green. $10.00–12.00

Seguaro Cactus Clay. Mexico. 1940s–1980s. Thick stands of hand-painted Seguaro cactus arise from brown earth-textured bases. $10.00–12.00

Cactus in Pots Clay. Mexico. 1940s–1980s. Dark green barrel cactus in terra-cotta pot ornamented with a sleeping peasant and cactus motif is paired with an assortment of cacti in a similarly decorated pot. $10.00–12.00

Mexican Peasant and Cactus Ceramic. Japan. A Mexican peasant in black pants, blue shirt, yellow scarf, and red sombrero sits sleeping next to a double-stemmed Sequaro cactus. $16.00–20.00

Chef and Brave Ceramic. Hand-painted. 1950s. A bare-chested Indian chief in a feathered headdress stands with arms crossed in his yellow buckskins. The brave beats a yellow tom-tom drum. $20.00–24.00

Cowboy on Bucking Bronco Ceramic. Japan. 1940s–1950s. This beautifully hand-painted nester consists of a boy-faced cowboy in red Stetson, blue shirt, and yellow chaps astride a bucking brown horse that is attached to a base textured to simulate grass. $30.00–35.00

Cowboy and Reclining Horse Ceramic. Japan. 1940s–1950s. This hand-painted pair features a boy-faced cowpoke in black hat, green shirt, red bandanna, and tan chaps sitting on the ground and a golden, saddleless horse lying down next to him. $30.00–35.00

Cowgirl on Bull Ceramic. Japan. 1940s–1950s. This two-piece nester features a brown bull with white horns and hooves and a cowgirl sitting astride him. She wears an orange Stetson, blue shirt, and red chaps. $30.00–35.00

Cowboy Boots Ceramic. Japan. 1940s–1950s. Yellow cowboy boots have brown trim and finely articulated design on sides. $8.00–10.00

Cowboy Boots Ceramic. Japan. 1940s-1950s. Beige cowboy boots with black soles have beautiful "sunrise" pattern embossed on sides and highlighted with orange. $8.00–10.00

Mexican Cowboys Ceramic. Identical, though differently painted, Mexican "charros" or cowboys in sombreros salute atop bowing horses. One "charro" wears blue vest, the other orange. $12.00–14.00

Cowboy and Rearing Horse Ceramic. A tan, heavy-bottomed cowboy with a blue bandanna tied around his face stands next to a beige rearing horse which barely reaches to the rim of the cowpoke's Stetson. $12.00–14.00

Teepees Ceramic. Japan. 1950s. Identical white conical teepees have black tips and vents, and sun and deer motifs on the sides. $10.00–12.00

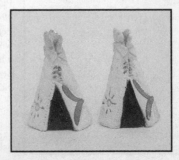

Cowboy Head and Stagecoach Ceramic. A white bust of a winding cowboy with red bandanna, black-dotted shirt, and floppy Stetson is teamed with a figurine of a beige stagecoach without horses. $12.00–14.00

Mexican Peasant and Hat Ceramic. Japan. White shakers with gold highlights depict a bald, large-headed Mexican, wrapped in a serape and sitting barefooted, flanked by his gold-banded sombrero. The peasant shows his teeth in a large grin. $12.00–14.00

Indian Chief and Teepee Ceramic. Japan. An Indian chief in a lush feather headdress, squats next to his white teepee which is capped with a gold tip. $20.00–22.00

Indian and Tepee Ceramic. Japan. An Indian with a single feather rising from the back of his long, black hair, sits wrapped in a red blanket. Next to him rises a beige tepee ornamented with green buffalo and man figures. $16.00–20.00

Three-Piece Mexican Peasant on Horse Ceramic. U.S.A. This three-piece set consists of a white horse and rider on an oval base, and two removable shakers that resemble cylindrical sacks and are inserted into the twin baskets on the horse's back. The set is basically white with black outlines and yellow, red, and blue wash on the rider's costume. $20.00–24.00

Sleeping Mexicans and Seguaro Cactus Ceramic. This three-piece set features a green, two-armed Seguaro cactus rising from a rectangular brown base. On either side are the sitting, sleeping figures of Mexicans in large sombreros. $10.00–14.00

Plains Couple Chalkware. U.S.A. 1940s. Chief in yellow and white headdress and white costume stands with arms crossed. The squaw, in white costume with red and blue design, has black braids. $22.00–26.00

Buffalo Ceramic. Japan. 1950s–1960s. Comical buffalo have deeply embossed bodies, white horns, and black, baby-doll eyes. $14.00–20.00

Sleeping Mexicans Ceramic. Identical figurines depict sitting Mexican peasants with arms tucked under red, yellow, and blue serapes and large sombreros completely covering their heads. $10.00–12.00

Mexican Couple Ceramic. Occupied Japan. Squat, simplified Mexican couple (3½") features the man in a yellow sombrero, green pants, and white scarf trimmed in red and blue. The señora is dressed completely in white and carries a flat plate-like hat on her head. $24.00–30.00

Child Cowboy with Horse Ceramic. U.S.A. A boy-faced cowboy in yellow chaps and green vest rests his hands on the black holsters of his gun. He is flanked by a white horse who stands, fully tacked, on a pale green oval base. $20.00–24.00

Iguanas Ceramic. Japan. 1940s–1950s. Realistic, colorful iguanas are depicted in different poses. The green one skulks on all fours on a base crafted to resemble a stick set into a desert floor. The yellow one climbs up a stick rising from a leafy floor and sticks out its tongue in pursuit of a luckless insect. $12.00–16.00

Comical Indian Chief and Squaw Ceramic. This comical, large-headed couple depicts a squinting chief in a white loin-cloth and Indian headdress, and his grinning squaw in green dress. $20.00–24.00

Chief and Squaw Children Ceramic. Japan. An Indian boy in a feather headdress and ornamented buckskins waves a hatchet. The girl beats a tomtom. $18.00–20.00

Dancing Indian Girls Ceramic. Japan. Identical figurines of Indian girls with bobbed black hair are depicted in dancing pose. One wears a red top, the other a black one. $12.00–14.00

Metal Buckaroos Metal. U.S.A. 1950s. Silver and gold painted metal buckaroos are beautifully detailed. The golden banners are inscribed "Idaho." $20.00–24.00

Cartoony Chief and Squaw Ceramic. Japan. Indian children with baby-doll faces represent a boy in black wearing an elaborate, multi-colored headdress, and a girl in red with eyes downcast with a yellow headband. $12.00–14.00

Sitting Indian Couple Ceramic. Japan. Small (3½") squaw and chief have white costumes and bright orange faces. Boy wears round, full feather headdress. $12.00–14.00

Chief and Squaw Heads with Feathers Ceramic and feathers. Deeply textured, realistically colored heads of squaw and chief have real feathers in headdresses. $16.00–20.00

Pale-faced Chief and Squaw Heads Ceramic. Japan. Realistically detailed heads of squaw and chief have pale faces, bright red lips, and black eyes. Chief has blue feathers at his ears. $14.00–16.00

Chief and Squaw Busts Ceramic. 1970s. Ruddy, realistic busts feature chief with red, blue, and yellow headdress, black braids, and yellow breast plate. Squaw wears blue and red band around her forehead, and a yellow, red, and blue necklace covers her bosom. $18.00–24.00

Chief and Squaw Busts Ceramic. Realistically detailed chief and squaw busts have classical, sculptural bases. Their dark brown faces contrast with the green, yellow, and red coloring of the ornaments and feathers. $14.00–16.00

Chief and Squaw Busts Ceramic. Small (3½") busts of squaw and chief sit on round bases. Squaw wears red dress. Chief in white and black headdress is bare-chested. $12.00–14.00

Chief and Squaw Busts Porcelain. White porcelain chief and squaw busts rise from green pedestal bases. Chief is detailed with red, yellow, blue, and green, while squaw has golden hair and red headband. $10.00–12.00

Totem Poles Ceramic. Identical totem poles represent two winged creatures atop each other. $10.00–14.00

Totem Poles Ceramic. Stylized totem poles are made in the shape of cylinders with faux-Indian motifs representing various large-eyed creatures crouching atop each other. $10.00–12.00

Chief with Teepee Ceramic. Late 1940s. A glum Indian chief in a yellow, red, and blue headdress sits cross-legged next to a white teepee with a green opening. $18.00–20.00

Chief in Canoe Ceramic. Japan. Late 1930s. A chief in a yellow shirt, blue trousers, and yellow and black headdress nestles in a white canoe painted with a brown cross-hatching pattern and green and brown border. $14.00–18.00

Chief with Totem Pole Ceramic. Japan. 1950s. A chief with a white face, reddish headdress with trousers, and blue shirt with winged fringe extends his arms. The totem pole has a brown base and a bird-motif "head." $20.00–24.00

Indian Couple in Canoes Ceramic. Japan. 1950s. Brave in white and blue outfit sits in a white canoe with brown trim. The squaw, holding a yellow paddle aloft, sits in a white canoe with green trim. $14.00–18.00

Navajo Chief and Squaw Chalkware. U.S.A. 1930s. Navajo couple in white and blue trim and orange faces stand on orange bases. $22.00–26.00

Indian Couple on Tray Chalkware. U.S.A. 1930s. Brown and white Indian couple in kneeling position nestle on a base tray embossed with petroglyphlike design. $22.00–26.00

Indian Children in Moccasins Ceramic. Japan. 1950s. Indian children sit inside beige moccasins. Girl wears red; boy, in lavish headdress, wears blue and carries a tomahawk. $26.00–30.00

Cartoonish Indian Couple Pottery. U.S.A. 1970s. Button-nosed Indian couple wear brown buckskins. They have large round heads, red headdresses, and tiny black feet. He holds an arrow, she holds an ear of corn. $14.00–16.00

Small Indian Children Ceramic. Japan. 1930s. Small (3") Indian children have baby faces and pastel-colored outfits. Girl, in yellow and white, has black beads around her neck. Boy, in pink, has a red, black, and white headdress. $12.00–14.00

Kneeling Chiefs Ceramic. Japan. 1940s. Small (3") figurines depict naked chief in large yellow headdress holding a spear. $10.00–13.00

Chief Busts Metal. Realistically sculpted busts of Indian chiefs with fanning feather headdress have a bronze finish. $10.00–12.00

Chief and Squaw with Child Wood composition. U.S.A. Late 1940s. Small figurines made of wood composition painted brown with dark brown paint on the carving depict a kneeling squaw cradling her papoose, and squatting chief holding a pipe. $12.00–16.00

Chief with Tomtoms in Base Ceramic. Japan. 1940s. This three-piece set consists of a chief in a red, white, and blue headdress attached to a white base with a crenelated green pattern running along the outside edge. In the base two matching yellow drums, the shakers, are nestled, fitting under the hands of the chief. $24.00–26.00

Chief, Squaw, Teepee and Drum Condiment Set Ceramic. Japan. This four-piece set consists of a base from the center of which rises a yellow and green teepee designed to hold toothpicks. On either side sit, cross-legged, a squaw in a yellow top, and a chief in a green top and red trousers. These

Conestoga Wagon with Team of Oxen Ceramic. U.S.A. 1950s. Beautifully hand-painted Conestoga wagon is teamed with a pair of spotted oxen. $16.00–18.00

Desperado and Rearing Horse
Ceramic. Occupied Japan.
1945–1952. A masked desperado
holds a golden six-shooter in one
hand. His rearing beige stallion
barely reaches to the bandit's chin.
$20.00–24.00

are the shakers. Between them stands a green tomtom drum–mustard pot. $24.00–28.00

Chief, Squaw with Child, and Canoe Tray Ceramic. Japan. Child-faced chief and squaw with baby nestle into a brown canoe. This is a nester made up of three pieces. $18.00–24.00

Sitting Braves Ceramic. Japan. 1950s. Child-faced braves squat. The one in blue with red trousers holds a brown arrow. The one in red with brown trousers holds a white tomtom. $10.00–12.00

Squaw Busts Ceramic. Japan. 1930s. Bare-breasted squaws rise from green pedestals. One has long, black braids framing her pale face, the other wears a red and blue headdress. $10.00–14.00

Chief and Brave, Sitting Ceramic. Japan. 1930s. Smiling, sitting brave wears red shirt, blue trousers, and yellow headband. Chief with blue chin feathers wears green and white. $10.00–14.00

Brave with Tomtom Ceramic. Japan. A pale brave with gold arm bands and belt, blue trousers, and red moccasins stands in dancing pose next to a yellow tomtom with green, red, blue, and yellow ornamentation and real twine ties. $12.00–14.00

Indian Child Perching on Teepee Ceramic. Japan. This cuddler set consists of a white teepee with red, yellow, and blue ornamentation and a smiling Indian child whose arms are clasped to form a circle which slips over the tip of the teepee. The legs straddle either side of the tent. $18.00–24.00

Indian Children Ceramic. Cartoony, naked Indian boy in large green, yellow, and red headdress sits cross-legged, holding a black pipe. The other child, in an even more elaborate head-dress, is wrapped to the chin in a white blanket with a red and blue border. $10.00–14.00

Chief Playing Banjo and Squaw Ceramic. Japan. A sitting chief in a yellow shirt and blue trousers strums a banjo. The squaw sits in her green top and red skirt. $10.00–14.00

Katchina Dolls Ceramic with feathers. Nicely detailed reproductions of Hopi Katchina dolls are decorated with real feathers. One represents a girl, the other, a bird deity. $20.00–24.00

Rattlesnake Nodder Ceramic. 1980s. A blue, pink, and green rattlesnake is composed of three parts: a coiled base, and a head and a rattler nodding shakers. $15.00–20.00

Cactus on Base Ceramic and dried cactus. U.S.A. 1950s. Ceramic barrel cactus in bloom nestles in a semicircular base made from a dried cactus. $14.00–18.00

CHILDREN'S WORLD

Donald Duck Heavy white pottery, hand-decorated over glaze. American Pottery Company. 1940s. White-bodied Donald Duck has blue bow tie and cap and stands with arms akimbo. Marked "Walt Disney." $30.00–38.00

Pluto Heavy white pottery, hand-decorated over glaze. American Pottery Company. 1940s. White sitting Pluto has red toenails, ears, and tongue and black eyes. Marked "Walt Disney." $30.00–38.00

Pluto Playing with Food U.S.A. Heavy glazed pottery. Bright yellow Pluto figures are unauthorized Disney knock-offs. Salt Pluto sits up on haunches and holds silver spoon in one paw and white bone in another. Pepper Pluto is down on his fours and balances a red plate on his nose. Both wear red bow ties. $20.00–30.00

Dumbo Heavy white pottery, hand-decorated over glaze. American Pottery Company. 1940s. White Dumbo with red or blue detailing stands up on back legs and curls up his trunk. Marked "Walt Disney." $30.00–38.00

Mickey and Minnie Glass Jars Glass and metal. Walt Disney Productions. 1960s–1970s. Glass jars with silver caps have decal faces of Minnie and Mickey. $24.00–26.00

Mickey Mouse on Cylinder Ceramic. U.S.A. Walt Disney Productions. Matching white cylinders trimmed in gold stripes are ornamented with mirror-image decals of Mickey Mouse in chef's toque sprinkling salt or pepper into a salad

Donald Duck Heavy white pottery, hand-decorated over glaze. American Pottery Company. 1940s. A white, sitting Donald Duck has red bow tie, buttons, and cap, and yellow feet and beak. Marked "Walt Disney." $36.00–44.00

Mickey and Minnie Heavy white pottery, hand-decorated over glaze. American Pottery Company. 1940s. Round–tummied Mickey and Minnie are white with red, black, and blue detailing. $40.00–45.00

bowl. The words "Walt Disney Productions" are found under the images. $16.00–20.00

Winnie the Pooh and Rabbit Ceramic. Enesco. 1960s. Winnie the Pooh and Rabbit are from the Disney character series by Enesco. $35.00–40.00

Donald Duck and Ludwig von Drake Ceramic. Disney. 1961. Designed by Dan Brechner. In mint condition, still boxed, this set fetches $115.00–120.00; without box, $40.00–55.00

Pinocchio and the Blue Fairy Ceramic. Disney. Pinnochio, in red shorts and feathered cap, is teamed with the Blue Fairy. $95.00–105.00

Pinocchio Ceramic. U.S.A. White ceramic Pinocchio figurines are beautifully painted in glowing primary colors. Salt Pinocchio wears black shoes, yellow shorts, blue gloves, green bow tie, and red cap. Pepper Pinocchio is in red shoes, blue shorts, yellow bow tie, green hat, and black gloves. $30.00–40.00

Figaro and Cleo Ceramic. Japan. These Disney knock-offs represent Pinocchio's pets, the cat Figaro and the fish Cleo. $60.00–65.00

"Dumbo" Firefighter Clowns Ceramic. Japan. These zany firefighter clowns are knock-offs of the characters in the Disney film *Dumbo*.

Musical Pigs Ceramic. Disney-like pigs that could be two of the Three Little Pigs play musical instruments.

Mad Hatter and the Mouse in the Teapot Ceramic. 1980s. Two of the zaniest characters from *Alice in Wonderland* are represented here as the Mad Hatter and the Mouse in the Teapot.

Gingerbread Boy and Girl and Napkin Holder Ceramic. 1970. Brown gingerbread boy and girl have white "frosting" scrollwork decorations and outstretched "bud" arms. The napkin holder consists of boy and girl joined at the hip. $28.00–34.00

Pinocchio Heavy porcelain. Japan. Hand-painted knock-off of the authorized Disney character, this set features two versions of Pinocchio, one in red shorts, yellow hat, and blue bow tie, the other in yellow shorts, red hat, and green bow tie. $35.00–40.00

Mickey and Minnie on Bench Heavy porcelain. Walt Disney Productions. 1960s. Beautifully painted Minnie in pink and Mickey in blue and yellow sit on a wooden bench. $40.00–45.00

Donald Duck Heavy porcelain. Walt Disney Productions. Beautifully painted matching Donald Ducks hold arms akimbo. White statuettes are trimmed in black, blue, yellow, and red. $35.00–40.00

Pluto Balancing Cup and Saucer Ceramic. Disney's antic dog Pluto is depicted balancing a cup and saucer on his nose and holding a spoon. $35.00–40.00

Mickey Mouse and Pluto Ceramic. Enesco. 1960s. Disney's lovable mouse and dog are represented in this 1960s set from the Enesco Disney series. $35.00–40.00

Doc and Dopey Shakers and Snow White Napkin Holder Ceramic. Two of the Seven Dwarfs flank the Snow White holder in this three-piece set. $40.00–50.00

Mickey Mouse Heads Ceramic. U.S.A. 1970s. Mickey Mouse heads are completely white, 5" tall. $28.00–32.00

Mickey Mouse Ceramic. Dan Brechner for Walt Disney Productions. 1961. The sprightly signature Disney Mouse sports its most recent look. $25.00–28.00

Donald Duck on Raft Ceramic. Japan. Walt Disney's Donald Duck stands on a raft, which is the pepper shaker. $20.00–25.00

Little Orphan Annie and Sandy the Dog Chalkware. 1940s. Dressed in yellow, with matching curly hair, Little Orphan Annie is in a kneeling position. Her reddish-brown dog Sandy has yellow snout and paws. $40.00–50.00

Schoolboy and Schoolgirl Ceramic. U.S.A. 1940s. A little girl in a white dress with red flowers and gold-trimmed collar wears red shoes and a blond bob haircut. The little boy is in a yellow and white T-shirt and blue shorts. Both are standing against a base of pale green textured to resemble grass. $16.00–20.00

Ball and Blocks Ceramic. U.S.A. A stack of A, B, and C blocks in white, pink, and red trim holds pepper, while a white ball with pink and blue spiral design holds pepper. $30.00–35.00

Woody and Winnie Woodpecker Ceramic. Walter Lantz Productions, Inc. Napco, Japan. 1958. Woody Woodpecker, in blue "suit," red "headdress," black tail, and yellow feet, holds a large white salt shaker. Winnie Woodpecker in a yellow dress and blue body holds a large white shaker. $30.00–35.00

Atchoo and Salt of the Earth Ceramic. Japan. Two monks in black robes, brown sandals, and white cords are named

Alice in Wonderland and the Mad Hatter Ceramic. U.S.A. 1950s. Alice, in her signature blond hair, blue dress, and white apron, holds her hands behind her back as she is addressed by the Mad Hatter in top hat, checkered trousers, and green cutaway. $35.00–40.00

"Atchoo" and "Salt of the Earth." Atchoo holds a red and white polka-dotted handkerchief to his nose, while Salt of the Earth piously folds his hands in prayer. $20.00–30.00

Butcher with Pigs Ceramic. A red-clad butcher in a yellow apron is flanked by two rotund yellowish pigs, one salt, the other pepper. All three are on a green base textured to resemble grass. $25.00–30.00

Dressy Ducks Ceramic. Long-necked ducks in pastel clothes with a nautical motif are dressed for strolling. She wears a pink jacket and lavender scarf. He is in a yellow jacket with a blue scarf. $12.00–16.00

Gnome Couple Ceramic. Marked "Made in Japan, QQ, 1979, Uniebok, B.V." (QQ stands for Quon Quon Company, Importers.) White-bearded, red-hatted gnome in yellow trousers and blue jacket sits and dozes. Blond girl gnome, in green cone hat and pink dress, sits and cradles her head in her clasped hands. $25.00–30.00

Gnome with Rabbit Ceramic. Marked "Made in Japan, QQ, 1979, Uniebok, B.B." (QQ stands for Quon Quon Company, Importers). White-bearded gnome in red cone hat and blue robe sits and pets a brown and white rabbit which sits up on its haunches. $25.00–30.00

Little Black Sambo and the Tiger Ceramic. U.S.A. A large-headed, grass-skirted Sambo shaker is paired with a bright yellow tiger. $20.00–25.00

The Jetsons Ceramic. Vandor. Manufactured as demos by the Vandor Company, the Jetsons were produced in only twelve sets, since Hanna Barbera withheld the license. $30.00–36.00

Spacely Sprockett and Pal Ceramic. Vandor. This Jetson set consists of Spacely Sprockett, George Jetson's boss, and his pal. $30.00–36.00

Chauncey Chirp Ceramic and rhinestones. Late 1940s. Brilliant yellow Chauncey Chirp wears white shirt, white bowler, and has rhinestone eyes and ornaments on feet and clothing. $30.00–36.00

Snoopy Ceramic. Japan. A white Snoopy wears a pink scarf. $30.00–35.00

Snoopy and Woodstock Ceramic. Snoopy, the white beagle from Daisy Hill Puppy Farm, and his bird friend Woodstock make up this set. $30.00–35.00

Howdy Doodie Bone china. Beswick China. England. The great children's television character stars in this set. $45.00–55.00

Laurel and Hardy Bone china. Beswick China. England. This two-piece set features the comic film duo of Laurel and Hardy. $45.00–50.00

Laurel and Hardy Three-Piece Set Bone china. Beswick China. England. The heads of Laurel and Hardy rest in a tray to which their bow ties are attached. $90.00–110.00

Robin Hood Ceramic. Robin Hood kneels on rock. The base is inscribed with the character's name. $38.00–42.00

Robin Hood and Maid Marian Ceramic. 1960s. Hip-height busts of Maid Marian and Robin Hood. $36.00–40.00

Robinson Crusoe Ceramic. The shipwrecked sailor Robinson Crusoe is shown sitting on a makeshift raft atop a collection of sundry supplies. The words "Robinson Crusoe" are written across the base of the raft. $36.00–40.00

Laurel and Hardy Glass and plastic. Laurel and Hardy's clear glass bodies and heads have black and red paint detailing and red and black bowler hats. $40.00–45.00

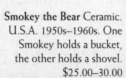

Smokey the Bear Ceramic. U.S.A. 1950s–1960s. One Smokey holds a bucket, the other holds a shovel. $25.00–30.00

Lilliputian Beer Drinker Ceramic. A Lilliputian bearded beer drinker sits inside a yellow laced shoe that must surely belong to Gulliver. $30.00–40.00

Tom Sawyer Ceramic. Tom Sawyer, dressed in chartreuse, sits in a beige rowboat. $30.00–34.00

Huck Finn Ceramic. Parkcraft. Huck Finn is on his raft. $30.00–34.00

Paul Bunyan and Babe Ceramic. 1960s. Paul Bunyan, 4½" tall, is teamed with Babe. $36.00–40.00

Stanley and Livingston Ceramic. The legendary African explorers are commemorated in this two-piece set. $26.00–30.00

Jonah and the Whale Ceramic. 1950s. A cheerful gray whale with a scooped-out middle section holds a despairing Jonah. $20.00–25.00

Jiggs and Maggie Chalkware. 1920s. Mason Jiggs and his washerwoman wife Maggie from George McManus's "Bringing Up Father" are shown in their rich old age, sitting. Maggie holds white rolling pin on her lap, ready for action. $50.00–75.00

Yosemite Sam Ceramic. U.S.A. 1940s. Yosemite Sam in green pants, black hat, and red bandanna reaches for his gun. $40.00–45.00

Paul Bunyan and Babe Ceramic. Hull. 1940s. The mythical American hero, 41/2" tall, is teamed with his beloved ox Babe, whose blue color matches Paul's trousers. The hero's name is printed on the base. $40.00–44.00

Popeye Ceramic. Japan. Licensed by King Features Syndicates, Hearst Corporation. 1980. A matched pair of Popeyes is shown in traditional colors. $22.00–28.00

Popeye and Olive Oyl Ceramic. Japan. 1980. Vandor. Licensed by King Features Syndicates, Hearst Corporation. This is a large-size set of the comic romantic pair, with Popeye holding an opened can of spinach and Olive Oyl rolling her big eyes. $28.00–36.00

Popeye and Swee'Pea in Rowboat Ceramic. Japan. 1980. A tough-looking Popeye sits with crossed knees in a small yellow rowboat. Facing him is Swee'Pea in yellow night-gown, looking glum. $22.00–28.00

Alice In Wonderland Ceramic. Regal China. This pair of *Alice in Wonderland* shakers is in white with gold trim. $40.00

Little Red Riding Hood Ceramic. Hull. 1943. Small set of Little Red Riding Hood in white dress has a bunch of flowers painted onto the middle of her dress. $35.00–40.00

Little Red Riding Hood Ceramic. Hull. 1943. Five-inch set of Little Red Riding Hood in white dress has a bunch of flow-ers painted onto the front of her dress. $40.00–45.00

Little Red Riding Hood Ceramic. Hull. 1940s. In red cape, white dress, and frilly white apron, Little Red Riding Hood holds black basket on one arm and a bouquet in the other hand. Shakers have gold trim at hemline and in cursive, the character's name along the base. $25.00–30.00

Snow White and Dwarf Ceramic. Hull. 1940s. Childish-looking Snow White in pink dress with green apron holds basket under one arm. Dwarf in blue, red, and yellow plays a bass. $30.00–35.00

King Midas Porcelain. Japan. 1950s. White-robed King Midas in gold crown and neck chain kneels over a bag of gold (pep-per shaker). $25.00–30.00

Tortoise and the Hare Ceramic. Hull. 1940s. A tan hare lies on his back sleeping while a green tortoise stands up on its hind legs. $25.00–30.00

Tortoise and the Hare Ceramic. 1960s. White tortoise with green belly and pale blue shell grins and holds out its flip-pers. The white hare with pink eyes and ears wears blue sneakers and holds out its forepaws. $12.00–16.00

Jonah and the Whale Ceramic. Japan. 1950s. A cheerful gray whale with a scooped-out middle section holds a despairing, tiny figurine of Jonah. $20.00–25.00

Fox and the Grapes Ceramic. Hull. 1940s. A brown fox with black eyes sits next to a clump of green grapes. $20.00–25.00

Little Mermaid Ceramic. Hull. 1940s. Blond mermaid reclines, her green tail flipped up at the end. $20.00–25.00

Little Mermaid Ceramic. Japan. 1950s. White torsoed, bare-breasted mermaids with blue tails have long blond hair. Salt holds pink seashells to ear, Pepper holds pink seashells to knee. $35.00–40.00

Tom Tinker and Dog Ceramic. Hull. 1940s. A white-stockinged, sitting Tom Tinker is flanked by a white poodle with a red bow. $20.00–24.00

Ladybug Ceramic. Hull. 1940s. Hatted Ladybug in yellow coat sits atop a pale pink rose. $20.00–26.00

Fisherman and the Fish Ceramic. Hull. 1940s. The fisherman from the story "The Fisherman and His Wife" lies on his stomach and holds in his arms a yellow and brown speckled, fat-lipped fish. $30.00–35.00

Genie with Lamp Ceramic. Hull. 1940s. A cross-legged genie, in costume that varies in color from pale green to white, has gold trim and real rhinestone on turban. His golden lamp sits between his knees. $20.00–30.00

Praying Genie and Lamp Ceramic. U.S.A. Genie, his head down, is praying as next to him rests his magic lamp. $15.00–20.00

Noah's Ark Ceramic. U.S.A. Noah's ark has two sets of animals as shakers. $52.00–60.00

Noah's Ark in Box Ceramic. U.S.A. Noah's ark with shaker animals in original box with label. $62.00–70.00

Man in the Moon Ceramic. Hull. 1940s. This stacker depicts the man in the moon as a round-faced, bald gentleman winking with one eye. $45.00–55.00

Cat and the Fiddle Ceramic. Hull. 1940s. A gray cat holds a brown fiddle. $22.00–24.00

Cat and the Fiddle Ceramic. Japan. 1950s. The gray and white cat fits into the fiddle. $26.00–30.00

Cat and the Fiddle Ceramic. Japan. 1950s. A brown cat in a large-collared blouse holds a fiddle. The brown jumping cow is attached to the crescent moon. $26.00–30.00

Cow and the Moon Ceramic. Hull. 1940s. The smiling brown cow leans its right "arm" on the sleeping, yellow crescent moon. $22.00–25.00

Cow and the Moon Ceramic. 1930s. Yellow moon is shown in profile and the black and white cow is up on her haunches in this rendition from "Hey, Diddle Diddle." $25.00–30.00

Hickory, Dickory, Dock Mouse Ceramic. 1930s–1940s. A brown grandfather clock is topped by a detachable gray mouse. $22.00–25.00

Little Bo-Peep Ceramic. Hull. 1940s. Bo-Peep is accompanied by her sheep. $38.00–44.00

Mary and Her Little Lamb Ceramic. 1950s. White Mary and her lamb both have closed eyes and pink and black detailing. $30.00–35.00

Humpty Dumpty Ceramic. 1950s. A white Humpty Dumpty fits into a white "brick" wall ornamented with one red daisy. He is smiling. $25.00–30.00

Humpty Dumpty on Wall Ceramic. 1950. Egg-shaped Humpty in a green, yellow, and pink outfit perches on a white and orange brick wall that has a yellow top surmounted, at either end, by green "knewels." The character and the wall are each shakers. $18.00–24.00

Mary and Her Little Lamb Ceramic. Hull. 1940s. A green-skirted, brown-haired Mary clutches a pink daisy as her white curly lamb cavorts on a piece of green turf. $40.00–45.00

Mary and Her Little Lamb and Schoolhouse Ceramic. Japan. 1950s. Mary and her lamb with green stripes are accompanied by a maroon schoolhouse. $25.00–30.00

Old Lady Who Lived in a Shoe Ceramic. 1940s. Old Lady in green apron, red jacket, and black hat towers over brown shoe with white spats. $25.00–30.00

Sad Sack Ceramic. Norcrest Company. Japan. Marked H-96 and George Baker Copyright. 1950s. George Baker's inept World War II private is represented here in two 4" figurines with "Sad Sack" appearing on the base fronts. The one in dress uniform salutes limply, while the one in fatigues slogs miserably under his heavy load. $80.00–90.00

There Was An Old Lady Ceramic. 1940s. Old Lady in red bonnet and pale green apron sits in a large basket inscribed with the text "There Was An Old Lady." $25.00–30.00

Churchmouse and Money Bag Ceramic. Japan. The mouse who stole money from the church has a money bag with red lines and "PW." $20.00–25.00

Two of the Three Little Kittens Ceramic. Hull. 1940s. Two standing calico little kittens with brown and black spots hold up their paws. One has pink mitten, the other white, and one mitten on each paw is missing. $40.00–45.00

Two of the Three Little Kittens Ceramic. Hull. 1940s. Two calico kittens are lying down and with huge grins on their faces hold up pink or blue mittens. $40.00–45.00

Pussy Cat, Pussy Cat, Where Have You Been? Ceramic. Hull. 1940s. A blue-dressed, white aproned maid addresses a large gray cat clutching a fish. $40.00–45.00

Queen of Hearts Ceramic. Hull. 1940s. Gold-crowned Queen of Hearts in red bustle and skirt ornamented with red hearts holds tray full of tarts. Along the base, the character's name is written in gold. $22.00–28.00

Old King Cole Ceramic. Hull. 1940s. A rotund Old King Cole stands atop an overstuffed green armchair. $20.00–26.00

Goose and Golden Egg Ceramic. 1940s. A white goose with gold trim sits beside a shiny gold egg. $10.00–16.00

Goose and Golden Egg Ceramic. 1960s. Mother Goose's long-necked white goose is featured with her golden egg sitting on a yellow base. $24.00–28.00

Mouse and Cheese Ceramic. 1940s. A black and gray mouse with red ears sits up next to a piece of Swiss cheese. $12.00–18.00

Mouse and Cheese Ceramic. 1940s. The mouse from "The Farmer in the Dell" wears a gray mask and green hat. $15.00–18.00

Mouse and Cheese Ceramic. 1950s. The gray mouse from "The Farmer in the Dell" holds right hand up to right ear and sits next to piece of cheese. $12.00–16.00

Bobby Shaftoe Ceramic. 1940s. Bobby Shaftoe sits on top of box with his name on it. $41.00–46.00

Puss in Boots Ceramic. 1940s. A gray Puss scrambles out of the ornate yellowish pepper-shaker boot. $20.00–24.00

Benjamin Bunny and Peter Rabbit Ceramic. Japan. This set of large Beatrix Potter's characters is unusual and striking. $25.00–30.00

Garfield and Odie Ceramic. Japan. Late 1980s. Bright-yellow Garfield in a brown pilgrim hat and holding a blunderbuss is teamed with a yellow Odie, whose black ears are in an "alert" position and whose red tongue flops out of his gaping mouth. $15.00–20.00

"A Nod to Abe Lincoln" Ceramic. Regal China. 1991. This "nodder" set features a bust of Abraham Lincoln flanked by a Black boy and Black girl nodders. It is signed by artist Betty Harrington. $1,100.00

Adam and Eve Wood. U.S.A. Wooden Adam and Eve, when placed together, are held to each other by a wooden peg which has been placed in the anatomically correct position. $25.00–28.00

Little Red Riding Hood and Wolf Ceramic. Hull. 1940s. Little Red, completely swathed in her red cape, holds a gray basket. She converses with Big Bad black wolf, who sits on his haunches and licks his chops. $30.00–35.00

Pan-Faced Fauns Ceramic. Japan. 1960s. Pan-faced fauns in pink have maroon and blue arms each. $26.00–28.00

Jerry Colonna Ceramic. The character Jerry Colonna is depicted as the porter pushing the luggage cart. $18.00–24.00

John F. Kennedy in Rocking Chair Ceramic. U.S.A. 1962. In this nester set, John F. Kennedy in black trousers sits on white rocker with his initials in gold. $50.00–65.00

John F. Kennedy in Rocking Chair Ceramic. U.S.A. 1960s. John F. Kennedy in brown trousers rocks on chair with his initials. $45.00–50.00

Jimmy Carter Peanuts Ceramic. U.S.A. 1970s. Smiling peanuts with huge teeth impersonate President Jimmy Carter. $30.00–40.00

Snowflake Ceramic. Light or dark-skinned pair of German comic characters from the 1930s. $80.00–85.00

Mugsy Dogs Ceramic. Shawnee Pottery. Zanesville, OH. 1937–1961. The matching set of small Mugsy dogs shows signature white terrier on all fours with big blue bandanna wrapped around its head and a doleful expression on its face. $15.00–20.00

Large Mugsy Dog Ceramic. Shawnee Pottery. Zanesville, OH. 1937–1961. This large set of Mugsy dogs shows them sitting up on haunches with black-nailed paws and large blue bandannas around the heads. $26.00–30.00

Teddy Bear and Raggedy Ann Ceramic. 1950s. Brown teddy bear with yellow bow and stitching down the middle raises one paw. The blond Raggedy Ann wears a white dress with blue dots and red and white stockings. $12.00–16.00

Stuffed Elephants Ceramic. 1950s. White matching elephants with upturned trunks wear collars with gold trim and pink bows. Their stitch marks are done in gold and they have pink and blue flower design on their bodies. $10.00–12.00

Hare and Tortoise Ceramic. Japan. The white rabbit sits and naps, resting his head on paw. The orange tortoise stretches out its smiling face. $12.00–14.00

White Rabbit and Magician's Hat Ceramic. Japan. A white rabbit with pink ears nests atop a big, black top hat of the sort magicians use. $18.00–22.00

Magician and Box Ceramic. Japan. This nester consists of a magician in yellow turban, green jacket, and white trousers sitting cross-legged and holding a yellow handkerchief. He sits atop a brown box embossed with the word "Magic." $20.00–24.00

Dumbo the Mice Red clay. Black mice with gigantic ears and red bows have a shiny, black glaze. One sits, the other lies down. $10.00–12.00

Dumbo the Elephant in Red Clay Red clay. Japan. 1940s. This replica of Dumbo, the large-eared elephant, is made in red clay with a deep black glaze and red and gold highlights. $12.00–14.00

Chalkware Dumbo Chalkware. U.S.A. 1940s. Pink baby Dumbo sits, raises his trunk, and exhibits large ears. $14.00–20.00

Dumbo Ceramic. American Pottery Company. "Walt Disney" embossed. White Dumbo figurines have blue highlights, black shoes, and red mouths. These were also made with red trim. $24.00–30.00

Heckle and Jeckle Ceramic. Japan. Beautifully painted set of the black crows Heckle and Jeckle stand on green, pebbled bases. $25.00–35.00

Pluto Ceramic. American Pottery Company. "Walt Disney" embossed. Sitting Pluto has red and black trim. $24.00–30.00

Mickey and Minnie Ceramic. American Pottery Company. "Walt Disney" embossed. White figurines of Mickey and Minnie are highlighted in red, black, and blue. $24.00–30.00

Humpty Dumpty Ceramic. 1950s. A pair of "before" and "after" Humpty Dumpties sits on a wall. The "before" looks smug. The "after" is broken and frowns. $26.00–30.00

Mickey and Minnie on Bench Ceramic and wood. Disney. 1952. Minnie in pink and Mickey in blue pants and yellow shirt sit on a wooden bench. $40.00–50.00

Disneyland Bells Ceramic. Japan. Disney. White bells with golden trim have an image, in blue, of Cinderella's castle and the word "Disneyland" on the side. $14.00–20.00

Mouse from Dumbo Ceramic. Japan. 1950s. Small gray mice in circus master costumes resemble Dumbo's mouse friend from the Disney movie. One wears green jacket with blue cap, the other wears a pink jacket with a blue cap. $16.00–20.00

Chip and Dale Ceramic. Japan. 1960s. Replicas of the Disney characters feature one standing and one crawling chipmunk with the cartoon character's frolicsome faces. Chipmunks are rich brown with white stripe on face and belly. $14.00–18.00

Bambi Ceramic. Japan. 1960s. Replicas of Disney character depict a crouching Bambi, brown with white spots, sticking up its tail. $12.00–14.00

Bambi on Grassy Base Heavy ceramic. Japan. Disney knock-off. 1940s. Bambi and Feline sniff each other. They stand on brassy bases with embossed flowers. $20.00–24.00

Thumper Chalkware. U.S.A. 1940s. Small, white Thumper sits up on hind legs and begs. $14.00–20.00

Thumper in a Jacket Ceramic. Japan. White, standing Thumper with long eyelashes wears a blue jacket. $14.00–18.00

Bullwinkle the Moose Ceramic. Japan. 1960s. Identical figurines of Bullwinkle the Moose have deeply embossed yellow bodies with brown highlights and real plastic eyes. $12.00–14.00

Old MacDonald and His Wife Ceramic. Regal China. The head of Old MacDonald in a yellow hat is matched by the head of a girl in yellow pigtails with a blue-outlined collar. $22.00–30.00

Nursery Rhyme Miniatures by Parkcraft Bone china. Parkcraft Company. Twelve nursery rhyme sets were made by Parkcraft in miniature size. These are Little Boy Blue and the cow; Mary and her little lamb; Old King Cole and his fiddlers three (in one shaker); Little Jack Horner and plum pudding; Old Woman Who Lived in a Shoe and shoe; Jack and

Jill; the cow jumping over the moon and the cat playing the fiddle; two views of Humpty Dumpty; Little Miss Muffet and tuffet; Little Bo-Peep and sheep; Red Riding Hood and wolf; and Peter and pumpkin. $24.00–30.00

Goose and Golden Egg Ceramic. Japan. A white goose with a golden beak, yellow-tipped wings, and brown feet is flanked by a reflective, golden egg. $14.00–18.00

Goose with Golden, Embossed Egg Ceramic. Japan. A large white goose with a yellow beak and black eyes is teamed with a large, shiny golden egg that is embossed with a floral motif. $12.00–18.00

Goose and Two Golden Eggs Plastic. Japan. A large white goose with a yellow beak and black eyes is teamed with a large, shiny golden egg that is embossed with a floral motif. $12.00–18.00

Small Goose with Golden Egg China. Japan. A small white goose with a painted green wreath around her neck is teamed with a small, golden egg. $12.00–18.00

Mother Goose Condiment Set Ceramic. Japan. This four-piece set consists of a brown, grass-trimmed tray with the name of the character embossed on the side. On one side stands a red-hatted, black-dressed Mother Goose. On the other stands the white goose and between them is the white house with yellow thatched roof which opens to reveal the mustard jar. $30.00–40.00

Little Boy Blue and Haystack Ceramic. Japan. A supine Little Boy Blue sleeps under his yellow hat and fits into the opening of a yellow haystack. $20.00–30.00

Old Woman and Shoe Ceramic. Japan. A white Old Woman with pale blue hair and blue-trimmed dress is flanked by a brown shoe with a blue roof. $20.00–24.00

Humpty Dumpty on Stump Ceramic. Japan. 1940s. One Humpty Dumpty wears a yellow cap and shoes, and a black suit with red bow tie. The other Humpty Dumpty wears a red suit and black cap. Each sits on a brown stump. $18.00–24.00

White Humpty Dumpty Ceramic. Japan. 1940s. White Humpty Dumpty with short legs attached to a two-course brick wall has red hand-painted lips and pink cheeks. These are the only spots of color. $14.00–20.00

Humpty Dumpty Couple Ceramic. Japan. 1940s. Completely bald Humpty Dumpties have baby-doll eyes and round lips. He wears a green suit. She wears a red dress. The bodies are two-thirds the size of the heads. $12.00–16.00

Humpty Dumpty Couple Ceramic. Japan. 1950s. Splay-legged Humpty Dumpty couple features large, smiling faces set into colorful bodies. He wears a red hat and shoes to match and pink pants. She wears spotted cap, blue shoes, and yellow pants. $14.00–18.00

Humpty Dumpty Couple on Wall Ceramic. Japan. 1950s. Egg-headed, white Humpty Dumpty couple sits on green-topped circular bases that feature three courses of white bricks. She wears a yellow dress and a daisy on her bald head. He wears blue sleeves and trousers and red bow tie. $13.00–15.00

Tallboy Humpty Dumpty Couple Ceramic. Japan. 1950s. Tall (8½") Humpty Dumpty couple sits on yellow brick walls. They have very fetching expressions: large baby-doll eyes, grinning, red mouths, and tiny little hats perched at a rakish angle on their bald heads. Salt wears a green hat with a pink ribbon and a pink, polka-dotted dress. Pepper wears a pink hat and suit. $20.00–30.00

Humpty Dumpty Couple, Middle-Aged Version Ceramic. Japan. 1950s. White Humpty Dumpty couple has feet embossed onto a conical base that resembles poisonously green grass. She has a pink bonnet and dress and carries a red handbag. He has a green hat and carries a black cane. $14.00–18.00

Humpty Dumpty Ceramic. U.S.A. Identical figurines of Humpty Dumpty depict a white egg in white pants and short, splayed legs wearing black shoes and blue mittens and bow tie. $16.00–20.00

Humpty Dumpty, Plastic Plastic. U.S.A. Identical figurines depict a large-headed Humpty Dumpty with a sticklike body perched on a low, brick-textured wall, which, in turn, sits on an oval base embossed with the character's name. Humpty Dumpty wears a swirly, turban-style hat in a color that contrasts with the body color. These plastic shakers were available in a range of colors such as black, white, red, and yellow. $20.00–24.00

Humpty Dumpty and Wall Ceramic. U.S.A. This nester consists of a rectangular brown, yellow, and white speckled wall that includes the character's feet and legs. The egg, wearing a black bow tie, sits atop the wall. $18.00–24.00

Rub-a-Dub-Dub, Three Men in a Tub Ceramic. Japan. 1940s. This three-piece nester set consists of a base that is composed of a white stand to which is attached a brown tub, to which is attached a cook. On either side of him nestle the tailor and the candlestick maker. The title of the nursery rhyme is written on the side of the tub. $40.00–45.00

Hey Diddle Diddle, The Cat and the Fiddle Ceramic. Japan. A white and gray kitten with closed eyes smugly pokes its foot through a pink fiddle. The foot is visible through a hole in the pink violin. $18.00–22.00

Hey Diddle Diddle, The Cat and the Fiddle Ceramic. U.S.A. A standing, white Angora cat holds a brown fiddle, which rests on the floor. This is a nester. $20.00–24.00

Hey Diddle Diddle, The Cat and the Fiddle Ceramic. U.S.A. A gray, simplified cat holds a brown fiddle by supporting it on one foot and cradling it in one paw. This is a nester. $20.00–24.00

Cow and the Moon Ceramic. Kreiss Distributor. Japan. A yellow moon profile goes with a black and white standing cow. $20.00–24.00

Peter the Pumpkin Eater and Wife Ceramic. Arcadia, CA. Peter the Pumpkin Eater wears blue suspendered trousers and yellow hat. His wife's head emerges from a yellow pumpkin. $30.00–35.00

Goldilocks Ceramic. Relco. Japan. Mirror-images of Goldilocks with yellow hair, red bows, blue-black dress, and bouquet hold a book inscribed "The Three Bears." $25.00–30.00

Barber and Pig Ceramic. Japan. A green-jacketed barber holds a razor. The green-trousered, white-faced pig sits back on the barber chair. $18.00–24.00

Relco Nursery Rhyme Sets Ceramic. Relco. Japan. A series of six nursery rhyme characters depicts the following: Red Riding Hood, Goldilocks, Queen of Hearts, Little Bo-Peep, Little Miss Muffet, and Mary and her Little Lamb. They all have the name written on the front of the base. $25.00–30.00

The Hurdy Gurdy Man
Ceramic. Hull. 1940s–1950s. A mustachioed hurdy-gurdy man in a pink bow tie and striped trousers cranks up a yellow hurdy-gurdy, while a dressed monkey holds out a tin cup.
$40.00–45.00

Red Riding Hood Ceramic. Hull. China. White Red Riding Hood in a dress with floral motif has gold highlights. The same figurine was available in a mustard pot and cookie jar. $24.00–34.00

Mary and Her Lamb on Tray Ceramic. Japan. 1940s. A green tray holds Mary in a long red skirt and yellow apron, holding a book, and an embossed white lamb with a black bow. $20.00–24.00

Church Mouse and Church Ceramic. Japan. A gray mouse with a pointed face is teamed with a white, New England-style church. $18.00–22.00

Blackbird in Pie Ceramic. Japan. A small blackbird nestles on a slice of pie. $14.00–18.00

Rockaby Baby Ceramic. Japan. This nester consists of a yellow-diapered baby and a white crib with brown trim and a blue-edged blanket. The words "Rockaby Baby" are found on the crib. $30.00–34.00

Tinkerbell on Flower Ceramic. Japan. This nester set consists of a yellow-haired Tinkerbell in a dark blue dress with yellow wings. She perches on a pink flower. $18.00–24.00

Pinocchio and Girlfriend Heavy porcelain. Disney. Japan. Beautifully painted depictions of Pinocchio, sitting and waving a green-gloved hand, and his puppet girlfriend, who mimics his gesture. $40.00–45.00

Popeye and Olive Oyl Ceramic. Vandor imports. Japan. 1980. This large set depicts a scowling Popeye holding a can of spinach, and an admiring Olive Oyl. $50.00–60.00

Donald Duck Ceramic. Dan Brechner. Disney. Early 1960s. Disney's Donald Duck straightens out his red bow tie and stands on a round pedestal on which his name is inscribed. $42.00–48.00

Donald Duck Sitting Heavy porcelain. Leeds China. 1944–1954. Donald Duck sits, holding on to his feet, and rolls his eyes. The colors are muted. $45.00–50.00

Donald Duck and Daisy Duck Porcelain. Japan. These Disney knock-offs depict Donald in a bow tie, holding his yellow hand to his heart and wearing a flower-petal hat. Daisy Duck wears a white and blue scarf, carries a handbag, and sport an identical flower-petal hat. $30.00–35.00

Donald Duck on Raft Ceramic. Japan. A yawning Donald Duck in a dark navy sailor costume reclines on a pink, blue, and white raft. This is a nester set. $45.00–55.00

Mickey Mouse and Minnie Mouse Ceramic. Dan Brechner. Disney. Japan. Mickey Mouse wears a pink shirt, blue pants, and brown shoes and stands atop a stack of yellow books inscribed "Mickey Mouse." Minnie wears a yellow dress and pink shoes, and sits atop a stack of blue books inscribed "Minnie Mouse." $50.00–55.00

Snow White and the Seven Dwarfs Series Ceramic. Enesco Distributor. Japan. The Disney version of Snow White (in yellow skirt, blue body, pale-blue sleeves, and tall, white collar) is teamed in each set with one of the seven dwarfs as depicted in the Disney film. $45.00–55.00

Raggedy Ann and Andy Ceramic. Japan. 1970s. Raggedy Ann and Andy have brown embossed curly hair, baby-doll eyes, and red mouths. She wears a pink blouse with white dots and a blue short skirt. He wears a green shirt with white dots and blue pants. $22.00–24.00

Raggedy Ann and Andy in Blue Ceramic. U.S.A. White, heavy figurines of Raggedy Ann and Andy depict the characters sitting in a splay-legged position. They wear deep blue and white costumes and have reddish-brown hair. $35.00–40.00

Raggedy Ann and Andy Ceramic. Japan. 1970s. Standing Raggedy Ann and Andy have red, curly hair. She has flow-

Dick Tracy and Junior Chalkware. Late 1930s. A yellow-raincoated and behatted Dick Tracy is flanked by an orange-suited and crouching Junior. $100.00–110.00

ered, blue dress and white pinafore. He has red checkered shirt, blue pants, and red-and-white-striped socks. They stand on brown bases. $15.00–20.00

Raggedy Ann and Andy Ceramic. Japan. 1970s. Red-haired Raggedy Ann and Andy are sitting and have short, stumpy arms. She wears a deep blue dress and white pinafore. He wears a pale blue set of trousers. $16.00–18.00

Woody Woodpecker Ceramic. Signed "Walter Lantz." Busts of Woody Woodpecker show the bird clasping his hands and rolling his eyes. $40.00–45.00

Woody Woodpecker Ceramic. Squat Woody Woodpecker is white with impressionistic paint job: blotches of brown on the elbows, spots of blue on the feet, hands, and collar. $15.00–28.00

Ziggy and Dog Ceramic. Korea. Enesco Distributor. 1970s. Ziggy stands on a blue base. His dog stands on a slightly higher blue base. $22.00–24.00

Oswald and Willy Ceramic. Walter Lantz Productions, Inc. 1958. Oswald holds a cylindrical shaker, as does Willy. Both are on stands inscribed with their names. $40.00–45.00

Sylvester the Cat Ceramic. Warner Brothers. Identical figurines of Sylvester the Cat show him waving with one hand and smiling a wobbly smile. $40.00–45.00

Tweetie Bird Ceramic. Warner Brothers. Identical figurines of Tweetie bird have baby-doll eyes and red beaks. $30.00–40.00

Tweetie Bird Ceramic. Japan. Knock-offs of Warner Brother's character, this Tweetie Bird wears a white shirt with blue trim and a white bowler with a blue band. $18.00–22.00

Bug Bunny Ceramic. Warner Brothers. White Bugs Bunny waves one yellow-gloved hand, and holds a carrot in the other. $30.00–40.00

Yosemite Sam Ceramic. Warner Brothers. Yosemite Sam wears yellow hat and waves black six-shooter. $30.00–40.00

Snoopy and Woodstock Ceramic. Japan. 1970s. Snoopy wears a chef's toque. Yellow Woodstock also wears a toque and sits atop a trash can. $25.00–30.00

Snoopy in Pink Bow Ceramic. Japan. 1970s. Identical figurines of Snoopy in aviator glasses show him wearing a pink bow. $20.00–24.00

Pebbles, BamBam, and Dino Ceramic. Japan. Mid-1980s. This three-piece set consists of a green base to the middle of which is attached a deep blue Dino, hollowed out to hold toothpicks. On either side sit BamBam and Pebbles. $25.00–30.00

Pebbles and BamBam Ceramic. Vandor. 1980s. Pebbles and BamBam are either crawling or standing up. $18.00–20.00

Paul Bunyan and Stump Ceramic. Japan. Paul Bunyan, in blue pants, red shirt, and black boots, holds an axe. He is accompanied by a yellow stump with brown trim. $30.00–35.00

Paul Bunyan and Ox Babe Ceramic. Japan. A standing Paul Bunyan is matched with his ox Babe in brown. $30.00–35.00

Paul Bunyan and Babe Ceramic. Japan. A sitting Paul Bunyan is flanked by a blue ox. $30.00–35.00

Tom Sawyer and Huck Finn Ceramic. Japan. Tom Sawyer and Huck Finn, both in straw hats, either hold a cat up by its tail or carry school books. $25.00–30.00

Pirate and Treasure Chest Ceramic. Japan. A pirate in a yellow headscarf, black eye patch, white shirt, and gray pants sits cross-legged. The trunk by his side is embossed with a swirly pattern. $18.00–24.00

Beatrix Potter's Mice Ceramic. England. Beatrix Potter's mice are found in a variety of costumes. Usually, they are teamed as a couple with one trousered and one skirted version in complementary colors with gold highlights. The mice themselves are gray. $25.00–28.00

Beatrix Potter's Characters Ceramic. Japan. Japanese spin-offs of British-made Beatrix Potter characters include

Benjamin Bunny, Samuel Whiskers, Jemima Duck, and Mrs. Tiggywinkle. $16.00–20.00

Bonzo the Dog Porcelain. Japan. Late 1940s. Standing figurines depict Bonzo with one black ear and one golden ear, golden paws, and the words "I'm Salt" or "I'm Pep" on the tummy. $20.00–24.00

Angel and Devil Ceramic. Japan. A white angel with yellow hair and long robes is flanked by a red devil holding a black pitchfork. $15.00–18.00

Angel and Devil Ceramic. Japan. An angel in a long, wide skirt and yellow hair holds a black prayer book. The devil, with a boy's face, wears a red devil costume, huge white bow tie, and holds a black pitchfork. $18.00–24.00

Winnie the Pooh and Rabbit Ceramic. Brown Winnie the Pooh is teamed with yellow Rabbit. $30.00–40.00

Maggie and Jiggs Ceramic. Japan. 1930s. White set of Maggie and Jiggs is hand-painted. Maggie has yellow hair, blue and yellow dress with red trim. Jiggs wears black top hat and jacket over red vest. $40.00–50.00

Betty Boop and Bimbo in Wooden Boat Ceramic and wood. Vandor. 1980s. Betty Boop plays a guitar. Her dog Bimbo listens. Both nestle in a wooden boat. $20.00–22.00

Betty Boop on Roller Skates and Bimbo Ceramic. Vandor. 1980s. Betty Boop in green wears roller skates and sells a hamburger. Bimbo rides a red bumper car. $20.00–22.00

Shmoo Ceramic. Japan. Al Capp's Shmoo from the Li'l Abner strip has either a red or a blue bow tie. $18.00–24.00

Howdy Doody in Cadillac Convertible Nester Ceramic. Vandor. 1980s. Howdy Doody bust fits into a pink Cadillac convertible. $18.00–22.00

Kit and Kat Ceramic. Vandor. 1980s. Kit and Kat, each figurine labeled with the characters' names, are dressed as short-order cook (Kat) and waitress (Kit). $18.00–22.00

Moon Mullens Glass with plastic. The Moon Mullens character is rendered in glass with a black plastic bowler hat. $14.00–22.00

Wizard of Oz Series Ceramic. Clay Art. Portero, CA. 1989. To commemorate the fiftieth anniversary of the movie *The Wizard of Oz*, Clay Art produced the following sets of shakers: Wicked Witch of the West and Glinda, the good Witch of the North; Dorothy with Toto and the Scarecrow (one shaker) and Cowardly Lion and the Tin Man (one shaker). $18.00–22.00

Princess and the Frog Ceramic. Clay Art. Potero, CA. 1980s. A blue-dressed princess leans over to kiss a green frog sitting on a brown stump. $18.00–22.00

Paddington Bear Ceramic. Japan. 1970s. Two versions of Paddington Bear in blue raincoat and yellow hat show him standing and holding a suitcase or sitting with a pair of binoculars. $20.00–24.00

Garfield the Cat Ceramic. Japan. 1980s. The orange Garfield cat is shown cooking (in toque and apron) and eating (in bib and holding utensils). $20.00–24.00

Aladdin and the Lamp Ceramic. Japan. Aladdin, in white robes and turban and playing a golden lute, is flanked by a golden lamp. $20.00–24.00

Noah and the Ark Ceramic. Japan. A brown ark is teamed with a white Noah reading from a scroll. $24.00–28.00

Noah's Ark Condiment Set Ceramic. Japan. This three-piece set consists of a sugar bowl in the shape of Noah's ark. The lid lifts off. On the lid sits two shakers, each depicting a pair of animals: a rooster/goose combination and a cow/horse combination. $25.00–35.00

Smokey the Bear Ceramic. Japan. Smokey wears green pants and yellow hat. One holds bucket, the other holds a shovel. $18.00–24.00

Calico Dog and Cat
Ceramic. Japan. 1950s.
Yellow cat with blue dots has
an orange bow. The yellow
puppy has blue checks.
$15.00–18.00

Mermaids Ceramic. Japan. Pale pink, bare-breasted mermaids caress their brown hair. $12.00–18.00

Spuds McKenzie Ceramic. Sarsaparilla. 1980s. White dogs with black-tipped ears lean on yellow bones. $18.00–22.00

Rocking Horse Ceramic. Josefs Originals. 1980s. White rocking horses on red rockers have red saddles and red and green plaid blankets. $10.00–12.00

"Stuffed" Horses Ceramic. U.S.A. 1950s. Stuffed horse shakers have prominent stitch marks and appear to be pieced together from a variety of colorful fabrics. These are available in pastel or primary combinations with floral or geometric prints. $18.00–24.00

"Stuffed" Elephants Ceramic. Japan. 1950s. Stuffed elephant shakers have prominent stitch marks and appear to have been pieced together from a variety of colorful fabrics. They are available standing on all fours or rearing up. $18.00–24.00

"Stuffed" Donkeys Ceramic. U.S.A. 1950s. Stuffed donkey shakers have prominent stitch marks and appear to have been pieced together from a variety of colorful fabrics. $18.00–24.00

"Stuffed" Teddy Bears Ceramic. U.S.A. 1950s. Sitting, stuffed teddy bears have prominent stitch marks and appear to have been pieced together from a variety of colorful fabrics. $18.00–24.00

"Stuffed" Bunnies Ceramic. U.S.A. 1950s. Sitting, stuffed bunnies have prominent stitch marks and appear to have been pieced together from a variety of colorful fabrics. $18.00–24.00

"Stuffed" Plaid Dogs or Cats Ceramic. Japan. 1950s. Sitting dogs or cats have subtle stitch marks and are painted in a plaid design. Salt is white with red, pepper is black with yellow or white. $15.00–18.00

"Stuffed" Floral Bunnies Ceramic. Japan. 1950s. Running, white bunnies with subtle stitch marks have pink ears and bows. $15.00–18.00

Bears on Wheels Ceramic. Josefs Originals. 1980s. Brown teddy bears in red bows with white dots stand on green bases on red wheels. $10.00–12.00

Teddy Bears Ceramic. Japan. 1950s. White teddy bears sit, splay-legged, and wear colorful bows around their necks. Their round ears are the same color as their claws. These bears come in various color combinations. $10.00–12.00

Black Teddy Bears Red clay. Black teddy bears have golden and red highlights. One lies, resting on a paw, the other sits, splayed-legged, and holds up its hands. $10.00–12.00

Elephants Lusterware. Lusterware elephants are made to look as though they were assembled from simple geometrical forms. The head is a ball, the trunk a trio of increasingly bigger balls, the ears two triangles, and so forth. The elephants are painted with a colorful spiral design and have red, blue, and yellow ornamentation. $12.00–14.00

Elephants Ceramic. Japan. 1950s. White elephants are extremely simplified and look as though they might have been sewn. They have upturned trunks and pink, red, and black ornamentation, borders of gingham squares. $10.00–12.00

Flowered Elephants Ceramic. Japan. 1950s. White elephants with floral bodies and pink cheeks stand on their hind legs. $10.00–12.00

Elephants Ceramic. Japan. 1950s. Very shiny elephants, one pink, the other gray, look as though they might be intended to resemble squeak toys. Their trunks stick out, and their fanlike ears protrude on either side of their heads. $10.00–12.00

Stitched Elephants Ceramic. Japan. 1950s. White elephants have bodies fashioned to appear as though they had been sewn. Stitch marks run along legs, ears, and heads. Pink ceramic bows are at the chins. $12.00–14.00

Polka-Dot Cats Ceramic. 1950s. White, stylized cats are painted with yellow circles outlined in blue and have stripes in the same color combination on their tails. $10.00–12.00

Stuffed Dog Ceramic. Japan. 1950s. White dogs with large baby-doll eyes and yellow V-shaped snouts have ears outlined in green stitching and a design of dots and zig-zags on their bodies. $12.00–14.00

Drummers Ceramic. Japan. 1940s. Stylized figurines of uniformed drummers emerging from their round drum sets are white with an orange and green costumed drummer. $14.00–18.00

Tin Soldiers Ceramic. Japan. 1940s. Tin soldiers, marching and holding guns, have childish faces. $14.00–20.00

"Wooden" Lions Ceramic. Japan. 1950s. Brown lions with pink faces and black manes have bodies that appear to have been cut out of wood. $16.00–20.00

Raggedy Ann and Andy Dolls Ceramic. Japan. 1950s. Large shakers represent Raggedy Ann and Andy dolls with prominent black stitching along arms, tummies, and faces. $35.00–40.00

CELEBRITIES

Benjamin Franklin Ceramic. Parkcraft. Taneycomo Ceramic Factory. Hollister, MO. Brown bust of Benjamin Franklin is teamed with a white scroll inscribed with his vital statistics. This is one in a series of seven famous people by Parkcraft. $18.00–25.00

Charles Lindbergh Ceramic. Parkcraft. Taneycomo Ceramic Factory. Hollister, MO. Orange and buff bust of Charles Lindbergh is teamed with a white scroll inscribed with his vital statistics. This is one in a series of seven famous people by Parkcraft. $18.00–25.00

Betsy Ross Ceramic. Parkcraft. Taneycomo Ceramic Factory. Hollister, MO. Buff, red, and blue bust of Betsy Ross is teamed with a white scroll inscribed with her vital statistics. This is one in a series of seven famous people by Parkcraft. $18.00–25.00

George Washington Ceramic. Parkcraft. Taneycomo Ceramic Factory. Hollister, MO. White bust of George Washington is teamed with a white scroll inscribed with his vital statistics. This is one in a series of seven famous people by Parkcraft. $18.00–25.00

Christopher Columbus Ceramic. Parkcraft. Taneycomo Ceramic Factory. Hollister, MO. Orange bust of Christopher Columbus is teamed with a white scroll inscribed with this vital statistics. This in one in a series of seven famous people by Parkcraft. $18.00–25.00

Will Rogers Ceramic. Parkcraft. Taneycomo Ceramic Factory. Hollister, MO. Buff, orange, and blue bust of Will Rogers is teamed with a white scroll inscribed with this vital statistics. This is one in a series of seven famous people by Parkcraft. $18.00–25.00

Marilyn Monroe Ceramic. Clay Art. 1980s. Two three-quarter figurines of Marilyn Monroe depict her in famous poses. One wears black strapless gown, the other, white halter top. $18.00–20.00

Marilyn Monroe in Cake Ceramic. Clay Art. A Marilyn Monroe look-alike in black gloves and strapless gown erupts out of the top of two-layer cake. She is attached to the top layer. The bottom layer is another shaker. The cake is white and festooned with pink. $16.00–20.00

Laurel and Hardy Heads on Tray Composition. Greece. Dark brown heads of Laurel and Hardy with black hats sit in a brown tray and black and white bow ties. $18.00–30.00

Laurel and Hardy Heads Ceramic. White ceramic heads of Laurel and Hardy have pink bow ties, black collars, and bowlers with gold bands. Their faces are fairly realistically detailed. $18.00–22.00

Betsy Ross and George Washington Ceramic. Japan. A blond, blue-dressed Betsy Ross holds a colonial flag in one hand. The red-frocked, black-hatted George Washington holds up a scroll with the words "Bill of Rights" inscribed on its face. $10.00–14.00

Herbert Hoover and Birthplace Ceramic. Rounded, trapezoidally shaped shakers are decorated with blue bust portrait of President Herbert Hoover and with a drawing of his birthplace. $12.00–16.00

J.F. Kennedy and Wife Ceramic. Rounded, trapezoidally shaped shakers are decorated with bust portraits of President John F. Kennedy and Mrs. John F. Kennedy. $12.00–16.00

Lyndon Johnson and Wife Ceramic. Rounded, trapezoidally shaped shakers are decorated with bust portraits of President Lyndon B. Johnson and Mrs. Lyndon B. Johnson. $12.00–16.00

Venus de Milo Ceramic. 1960s. The famous Venus de Milo is reproduced here in an all-white and an all-black version. $12.00–16.00

Big Boop and Betty Boop Ceramic. Japan. 1940s. Betty Boop in red skirt and chef's hat is teamed with Big Boop in black pants and chef's hat. $18.00–20.00

Priscilla and John Alden Ceramic. Finely detailed representations of Priscilla and John Alden have "Boston Mass." inscribed on the brown bases. Priscilla wears brown with a white apron. John is in dark blue with brown hat. $12.00–14.00

Priscilla and John Alden Ceramic. Small (3½") versions of Priscilla and John Alden stand on square bases. Priscilla wears lavender cape over her beige dress. John wears red cape over his beige clothing. $10.00–12.00

Cartoonish Pilgrim Couple Metal. Small (3") stylized figurines of pilgrim couple shows girl in gray extending her arms to the boy in gray with a black puddin'-head haircut. $10.00–12.00

Priscilla and John Alden Ceramic. Large (5½") figurines of Priscilla and John Alden stand on white bases inscribed with their names. Priscilla wears a pink dress and blue cape and carries a black prayer book. John wears typical brown pilgrim costume. $12.00–14.00

General Eisenhower Bust Nodder Ceramic. 1950s. A grinning head of General Eisenhower is inserted into the brown, uniformed bust. The bottom says "I Like Ike. $25.00–35.00

Carter Peanut Faces Ceramic. 1970s. Beige peanuts with the famous Jimmy Carter smile are marked "S" or "P." $16.00–20.00

Plains, Georgia Shakers Ceramic. 1970s. Cylindrical, white bottles with "hourglass" stoppers bear the smiling peanut figurine beneath the words "Plains, Ga." and over the words "Home of Jimmy Carter." $10.00–14.00

Presidential Cylinders Ceramic. White cylinders, pinched in two-thirds up the side, bear decals with images of various presidents, among them Harry S. Truman, D.D. Eisenhower, Grover Cleveland, F.D. Roosevelt, Thomas Jefferson, and Andrew Jackson. $10.00–12.00

Presidential Cylinders Ceramic. Bell-shaped cylinders, in white, bear decals of Robert and John Kennedy, Richard Nixon, and Richard Nixon and Pat Nixon. $8.00–12.00

John F. Kennedy in Rocking Chair Ceramic. Japan. This two-piece set consists of a rocking chair in which nestles a figurine of John F. Kennedy in white shirt and black tie. $35.00–45.00

Presidential Urn Shakers Ceramic. White, urn-shaped shakers with gold trim have decals of presidents and their wives. $14.00–18.00

Presidential Truncated Obelisk Shakers Ceramic. White ceramic shakers in the shape of truncated obelisks are ornamented with gold and bear the decal portraits of presidents and their wives. $12.00–14.00

Presidential Truncated Obelisk Shakers Ceramic. Large (5½") white ceramic shakers in the shape of truncated obelisks with rounded tops are ornamented with gold and decal portraits of presidents and their wives. $14.00–16.00

Republican Elephant and Democratic Donkey Ceramic. Japan. A laughing gray elephant falls back on the ground, raising its trunk and flapping back its ears. The gray donkey sits back and opens wide its mouth, revealing white teeth and a salmon tongue. $30.00–35.00

Hear No Evil, See No Evil Monkeys Ceramic. Japan. 1950s. Pale yellow Capuchin monkeys sit. One covers its ears, the other covers its eyes. $20.00–24.00

Rodin's "The Thinker" as Monkey Ceramic. Japan. 1950s. This nester sets consists of a wood stump on which sits a yellowish monkey in the pose of "The Thinker." $14.00–18.00

Katzenjammer Kids Goebel. 1920s. Hans and Fritz are featured in their striped and checkered trousers. $25.00–35.00

ADVERTISING AND PROMOTIONAL GIVEAWAYS

Aunt Jemima and Uncle Moses, Quaker Oats Company Plastic. Fiedler and Fiedler Mold and Die Works. Dayton, OH. 1950s. Black "Aunt Jemima" in red kerchief and dress, white apron and neckerchief, holds a white plate of pancakes. Black, bald "Uncle Mose" has white eyebrows, wears a red frock coat over a white shirt, yellow bow tie, and yellow trousers, and holds a black top hat. F & F logo is imprinted on the bottom of each piece which was produced to promote the Aunt Jemima Pancake Mix. Small size. $36.00–44.00

Ball Mason Minis Glass and metal. Matching miniatures of Ball Mason canning jars, complete with embossed logos. $30.00–38.00

Barbarossa Beer Bottles Plastic. Dark brown elongated beer bottles have gold "Barbarossa" labels. $16.00–19.00

Bill's Novelty Beer Bottles Glass and metal. U.S.A. Small, clear glass bottles, topped with metal caps, have elongated shape and red, white, and blue labels reading "Bill's Novelty Beer" and "Souvenir, Milwaukee, Wis." $10.00–12.00

Blatz Pilsener Beer Bottles Plastic and metal. Edward A. Muth & Sons, Inc. Buffalo, NY. Auburn elongated plastic bottles (4") with gold-tone metal caps. Body and neck labels in black, red, and gold read "Blatz Pilsener Beer." $32.00–40.00

Blatz Pilsener Beer Bottles Plastic and metal. Edward A. Muth & Sons, Inc. Buffalo, NY. Auburn squat plastic bottles (3") with metal caps and beige, black, and red labels bearing "Blatz Beer" logo. $24.00–36.00

Aunt Jemima and Uncle Moses, Quaker Oats Company Ceramic. Fiedler and Fiedler Mold and Die Works. Dayton, OH. 1950s. Black "Aunt Jemima" in red kerchief and dress, and white apron and neckerchief, holds a white plate of pancakes. Black, bald "Uncle Moses" has white eyebrows, wears a red frock coat over a white shirt, yellow bow tie, and trousers, and holds a black top hat. F&F logo is imprinted on the bottom of each piece, which was produced to promote the Aunt Jemima Pancake Mix. $44.00–50.00

Acme Beer Bottles Plastic and metal. Edward A. Muth & Sons, Inc. Buffalo, NY. Auburn, plastic squat bottles (3") with metal caps and yellow, navy, red "ACME Beer" label. $16.00–24.00

Blatz Old Heidelberg Beer Bottles Plastic and metal. Edward A. Muth & Sons, Inc. Buffalo, NY. Burnt sienna squat plastic bottles (3") with metal caps and navy, gold, and red labels inscribed with "Blatz Old Heidelberg Beer." $16.00–24.00

Blatz Pilsener Beer Bottles Plastic and metal. Edward A Muth & Sons, Inc. Buffalo, NY. Auburn elongated plastic bottles (4") with metal caps. Body and neck labels in navy, red, and yellow read "Blatz Pilsener Beer." $16.00–24.00

Budweiser Beer Bottles Plastic and metal. Edward A Muth & Sons, Inc. Buffalo, NY. Auburn elongated plastic bottles (4") with gold-tone metal caps have paper labels bearing "Budweiser Beer" slogan. $16.00–24.00

Bud Man Beer Bottles Ceramic. U.S.A. 1970s. "Bud Man" shakers, sold in Busch Gardens in 1970, depict a bulbous-nosed hooded, masked, and caped hero with turned-in-at-the-toes feet. $35.00–55.00

Dehler's Beer Bottles Plastic and metal. Edward A. Muth & Sons, Inc. Buffalo, NY. Auburn elongated plastic bottles (4") with metal caps. Red neck labels and white, red, and gold body label with "Dehler's Beer" logo. $24.00–26.00

E & O Pilsner Beer Bottles Plastic and metal. Edward A. Muth & Sons, Inc. Buffalo, NY. Burnt sienna elongated bottles (4¼") with black metal caps. Black, gold, and beige labels read "E & O Pilsner Beer." $75.00–125.00

Falstaff Beer Bottles Plastic and metal. Edward A. Muth & Sons, Inc. Buffalo, NY. Auburn elongated plastic bottles (4") with black metal caps. Body and neck labels in beige, red, and gold bearing "Falstaff Beer" logo. $10.00–16.00

Falstaff Pale Beer Bottles Plastic and metal. Edward A. Muth & Sons, Inc. Buffalo, NY. Bright auburn elongated plastic bottles (4¼") with metal caps and beige, red, and black labels in shield shape bearing "Falstaff Pale Beer" logo. $40.00–60.00

Fort Pitt Beer Bottles Plastic and metal. Edward A. Muth & Sons, Inc. Buffalo, NY. Dark auburn elongated plastic bottles (4") with metal caps. Neck and body labels in gold, beige, and rust bear motto reading "Fort Pitt Special." $16.00–24.00

Fort Pitt Beer Bottles Plastic and metal. Edward A Muth & Sons, Inc. Buffalo, NY. Dark brown plastic squat bottles (3") with metal caps and red, gold, and yellow "Fort Pitt Special Beer" labels. $10.00–16.00

Koehler's Beer Bottles Plastic. Squat brown beer bottles with black lids have "Koehler's" labels. $14.00–16.00

Koehler's Beer Bottles Glass. Elongated brown beer bottles with brown caps have "Koehler's" labels. $14.00–16.00

Lone Star Beer Bottles Glass and plastic. U.S.A. Clear glass bottles with white plastic caps have stencilled in red the Lone Star label. $10.00–14.00

Miller High Life Beer Bottles Plastic and metal. Edward A. Muth & Sons, Inc. Buffalo, NY. Yellow tapering plastic bottles (4") with metal caps and gold neck bands, bold neck, and body labels bearing "Miller High Life" imprint. $24.00–32.00

Old Export Beer Bottles Plastic and metal. Edward A. Muth & Sons, Inc. Buffalo, NY. Auburn elongated plastic bottles (4") with metal caps. Neck and body labels are in white and brown and bear "Old Export" motto. $16.00–24.00

Old Gold Beer Bottles Plastic and metal. Edward A. Muth & Sons, Inc. Buffalo, NY. Auburn elongated plastic bottles (4¼") with metal caps. Neck and body labels in yellow, gold, red with "Old Gold Special" motto. $100.00–150.00

Old Milwaukee Beer Bottles Metal. U.S.A. Silver beer cans with perforated tops are wrapped in the "Old Milwaukee" labels. $10.00–14.00

Old Shay Ale Beer Bottles Plastic and metal. Edward A. Muth & Sons, Inc. Buffalo, NY. Dark auburn elongated plastic bottles (4") with black metal caps. Oval neck and body labels in gold, red, yellow, and black bear words "Old Shay Ale." $16.00–24.00

Old Shay Beer Bottles Plastic and metal. Edward A. Muth & Sons, Inc. Buffalo, NY. Dark brown squat plastic bottles (3") with metal caps and black, gold, red label bearing "Old Shay Beer" slogan. $24.00–32.00

Pabst Blue Ribbon Beer Bottles Plastic and metal. Edward A. Muth & Sons, Inc. Buffalo, NY. Auburn elongated plastic bottles (4") with gold-tone metal caps. Body and neck labels bear blue-ribbon "Pabst Blue Ribbon" motto in blue, white, and gold. $16.00–24.00

Piels Real Draft Beer Bottles Plastic. Brown beer bottles with white lids have "Piels Real Draft" labels. $14.00–16.00

Ruppert Beer Bottles Plastic and metal. Edward A. Muth & Sons, Inc. Buffalo, NY. Bright auburn elongated plastic bottles (4") with metal caps. Neck and body labels in auburn, red, and yellow bear "Ruppert Beer" logo. $16.00–24.00

Schlitz Beer Bottles Plastic and metal. Edward A. Muth & Sons, Inc. Buffalo, NY. Burnt sienna elongated bottles (4") with brass-colored metal caps. Brown and gold labels read "Schlitz Beer." $24.00–32.00

Schlitz Beer Bottles Plastic and metal. Burnt sienna elongated plastic bottles (4") with metal caps. Neck and body labels are in white and brown rectangle emblazoned with the "Schlitz" logo. $6.00–10.00

Schlitz Beer Cans Miniature versions of Schlitz beer cans nestle in a cardboard holder. $8.00–10.00

Utica Club Brewery Beer Steins Ceramic. 1950s–1960s. Webco. Brazil. Replicas of "Schultz" (large) and "Dooley" (small), the figurative old steins made by the Utica Club Brewery, feature tops crafted to resemble the faces of characters. $16.00–18.00

Big Boy Ceramic. The pert, red-haired "Big Boy" of the eponymous restaurant chain holds on to his red and white checkered overalls. $25.00–30.00

Black and White Scotch Ceramic. U.S.A. The black and white terriers are mascots of Black and White Scotch. $12.00–16.00

Blue Nun Wine Ceramic. U.S.A. Early 1980s. Matching Blue Nuns in white headdresses and collars hold baskets of green grapes. The white bases are inscribed with the words, "BLUE NUN. Correct with any dish." $22.00–30.00

Bob's Big Boy Ceramic. Bob's Big Boy is available in two different sizes. The checks in Bob's outfit differ somewhat in the small and the large sizes.

Bride and Groom Radio Show Ceramic. U.S.A. 1930s. White bride and groom have black detailing (eyes and hair) with the words "Bride and Groom" written on the bottom, identifying the set as a premium from the "Bride and Groom" radio show. $30.00–35.00

Bromo Seltzer Glass. U.S.A. Cobalt-blue glass bottles with black stoppers are embossed with "Bromo Seltzer." $12.00–15.00

Burt and Harry Peil Ceramic. 1970s. Burt and Harry Peil, the mascots of Peil's Beer, are dressed in black. Both bald, Bert is short in a yellow and red vest, while Harry is tall and bow-tied. The set is very scarce. $28.00–33.00

Burton's Whiskey Glass and metal. Brown whiskey bottles with metallic lids have "Burton's 51" labels. $10.00–12.00

Campbell Kids, Campbell Soup Company Plastic. Fiedler and Fiedler Mold and Die Works. Dayton, OH. 1950s. Boy and girl "Campbell Kids" in red outfits with white aprons and white chef hats emblazoned with a red "C" on the brim. The girl holds a soup spoon and bowl, while the boy holds a

Carey Salt Cardboard and plastic. Scaled-down versions of the Carey Salt box have red lids. $8.00–12.00

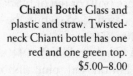

Chianti Bottle Glass and plastic and straw. Twisted-neck Chianti bottle has one red and one green top. $5.00–8.00

spoon. The "F & F" logo is embossed on the bottom of the figures. $36.00–40.00

Campbell Kids Ceramic. U.S.A. 1950s. Figural set of Campbell Kids was made in the 1950s. $18.00–24.00

Campbell Kids Porcelain. U.S.A. 1983. Whitish-ivory, 3" high shakers are trimmed in gold and decorated with a Campbell Kid (one boy, one girl chef) as they appeared in the 1930s. $25.00–33.00

Campbell Soup Company Wooden Cans Wood. U.S.A. 1950s. Wooden salt and pepper mills, 5¾" tall, were painted over to represent Campbell Soup cans. $18.00–22.00

Campbell Soup Company Glass Glass. U.S.A. 1980s. The clear glass shakers, 3½" tall, have "Campbell" written in red. $8.00–10.00

Campbell Soup Company Soup Cans Plastic. U.S.A. 1980s. Plastic shakers, 3½" tall, closely resemble the Campbell's soup can. $10.00–12.00

Campbell Soup Company Barbecue Cans U.S.A. 1980s. The classic Campbell's Soup can, clearly labeled "Salt" and "Pepper," is identified as "Barbecue." $16.00–20.00

Cathedral Ink Glass. U.S.A. 1970s. Deep red glass bottles with white stoppers are replicas of the "Cathedral Ink Bottle." $6.00–8.00

Chicken Of the Sea Ceramic. 1940s. Matching pair of open-mouthed tuna, one blue, one yellow, embossed with flippers, scales, and gills. The words "Chicken of the Sea" are imprinted on the bottom. $20.00–24.00

Coca-Cola Bottles Ceramic. U.S.A. Unusual ceramic replicas of Coca-Cola bottles are painted red and silver. $15.00–18.00

Coke Cans Metal. 1970s. Accurate replicas of red and white Coke cans have silver tops. $8.00–12.00

Colonel Sanders' Kentucky Fried Chicken Ceramic. A white replica of Kentucky Fried Chicken mascot Colonel Sanders, stands on a white base (salt) or red or black one (pepper). The black-based set is dated 1965, while the red-based carries the date 1971. $20.00–30.00

Coppertone Suntan Lotion Ceramic. U.S.A. 1940s. The signature "Coppertone Suntan Lotion" girl, pink ribbons on her pigtails and feet in oversize pink slippers, turns back to look at the yellow terrier pulling at her panties. $20.00–24.00

Dairy Queen Cones Ceramic. Vanilla (salt) and chocolate (pepper) ice cream swirled with the distinctive Dairy Queen curl atop yellow "Safe-T-Cups." $16.00–20.00

Dairy Queen Dutch Girls Ceramic. Matching Dutch girls in blue dresses and caps, white aprons and blouses, have yellow hair and hold up their white arms. "Dairy Queen, trademark" is on the black. $12.00–15.00

Elmer and Elsie Ceramic. U.S.A. 1940s. Waist-up figurines of Elsie and Elmer, the Borden Company mascots, have names written on bottom of base. Both look pensive. Elmer wears a chef's hat. $35.00–45.00

Elsie the Borden Cow Nodder
Ceramic. U.S.A. 1940s. Elsie's head balances on her bust. The yellow daisy ring is part of the neck. $32.00–36.00

Elmer and Elsie Ceramic. U.S.A. 1940s. Tan versions of Borden's Elsie and Elmer are highlighted in a soft shade of brown. $32.00–42.00

Exxon Tiger Plastic. U.S.A. Whirley Industries. Warren, PA. 1970s. The Exxon Company tiger is represented in this cleverly designed shaker composed of a rectangular box as the body to which are affixed a tail and a plastic head. A black button in the middle of the back activates the salt and pepper dispensers. $15.00–20.00

Film Canisters Plastic. Hall Brothers, Morgan, UT. Snap-on salt and pepper tops sit atop black film canisters. $6.00–8.00

Firestone Tires Ceramic. Matched pair of whitewall tires with black outer rim, yellow body, white hubcaps with yellow-orange centers. The logo "Firestone" is inscribed on the upper whitewalls. $12.00–16.00

Flour Fred Ceramic. England. The "Flour-Fred" mascot in black with white chef's hat is a mustard pot and is teamed with black and white pepper shakers and matching pie bird. $20.00–25.00

Esso Gas Pumps Plastic. The blue and white and red and white gas pumps have the "Esso" label on the front. $20.00–25.00

Fido and Fifi, Ken-L Ration Pet Food Company Plastic. Fiedler and Fiedler Mold and Die Works. Dayton, OH. Yellow "Fido" dog and black "Fifi" cat sit up on their haunches and lick their muzzles with red tongues. "F&F" logo is inscribed on white on the top. $20.00–24.00

Filter Queen Plastic. U.S.A. Red plastic canister vacuum cleaners have "Filter Queen" inscribed in white on the top. $12.00–18.00

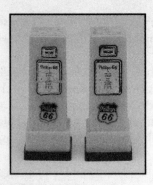

Gas Pumps, Phillips 66 Plastic. Deco-inspired red plastic pumps have the Phillips 66 label on the front. Gas pumps were made in a number of shapes and colors and carried the labels of gasoline companies. $20.00–25.00

Gulf Gas Pumps Plastic. Orange gasoline pumps have Gulf decal. $20.00–25.00

Mobil Gas Pumps Plastic. White and red gasoline pumps bear the Mobil gas label. $20.00–25.00

Pure Gas Pumps Plastic. Red and white gas pumps have "Pure" decal. $20.00–25.00

Self Service Gas Pumps Ceramic. 1970s. White, new-style gasoline pumps with coiled hoses on the side bear the label "Self-Service" and "Super Premium Salt" and "Super Premium Pepper." $16.00–20.00

Sinclair Gas Pumps Plastic. White and red gasoline pumps bear Sinclair label. $20.00–25.00

General Electric Coil Top Refrigerator Milk glass and metal. 1920s. White milk glass replicas of the G.E. Coil Top Refrigerator with metal caps made to resemble coil tops and G.E. logo stickers set in the front. $70.00–80.00

General Electric Two-Door Refrigerator Plastic. 1960s. Aluminum Housewares Company. Tan, gold, or cream two-door refrigerator with ice-maker in upper door has "wood-grained" door handles. $25.00–30.00

General Electric Coil Top Refrigerator Plastic. 1960s. Aluminum Housewares Company. White old-fashioned, coil-top refrigerator has "silver" hinges and handle. $25.00–30.00

Greyhound Buses Metal. 1930s. Scaled-down replicas of Greyhound Scenicruiser buses, complete with movable rubber wheels, and painted blue, white, and gold. $36.00–50.00

Greyhound Buses Ceramic. 1940s. Red, white, and blue double-decker greyhound buses are inscribed with their name on the side. $30.00–35.00

Guckenheimer Whiskey Glass and metal. Brown glass replicas of Guckenheimer Whiskey bear the appropriate labels and silver screw-on caps. $8.00–12.00

Hamm's Bears Ceramic. The bears are mascots of Hamm's Beer.

Handy Flame Ceramic. 1940s. Matching pair of blue gas flames, tear-drop shaped, with triangular black eyes, round cheeks and noses, and smiling, red lips. "Handy Flame" is impressed on most sets. $40.00–44.00

Harvestore Silos Ceramic. U.S.A. Matching royal blue Harvestore silos are inscribed, at the top, with the works "A O Smith Harvestore System."

Heinz Ketchup Bottles Plastic. Hong Kong. Late 1970s. Matching red plastic tapering bottles with white plastic caps and labels reading "Heinz Tomato Ketchup." $6.00–10.00

Heinz Shakers Glass and metal. Squat glass bottles, not replicas of the ketchup bottles, have silver, bell-shaped caps and bear red "Heinz" logo. $6.00–8.00

Hershey Chocolate Kisses Ceramic. Matching pair of chocolate Hershey kisses in the distinctive cone shape, one embossed "S," the other "P." $12.00–18.00

Hershey Milk Chocolate Mugs Ceramic. 1970s. White ceramic jugs have brown "Hershey's Milk Chocolate" labels wrapped around their middles and the words "Salt" and "Pepper" written on the white mound lids. $12.00–15.00

Hershey's Unsweetened Baking Chocolate Ceramic. Realistic renditions of packages of Hershey's Unsweetened Baking Chocolate have "Salt" and "Pepper" inscribed on the white bases. $12.00–15.00

Italian Swiss Colony Chianti Glass, metal, and straw. Clear glass Chianti bottles in straw bottles rest on green or red bases. $4.00–6.00

Kahiki Heads Ceramic. U.S.A. Brown Easter Island head sculptures are from the Kahiki restaurant chain. $14.00–18.00

Kellogg's Rice Krispies, Snap and Pop Ceramic. Japan. Kellogg's Rice Krispies mascots Snap and Pop are brightly colored elves with chef's toque ("Snap") and brimmed cap ("Pop"). The third member of the Kellogg's Rice Krispies clique, Crackle, was originally made as the mustard dish. $35.00–40.00

Ken-L Ration Dog and Cat Plastic. Fiedler & Fiedler Mold and Die Works Company. Dayton, OH. The yellow puppy with red tongue and black and white cat both sit up and beg with eager, mouth-watering expressions on their faces. $20.00–24.00

Lancers White and Rose Wines Plastic. Replicas of Lancers White and Rose wine bottles, in rust and gray, carry appropriate labels. $8.00–10.00

Lenny Lennox Ceramic. U.S.A. 1950s. Lenny Lennox, the captivating mascot of Lennox furnaces, wears a blue shirt and gray trousers. $40.00–50.00

Lightbulbs Glass and metal. U.S.A. Replicas of clear glass lightbulbs have metal screw-on caps at the socket end. $10.00–12.00

Luzianne Mammy, Luzianne Coffee Company Plastic. 1950s. Fiedler & Fiedler Mold and Die Works. Dayton, OH. Matching pair of black "Luzianne Mammy" figurines in black-and-white-striped kerchief, yellow shirt, and green, floor-length skirt, holding a tray with a blue and white speckled coffeepot and steaming cup of coffee. "F & F" is embossed on the bottom and the words "Luzianne Mammy" are impressed on the figurines. $70.00–86.00

Luzianne Mammy, Luzianne Coffee Company Plastic. Reproductions of the original Luzianne Mammy have bright red skirts. $12.00–14.00

Magic Chef Plastic. 1940s. Matching Magic Chef plastic chefs have white bodies, with hands clasped on their bellies, black pencil moustaches, and bright red, octagonal chef's toques. A red crown with "S" or "P" is in the bottom center of their aprons. $20.00–26.00

Mason Jars Glass and metal. U.S.A. Miniature versions of the Mason glass canning jar have metal screw-on caps. $12.00–14.00

Mr. Peanut U.S.A. Salt and pepper shakers in the shape of the Planters Peanut Company mascot have been produced since the 1930s in a variety of sizes, colors, and materials, including ceramic and plastic. The design of Mr. Peanut has changed, with the monocle migrating from the right eye to the left and the string lengthening. Both eyes have variously been visible or one has been concealed by the monocle. Leg and arm positions have been altered, the top hat size has been changed, the nose modified, the spat buttons have disappeared. The body has been trimmed and the smile has broadened. Cost depends on style, date, and condition. $8.00–40.00

Mr. Peanut Plastic. U.S.A. Late 1930s. The top-hatted mascot of the Planters Peanut Company is 3⅛" tall and comes in red, yellow, peach, blue, pink, silver, gold, creamy yellow, and black. $8.00–12.00

Mr. Peanut Plastic. U.S.A. Late 1930s. Mr. Peanut, 4½" tall, was available in red, yellow, peach, blue, pink, silver, gold, creamy yellow and black. $8.00–10.00

Mr. Peanut Ceramic. Yellow-bodied and spatted Mr. Peanut has black arms, top hat, and shoes. He has monocle in right eye. $20.00–25.00

Mr. Peanut Ceramic. This 4½" tall Mr. Peanut has a rhinestone monocle in his left eye. $55.00–65.00

Mr. Peanut on the "Half Shell" Ceramic. U.S.A. Typical Mr. Peanut stands on the lower half of a peanut shell. $20.00–22.00

Mitchell's Dairy Milk Bottles Glass and metal. U.S.A. 1940s–1950s. Mitchell's Dairy milk bottles appeared in two

Straight-Legged Mr. Peanut Ceramic. U.S.A. Straight-legged Mr. Peanut holds his cane in front of him. He wears a squarish top hat. Mr. Peanut's posture, shape, top hat, features, and accessories have changed since 1930, when the Planters Peanut Company mascot was launched. $18.00–22.00

versions: one clear glass, the other white glass. Both have "Mitchell's" emblazoned across the front in red script and silver caps. $18.00–24.00

Mixmaster Plastic. 1960s. The movable Mixmaster has a sliver motor casing, black base, and clear plastic bowl and shaker "beaters." $20.00–25.00

Mixmaster Plastic. 1960s. The Mixmaster is entirely white with black trim. $15.00–20.00

Mobil Oil Cans Cardboard and metal. U.S.A. Matching cans with silver perforated tops are emblazoned with the text "Mobiloil Special" under the trademark Pegasus. $12.00–14.00

Muth, Buffalo Souvenir Bottles Glass and metal. U.S.A. 1940s. Squat brown beer bottles have colorful label featuring a sitting blond in a blue two-piece bathing suit posing against a lake on which a sailboat is framed by fluffy clouds. The bottles are marked Muth, Buffalo. $12.00–14.00

New York City Souvenir Bottles Glass and metal. U.S.A. 1940s. Brown beer bottles have polychrome stickers, one with an image of the Rockefeller Center, the other of the Statue of Liberty. The beautiful illustrations have "New York" below the respective monuments. $10.00–12.00

New York State Thruway Metal and ceramic. 1940s. An Art-Deco-inspired ovalish dish textured to resemble grass and painted a pale green holds small gold clubs and two realistic golf balls, each with three holes. $25.00–30.00

New York World's Fair, 1939 Plastic. U.S.A. The trylon and hemisphere of the New York World's Fair of 1939 are ren-

Millie and Willie, Kool Cigarettes Plastic. Early 1940s. Fiedler & Fiedler Mold and Die Works Company. Dayton, OH. Black and white "Millie" penguin wears a red bow on her head and fingers a red necklace, while "Willie" penguin sports a black bow tie. Both have bright yellow beaks and white and black googly eyes. The "F & F" logo is on the bottom of each piece. $30.00–40.00

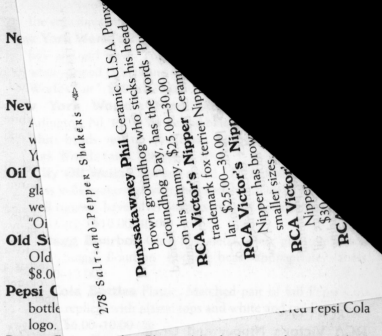

Punxsatawney Phil Ceramic. U.S.A. Punx... brown groundhog who sticks his head "Pu... Groundhog Day, has the words "Pu... on his tummy. $25.00–30.00

RCA Victor's Nipper Cerami... trademark fox terrier Nipp... lar. $25.00–30.00

RCA Victor's Nipp... Nipper has brow... smaller sizes...

RCA Victor... Nipper... $30...

RC...

Ne...

Nev York Wo...
A...
w...
Y...

Oil C...
gla...
we...
"Oi...

Old S...
Old...
$8.0...

Pepsi C... Bottles Plastic. Matched pair of... bottle... with plastic tops and white and red Pepsi Cola logo. ...

Pepsi Cola Bottles Plastic. Matched pair of empty (clear) Pepsi Cola bottle replicas with plastic tops and white and red Pepsi Cola logo. $6.00–10.00

Poppin' and Poppie Fresh Plastic. Pillsbury doughboy and girl, Poppin' and Poppie Fresh, in white plastic with blue eyes and dot (Poppin's on hat, Poppie Fresh's on dress) stand on round bases on which their names are inscribed. $16.00–20.00

Poppin' and Poppie Fresh Ceramic. Pillsbury's Poppin' and Poppie Fresh are made of white ceramic with blue neckerchiefs and dot on toque. $12.00–16.00

Possem Hollar Whiskey Glass and metal. U.S.A. Clear glass "teardrop"-shaped bottles with two dimples just above the base have metal caps and the worlds "Possem Hollar" emblazoned on them. $4.00–6.00

Precision Sweepers Plastic. U.S.A. 1950s. Matching plastic canister vacuum cleaners from Precision Sweepers are red (pepper) and white (salt). $16.00–20.00

...satawney Phil, the
...out of his hole every
...nxsatawney, PA" written

...c. U.S.A. 1940s. RCA Victor's
...er is white with black ears and col-

...er Ceramic. Japan. 1940s. Off-white
...ears and brown collar. Comes in larger and
...$25.00–30.00

s Nipper Lexon china. 1930s. This fine set of
...finely detailed and delicate, is white with black trim.
...00–40.00

Victor's Nipper and Gramophone Ceramic and plastic. U.S.A. 1950s. White Nipper with brown ears and black-gold collar sits on a black plastic base listening to a gramophone record "to his master's voice." The base has a black-gold label that reads, "His Master's Voice." Dog and gramophone both have paper labels that read "Nipper" TM RCA CORP. MADE IN JAPAN." $20.00–25.00

RCA Victor's Nipper and Gramophone Plastic. U.S.A. 1950s. A plastic Nipper sits next to a finely detailed gramophone, complete with crank. Both are marked on the bottom with the RCA trademark. $20.00–25.00

Regina Vinegar Glass and plastic. One green (pepper) and one clear (salt) glass bottle bear the labels "Regina Champagne Vinegar" and "Regina Wine Vinegar." $8.00–10.00

Ritz-E Plastic. Miniature versions of Ritz-E Sparkling Beverages team up one green and one clear bottle with the label. $10.00–12.00

Safe-T-Cup Ice Cream Cones Ceramic. U.S.A. Replicas of Safe-T-Cup cones have one vanilla- and one chocolate-dipped ice cream. $15.00–22.00

Samovar Vodka Bottles Glass and metal. U.S.A. Scaled down versions of Samovar Vodka bear all appropriate labels. $8.00–12.00

Sandeman Port Wine Ceramic. Black figurines of the black-caped and hatted figure are miniatures of the Wedgewood Sandeman decanter. $28.00–36.00

Sealtest Dairies Minis Plastic and metal. Matching transparent amber bottles with metal caps, yellow and red neck bands, and oval seals inscribed with "Sealtest." $30.00–36.00

Sealtest Milk Bottles Glass and metal. Clear glass milk bottles with metal caps have red "Sealtest" label. $15.00–18.00

Sears Kenmore Washers and Dryers Plastic. Cooks Corporation. Hong Kong. This blue plastic rectangular box sits on a white base, with the salt and pepper shakers on the sides. The top slides over to reveal the shaker holes. The front center is transparent plastic, encasing water and soapsuds. In the interior, a green-dressed housewife presides over a Kenmore washer and dryer. When the shaker is agitated, the soap suds up. $18.00–26.00

Seven-Up Bottles Plastic or glass with metal. Matching pair of green 7-Up bottle replicas with plastic tops and "7-UP" logo on body and neck. The glass and metal versions are priced higher than the plastic ones. $10.00–15.00

Sheraton Hotel Bellhop Ceramic. Goebel. 1953. Designed by Zetzmann, a sculptor, the Sheraton Hotel bellhop is dressed in red and carries in his hands a pair of brown, detachable suitcases with real leather handles. The salt and pepper shakers are the suitcases. $35.00–50.00

Shoe House Ceramic. White ankle-high lace-up shoes with black soles have doors and windows drawn on the sides to advertise The Shoe House of York, PA. $10.00–14.00

Squirt Glass and plastic. U.S.A. 1950s–1960s. Green, squiggly-sided Squirt bottles have yellow lids and labels. $12.00–14.00

Squirt Glass. U.S.A. 1940s. Green, larger-sized Squirt bottles have metal lids. $12.00–14.00

Stanley Products Plastic. U.S.A. 1940s–1950s. Bullet-shaped plastic shakers have transparent bodies and colored tops and bottoms. $10.00–16.00

Steam Irons Plastic and metal. Matching steam irons—without brand names—sit atop an ironing board. $20.00–24.00

Stokely's Products Plastic. U.S.A. 1940s–1950s. Red, kissing strawberries from Stokely Products are plastic and magnetic. One looks down, the other rolls its eyes. $10.00–16.00

Dino the Dinosaur, Sinclair Gasoline
Ceramic. Green "Dino the Dinosaur," the friendly brontosaurus, is the mascot for Sinclair Gasoline. $15.00–20.00

Sunshine Bakers Ceramic. White ceramic bakers have rotund bellies encased in aprons, yellow bow ties, and pencil-thin moustaches. Gold detailing and pink cheeks enliven the design of these tiny shakers. "Sunshine" is inscribed on the toques. $12.00–15.00

Tappan Range Plastic. U.S.A. 1976. An almond-yellow Tappan range is a single-piece shaker with perforated sides to dispense salt and pepper. $30.00–34.00

Tappan Range Chefs Ceramic. Tappan Range chefs in white uniforms, blue neckerchiefs, red shoes, and black hair have the word "Tappan" on the front of their toques. $12.00–16.00

Tappan Chefs Plastic. 1950s. Stylized chefs with goatees, flattened toques, and bell-shaped bodies come in a range of colors, from white to red to chartreuse. $10.00–12.00

Television Set Plastic. U.S.A. 1960s. A brown console TV stands on spindly legs and, on its screen, may carry the manufacturer's advertising sticker. The salt and pepper containers slip into the top of the appliance. $25.00–30.00

Tee and Eff (Tastee Freez Kids) Ceramic. Tee and Eff are the Tastee Freez mascots. $25.00–28.00

Tipo Sherry Bottles Glass and plastic. U.S.A. 1950s. Clear glass bulbous bottles sit on plastic bases, one black, the other red, and have plastic caps (one red, the other green). Both bear the Tipo Sherry Label. $10.00–12.00

Toaster Metal and plastic. Miniature replica of rounded pop-up toaster in "chrome" with black plastic base. White (salt) and brown (pepper) slices of toast protrude from top slits. $24.00–30.00

Tony the Tiger Plastic. U.S.A. Rectangular plastic box with white and black buttons in the center is stencilled with an orange, black, and white tiger body, and has an orange modeled tiger head and tail tacked at the far ends. One-piece shaker. $8.00–12.00

Trader Vic's Ceramic. U.S.A. Brown totemic figures from the Trader Vic's restaurant chain clasp hands over stomachs. $12.00–16.00

TWA Shakers Plastic. U.S.A. 1950s. Miniature red plastic shakers, cylindrical with broader, rounded bottoms, bear a circle with the letters "TWA" stencilled on them. Salt has white top, pepper has red top. $12.00–14.00

Vermouth Glass and plastic. Clear glass bottles stoppered with red and green plastic caps bear the labels "Le Jon Sweet" and "Le Jon Dry" Vermouth. $8.00–10.00

Vess Soda Glass and plastic. One clear and one green glass bottle of Vess soda carry the slogan "Vess Billion Bubble Beverage." Plastic lids are red or white. $8.00–12.00

Westinghouse Washer/Dryer Plastic. Matching pair of white plastic appliances sit on white bases and have turquoise controls and transparent, plastic ports. Beneath the "Westinghouse" logo appear the words "Laundromat" (salt) and "Clothes Dryer" (pepper). $24.00–30.00

Virginia Dare Beverages Glass and plastic. U.S.A. Clear glass bottles with plastic tops are stencilled in white and blue ink and bear the labels of Virginia Dare. $10.00–12.00

Volkswagen Bus Plastic. 1985. A cheerful, bright red VW has a white "crepe station" carved into its side. Clear glass and metal salt and pepper shakers protrude from the top. $18.00–25.00

Wade's Dairy Milk Bottles Glass and plastic. U.S.A. 1950s. Glass, squat milk bottles with plastic shaker tops have the motto "Wade's Dairy, Fairfield, Conn." emblazoned across the front in orange script. $15.00–18.00

Waring Blenders Plastic. The original Waring Blender features a silver base, clear blender, and tops in yellow, red, or black. $15.00–20.00

SPORTS AND CELEBRATIONS

SPORTS

Baseball Glove and Baseball Ceramic. 1960s. U.S.A. A brown baseball glove is teamed with a realistically detailed baseball. $6.00–8.00

Football and Megaphone Ceramic. 1950s. U.S.A. A brown football is matched with a yellow cheerleader's megaphone. $9.00–11.00

Fishing Creel and Waders Ceramic. 1940s–1950s. U.S.A. A fishing creel is accompanied by a pair of brown hip boots (waders). $12.00–14.00

Football and Helmet Ceramic. 1950s. A brown football is paired with a white football player's helmet. $8.00–10.00

Golf Bag and Clubs Ceramic. Japan. 1950s. A gold bag has two shakers in the shape of two yellow clubs resting on it. $22.00–25.00

Golf Bag and Ball Ceramic. Japan. 1950s. A brown golf bag is paired with a white golf ball. $14.00–16.00

Golf Bag and Ball Ceramic. U.S.A. 1960s. This largish set consists of a brown golf bag and white golf ball. $12.00–14.00

Golf Ball on Tee Ceramic. Japan. 1950s. A golf ball sits on a tee. The set may cary a Rossware "Birdie" label. $18.00–24.00

Fishing Creel and Fish Ceramic. Japan. 1940s. A brown fishing creel is teamed with a pinkish fish to go inside it. $12.00–14.00

Football Player's Head and Football Ceramic. 1940s. U.S.A. A broadly grinning football player's head, encased in a tan, old-fashioned helmet, is teamed with a sepia-colored football. $10.00–15.00

Golf Green, Balls and Flag Wood. U.S.A. 1930s. A pair of gold balls, painted with gray speckles, rests on red tees that sprout from an oval base of turf. Between them a banner with the number 8 is planted.

3 Cricket Bats and Golf Clubs Metal. England. 1940s–1950s. This heavy, metal set features a golf ball and a cricket ball that are cradled atop, respectively, a trio of golf clubs and a trio of cricket bats. $18.00–22.00

Fishing Creel and Fisherman's Hat Ceramic. Japan. 1940s. A fishing creel is matched with a fisherman's hat. $12.00–14.00

Fisherman in Boat Ceramic. Japan. 1940s. A fisherman dressed in a yellow outfit is inserted in his fishing boat. Elbee Art sticker may be attached. $24.00–26.00

Gun with Bullet Ceramic. Japan. 1940s–1950s. A brown and black gun is paired with a gray bullet. $18.00–24.00

Racing Cars Ceramic. Japan. 1950s. A pair of racing cars is painted pink (salt) and blue (pepper). $12.00–15.00

Connaught Rolling Race Cars Ceramic and metal. Green Connaught set has metal wheels. $24.00–26.00

Triumph Tr2 Rolling Cars Ceramic and metal. Blue Triumph Tr2 set has metal wheels. $24.00–26.00

Binoculars and Case Ceramic. Japan. 1940s–1950s. Black binoculars are teamed with a black case. $10.00–12.00

Saddle and Cowboy Boots Ceramic. Japan. 1950s. Saddle and cowboy boots are both brown. $12.00–15.00

Western Saddles Ceramic. Japan. 1940s. A pair of brown Western saddles rests on saddle trees. $10.00–12.00

Football Boys Ceramic. Japan. 1940s–1950s. A pair of football boys in white jerseys and black pants wears brown old-fashioned football helmets. "S" hefts football to shoulder, while "P" holds it under his arm. $24.00–26.00

Tennis Boys Ceramic. Japan. 1940s–1950s. Cute boys in white trousers hold tennis rackets. One has white cap and red top, the other a red cap and blue top. $20.00–24.00

Hockey Players Ceramic. Japan. 1940s–1950s. Gloved and helmeted ice hockey players are frozen in dynamic action. The matching figurines are available in a range of colors, from chartreuse to orange to brown. $18.00–20.00

Matador and Bull Ceramic. Japan. 1950s. Dashing, black-faced matador swings his red cape at a squat yellow bull. $20.00–24.00

Matador and Bull Ceramic. Japan. 1950s. A white-faced matador faces a charging bull. $12.00–16.00

Baseball Pitcher and Batter Ceramic. Japan. 1940s–1950s. A white-and-blue uniformed pitcher snarls at a batter in the same colors with a surly frown on his face. $24.00–26.00

Bowler with Pins Ceramic. Japan. 1940s–1950s. A yellow bowler crouches over a black bowling ball. The mate to this shaker is a set of yellow bowling pins. $20.00–25.00

Umpire and Hitter Ceramic. Japan. 1940s–1950s. A black-jacketed, green-trousered umpire stands aloof, arms behind his back, as a white-and-black-stripped hitter in a yellow and red cap looks down grumpily. $24.00–26.00

Boxers Ceramic. Japan. 1940s–1950s. A hand-painted pair of hulking, white boxers—one in red trunks, the other in black—face off with black boxing gloves. $24.00–28.00

Wrestlers Ceramic. Japan. 1940s–1950s. Muscled wrestler holds the other over his head. $22.00–25.00

Boy Boxers Ceramic. Japan. 1940s. Two hand-painted red-headed boys, one in red, the other in blue overalls, face each other with raised fists in brown boxing gloves. $20.00–22.00

"8" Ball Ceramic. Japan. 1940s. A matching set of "8" balls features a white number on a black background. $10.00–14.00

Kingpins with Faces Ceramic. Japan. Red kingpins with white "trousers," buttons, bow ties, and faces, frown. They are inscribed "PIN–SALT" and "PIN–PEPPER." $18.00–20.00

Canoeists Ceramic. Japan. 1940s. This lovely pair of hand-painted canoeists nestles in a brown canoe. One of the boys wears green trousers with a red and white checkered shirt and brown stocking cap, the other is in yellow trousers, green and black shirt, and brown cap. $20.00–24.00

Boy Golfers Ceramic. Japan. 1940s. Hand-painted, cute boy golfer figurines show one swinging a club and the other toting his golf bag. $20.00–24.00

Swimmers' Legs Ceramic. Japan. 1940s–1950s. A comely pair of female legs emerges, from the knees up, from sea-wave bases. Toenails are painted bright red. $18.00–24.00

Male and Female Headless Torsos Ceramic. Japan. 1960s. Muscular male and female torsos, headless and limbless, are dressed in skimpy black and yellow polka-dotted swim trunk and bikini, respectively. $16.00–18.00

Football Players Ceramic. Japan. 1940s–1950s. Player on the ground is holding the ball for the kicker and has no head. The kicker is holding the other player's head in his hands. $38.00–42.00

Diving Legs and Torso Ceramic. Japan. 1960s. A pair of flesh-toned legs dives into the water in one piece that accompanies a naked upper torso. $18.00–24.00

Hunter and Rabbit Ceramic. Japan. 1940s–1950s. A hunter is teamed with a little white rabbit. $18.00–24.00

Croquet Set Plastic. U.S.A. Yellow croquet mallets are tipped in red and nestle in a bright green "stand" which holds a stack of balls. $36.00–38.00

Boxing Gloves Ceramic. Japan. 1950s. Brown boxing gloves have embossed laces. $10.00–12.00

Wrestlers Ceramic. Sarsaparilla. 1980s. This nester set is made up of a long-haired blond wrestler in yellow trunks and shoes who balances on his shoulders a bald wrestler in a mask and red trunks and shoes. $18.00–20.00

Fishing Waders and Creel Ceramic. U.S.A. 1950s. Brown fishing creel goes with black, shiny waders. $16.00–24.00

Arm and Dumbell Ceramic. U.S.A. 1960s. A white arm with a giant muscle and open hand is teamed with a black dumbbell. The dumbbell may be balanced on the open palm. This is a nester. $20.00–24.00

Football and Helmet Ceramic. U.S.A. 1960s. A brown football is teamed with a white helmet. $16.00–20.00

Footballs Ceramic. Japan. 1960s. Very realistic footballs have pigskin-textured bodies, white stitching, and even black lines. $14.00–18.00

Footballs on Metal Stand Ceramic and metal. Shafford. Japan. Two dark-brown footballs, realistically rendered, are lodged at the two ends of a black metal stand that has a rectangular representation of the gridiron between the two rings that house the balls. $20.00–24.00

Football and Player's Head in Helmet Ceramic. U.S.A. 1950s. A brown football goes with a beige player's head encased in a helmet. Player grins. $16.00–20.00

Golf Club and Ball Ceramic. Extraordinarily realistic reproductions of a gold ball and a gold club house salt and pepper. The club is brown and black, while the dimples on the white ball are highlighted with yellow. $16.00–20.00

Golf Ball and Bag Ceramic. Japan. A very white golf ball, complete with realistic dimples, goes with a yellowish-brown golf bag with the ends of two clubs emerging from the top. $14.00–18.00

Wooden Golf Balls on Stand Wood. 1950s. White wooden golf balls balance on red tees which are anchored to a green. $18.00–24.00

Golf Balls on Metal Stand Ceramic and metal. Shafford. Japan. Realistic golf balls are housed in a metal stand in the center of which two wire golf clubs are crossed. $20.00–24.00

Golf Ball on Tee Ceramic. U.S.A. 1950s. A white golf ball balances on a white tee that is attached to a green, turf-simulating tray. $20.00–24.00

Baseballs on Metal Stand Ceramic and metal. Shafford. Japan. Two realistic white baseballs are lodged in a metal stand in the center of which two wire bats are crossed. $20.00–24.00

Pittsburgh Pirates Baseball Glove Ceramic. U.S.A. 1960s. A buttery yellow baseball mitt, with red stitching has the name "Pittsburgh Pirates" across the end of the mitt. The ball which nestles in it is the same color and also has red stitching. $20.00-24.00

Baseball Mitt and Ball Ceramic. U.S.A. 1960s. A brown baseball mitt, without top stitching, cradles a white ball with stitching, though not highlighted by any color. $16.00–20.00

Baseball Players Ceramic. Clay Art. 1980s. A pitcher and a catcher wear white and blue uniforms. $15.00–18.00

Bowling Pin with Bowling Ball
Ceramic. U.S.A. 1940s. A yellow
bowling pin goes with a black bowling ball. There is an entire series of
sports "go withs" that team up the
emblems of a sport, such as fish and
fishing creel, baseball and glove, 8
ball and billiard ball, golf ball and
golf club, etc. $20.00–24.00

Matador with Red Bull Ceramic. Japan. 1950s. A boy-faced
matador in black and white holds a red cape. The bull is blood
red with golden hooves and horns. $24.00–30.00

Tennis Racket and Ball Ceramic. Japan. 1950s. A yellow tennis racket, quite crude, is teamed with a white tennis ball.
$10.00–14.00

Tennis Balls in Metal Stand Ceramic and metal. 1980s.
Yellow tennis balls are lodged at either end of a golden metal
stand that has as its handle a wire tennis racket. $10.00–14.00

Boxing Gloves Ceramic. U.S.A. Brown boxing gloves are darker
at the top. One has green laces, the other, tan. $10.00–14.00

Boxing Gloves and Bag Ceramic. Japan. 1950s. Red boxing
gloves, one atop the other, are paired with a red boxing bag.
$10.00–14.00

Pool Balls Ceramic. U.S.A. Both the white ball and the "8" ball
sit on a triangular, green base. $12.00–14.00

Basketballs on Metal Stand Ceramic and metal. Shafford.
Japan. Realistic basketballs are housed at either end of a black
metal stand at the center of which rises a metal backboard.
$20.00–24.00

Soccer Balls on Metal Stand Ceramic and metal. Shafford.
Japan. Realistic soccer balls are lodged at either end of a black
metal stand from the center of which rises a black mesh
screen. $20.00–24.00

Soccer Balls and Leg in Stand Ceramic and metal.
Shafford. Japan. Realistic soccer balls are lodged at either end
of a black metal stand from the center of which rises a black
mesh screen. $20.00–24.00

Fisherman's Hat and Creel Ceramic. Japan. 1960s. A "straw" fisherman's hat with a yellow hatband and a green feather is teamed with a green fishing creel. $14.00–18.00

Parachute and Flier Ceramic. Vandor. 1980s. A flier in a yellow jumpsuit with a blue harness stands in a cloud. His white and pink parachute is attached to his arms by means of plastic cylinders. The flier and the parachute are separate shakers. $18.00–22.00

Jockey and Rearing Horse Ceramic. Japan. 1940s. A jockey in yellow jodhpurs and blue and white cap is teamed with a pinkish rearing horse. The jockey has a childish face. $14.00–20.00

Baby Sportsmen Ceramic. Japan. 1950s. Toddlers in red overalls wear the headgear appropriate to a particular sport and brandish its emblems. Thus there are sets of golfers, football players, skiers, baseball players. $24.00–30.00

CIRCUS

Clowns on Donkeys Ceramic. Japan. Identical white clowns in spotted costumes straddle small beige donkeys. $10.00–14.00

Clown Heads Ceramic. Identical heads of clowns with blue eyes, red triangular noses, and yellow hair wear white tall hats with red dots. Salt is in green collar, pepper is in pink collar. $12.00–14.00

Clown and Ball Nester Ceramic. Japan. A grinning, green clown holds up one hand into which fits a ball. $28.00–32.00

Glee and Glum Clowns Ceramic. Black "Glum" in top hat, frock coat, trousers, and umbrella scowls. White "Glee" in clown suit laughs. He is fat, round, and sits on his round bottom, supported by his stumpy hands. The names "Glum" and "Glee" are inscribed on their heads in gold. $20.00–24.00

Clown Firemen Ceramic. Cute, boy-faced clowns with red noses, red caps, and yellow hair wear gray jackets. One holds a ladder, the other holds a pick. $14.00–18.00

Lion Tamer and Lion Ceramic. A handsome, sitting lion tamer in blue pants and red top with yellow "frogs" sits on a taboret holding a whip and pointing with his thumb. The orange lion sits and merely rolls his eyes. $20.00–24.00

Tigers on Balls Ceramic. Japan. Kittenish tigers perch on red, white, and blue balls. $12.00–18.00

Frolicking Clowns Ceramic. One white clown stands on his hands, in which he cradles his snowball head with "X" eyes. The other clown sits on his bottom and waves one hand. $14.00–18.00

Clown with Dog Ceramic. Japan. A white clown with red lips and costume detailing sits cross-legged. In his lap is balanced a small white dog dressed in a clown costume. $20.00–25.00

Clowns Ceramic. C. Miller. Regal China Company. Matching white ceramic clowns are hand-painted. The clowns have bright red lips and noses and are wearing white hats with red dots, green collars, yellow trousers, and hold brown circles. $25.00–30.00

Clown Garbage Cans China. Taiwan. 1970s. White garbage cans have clown faces. $12.00–16.00

Ringmaster Dog on Ball Ceramic. Shafford. This two-piece shaker consists of a red, white, and green ball (salt) on the top of which stands a little brown dog in white formal attire, black top hat and cane, and yellow bag. $22.00–24.00

Blue Monkeys Ceramic. Japan. 1940s. Matching pale blue monkeys with gold trim sit holding their knees and tilting their smiling faces to the right side. They are wearing bellhop-style hats. $12.00–14.00

Blue Elephant Musicians Ceramic. Japan. 1940s. Blue elephants with upturned trunks play musical instruments that are painted gold. One plays the drums, the other a bass fiddle. $12.00–14.00

Elephant and Tent Ceramic. Japan. 1940s. A gray elephant in a red clown hat goes with a white circus tent with blue lines, red banner, and red tent flap. $24.00–28.00

Dancing Elephants Ceramic. Japan. 1940s. Gray elephants in headdresses and blankets perform, raising their trunks. One stands on its hind legs, the other lifts a foot. $24.00–28.00

Lusterware Elephants Luster-finish porcelain. 1940s. One yellow and one white elephant in circus garb stand up on pale blue bases. $18.00–24.00

Monkey on Base Ceramic. Japan. 1950s. This nester consists of a white cylindrical base ornamented with red and blue dots and a sitting brown monkey with pink face who tips his red sailor cap. $12.00–14.00

Lion on Base Ceramic. Shafford. Japan. 1950s. This nester consists of a white cylindrical base ornamented with red and blue dots and a rampant, luxuriously maned lion in shades of tan and brown. $18.00–24.00

Elephant on Trampoline Base Ceramic. Japan. 1960s. This nester consists of an egg-shaped base made in the form of a trampoline held by straps to a flattened ball and a gray simplified elephant in a red and blue cap, turning up his trunk. $12.00–14.00

Clown on Drum Nester Ceramic. Japan. 1960s. A brown and tan drum serves as the base for a clown with "X" eyes, green cap, and white costume with red dots. The clown lies on his back and kicks up his legs. $24.00–28.00

Dressed Dog on Ball Ceramic. Shafford. Japan. A white, star-studded ball is the base to a fuzzy, brown-faced dog in girl clown costume. In its hands, the dog holds golden cymbals. The clown-dog's base is the semispherical top to the ball. There is an entire series of shakers in this vein. $20.00–24.00

Clowns Ceramic. U.S.A. Identical fat white clowns with white "army" caps pose red-nailed hands on their fat bellies. Salt has blue trim, Pepper has red trim. Clowns have black crow's feet lines on either side of their beady eyes that are surmounted by large, arched eyebrows. $12.00–14.00

Seal Balancing Red Ball
Ceramic. Japan. 1940s–1950s.
A black seal balances a red ball
on its nose. This is a nester
$20.00–24.00

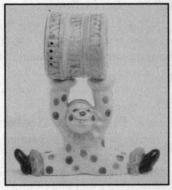

Clown Holding Drum Nester
Ceramic. Japan. The light-brown
drum balances on the clown's outstretched arms. The clown is
dressed in a white jumpsuit with red
and green dots and a yellow ruff.
$24.00–28.00

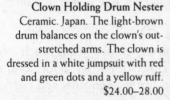

Clown Heads in Hats Ceramic. 1960s. A "bum" clown's head
in a very tall black top hat rises out of a green ruffle. A "harlequin" clown's head in a blue-and-white-striped cone hat rises
out of a pink ruffle. $12.00–14.00

Clown Reamer Heads Porcelain. White-faced clowns in
orange and yellow costumes sit in identical positions. On
their heads they wear orange and yellow cone-shaped hats
that are ridged like lemon juicers. These sets are also found in
white with red and blue dots. $14.00–18.00

Clown Reamer Heads Porcelain. Small (3½") pink-faced
clowns in white costumes with red and blue dots sit in identical positions. On their heads they wear yellow and white
cone-shaped hats that are ridged like lemon juicers.
$12.00–14.00

Clown Girls in Garden Holder Ceramic. Japan. 1940s. This
three-piece set comprises a blue, peanut-shaped basket textured to resemble grass with a columnar stem rising from the
middle and capped by a red daisy with yellow center. Into
each side fit identical figurines of yellow-dressed and capped

girl clowns holding flowers and wearing deep blue ruffs around their collars. $12.00–14.00

Monkey Drummer Ceramic. Two-piece shaker set comprises a white and pink drum on a blue base and a sitting monkey in a blue cap, red, blue-trimmed jacket, and yellow pants with both arms at sharp angles. In his hand he holds yellow drumsticks with red heads. $20.00–24.00

Monkey Accordionist Ceramic. A crouching red-lipped monkey in blue cap and trousers and red jacket holds a detachable white accordion with blue ends. $18.00–20.00

Monkey on Drum Ceramic. Shafford. Japan. A dressed monkey balances on two balls which are attached to the semispherical top of a white drum. The monkey is one shaker, the drum is another. $18.00–24.00

Clown Piggyback Nesters Ceramic. Japan. 1940s–early 1950s. White, hand-painted nester clowns fit atop each other in piggyback fashion. Top clown leapfrogs across bottom clown. They wear white suits with green ruffs and red and green dots and black shoes. Cone hats are green and orange, and yellow and black. $40.00–48.00

Black Elephant on Base Red clay. A shiny black elephant sits on a detachable rectangular base. Elephant's trunk is thrown back over the head. $10.00–12.00

Clowns Playing Wheelbarrow Ceramic. Japan. 1940s–1950s. White clowns in skirt and pant outfits with black dots and bright yellow trim and conical yellow hats play human wheelbarrow with one holding on to the upraised legs of the other. $22.00–28.00

Turnabout Clowns on Taborets Ceramic. Japan. 1940s–1950s. These turnabout clowns have smiling faces on one side, frowning on the other. Pink clown with blue hat stands on his hands on a blue and white taboret. Green clown with red hat balances on one leg atop a red and white taboret. $24.00–28.00

Turnabout Clowns Doing Handstands Ceramic. Japan. 1940s–1950s. These turnabout clowns have smiling faces on one side, frowning on the other. White clown is in a red, yellow, and blue polka-dotted costume and yellow hat, while the yellow and white clown wears a green hat. $24.00–28.00

Clowns Riding Pigs Ceramic. Japan. 1940s–1950s. Identical white figurines depict child-faced clowns in red hats and with red sports riding stiff-legged white pigs. $22.00–26.00

Clowns Doing Handstands Ceramic. Japan. 1940s–1950s. Identical clowns relax on their elbows, supporting their smiling faces on their hands, and hold their red-clad legs in the air. $22.00–26.00

Laughing Clowns Ceramic. Japan. 1940s–1950s. Identical pink-shirted, blue-trousered, and red-shoed clowns sit on striped taborets and hold up white-gloved hands at either side of their grinning mouths. $22.00–24.00

Conversing Clowns Ceramic. Japan. 1940s–1950s. A "lady" clown in red bowler hat, yellow skirt with brown dots, and blue ruffled blouse clasps gloved hands to heart as she inclines her ear to her suitor, a blue-hatted, yellow-trousered, green-shirted clown who holds one hand to heart and raises with other. $22.00–24.00

Laughing Clowns Ceramic. Japan. 1940s–1950s. Identical grinning clowns in pin hats, red ruffs, blue shirts, and white shorts expose their pink bare legs on either side of a bland red and yellow ball they straddle. $22.00–24.00

Harlequin Heads Ceramic. Japan. 1940s–1950s. Identical white harlequin heads in green ruffs and conical hats with yellow ruffles and red pompoms have patches of red hair and red, comma-shaped ornaments on cheeks. $18.00–22.00

Clown Heads in Top Hats Ceramic. Japan. 1940s–1950s. Identical white clown heads with O-shaped mouths and eyes and orange eyebrows and hair wear blue ruffs and undersize black top hats. Each cheek is ornamented with a single red vertical stripe. $18.00–22.00

Clown and Gray Drum Nester Ceramic. Japan. The clown sits splay-legged on the top of a gray-sided drum. The clown's suit is white with red and green dots and a red ruff. $24.00–28.00

Clown Heads on Drums Ceramic. Japan. 1940s–1950s. Identical shakers feature white round clown heads with delicate orange eyebrows, red cone hats, and blue ruffs emerging from the top of white drums banded in black. $18.00–22.00

Clowns with Emmett Kelley Faces Ceramic. Japan. 1940s–1950s. Identical clown heads in white cone hats with red dots and identically painted, Emmet-Kelley-style, faces rise from ruffs that are painted pink (salt) and blue (pepper). $18.00–22.00

Metal Clowns Metal. Rare painted metal clowns are identical except for the fact that one is black with gold, red, and white trim, and the other white with red and black trim. $20.00–24.00

Clown Busts Ceramic. Japan. 1940s–1950s. Emmett Kelley and harlequin-type clowns are featured in these shakers. The harlequin—in whiteface with extravagantly arched eyebrows, red lips, and side tufts of hair—wears an orange cone hat, a white and blue ruff, and a polka-dotted costume. The Emmett Kelley type wears a tiny orange bowler atop his bald head, a suit-and-tie combo that involves a blue suit, red tie, and white shirt. These shakers terminate at mid-chest. $20.00–24.00

Clown on Barrels Ceramic. Japan. 1940s–1950s. Skinny, comical clowns cling to the sides of two brown, wood-grained barrels. The clowns' bodies arch between their ankles and necks into the bow of the letter "D." One clown wears yellow cap, the other a red cone hat. $14.00–20.00

Sitting Clowns Ceramic. Japan. 1940s–1950s. Identical white clowns sit straddle-legged. They have orange buttons, hair, cheeks, and noses, and blue ruffs and ruffles. $14.00–18.00

Clown Head Pots Ceramic and metal. Japan. 1950s. Identical stylized clown heads in black with large pink noses, blue lips, and yellow porkpie hats sit on three tiny "feet." From either temple emerges a metal handle. Initials "S" and "P" appear on the hat. $12.00–18.00

Bum Clown Head Pots Ceramic and metal. Japan. 1050s. Red Skelton look-alike heads with bald pates, red noses, and lips that are outlined in white and set into a black unshaven lower face sit on three tiny black legs. Out of each temple protrudes

Blue Elephant Nester Ceramic. Hull. 1940s. A blue elephant sits on a blue drum. The elephant's trunk is triumphantly curled. $24.00–28.00

a metal wire handle. Tiny red cylindrical hats jut out of the right side of the heads. $12.00–18.00

Seal Balancing Ball Nester Ceramic. Japan. 1940s–1950s. A black seal balances a red and white ball. This is a nester. $18.00–24.00

Brown Seals Ceramic. Japan. Small brown seals have red balls attached to their noses and red collars around their necks. $14.00–18.00

Gray Seal Atop Brown Discs Nester Ceramic. Japan. 1940s–1950s. A gray seal balancing a red ball sits atop a stack of three brown disks. $16.00–20.00

Holidays

valentine's day

Season With Love Plastic and fabric. U.S.A. 1970s. Padded red hearts, trimmed with lace and red bow, are embellished with the words "Season With Love." Clear shakers in red holder are hidden behind the hearts. $10.00–14.00

Engagement Ring and License Ceramic. A black and white "Certificate of Marriage" is paired with a jeweler's box opened to reveal a gold band with sparking rhinestone. $15.00–18.00

Pierced Heart Ceramic. A divided red heart rests on a base and is pierced by a gold arrow. The shakers form each half of the heart. $15.00–18.00

st. patrick's day

Leprechauns Ceramic. U.S.A. Rosy-cheeked leprechauns in green and brown traditional attire play and dance an Irish jig on a base of clover and toadstools. $18.00–24.00

easter

Ducks in Purple Wooden Basket Ceramic and wood. U.S.A. Yellow ceramic ducks sit in purple wooden basket with pink bows, handle, and painted patterns of dot clusters. $12.00–14.00

Glass Shakers in Pink Wooden Napkin Holder Glass and wood. A pink wooden napkin holder in the shape of a picket fence flanked by planters is filled with a bunny, flowers, and butterfly, and, in the planters, holds glass shakers. $13.00–16.00

Easter Bunnies in Basket Ceramic and straw. U.S.A. White Easter bunnies in pink dresses and white aprons nestle in a white wicker basket with green grass and dried flowers. $16.00–18.00

Fat White Bunnies Ceramic. U.S.A. White boy and girl bunnies are squat and round. She wears a pink, blue, and yellow dress with a maroon bow, while he is in blue and yellow overalls. $14.00–18.00

Bunnies in Ceramic Basket Ceramic. U.S.A. 1950s. One white, one bluish-gray bunny nestle in a white and pink or white and blue ceramic basket. $14.00–16.00

Ballerina Bunnies Ceramic. U.S.A. 1970s. Smiling ballerina bunnies in pink dresses wear pink ballet slippers. $14.00–16.00

Easter Egg Bunnies Ceramic. White rabbits, with bodies in the shape of yellow, green, and white Easter eggs, wear bows. One sits up, the other lies down. $10.00–14.00

Chicks Hatching from Easter Eggs Ceramic. Pastel chicks appear from the tops of painted Easter eggs in shades of yellow, green, and white. One lies on its side, the other stands up. $10.00–14.00

"Easter Parade" Bunnies Ceramic. U.S.A. Cartoonish-faced white rabbit with pink ears rests his elbows and head on a large orange carrot. $14.00–16.00

"Easter Parade" Bunny with Carrot Ceramic. U.S.A. Pensive, cartoonish-faced white rabbit with pink ears rests his elbows and head on a large orange carrot. $14.00–16.00

"Easter Parade" Bunny with Cabbage Ceramic. U.S.A. Cheerful, cartoonish-faced white rabbits with pink ears hold bouquets of tulips. One sits up, the other lies down. $14.00–16.00

Easter Bunny and Chick Hatching from Eggs Bisque. Two beribboned, pastel-colored Easter eggs have windows punched out of the sides out of which protrude the heads of a bunny and a chick (one per shaker). $14.00–16.00

mother's day

Mother's Day Ceramic. U.S.A. White cylinders highlighted with gold are painted with pink, blue, and green posies, the word "Mother" in blue script, and an appreciative paragraph devoted to Mother. $10.00–14.00

halloween

White Ghost, Black Cat, and Jack-O-Lantern Votive Ceramic. U.S.A. A wooden tray holds a smiling jack-o-lantern votive candle, flanked, on each side, by white ghost and black cat shakers. $15.00–18.00

Skulls in Graveyard Ceramic and wood. U.S.A. A pair of ceramic skull shakers sit inside a gray wooden graveyard. $15.00–18.00

Skeletons/Ghosts Ceramic. Japan. 1950s. Skeleton covered in a tan shroud grasps one edge of shroud with bone hand. Skull features are depicted on the face, and the word "Poison" appears across the front of each figurine. $12.00–14.00

Spooky and Scary Pumpkins Ceramic. One elongated, standing orange pumpkin with an "O" mouth and "apostrophe" eyes is teamed with a round, grinning, gap-toothed pumpkin. $12.00–14.00

Pumpkin and Black Cat Ceramic. U.S.A. A round-eyed black cat is paired with a grinning orange jack-o-lantern. $14.00–16.00

Grinning Jack-O-Lanterns Ceramic. U.S.A. Happy-faced jack-o-lanterns are a deep orange color with black faces. $12.00–15.00

Pumpkins in Pilgrim Hats Ceramic. U.S.A. 1980s. Smiling jack-o-lanterns are wearing black pilgrim hats. $10.00–12.00

Stacked Pumpkins Ceramic. Seven smiling jack-o-lanterns are piled up in two harvest stacks. $10.00–12.00

Witches Ceramic. U.S.A. 1980s. Witches in black dresses and conical hats hold beige brooms and have orange hair. $10.00–12.00

Thanksgiving

Turkeys Bisque. Colorful, finely detailed turkeys with full opened tail feathers are in shades of brown and aqua. $16.00–18.00

White Pilgrim Hats Ceramic. White pilgrim hats have black belts and gold buckles. $10.00–12.00

Pilgrim Couple Ceramic. Cartoon-faced pilgrim couple is dressed in gray with black shoes. She holds red purse. Both have heart-shaped red lips. $12.00–14.00

Pilgrim Couple Ceramic. Japan. 1960s. Blond, freckle-faced couple in white tights represents cheerful versions of pilgrims. Boy wears black hat and jacket, girl wears red dress with white apron and cap. $12.00–14.00

Turkeys Ceramic. Plump brown, yellow, and green turkeys have curly pink necks and white heads. $10.00–12.00

Boy and Girl Pilgrims Ceramic. Chubby boy and girl pilgrims are dressed in brown and have "Give Thanks" inscribed on their fronts. $10.00–12.00

Pilgrim Bears Plastic. Brown plastic bears wear brown and white pilgrim attire. He holds blunderbuss, she carries fruit-and-vegetable-filled basket. $8.00–10.00

Praying Pilgrim Children Ceramic. Blond boy and girl pilgrims kneel in their blue outfits. $8.00–10.00

Cornucopia Ceramic. Brown "wicker" cornucopias are overflowing with harvest produce: corn, pumpkins, apples, grapes, and squash. $12.00–14.00

John and Priscilla Pilgrim Bears Ceramic. John and Priscilla Pilgrim bears are dressed in traditional costume. She is in blue and white and holds a pie. He is in black and holds a pumpkin. $15.00–17.00

christmas

Roly-Poly Santas Ceramic. Pear-shaped, roly-poly Santas clasp hands over their fat stomachs in their red and black outfits and red and white hats. $14.00–16.00

Santa, Sleigh, and Elf Bisque. White bisque sleigh holds an elf hiding in Santa's toy bag and a rotund Santa in the driver's seat. $14.00–16.00

Elves With Baskets Ceramic. Bearded, colorful elves rest against huge wicker baskets. $15.00–18.00

Elves with Acorns Ceramic. Bearded, whiskered elves shoulder giant acorns. $15.00–18.00

Elf Bakers Ceramic. Bearded, serious elves wear chef's toques. One holds a mixing bowl and wooden spoon, the other hefts a rolling pin. $15.00–18.00

Elf Wizards Ceramic. Bearded elves are dressed in wizard cone hats and robes. The one with the floor-length beard stands and holds a pensive index finger under his nose, while the short-bearded one sits in a meditative pose. $15.00–18.00

Mr. and Mrs. Claus Ceramic. Dot-eyed Mr. and Mrs. Claus wave one hand and stand in their red and white outfits. $10.00–12.00

Wooden Santa Tray with Shakes Wood and glass. A wooden holder shaped like the top of a chimney, out of the back of which emerges a wooden cutout of Santa, holds two glass and metal shakers. $15.00–16.00

Wooden Mrs. Santa Tray with Shakes Wood and glass. A wooden holder shaped like the top of a chimney, out of the back of which emerges a wooden cutout of an aproned Mrs. Claus, holds two glass and metal shakers. $15.00–16.00

Seasoned Greetings Santa and Mrs. Claus Ceramic. Red and white Mr. and Mrs. Claus smile in their cooking outfits. He is in a chef's hat and holds a wooden spoon and fork, while she holds a pastry. His apron is inscribed "Seasoned," hers, "Greetings." $14.00–16.00

Saint Nick and Toy Bag Ceramic. A red and white bearded Saint Nick is flanked by a sack crammed with toys such as teddy bear, clown, and bunny. $20.00–24.00

Bumpkin Santa and Mrs. Claus Bisque. Fabrizio. Country bumpkins Santa and Mrs. Claus have round heads with dot eyes. Mrs. Claus wears a country bonnet and a white frilly apron and holds a wooden spoon. $12.00–14.00

Santas in Red Basket Ceramic. Small Santas with "S" or "P" on their belt buckles nestle in a red basket. $12.00–14.00

Santas with Toys Ceramic. Standing Santa in full costume holds up a brown teddy bear, while seated Santa in green and white shirt and suspenders holds a yellow ball with a heart. $15.00–17.00

Clarinetist Santa with Dog Ceramic. Hand-painted Saint Nick in fur-trimmed coat stands and blows into his clarinet while a white, floppy-eared hound sits on his haunches and points his snout soulfully into the air. $24.00–26.00

Kissing Claus Couple Ceramic. Cute Mr. and Mrs. Claus bend toward each other at the waist and pucker their lips. $12.00–14.00

Casual Santa Ceramic. A rotund Santa with gold spectacles hugging his red nose holds on to his bulging tummy. He wears red-and-white-striped shirt and green suspenders. $15.00–17.00

Saint Nicholas and Tree Ceramic. Saint Nicholas in floor-length, fur-trimmed red coat holds a small pine tree over one

Mr. and Mrs. Claus in Rockers Ceramic. Mr. and Mrs. Claus recline in white and gold rockers and conversationally hold out one hand to each other. $10.00–12.00

shoulder and a bulging sack in another. The second shaker is a snow-colored pine tree. $18.00–24.00

Christmas Carolers Ceramic. A pair of kids in green and red outfits smile pleasantly from beneath their pompommed stocking hats. $10.00–12.00

Dickensian Christmas Couple Ceramic. A plump, middle-aged Victorian couple features a lady in a red dress, white apron, green hat, and gold purse and a gentleman in black, white, and red with a black top hat and gold cane. $14.00–16.00

Gingerbread Kids and Frying Pans Ceramic. Flat boy and girl gingerbread cookies in brown with brown and red icing features hold frying pans. $10.00–13.00

Gingerbread Children Ceramic. Adorable round gingerbread kids have plump, golden-brown bodies with red icing eyes and chocolate icing hair. Sitting girl, her skirt trimmed with icing rick-rack, holds hands on lap, while sitting boy, three buttons down his front, holds up both arms. $12.00–14.00

Flat Gingerbread Kids Ceramic. Small, flat gingerbread kids are decorated with red, white, and brown icing. $10.00–12.00

Gingerbread Houses with Kids Ceramic. Two gingerbread houses are decorated with white icing and colorful candy. Facade of each house features a flat, cookie-shaped image of brown gingerbread boy or girl decorated with white icing and bright candles. $16.00–18.00

Praying Children Ceramic. White, kneeling boy and girl with gold trim lower their eyes and fold their hands in prayer. $8.00–10.00

Shaker Candles with Choir Angel Ceramic. A pair of white ceramic candlesticks anchored to an oblong base flank a white angel holding a black song book. Red-flamed candles are the shakers. $10.00–12.00

Cartoon Squirrels in Santa Hats Ceramic. Cute brown cartoon squirrels with white tummies and faces and red mittens and Santa caps roll their blue eyes. $8.00–10.00

Cartoon Mice in Santa Hats Ceramic. Cute gray sitting mice with pink ears wear red Santa hats. $8.00–10.00

Candy Cane People Ceramic. Candy cane "S" and "P" have cute cylindrical heads and stick arms and legs. $10.00–14.00

Conical Santas with Emerald Eyes Ceramic. Conical busts of Santa with stylized white beard, round red cap, and red noses wink, revealing one emerald rhinestone eye. Pepper has black pompom, Salt has white. $8.00–10.00

Angels with Poinsettia Hats Ceramic. Girl angels in long red dresses wear red poinsettia hats. The pig-tailed angel has large snowflake "apron," the pageboy angel holds an open book. $8.00–12.00

Christmas Bells Ceramic. Red and white ornamented Christmas bells are topped with green wreaths of holly. $6.00–8.00

Santa Claus Heads Ceramic. High-gloss ceramic heads of a red-lipped Santa show him winking and flashing one blue eye. The red caps of this version flap over to the chin, creating a handle effect. $8.00–10.00

Santa Claus Heads Ceramic. Bearded heads of Santa in a short-tailed red hat depict one with parted lips and wide-open eyes, the other with a tight mouth and winking eye. Gold glitter is scattered on the fur trim of the hat. $8.00–10.00

Santas with Candy Cane and Bell Ceramic. Standing Santas in black boots hold up one arm. One holds a candy cane, the other a yellow bell. $8.00–10.00

Chimney Santas Ceramic. Three-quarter figure Santas pop out of snow-capped chimney. They hold a stuffed sack with one hand and wave with the other. $8.00–10.00

Small Santas Ceramic. Small figurines of a grinning, white-faced Santa show lips, eyes, and cheeks in red or black highlight. $8.00–10.00

Santas with Letters Ceramic. Cute red and white Santas in black boots hold wads of letters to their chests. $8.00–10.00

Christmas Boat Ceramic. Red ceramic boat carries name "S-Noel" on bow and files red "Noel" flag. A whiskered captain in a red uniform and white cap with "S" on the bill holds a monocle to his eye, while his "Pepper" crew, a white doglike creature, wears a red bandanna. Each removable figure flanks a green and white "smokestack" mustard pot. $24.00–26.00

Mr. and Mrs. Claus Chalkware. U.S.A. 1940s. Serious-looking Santa and Mrs. Claus wear red-orange costumes with yellowish fur trim. $20.00–24.00

Gold-Trimmed Mr. and Mrs. Santa Ceramic. Gold-trimmed Santa in red hoists black sack across his back, and white-clad Mrs. Santa holds a red and white stuffed stocking. $20.00–24.00

Rocking Mr. and Mrs. Santa Ceramic. Seated in their rocking chairs, Mr. and Mrs. Santa hold toys in their laps. Mrs. Santa is in green, while Santa is in his traditional garb. $14.00–16.00

Mr. and Mrs. Claus with Sacks Ceramic. Shiny, ceramic, gold-trimmed Santa couple holds toy sacks. His is white, hers is black. She wears her hair in a topknot. $10.00–14.00

Mr. and Mrs. Claus with Sacks Ceramic. Gold-trimmed Mr. and Mrs. Santa Claus prepare to distribute presents. The red aproned Mrs. Claus—in a white dress with gold dots—reaches into a green bag of letters, while Santa looks sternly, one arm akimbo, the other hefting the sack. $10.00–12.00

Christmas Snowmen Ceramic. Occupied Japan. Beautiful detailed white snowboy and snowgirl grin jovially. She wears poinsettia-topped kerchief and holds holly berries. He wears an orange hat and red scarf. $16.00–20.00

Angel Musicians Ceramic. White ceramic angels with golden haloes (containing the holes) and accents are available in twelve different poses: conducting, playing the tambourine, the harp, the clarinet, the violin, the drum, the recorder, and four holding sheet music. $12.00–14.00

Santa's Packages (Santa with Sack) Ceramic. A red, white, and black Santa, the word "Santa's" on his tummy, has oval eyes and stands next to a white sack bulging with gift-wrapped boxes and labeled "Packages." $12.00–14.00

Bell-Ringing Santas with Cauldron Ceramic. Two bell-ringing Santas flank a red cauldron mustard pot labelled "Christmas Cheer." $14.00–16.00

Santas with Bells and Candy Canes Ceramic. Shafford. Japan. Standing Santas with beige-highlighted hair wear traditional costume. One holds a large candy cane, the other holds up a green wreath with two golden bells. $22.00–24.00

Santas with Sacks Ceramic. Shafford. Japan. Standing Santas with gray-highlighted hair wear traditional costumes. Both hold sacks, but over opposite shoulders, and have glitter highlights on fur trim. $18.00–20.00

Santa Astride Packages Ceramic. Holt-Howard. Stamford, CT. 1950s–1960s. A stylized, cute Santa with a round, fat, oversize head grins as he sits astride a stack of two gift-wrapped packages. He holds a little box in his hands. A magnet holds Santa atop the stack. $18.00–24.00

Santa Climbing Out of Chimney Ceramic. A realistic-looking Santa hoists himself out of a snow-rimmed brick chimney and holds his sack over one shoulder. $12.00–14.00

Santa with Bell-Hat Nester Ceramic. Shafford. Japan. 1950s. The head of a fat Santa—with a beard full of white tendrils, a red nose, and tightly shut eyes—supports a red, yellow, and gold bell topped with a red bow. $18.00–20.00

Sitting Santas Ceramic. Shiny red and white ceramic Santas are depicted in sitting position. One sits spread-legged and holds out his arms, the other sits cross-legged and waves one hand. Both have glitter on the fur trim. $14.00–16.00

Mr. and Mrs. Santa Ceramic. Japan. 1940s–1960s. Santa, dressed in a floor-length, fur-trimmed robe, waves with one hand and holds a gift in the other. His gloves and ribbon are pale blue. Mrs. Claus holds a sprig of ivy and smiles ecstatically. Both have glitter on fur trim. $14.00–16.00

Blue-Gloved Santas Ceramic. Japan. 1940s–1960s. Small, blue-gloved Santas in otherwise traditional costume hold a pair of golden bells in one case and the neck of a bulging sack in the other. $12.00–14.00

Waving Santas Ceramic. Japan. 1940s–1960s. Red-cheeked, fat-bellied Santas wave with one hand and hold a green sack of toys with the other. The sack is slung over opposing shoulders. $14.00–16.00

Sitting Mr. and Mrs. Claus Ceramic. Taiwan. Mr. and Mrs. Claus sit on black chairs and face each other. Both hold wrapped gifts in their laps. $12.00–14.00

Waving Mr. and Mrs. Claus Ceramic. Japan. 1940s–1960s. A curly-bearded Santa in a long, fur-trimmed robe waves with one green-gloved hand while bespectacled Mrs. Santa, in green dress with white apron, waves her red-gloved hand. $16.00–19.00

Sitting Santa and Kneeling Mrs. Claus Ceramic. Japan. 1940s–1960s. Straddle-sitting Santa with holly in his hat holds out his arms to kneeling, red-dressed Mrs. Claus whose gold-rimmed spectacles are slipping off her nose. $12.00–14.00

Cowboy Mr. and Mrs. Claus Ceramic. Japan. 1940s–1960s. White-bearded Santa in a tan Stetson and chaps and red shirt holds on to his holster, while Mrs. Claus, in red dress and white apron, hefts a shotgun. $20.00–24.00

Aged Mr. and Mrs. Claus Ceramic. Japan. 1940s–1960s. Wrinkled Mr. and Mrs. Claus smile benignly. She has blue spectacles and a red Santa hat. $12.00–14.00

Wild West Mr. and Mrs. Claus Ceramic. Santa, in a white Stetson ornamented with holly and red shirt, holds a white frying pan. Mrs. Claus, in a red dress and white apron, holds out a coffeepot and a mug. $18.00–24.00

Christmas Rocking Horses Ceramic. Lefton Company. 1940s. White rocking horses with green and red saddles are ornamented with red bows and sprigs of holly. $14.00–16.00

Christmas Trees Ceramic. Japan. 1950s. Dark green Christmas trees are decorated with snow and colorful balls and topped with golden stars. $12.00–14.00

Elves on Rockets Ceramic. Japan. 1940s–1960s. Red-dressed elves with white cone hats sit astride white rockets highlighted with gold. $14.00–18.00

Rudolf the Red-Nosed Reindeer Head Ceramic. Lefton Company. 1940s. Brown busts of Rudolf the Red-Nosed Reindeer show a flirtatious, cartoonish animal. $12.00–14.00

Frosty the Snowman and Friend Ceramic. Japan. 1940s–1960s. Frosty the Snowman, in a black top hat, bow tie, and shoes waves one red-mittened hand, as his rotund white friend stands by, wearing a green necktie and holding a gold and red broom. $16.00–24.00

Mr. and Miss Snowman Heads Ceramic. Japan. 1940s–1960s. Sloe-eyed, pink-cheeked snowman wears red top hat and red- gold- and white-striped scarf. Miss Snowman wears an identical scarf and red conical hat. Both have golden noses. $16.00–18.00

Poinsettia Angel Children Ceramic. Japan. 1940s–1960s. Girl angel wears red poinsettia dress and hat, while boy angel wears green outfit with green poinsettia blossom on head. He plays an accordion. $12.00–16.00

"Noel" Children Ceramic. Japan. 1940s–1960s. Boy and girl in red, fur-trimmed conical hats and red coats over white gowns hold up holly-trimmed letters. He holds "NO," she holds "EL." $14.00–18.00

Angel Girls with Bells and Muff Ceramic. Holt-Howard. Adorable angel girls with white hair and long coats cast down their eyes. The gold-trimmed figurines show one angel holding a pair of red bells, and the other slipping her green-gloved hands into a muff. $14.00–18.00

White Mice in Christmas Hats Ceramic. White mice with smiling faces and closed eyes sit up on their haunches. Their red and white Santa hats are trimmed with holly and sit low on their foreheads. $10.00–12.00

Large Red Elf Booties Ceramic. Japan. 1940s–1960s. Red elf booties are trimmed with "ermine" and gold and have gold stars on their upturned toes. $10.00–14.00

Christmas Chipmunks Ceramic. Japan. 1940s–1960s. Gray sitting chipmunks wear red Santa hats and gloves. $10.00–14.00

Christmas Candles Ceramic. Japan. 1940s–1960s. Green candle stubs in candlesholders decorated with holly have red "wax" dripping down the top. There are no flames. $8.00–12.00

Deer on Tray Metal. A metal tray with a scene of Santa at the North Pole holds two silver-coated reindeer, one standing, the other lying down. The deer are the shakers. $16.00–20.00

Christmas Mice on Wedges of Cheese Ceramic. Japan. 1940s–1960s. Yellow wedges of Swiss cheese are topped with heads of gray, large-eared mice in Santa hats. Wedges are marked "S" and "P" and squeak when turned over. $12.00–16.00

Santa and Rudolf the Red-Nosed Reindeer in Bed
Ceramic. Japan. 1940s–1960s. Stylized Santa and Rudolf the
Red-Nosed Reindeer heads rest on a white-sheeted, brown-
framed bed with a green coverlet ornamented with a holly
design. $14.00–18.00

Santa and Christmas Tree Ceramic. Old-fashioned-looking
Santa with a realistic face stands next to a green pine tree.
$14.00–18.00

Christmas Reindeer Ceramic. Japan. 1960s. Cartoonish white
reindeer with pink cheeks, red bows, and holly hold up one
yellow hoof for inspection. Their stylized horns match the
hoof color. $8.00–12.00

Snowmen on Christmas Tree Tray Ceramic. White snowmen's bodies resemble lightbulbs with red conical caps and
red and white polka-dotted scarfs. The snowmen stand on a
red, Christmas-tree-shaped tray. $20.00–24.00

Sitting Santas Ceramic. Japan. 1940s–1960s. Two jolly Santas
with blue eyes and "gingerbread" trim sit, showing their white
boots. $12.00–16.00

Bearded Santas Ceramic and fake fur. Thin, childish-faced
Santas in gold boots have real fur beards. $14.00–16.00

Mr. and Mrs. Claus in Rockers Ceramic. A pipe-smoking
Santa sits in a brown rocking chair, while a green-dressed Mrs.
Santa sits in her rocker holding a red-and-white-striped candy
cane. $14.00–16.00

Saluting Santa and Rudolf Ceramic. A pert Santa salutes
smartly, holding a holly-decorated toy bag behind his back.
He is flanked by an attentive yellow and white Rudolf who
wears a bright red bow around his neck and stands in a clump
of dark green holly. $14.00–16.00

Mrs. Claus Helps Dress Mr. Claus Ceramic. Mrs. Claus in
a green dress with "gingerbread" trim highlighted with glitter
holds out red mitten to Mr. Claus, who sits in a green chair
holding his cap in one hand. $14.00–16.00

Santa and Pine Tree Ceramic. A small, shiny ceramic Santa
stands next to a spiral bright green pine tree ornamented with
red dots. $12.00–14.00

"S" and "P" Snowmen Ceramic with flat, bisque finish. Round, white snowman in green top hat holds a red "S," and snowwoman, in red Edwardian motoring bonnet, holds green letter "P." $12.00–14.00

Mr. and Mrs. Claus Chalkware. Small figurines depict scruffy Santa and pleasantly smiling Mrs. Claus in a long coat and white muff. $20.00–24.00

Gift-Wrapped Packages Ceramic. Cylindrical packages are wrapped in white and gold snowflake motif "paper" and tied with red ribbon, with pompoms on top. Each carries a label, one "pepper," the other "salt." $10.00–12.00

Mr. and Mrs. Snowman with Gifts Ceramic. Shiny ceramic Mr. Snowman wears black top hat and carries black and gold gift in his red-mittened hands. Mrs. Snowman has black accessories, including holly-ornamented hat, and carries red package. $12.00–14.00

High-Heeled Boots Ceramic. High-heeled black ankle boots sit on black and white bases. $8.00–12.00

Geese with Christmas Ribbons Ceramic. 1980s. White Christmas geese wear red and green ribbons around their necks. $12.00–14.00

Ornamented Christmas Tree Ceramic. Ornamented Christmas trees sit on red bases. $10.00–12.00

Hugging Santa and Mrs. Claus Ceramic. A squat, plump Santa kneels and reaches out his arms to an equally plump, bespectacled Mrs. Santa with a green ribbon in her white hair. $10.00–12.00

Christmas Pigs Ceramic. Kreiss. Hilarious pig couple in white ceramic depicts inane-looking Mr. Pig sitting on his haunches, laughing, and wearing a bright red bow tie which matches his crimson lips, tongue, and snout. Mrs. Pig looks identical, but has black bow on her head and a skirt fashioned of holly leaves and berries. $10.00–12.00

Santa in Sleigh Ceramic. A plump Rudolf the Reindeer with candy-cane-striped antlers has a harness of green holly leaves. Santa sits in a white candy-cane-trimmed sleigh, and wears an ermine-trimmed red suit. $12.00–16.00

Kissing Mr. and Mrs. Claus on Bench Ceramic and wood. Elderly Mr. and Mrs. Claus sit on a small wooden bench. He holds a candy cane in one hand, she clutches a stack of wrapped presents. $12.00–14.00

Mr. and Mrs. Claus with Gingerbread Trim Ceramic. A hatless, tired-looking Santa sits back on his green arm chair, holding his cap in his hand. Mrs. Claus, looking positively regal in her red and green frock and white ermine muff, peers over her half-moon spectacles. Both are trimmed with gold-speckled gingerbread. $12.00–14.00

Church and Preacher Ceramic. A small, white church with a red roof and brown door is capped with a yellow cross. Standing next to it is a snowman-shaped preacher in black with red bow tie and black porkpie hat. $12.00–14.00

Gold-Capped Santa Heads Ceramic. Pre-1960s. Japan. Matching heads depict a full-bearded Santa with pink cheeks, red lips, and black-tasselled golden caps. $12.00–14.00

Father Christmas Heads Ceramic. Pre-1960s. Japan. Blissfully smiling Father Christmas heads rest on long, snowy beards. The red caps are trimmed in gold-speckled gingerbread. $14.00–18.00

Santa Heads Ceramic. Pre-1960s. Japan. A lumberjack-y-looking Santa in a red cap with red lips in a white beard is featured from chin up. $10.00–12.00

Mr. and Mrs. Claus on Mailboxes Ceramic. Pre-1960s. Japan. Small Mr. and Mrs. Claus in traditional costumes are reclining cheerfully atop white ceramic mailboxes ornamented with red flags, holly and berry sprigs, the letters "S" and "P," and the words "Happy Holiday" on the sides. $10.00–12.00

Mr. and Mrs. Claus with Gingerbread Trim Ceramic. Pre-1960s. Japan. Jolly, red-suited Santa has a garland of gingerbread trim around his head, at his cuffs, and around his waist. Mrs. Claus, in a white and red polka-dotted blouse and red skirt, has gingerbread trim around her collar and hem. $14.00–16.00

Mr. and Mrs. Claus Distributing Presents Ceramic. Pre-1960s. Japan. Traditional Santa holds up jingle bell, while Mrs. Claus, in a black apron, holds a stack of presents. $14.00–16.00

Plastic Mr. and Mrs. Claus Plastic. Pre-1960s. Red, button-nosed Mr. and Mrs. Claus have round faces and stylized, rotund bodies. He wears a yellow belt around his waist. $10.00–12.00

Comical Santa Couple Ceramic. Pre-1960s. Japan. Tiny set of Santas depicts one with hat drooping over one eye and the other squinting and holding one hand up to his ear. $8.00–10.00

Santas on Pig-Back Ceramic. Pre-1960s. Japan. Fat, round Santas holding golden bells in their hands sit astride white ceramic pigs. $14.00–16.00

Candy Cane and Bell Santas Ceramic. Pre-1960s. Japan. Matching traditional Santas in black boots and belts hold aloft different emblems. One holds yellow bell, the other a striped candy cane. $14.00–16.00

"Merry Christmas" Santas Ceramic. Pre-1960s. Japan. Stylized, conical Santas with red O-mouths hold up the words "Merry" and "Christmas," each exhibiting one. $14.00–16.00

Mr. and Mrs. Snowman Ceramic. Pre-1960s. Japan. Round white ceramic snowman couple depicts the Mrs. in a yellow bonnet with bow tie and black muff, and Mr. in a black top hat, lantern, and yellow scarf and vest. $12.00–16.00

Christmas Snowmen Ceramic. Pre-1960s. Japan. Small white snowmen with black buttons and red scarves wear miniature conical Christmas trees ornamented with colorful balls as hats. One holds a golden broom. $10.00–14.00

Debonair Snowman Couple Ceramic. Pre-1960s. Japan. White snowman couple consists of the lady holding a green umbrella and the gent in a black and yellow top hat and brown cane. $10.00–12.00

Baroque Angels with Gifts Ceramic. Pre-1960s. Japan. White child angels, baroque in inspiration, have small golden wings and gold-highlighted "diapers." They sit on red-rib-boned, holly-leaf-ornamented presents, and hold wrapped boxes on their shoulders. $16.00–24.00

Girls with Snowflakes Ceramic. Pre-1960s. Japan. Blond girls in white coats with bell-shaped skirts wear red Santa hats and hold gold-ornamented snowflakes. $12.00–14.00

Gift-Bearing Couple Ceramic. Pre-1960s. Japan. Blond couple consists of red-coated lady with hands in white muff, and black-clad gent in black top hat holding presents. His hat is decorated with holly leaves and berries. $12.00–14.00

Santa Kids in Sleighs Ceramic. Pre-1960s. Japan. Cute children in red and white Santa suits sit in tiny white sleighs. Pepper has black hair, Salt has orange. $12.00–14.00

Reindeer with Jingle Bells Ceramic. Pre-1960s. Japan. Fawn-colored deer pair consists of an antlered standing adult and a sitting youngster, both with golden jingle bells around their necks. $10.00–12.00

Stylized Santa and Rudolf Ceramic. 1950s. Japan. A lemon-shaped Santa head emerges from a squat, red and white boy with green gloved hands. Santa's beard is decorated with golden swirls in the shape of "6s." Rudolf is hourglass-shaped with pink ears, golden nose, and a necklaces of holly leaves and berries. $12.00–14.00

Leaping Reindeer Ceramic. 1950s. Japan. Two prancing, white ceramic reindeer wear golden bells around their necks and have golden antlers. Both leap over a white base ornamented with holly leaves and berries. $12.00–14.00

Christmas Trees Ceramic. 1950s. Japan. Four-tiered Christmas trees sit on white and gold bases and have, among their ornaments, red balls, candy cane stockings, and gold stars. $12.00–14.00

Christmas Candles Ceramic. Pre-1960s. Japan. White candles with yellow flames sit in white bases ringed with green and with green carrying handles. A cluster of holly leaves and berries flanks the side of each candle. $12.00–14.00

Christmas Boots Ceramic. Pre-1960s. Japan. Red high-heeled boots with upturned toes are ornamented with gold bells and trim. $12.00–14.00

Christmas Cow Ceramic. Vandor. 1980s. A white cow with black spots and yellow horns and a red muffler around her neck lounges in a green holly wreath sprinkled with red berry clusters and shaped to resemble a rubber tire. $18.00

Chalkware Devils Chalkware. 1940s. Red chalkware devils in capes sit cross-legged. One has yellow beard and eyebrow detailing and green gloves; the other reverses the color combination. $10.00–12.00

Angel and Devil Ceramic. Japan. 1950s. White angel with gold trim and yellow hair folds hands in prayer. White devil with red horns, black hair, malicious expression, and hairy, satyr-like legs raises fists menacingly. $10.00–12.00

Large Red Devil Ceramic. 1950s. Large red devil shakers depict a horned, caped figure with black features holding a black pitchfork. $8.00–12.00

Blue and White Angels Porcelain. Girl angels with pageboy haircuts, long dresses, and long wings stand in praying poses. Their dresses and hair are pale blue. $12.00–14.00

Food and Music Angels Ceramic. 1950s. Little girl angels with brown hair and green polka-dotted dresses have tiny wings. Salt, with apron and dishcloth, holds a teapot in one hand and a plate in the other. Pepper plays a brown accordion. $12.00–14.00

Food and Music Angels Ceramic. 1950s. Little girl angels with brown hair and brown polka-dotted dresses have tiny wings. Salt, in chef's toque and white apron, holds a loaf of bread. Pepper holds trumpet. $12.00–14.00

weddings

Bride and Groom Bench Sitters Ceramic and wood. Bride, in white veil and gown highlighted with gold, closes her eyes and purses her lips, while groom, in black cutaway and striped trousers, does the same as he cradles a top hat in his arms. Both sit on a wooden bench. $24.00–26.00

Bride in Net Dress and Groom Ceramic and net. Blond nuptial couple bends at the waist and can be positioned to kiss. She wears real net skirt over white ceramic dress. He is in white-and-black-striped trousers and black cutaway. $22.00–26.00

Bride and Groom on Brass Wire Altar Ceramic, net, and brass wire. Dan Brechner and Co. Traditional bride and groom stand in a brass holder shaped to look like the arched window of a church. Bride wears real net skirt and veil. $25.00–30.00

Wedding Bells Ceramic and satin. U.S.A. 1940s. White ceramic bells are in the shape of cowbells. Tied with a satin white bow, they are inscribed with the names of the couple and the date of the wedding ceremony. $14.00–18.00

Bridal Cooks Ceramic. 1940s. A smiling male and female cook in aprons. She holds a frying pan, he looks sheepish. Both have the names of the bride and groom inscribed on the hat. $8.00–10.00

Anniversary Hearts Bone china. White hearts on four golden feet are decorated with bows, flowers, and doves and inscribed, in gold, with "Happy Anniversary." $10.00–12.00

Standing Hearts Porcelain. Japan. Matching white hearts with pink roses and gold trim stand on tiny feet and are inscribed "My love for you is ever true." $10.00–12.00

Bridal Cookbooks Porcelain. Japan. White books with lavender flowers and gold swirling leaves are inscribed either "This way to his heart" or "Bride's Cookbook." $10.00–12.00

Bride and Groom in "Just Married" Car Ceramic. U.S.A. 1950s. This two-piece set consists of a bride and groom unit that fits into a green car with pink wheels inscribed with "Just Married" and "Niagara Falls." Bride wears pink dress with white veil, groom is in black. $20.00–24.00

Bride and Groom Ceramic. Occupied Japan. 1945–1952. Bride, in white, has pale yellow hair, and carries a green and red bouquet. The groom wears a black cutaway, striped trousers, and green tie. $18.00–24.00

Goebel Bride and Groom Ceramic. Goebel. Carl Wagner design. 1951. Small bridal pair includes bride in white with blond hair and pink flowers. The groom is in top hat and a gray suit. $25.00–30.00

Bride and Groom Ceramic. Japan. 1930s. The bride wears white with pink flowers on her veil and in her bouquet. The groom is stout with blue vest, black jacket, white trousers, and wears glasses. $24.00–28.00

Groom Carrying Bride Ceramic. Japan. 1940s. This nester set represents a groom holding a bride figurine. Her veil and

Pig Bride and Groom Ceramic. Japan. 1940s. Blushing bride and groom have brilliant red lips. Pig bride wears gold necklace and pink scarf, and carries bouquet of pink and blue flowers. Pig groom has golden buttons. $20.00–24.00

gown have highlights of gold glitter. Both figurines have gold outlining. $25.00–35.00

Bride and Groom Ceramic. Japan. 1950s. Blond bride and groom are in white with golden detailing. $15.00–25.00

Bride and Groom Ceramic. Japan. 1960s. Bride in a white off-the-shoulder gown and veil with pink rosebuds, closes her eyes. The groom has a JFK haircut, black suit, and gray hat. $15.00–25.00

Bride and Groom in Convertible Ceramic. Japan. 1950s. Busts of childlike bride and groom sit inside a yellow 1950s convertible. The hood lifts off to reveal a mustard pot. The bride has real veiling. $20.00–24.00

Wedding Couple Turnabout Ceramic. Japan. 1940s. The "before" side shows a young bride with gold-tipped hair and dress, clutching a pink bouquet. The groom wears black cutaway, white vest with gold buttons, and white pants with black stripes. The "after" side shows the aged couple, wrinkled and in tatters. There is no base. $35.00–40.00

Wedding Couple Turnabout Ceramic. Japan. 1950s. The "before" side depicts a bride and groom dressed entirely in white. His trousers have black stripes, and he wears a yellow bouttonniere on his lapel. She holds a black prayer book and has red shoes. When the shakers are turned around, a later stage in their life is revealed. He is in his pajamas, which are unbuttoned to reveal a protruding, pink belly. She is in a dotted nightgown holding a baby. The base of the groom is inscribed "Love!!!" (groom side) and Marriage???" (husband side), and "Marriage???" (bride side) and "Love!!!" (mother side). $40.00–45.00

Wedding Couple Turnabout Ceramic. Japan. 1940s. The "before" side depicts the groom in black pants, white jacket, and slim figure. The "before" bride wears a white dress and carries a bouquet of red flowers. The "after" side reveals a middle-aged husband, bald, potbellied, in green trousers barely held up by suspenders. The wife wears a head scarf, has an ample, green bosom, a large stomach, and a long, red skirt. $45.00–50.00

Wedding Couple Turnabout Ceramic. Japan. 1940s–1950s. The "before" groom wears black pants, red bouttonniere, and stands on a base with knee-high green grass. He is pyramidal in shape, with wide, flaring shoulders. The "before" bride wears a flaring, white dress and carries a bouquet of pink and red flowers. The husband on the "after" side is bald, with a bulging stomach, green, patched trousers, and yellow suspenders. Around his feet is curled a black and white dog. The wife is now pregnant, wearing a pink kerchief, a green apron, and has at her bare feet a hen and chicks. $40.00–45.00

Wedding Couple Turnabout Ceramic. Japan. 1940s–1950s. The groom wears a black pair of pants and tie. His hair is parted in the middle and slicked back. At his feet are two clumps of green grass. The bride wears a white, flaring dress and carries a pink bouquet. Her hair is red. On the "after" side, the husband has shifted the part on his hair to the side. He wears green trousers, held up by yellow suspenders. At his bare feet is curled up a gray hound dog. The wife wears a white kerchief and green apron, she holds her hands on her bulging stomach. The words "before" and "after" are inscribed on the base on the appropriate sides. $40.00–45.00

Wedding Couple Turnabout Ceramic. Japan. 1940s. The groom wears a black top hat and cutaway, and a white vest highlighted with gold. The bride wears a long, pale blue skirt and cap with a white blouse. Gold trim highlights the neckline and cap sleeves. She carries a pastel bouquet. On the "after" side, the groom has aged. He is dressed in the identical costume, but his face has rounded and his stomach now bulges. The bride is pregnant and has shifted her bouquet to the side. The words "before" and "after" appear on the base on the appropriate side. $40.00–45.00

Wedding Couple Turnabout Ceramic. Japan. 1940s. The groom wears black trousers and a white cutaway, and holds the black top hat in his left arm. He is flanked, at the base, by a green bush with red flowers. The bride wears a white, long-sleeved dress with a touch of lace at the collar and wrist. She carries pink flowers. Gold highlights the dress. In the "after" side, the husband has aged. His hair has turned gray, and he has grown a white beard. His figure has filled out. He is in brown pants and suspenders with a shirt tie. The same green bush surrounds his legs. The wife is also old, with white hair, a yellow shawl, gray skirt, and white apron. $45.00–50.00

Black Couple Turnabout Ceramic. Japan. 1940s. On the "before" side, the Black suitor wears a natty blue checked jacket, yellow cap, and black pants, and carries a gold cane. The young woman wears a yellow dres and a white apron and pink shawl, and holds a bouquet of flowers. On the "after" side, the husband has filled out and wears green trousers with blue suspenders, but no shirt. The wife holds twins, dressed in the same yellow skirt and pink shawl. The words "before" and "after" appear on the bases of the appropriate sides. $55.00 and up.

Wedding Couple Turnabout Ceramic. Japan. 1940s. The "before" side depicts a normal bride and groom. The "after" side shows the same couple, though now the husband has aged and the wife is pregnant. $40.00–45.00

FOODS

Hard-Boiled Egg Stacker Ceramic. Japan. 1940s–1950s. A hard-boiled egg, in two sections, top and bottom, stacks vertically. $8.00–10.00

Stuffed Eggs Ceramic. Japan. 1940s–1950s. A pair of hard-boiled egg halves is stuffed high with devilled filling. $8.00–12.00

Ham and Egg Ceramic. Japan. 1940s–1950s. A large white egg is paired with a rosy ham shank. $12.00–16.00

Eggs and Sausage Links Ceramic. Japan. 1940s–1950s. A pair of white fried eggs glistens on one side of a pale blue plate while a pair of brown "links" rests on the other. $16.00–18.00

Toaster and Toast Ceramic. Japan. 1940s–1950s. Two slices of toast nestle next to a white toaster. $10.00–12.00

Ice Cream Freezer and Cake Ceramic. Japan. 1940s–1950s. A greenish ice cream freezer sits next to a chocolate cake. $12.00–14.00

Egg in Frying Pan Ceramic Japan. 1940s–1950s. A fried egg nestles in a brown frying pan. $8.00–10.00

Steak in Frying Pan Ceramic. Japan. 1940s–1950s. A beef steak or a ham steak lies in a black frying pan. $18.00–24.00

Fish in Frying Pan Ceramic. Japan. 1940s–1950s. A yellow fish nestles in a black frying pan. $18.00–24.00

Freshwater Trout Chalk. U.S.A. 1930s. Two clusters of red-lipped freshwater trout rise up from their tails. $28.00–30.00

Pie a la Mode Ceramic. Japan. 1940s–1950s. A wedge of pie—in a variety of fillings—is topped by a scoop of ice cream in this nester set. $10.00–14.00

Turkey in Roaster Ceramic. Japan. 1940s–1950s. A golden turkey sits in a yellow roasting pan. $6.00–20.00

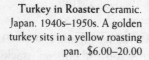

Ice Cream Cones Ceramic. Japan. 1940s–1950s. Two ice cream cones are topped with a scoop of strawberry and chocolate or vanilla ice cream, respectively. $9.00–11.00

Pancakes and Syrup Ceramic. Japan. 1940s–1950s. A pitcher of syrup accompanies pancakes on a blue trim plate. $22.00–26.00

Chocolate and Strawberry Milk Shakes Plastic. Japan. 1940s. Tall brown and pink glasses rest in "silver" holders and are capped with brown and white "foam" with straws. $20.00–24.00

Bread and Butter Ceramic. Japan. 1940s–1950s. A loaf of bread is accompanied by a yellow square of butter. $8.00–10.00

Braided Buns Ceramic. Japan. 1940s–1950s. A pair of braided dinner rolls is sprinkled with simulated poppyseeds. $10.00–14.00

Ice Cream Cones Ceramic. Japan. 1940s–1950s. Two ice cream cones are topped with scoops of chocolate ice cream. $7.00–9.00

Hamburgers Ceramic. Japan. 1940s–1950s. A pair of hamburgers is sandwiched between realistically painted lettuce leaf, tomato, and slice of cheese. $8.00–12.00

Hot Dogs Ceramic .Japan. 1940s–1950s. A pair of hot dogs juts out of mustard-smeared buns. $10.00–12.00

Baked Potatoes Ceramic. Japan. 1940s–1950s. These Idaho baked potatoes are split at the top to show yellow pats of melting butter. $14.00–16.00

Cupcakes Ceramic. Japan. 1940s–1950s. A pair of chocolate cupcakes in white "accordion-pleated" liners is topped with walnut halves. $10.00–14.00

Coffee and Donut Ceramic. Japan. 1940s–1950s. A cup of coffee is accompanied by a donut. $10.00–12.00

Trout on Scale Ceramic. Japan. 1940s–1950s. A gray trout with a pink mouth lies on a white old-fashioned scale whose printer is halfway between the fifteen and twenty marks. $24.00–28.00

Hot Chocolate in a Cup Ceramic. Japan. 1940s–1950s. A white cup brimming with hot chocolate has an image of a moustachioed, hatted man on the side and the word "PA." The saucer on which the cup rests has a scalloped decoration running along the edge. Each piece is a shaker. $16.00–18.00

Hot Dog and Hamburger Ceramic. Japan. 1940s–1950s. This realistically painted set features a hamburger in a bun and a hot dog, blanketed in mustard and tucked into a bun. $12.00–16.00

Stuffed Baked Potatoes Ceramic. Japan. 1940s–1950s. Idaho baked potatoes are squared off on the bottom, with skins peeled back on top to reveal a mound of mashed potatoes topped by a wedge of yellow butter. $15.00–16.00

Banana Split Ceramic. Japan. 1940s–1950s. A luscious banana split—complete with bananas, scoops of strawberry and chocolate ice cream, whipped cream, and cherry—nestles in a white, boat-shaped saucer. $14.00–16.00

Bagels With Comic Faces Ceramic and wood. This 5" tall set features bagels with comic faces stacking on each other on a wooden stand. $18.00–22.00

FRUITS

Green and Purple Pineapples on Tray Ceramic. Japan. 1940s–1950s. Matching green pineapples with purple foliage rest on a purple and green leaf-shaped tray. $24.00–28.00

Bananas Ceramic. Japan. 1940s–1950s. A pair of bright yellow bananas with brown spots lie on their sides. $8.00–10.00

Grapes and Leaves Ceramic. Japan. 1940s–1950s. A bunch of dark red grapes rest on a green leaf. $7.00–9.00

Oranges Ceramic. Japan. Brightly colored oranges rest on green leaf bases. $12.00–14.00

Tangerines Ceramic. A pair of bright orange tangerines with green stems. $8.00–10.00

Damson Plums Porcelain. Bright red plums rest on green leaf bases. $8.00–10.00

Pears Ceramic. Beautifully painted pears have yellow skins with rose-red blush and green leaves. $10.00–12.00

Peaches Ceramic. Delectable peaches, their skins shading from pale yellow to pink at the top, have green leaf on side. $8.00–10.00

Delicious Apples Ceramic. Matching red delicious apples have green leaves draped across the top. $10.00–14.00

Strawberries on Vine Porcelain. Hand-painted strawberries cluster amid dark brown leaves in these vertical shakers. $12.00–16.00

Macintosh Apples Ceramic. Red-orange Macintosh apples have yellow highlights at top. $10.00–12.00

Fruit and Bowl Plastic. U.S.A. 1950s–1960s. This three-piece set features a beige sugar bowl topped with an assortment of fruit. The orange and the lemon are detachable salt-and-pepper shakers. $14.00–18.00

Watermelon Wedges with Grasshoppers Ceramic. Japan. 1940s–1950s. Grasshoppers, beautifully hand-painted in shades of green and yellow, perch on pink wedges of watermelon that are detailed with black seeds and green rinds. $26.00–30.00

Roma Apples Ceramic. A pair of round red Roma apples feature orange stems. $8.00–10.00

Acorns Ceramic. Light brown acorns have darker brown cross-hatched caps. $6.00–8.00

Watermelons Ceramic. Whole watermelons are painted in alternating stripes of light and dark green. $10.00–12.00

Pineapples on Leaf Ceramic. This set of small pineapples rests on a bright green palm-leaf tray. The pineapples are draped with banners reading "Aloha." $12.00–14.00

Grapes Ceramic. A matcing pair of deep purple grapes has green leaves at top. $8.00–10.00

Tangerines on Tray Ceramic. Realistic pair of tangerines rests on white, scalloped-edged tray with deep red border. $16.00–18.00

Watermelon Wedges Ceramic. Japan. 1940s. The red, white, and green wedges of watermelon have a scattering of black seeds. $10.00–12.00

Watermelon Rounds Ceramic. Japan. 1940s–1950s. Two round watermelons have ends sliced off and show bright red interiors studded with black seeds. $12.00–14.00

Fruit Bowl Ceramic. A green-stemmed fruit bowl with red flower design holds an assortment of fruit. The apple and the orange lift out to dispense salt and pepper. $16.00–18.00

White Pineapples Porcelain. Late 1950s. White porcelain pineapples sparkle with 22-karat-gold paint highlights on tips of foliage and sprout pink blossoms from each facet. $24.00–26.00

Strawberries Ceramic. Japan. 1940s–1950s. Juicy red strawberries with yellow "seeds" sit atop green foliage bases. $10.00–12.00

Lemons Ceramic. Japan. 1940s–1950s. Bright yellow lemons have green stem stumps. $10.00–12.00

Yellow Pumpkins Ceramic. Japan. 1930s–1940s. Miniature yellow pumpkins have yellow stems. $8.00–10.00

Corn on the Cob Ceramic. Japan. 1950s. Two ears of corn, half exposed, rest on their bases. $8.00–10.00

Beets Porcelain. Japan. 1950s. Bright red porcelain beets with green tops rest on their sides. $8.00–10.00

Ears of Corn Ceramic. Japan. 1940s–1950s. Two stripped ears of corn lie on their sides. $8.00–12.00

White Asparagus Porcelain. Japan. 1950s. Two standing bunches of white asparagus are tied with two dark green strings and have deep purple tops. $10.00–12.00

Hubbard Squash Ceramic. Japan. 1940s. Two green and yellow hubbard squashes lie on their sides. $10.00–12.00

Chanterelle Mushrooms Porcelain. Japan. 1950s. Green-stemmed, orange-capped Chanterelle mushrooms stand on rounded bases. $8.00–10.00

Cherries Carrara glass and lead. Red Carrara glass cherries have gray lead stems and leaves. $12.00–16.00

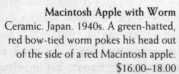

Macintosh Apple with Worm Ceramic. Japan. 1940s. A green-hatted, red bow-tied worm pokes his head out of the side of a red Macintosh apple. $16.00–18.00

Shiitaki Mushrooms Porcelain. Japan. 1950s. Clusters of white and brown Shiitaki mushrooms stand on rounded bases. $10.00–14.00

Porcini Mushrooms Porcelain. Japan. 1950s. White based clusters of porcini mushrooms have brown conical caps. $8.00–12.00

Russet Potato Porcelain. Japan. 1950s. Two brownish-red russet potatoes lie on their sides. $6.00–8.00

Cauliflower and Artichoke Ceramic. Japan. 1960s. A green artichoke accompanies a green-stemmed head of cauliflower. $10.00–12.00

Cabbage Heads Porcelain. Japan. 1950s. Realistically molded cabbage heads have finely detailed veining on green leaves. $10.00–14.00

Tomatoes Ceramic. Japan. 1950s. Bright red tomatoes have red leaves clinging to their bottoms. $8.00–10.00

Green Bell Peppers Ceramic. Japan. 1930s–1940s. Deep green bell peppers have short stems protruding from tops. $6.00–8.00

Yellow Pumpkins Ceramic. Japan. 1930s. Small, round yellow pumpkins have red lines indicating sections and two dark green leaves painted on sides. $6.00–8.00

Cabbage Heads Ceramic. Japan. 1940s–1950s. White and green cabbage heads have smooth, rounded shape. $10.00–12.00

Zucchini Squash Ceramic. Japan. Early 1950s. Lovely green zucchini squash with yellow ends have flattened blossom on stem side. $10.00–14.00

Plantains Ceramic. Japan. 1940s–1950s. Two clusters of yellowish-green plantains lie on their sides. $15.00–20.00

Tomatoes Ceramic. Japan. 1940s–1950s. Bright red tomatoes have green leaves draped across tops. $8.00–10.00

Iceberg Lettuce Porcelain. Japan. Early 1950s. Two finely articulated heads of iceberg lettuce are pale green in color. $10.00–12.00

Chili Peppers Porcelain. Japan. Early 1950s. Bright red chili peppers lie on their sides. $7.00–9.00

Indian Corn Ceramic. Japan. 1940s. Barely opened ears of Indian corn lie in dark green leaves. $10.00–11.00

Corn Cobs Ceramic. Japan. 1940s–1950s. Matching yellow ears of corn half emerge from green foliage $10.00–12.00

Orange Bell Peppers Ceramic. Japan. 1940s–1950s. Tubular orange-colored bell peppers lie on their sides. $7.00–9.00

Red Bell Peppers Ceramic. Japan. 1940s–1950s. Elongated red bell peppers with green stems lie on their sides. $6.00–8.00

Red Bell Peppers Ceramic. Japan. 1940s–1950s. Ovoid red bell peppers sit upright. $6.00–8.00

Corn Cobs Ceramic. Japan. 1940s–1950s. Yellow ears of corn have one dark green strip of foliage. $6.00–8.00

Chili Peppers Ceramic. Japan. 1940s–1950s. One green and one red chili pepper lie on their sides. $6.00–8.00

Pea Pods Ceramic. Japan. 1940s–1950s. Bright green peas burst from dark green pods. $8.00–10.00

Lunchbox and Thermos Ceramic. Japan. 1950s. A dome-topped laborer's lunchbox in tan is paired with a tan thermos bottle topped with a red cup. $10.00–15.00

Chianti Wine Bottles Glass, straw, and metal. U.S.A. Matching miniature Chianti wine bottles in clear glass are wrapped in straw and capped with red and green screw-on caps, respectively. $12.00–14.00

Popcorn and Pop Ceramic. Japan. 1950s. A box of popcorn is teamed with a bottle of pop. $18.00–22.00

Orange Condiment Set Ceramic. Japan. Hand-painted Maruhon Ware. Orange condiment sits on green long tray. $18.00–20.00

Apple and Grapes Condiment Set Ceramic. Japan. "PY Japan." An apple and a bunch of grapes sit on a leafy tray. $24.00–26.00

One-Piece Fish Ceramic. U.S.A. Signed "C. Miller." This one-piece set features fish standing on their tails and hats in light brown. $34.00–36.00

One-Piece Onions Ceramic. U.S.A. Two-tone onions are painted light yellow with green tops. $10.00–15.00

One-Piece Cabbage Ceramic. U.S.A. One-piece set depicts green and white cabbage. $9.00–15.00

One-Piece Corn Ceramic. U.S.A. One-piece set depicts yellow corn. $9.00–15.00

One-Piece Grapes Ceramic. U.S.A. A bunch of green grapes has a brown stem. $9.00–15.00

One-Piece Pumpkin Faces Ceramic. U.S.A. Orange pumpkin faces have green stems. $9.00–15.00

One-Piece String Beans Ceramic. U.S.A. Large green beans appear to be Kentucky wonder beans. $9.00–15.00

One-Piece Peas Ceramic. U.S.A. Peas peek out of green pods. $9.00–15.00

One-Piece Eggplant Ceramic. U.S.A. Eggplant has green and yellow stems. $9.00–15.00

One-Piece Carrots Ceramic. U.S.A. This one-piece set features red and yellow carrots. $9.00–15.00

Maxi Pie and Rolling Pin Ceramic. Japan. 1950s. This large-format set features a yellow pie and white rolling pin. $14.00–18.00

Fruit Baskets Ceramic. "Tilso." These 5" hand-painted white baskets are filled with colored fruit. $8.00–12.00

Ice Cream Sundae Ceramic. U.S.A. A blue dish (pepper) holds a scoop of pink ice cream with chocolate sauce. $16.00–20.00

Ice Cream Cones Ceramic. U.S.A. Two cones of shiny chocolate ice cream lie on their sides. $12.00–16.00

Popcorn and Pop Ceramic. U.S.A. A yellow bottle of soda, marked "Pop," is teamed with a brown box, marked "Popcorn," heaped with white popcorn. $14.00–18.00

Frying Pan with Egg Ceramic. Bernard Studios, Inc. Fullerton, CA. A brown frying pan (pepper) holds a sunny-side-up egg (salt). $14.00–18.00

Hard-Boiled Egg Ceramic. Japan. 1950s. Two halves of a hard-boiled egg have plain, white exterior. $12.00–14.00

Toaster and Toast Ceramic. U.S.A. A brown, buttered slice of toast is teamed with a white, streamlined toaster. $14.00–18.00

"Pa" Coffee Cup Ceramic. U.S.A. A white cup brimming with coffee has a drawing of a mustachioed man in a hat on the side and the word "Pa." The saucer is the pepper shaker. $16.00–18.00

Pie Wedge and Rolling Pin Ceramic. U.S.A. A yellow wedge of pie is teamed with a white rolling pin. $14.00–18.00

Cup and Donut Ceramic. U.S.A. A blue cup is accompanied by a brown, shiny donut. $12.00–14.00

Coffee Mug and Donut Ceramic. U.S.A. A white mug, marked "Coffee," is teamed with a shiny, fat donut. $12.00–14.00

Chocolate Cake and Present Ceramic. U.S.A. A chocolate cake on a plate goes with a white present tied with a yellow bow. $12.00–14.00

Suckling Pig on Platter Ceramic. U.S.A. A brown sucklng pig (salt) nestles on a yellow platter (pepper). $16.00–20.00

Chicken in a Pan Ceramic. U.S.A. A brown chicken nestles in an oval, yellow pan. $16.00–20.00

Stack of Crackers Ceramic. Medelman. Italy. Two identical stacks of crackers have cracker-textured tops. $12.00–16.00

French Loaf Halves Ceramic. Japan. 1980s. Two ends of a loaf of French bread are realistically detailed. $12.00–15.00

Hamburgers in Buns Ceramic. Japan. 1980s. Simplified yellow buns hold a textured, brown hamburger patty. $12.00–15.00

Salami Ends Ceramic. Japan. 1980s. Two chunks of what appears to be Polish sausage have dark brown skins and mottled pink and brown sides. $12.00–15.00

Cupcakes Ceramic. Japan. Chocolate cupcakes with white frosting and multicolored "sprinkles" have squarish red cherries on top. $10.00–14.00

Corn on the Cob on Tray Ceramic. Japan. Realistic corn on the cob, still in their husks, sit on a tray shaped like a flattened corn on the cob with husks. $12.00–14.00

Watermelon Slices Ceramic. Japan. 1960s. Wedges of watermelon have green rinds, white rims, and red fruit. $12.00–14.00

Pale Watermelon Slices Ceramic. Japan. 1950s. Large wedges of watermelon with pale orange flesh and large white rinds have beautifully striated dark and light green outer rinds. $12.00–16.00

Watermelon Wedges with Grasshoppers Ceramic. Japan. 1950s. Beautiful large grasshoppers with yellow bodies, green wings, and pink feet sit on pink watermelon wedges. $20.00–24.00

Apples Ceramic. Japan. Macintosh apples have one yellow and one red side. $10.00–14.00

Strawberries Ceramic. Japan. 1960s. Textured, deep-pink strawberries sit on three leaves. The leaves are attached to the screw-on ceramic cap. $12.00–14.00

Pea Pods on Tray Ceramic. Japan. Two pods, pale green shading into yellow, are open to reveal a row of peas each. The matching pods sit on a rectangular tray textured to resemble overlapping leaves. $18.00–24.00

Chrome Toaster and Toast Ceramic. Vandor. Marilyn and Gary Pelzman. 1980s. The Deco-era toaster has a chromelike finish. The slices of Wonder bread fit inside the opening and hold salt and pepper. $15.00–18.00

Strawberry Basket Ceramic. Japan. White baskets are heaped with red strawberries with green stems. $12.00–14.00

Bananas Ceramic. Japan. Matching yellow bananas have brown spots on one side, green stems on the other. $10.00–12.00

Bread Basket and Cheese Board Ceramic. Japan. A napkin-lined basket holds a loaf of crusty bread and is teamed with a "wooden" board holding a wedge of cheese and an apple. $14.00–20.00

Bowl of Fruit Ceramic. Japan. A brown fluted and stemmed compote holds an assortment of fruit, including an apple, a pear, a pineapple, banana, grapes, and strawberries. The pineapple has plastic leaves. The apple and the pear are the shakers. $14.00–20.00

Bowl of Fruit Ceramic. Japan. A elegant white hexagonal footed bowl is heaped with an assortment of fruit in pastel shades. Among the fruits are a cluster of grapes, a lime, apples, pears, pineapple, and a liberal scattering of leaves. Two fruit are salt and pepper shakers. $16.00–20.00

Ham in Frying Pan Ceramic. Japan. A black frying pan holds a pink slab of ham. $12.00–14.00

Pancakes and Syrup Ceramic. Japan. A blue plate holds a pale stack of pancakes with a melting square of butter. The syrup is in a standard pitcher with a black top, rather than the usual gray one. $12.00–14.00

Blackbird and Pie Ceramic. Japan. A slice of what looks like lemon chiffon pie is topped with a blackbird. $10.00–14.00

Double Slices of Pineapple Ceramic. Japan. Two overlapping slices of pineapple form each of these shakers. $12.00–16.00

Pie a la Mode Ceramic. Japan. This very crude set consists of a pinkish wedge of pie and an unarticulated scoop of vanilla ice cream. $8.00–10.00

Hot Dogs in Buns Ceramic. Japan. Hot dogs protrude from the ends of rectangular buns and are slathered under layers of something frothy that looks nothing like mustard. $12.00–14.00

Heads of Garlic Ceramic. Japan. Realistic-looking heads of garlic have green stems. $10.00–12.00

Pea Pods Ceramic. Longish green pods open along the middle to reveal a row of yellowish peas. Wavy lines predominate. $12.00–14.00

Small Peas in Pod Ceramic. Crudely formed pods have dark brown pods with yellow peas. $8.00–10.00

Straws and Ice Cream Soda Ceramic. Japan. A metallic-looking old-fashioned straw dispenser has its lid partially off, revealing a thicket of yellowish straws. The ice cream soda comes with a huge, swirling head of foam and sits in a white holder. $12.00–16.00

Heads of Lettuce Ceramic Japan. Spherical heads of lettce with realistic veining have borders of leaf ends. $12.00–14.00

Heads of Iceberg Lettuce Ceramic Japan. Spherical heads of iceberg lettuce have realistic details. $12.00–14.00

Purple Grapes Ceramic. Japan. A cluster of purple grapes with green leaves and brown stem lies on its side. $12.00–14.00

Pumpkins Ceramic. Japan. 1970s. Small orange pumpkins have green stems. $10.00–12.00

Apple on Tree Branch Ceramic. Japan. A red apple hangs from the branch protruding from tree trunk that is covered with leaves. $16.00–20.00

Grapes on Vine Ceramic. Japan. A cluster of grapes is suspended from a "C"-shaped vine with green leaves. $16.00–20.00

Pear on Tree Branch Ceramic. Japan. A yellow pear with red top hangs from a "C"-shaped tree trunk covered with leaves. $16.00–20.00

Baked Potatoes with Butter Ceramic. Japan. Idaho potatoes burst open at the top to reveal fluffy white flesh and yellow pat of butter. $10.00–12.00

Kingpin-Shaped Corn Cob Ceramic. Japan. Kingpin-shaped corn cobs have husks halfway up the sides. $10.00–12.00

Celery Bunches Ceramic. Japan. Large bunches of celery with small leaves on top resemble large and elongated bell peppers in shape. $10.00–12.00

Pumpkin and Gourd Ceramic. Avon. This very realistic, highly glazed set consists of a small, bright orange pumpkin and a larger gourd, green on the bottom, yellow on the top. $12.00–14.00

Cabbages in a Can Ceramic and tin. A pair of green cabbage heads comes in a tin can with a yellow label carrying a drawing of the cabbages and marked "A Pair of Cabbage Salt and Pepper Shakers." $25.00–30.00

Tomatoes in a Can Ceramic and tin. A pair of red tomatoes with green leaves comes in a tin can with a red label bearing a drawing of the vegetables and the words "A Pair of Tomato Salt and Pepper Shakers." $25.00–30.00

Onions in a Can Ceramic and tin. A pair of yellow onions with brown stripes and shadings, very realistic, comes in a tin can with a drawing of the vegetables and the words "A Pair of Onion Salt and Pepper Shakers." $25.00–30.00

Glass Ice Cream Cones Glass and metal. Brown glass cones in diamond platter have metal ice cream tops in white and brown. The cones slip into spiral wire constructions attached to a round base painted bright orange. A metal carrier rod between the cone holders terminates in a small ball. $24.00–28.00

Strawberries on a Tray Ceramic. Japan. Red strawberries with white dots and green stems sit in a leaf-ornamented tray. $16.00–20.00

Tomatoes on a Tray Porcelain. A pearly-white tray resembling a basket with scalloped edges and tapering handle holds tomatoes. $14.00–16.00

Tomatoes on Tray Ceramic. Japan. A double-leaf-shaped tray with a brown "stem" handle holds two tomatoes. $14.00–16.00

Red Delicious Apples Ceramic. Japan. Red delicious apples have yellow bases. $10.00–12.00

Bartlett Pears Ceramic. Japan. Yellow Bartlett pears have brown markings. $10.00–12.00

Fuzzy Peaches Ceramic. Japan. Yellow peaches with pink cheeks are coated with fuzz. $10.00–12.00

Watermelon Wedges Ceramic. Japan. Crudely painted watermelon wedges have deep green rinds. $8.00–10.00

Bananas Ceramic. Japan. Yellow bananas have green tips and brown stems. $10.00–12.00

Mushroom Pairs Ceramic. Japan. Each shaker is a large brown-capped mushroom, to the stem of which clings a small, entirely beige mushroom. $10.00–12.00

Asparagus Spears Ceramic. Japan. Green asparagus spears have white shafts and lie on their sides, one per shaker. $8.00–10.00

Idaho Potatoes Ceramic. Japan. Matte-brown Idaho potatoes have pebbled surface. $10.00–12.00

Boiling Potatoes Ceramic. Japan. Small brown potatoes with pink over-blush have scattering of dimples. $6.00–10.00

AT HOME

Ice Cream Parlor Chairs Ceramic and metal. Japan. Large
(6″) wire ice-cream-parlor chairs have ceramic cushions which
snap in as the shakers. Images of Niagara Falls may be found
on the "cushions." $14.00–18.00

Black Telephone Ceramic. Japan. 1960s. The black dial telephone comes in two parts with the receiver as one shaker, and
the base as the other. $16.00–20.00

Pot-Bellied Stove and Coal Bucket Ceramic. U.S.A. A
brown pot-bellied stove stands next to a brown bucket brimming with coal. $12.00–14.00

Stove and Refrigerator Ceramic. Japan. 1940s. A four-door
stove with red handles and knobs is teamed with a single-door
refrigerator. This set comes in various colors. $10.00–14.00

Pot-Bellied Stoves Ceramic. Japan. 1940s. White pot-bellied
stoves sit on red feet and are hand-painted with floral motif
and gold trim. $10.00–12.00

Chamber Pots Ceramic. Japan. 1950s. White-covered chamber
pots with black handles are inscribed with the slogans "Fill'er
up with S" and "Fill'er up with P." $10.00–12.00

Toilet and Water Tank Porcelain. Japan. 1950s. A white toilet
is teamed with a pedestal water tank. Both are trimmed in
gold. "Mine" is written on top of the tank, and "Your'n" on the
lid of the toilet. $10.00–14.00

Water Faucets Ceramic. Japan. 1960s. Bright blue matching
water faucets have cross-type spigots capped with a black lit-

tle dome. These are also available in white with red or blue domes. $16.00–18.00

Ladies' and Gents' Toilets Ceramic. Japan. 1950s. White toilets with brown lids are inscribed either "Ladies" or "Gents." $10.00–14.00

Bed with Pillow Nester Ceramic. U.S.A. A white twin bed, decorated with ribbons on the headboard, has a removable pillow on one end. $12.00–14.00

Dinette Table with Chairs on Base Ceramic. Japan. A yellow, pedestal-type table is attached to a blue base. On either side of the table are white and yellow chairs, the shakers. $18.00–20.00

Sofa and Armchair Ceramic. U.S.A. A pale blue sofa, with tufted back, is accompanied by a yellow armchair. $15.00–17.00

Telephone and Telephone Directory Ceramic. U.S.A. A black telephone is teamed with a white book inscribed "Telephone Directory." $10.00–14.00

Telephone and Directory Ceramic. Japan. A brown telephone with gold highlights is teamed with a pink, opened "Telephone Directory." $11.00–14.00

White Telephone Ceramic. Japan. 1950s. A white, dial telephone has green and red trim. The base is the salt shaker, the receiver the pepper shaker. $10.00–12.00

Fireplace and Logs Nester Ceramic. U.S.A. 1950s. White fireplace, complete with painted logs and flames, holds on its mantel a trio of logs. $15.00–18.00

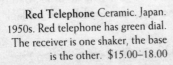

Red Telephone Ceramic. Japan. 1950s. Red telephone has green dial. The receiver is one shaker, the base is the other. $15.00–18.00

Chopping Block and Cleaver Ceramic. U.S.A. A brown chopping block serves as the base for a yellow-bladed cleaver. $12.00–14.00

Hammer and Nail Ceramic. U.S.A. A brown and black hammer goes with a huge gray nail. $14.00–18.00

Plane and T-Square Ceramic. U.S.A. A pink T-square accompanies a yellow and brown plane. $12.00–14.00

Hammer and Anvil Ceramic. Japan. A deep brown anvil serves as the base for a charcoal-gray anvil. $10.00–14.00

Flat Tire and Pump Ceramic. U.S.A. A gray, flat tire is teamed with a brown pump. $14.00–18.00

Screw and Bolt Ceramic. U.S.A. A black bolt goes with a black screw. $10.00–14.00

Thermos and Lunch Box Ceramic. U.S.A. A brown lunch box is teamed with a brown thermos with a red cap. The lunch box may also be black, and the thermos, green. $14.00–18.00

Fireplace and Rocker Ceramic. Japan. A yellow fireplace, complete with hanging pot and sleeping calico cat, is emblazoned "God Bless Our Home." The black rocker has white trim and a sleeping cat curled on the seat. $10.00–12.00

Red Fireplace and Rocker Ceramic. Japan. 1950s. A red fireplace with a yellow mantel and a red teapot with teacup is flanked by a black rocker on a yellow background. $10.00–12.00

Pot-Bellied Stoves Ceramic. Japan. 1950s. White pot-bellied stoves have pale blue rings around the middle and some gold detailing on the doors. Each has a truncated stovepipe marked with either an "S" or "P." $12.00–16.00

Telephones Ceramic. Japan. 1950s. Old-fashioned telephones are wood-grained, painted yellow, with red flower ornamentation. $10.00–12.00

Cannon and Drum Bugle Ceramic. Japan. 1960s. A black drum is topped with a yellow bugle. The brown cannon has dark brown wheels. $10.00–12.00

Watering Cans with Roosters Ceramic. Japan. 1970s. White watering cans with yellow spouts and handles have a colorful rooster motif painted on the side. $10.00–12.00

Watering Cans with Rooster Motifs Ceramic. Japan. 1970s. White watering cans have yellow handles, red spouts, and colorful roosters painted on the sides. $10.00–12.00

Watering Cans with Flowers Ceramic. Japan. 1960s. White watering cans with yellow and brown plaid spouts and handles have a floral, hand-painted design on the side. $10.00–12.00

Watering Cans with Inspirational Message Ceramic. Japan. 1950s. White watering cans with pink highlights are inscribed with the following poem:"The kiss of the sun for pardon/The song of the bird for mirth/One is nearer God's heart in a garden/Than anywhere else on earth." $12.00–14.00

Clocks with Smiling Faces Ceramic. Japan. 1960s. Identical alarm clocks with black "ringers" and three yellow feet have smiling faces. $10.00–12.00

Cooking Stoves Ceramic. Japan. 1960s. White stoves with oven doors have dual red tulip design painted on the front. $10.00–12.00

Meat Grinders Ceramic. Japan. 1960s. White meat grinders on yellow feet have brown handles and a pink flower bud painted on the flat surfaces. $10.00–12.00

Invertible Coffeepots Ceramic. Japan. 1960s. Identical coffeepots are white with pink flower on the upper half, and a yellow chick on the lower half. Spout is pink. $10.00–12.00

Tea Kettles Ceramic. Japan. 1970s. Conical tea kettles with straight, yellow spouts and handles are white with a blue and yellow pansy motif. $10.00–12.00

Squat Tea Kettles Ceramic. Japan. 1970s. Squat, rounded tea kettles with brown handles have a leaf design. $10.00–12.00

Wheelbarrows Ceramic. Japan. 1960s. Black wheelbarrow has yellow wheel and white tulip motif. White wheelbarrow has black wheel and pink and green tulip motif. $10.00–12.00

Scales Ceramic. Japan. 1960s. White scales have brown support and sit on a white base outlined in pale green with a floppy tulip design. $10.00–12.00

Irons Ceramic. Japan. 1960s. Old-fashioned irons have yellow handles, black "bulbs," and a floral motif on the white body. $10.00–12.00

Irons Ceramic. Japan. 1960s. White irons have blue handles, gold trim, and a scattering of tiny flowers and leaves on the top and sides. $10.00–12.00

Blue Seltzer Bottles Ceramic. Japan. 1950s. Bright blue seltzer bottles have gold nozzles. $12.00–18.00

Victrolas Ceramic. Japan. 1930s. Horned victrolas are painted either blue or yellow with a motif of lilies of the valley. This style shaker came in many color combinations and with a variety of hand-painted floral decorations. $10.00–12.00

Victrolas Ceramic. Japan. 1960s. Yellow-horned Victrolas sit on white bases with floral motif. $10.00–12.00

Victrolas Ceramic. Japan. 1950s. White, old-fashioned Victrolas have pink outlining, a scattering of pink, poinsettia-like flowers on the horn, and the inscription "Edison Home. Ft. Myers, FLA" on the base. $10.00–12.00

Spinning Wheels Ceramic. Japan. 1950s. Brown and blue spinning wheels have yellow and red spindles and sit on white bases decorated with red lilies of the valley. $10.00–12.00

Stove with Kettles Ceramic. Japan. 1940s. A lovely, hand-painted stove is the base for the shakers made in the shape of a teapot and a stewpot, both of which are decorated with floral motifs. The stove has a lavender body, green door, and orange backsplash. $15.00–18.00

Elephant-Headed Tea Kettles Ceramic. 1940s. Tea kettles in the shape of Dumbo, with large pink ears and trunk and big eyes have trunk as spout and sit on three tiny "feet." $14.00–18.00

Tea Kettles with Flowers Ceramic. 1950s. White teapots with metal handle sit on three small "feet" are hand-painted with graceful rose and leaf motif. $14.00–16.00

Chef With Fly on Nose Pot Ceramic. 1950s. A comical, cross-eyed chef head in a short white toque has a fly sitting on the nose. The head rests on three small black feet. $14.00–16.00

Black Teapots Red clay. 1960s. One spherical, one ovoid teapot have metal handles and three small "feet." The squat one is ornamented with a hand-painted floral design, while the spherical one is decorated with a rooster. Both are highly glazed. $10.00–14.00

Stove with Pots Condiment Set Red clay. A large black stove, with a deeply embossed design, has a removable lid on which sits the tea kettle and coffeepot shakers in highly glazed deep brown. $16.00–20.00

Small Black Stove with Burners Red clay. A small, old-fashioned cook stove in highly glazed black finish has two white cooktops which are the removable shakers. $10.00–16.00

Black Stove with Pots Red clay. Old-fashioned black stove with gold trim and the work "DOT" on the door, is the base for a coffeepot and a tea kettle, both highly glazed and black, with a gold trim. $12.00–16.00

Black Pig Tea Kettles Red clay. Big-eyed, hand-painted pig heads are fashioned into tea kettles with metal handles. Pigs wear pink bow ties and have blue eyes. The spouts sprout from the sides. $12.00–14.00

Bulldog Tea Kettles Red clay. 1950s. Deep brown bulldog heads have hand-painted white jowls with blue dots, red scowling lips, and white eyes. The lids are yellow stocking caps. Handles are made of metal. $12.00–14.00

Black Mice Tea Kettles Red clay. 1950s. Black mice heads with hot pink ears have bright red lips and blue eyes. The one with the blue cap is a boy, the one with a red bow on its lid is a girl. The heads sit on three little feet and have a metal handle. $12.00–14.00

Black Teapots Red clay. 1940s. Small round teapots have a golden rooster motif hand-painted on the side. They are finished in a deeply reflective black glaze. $10.00–12.00

Black Coffeepots Red clay. 1940s. Standard "home-on-the-range" coffeepots are deep black with the word "salt" or "pepper" hand-painted in white and surrounded by little flowers. $10.00–12.00

Tea Kettles Red clay. 1940s. Small tea kettles in a variety of shapes have metal handles and hand-painted sides, usually with the letters "S" and "P" in white. $10.00–12.00

Three-Tiered Teapot Ceramic. Japan. This three-tiered teapot features a large-bottom pot with a standard tea spout, a non-spouted central section, and a triangular spouted top section. The lowest part is a sugar bowl, the subsequent two parts are shakers. All three have handles. Various floral motifs are hand-painted on the sides. $14.00–16.00

Tea Kettle on Pot-Bellied Stove Ceramic. Japan. 1940s. A white, pot-bellied stove is the base for a white teapot with a pink flower in this nester set. $10.00–12.00

Teapot and Coffeepot Porcelain. White teapot and "bulb" coffee maker have pastel-colored porcelain and sculpted flowers clustering on the sides or on the top. Gold ornamentation is usual. $10.00–12.00

Teapot and Sugar Bowl Shakers on Tray Ceramic. Japan. 1940s. Round teapot and sugar bowl shakers sit in a gracefully undulating tray. The pots are ornamented with a repeating blue horizontal stripe and a green wash on the spout, lid, and parts of the body. $12.00–14.00

Oriental-Style Teapot and Bowl Ceramic. Japan. 1940s. Lovely, spherical teapot and bowl have blue, ear-shaped handles, spout, and lid and a blue and red pattern of cherry blossoms. $10.00–12.00

Coffeepot and Teapot Ceramic. Japan. 1950s. The pots are banded in pale green on the top and the bottom, framing a white field with a pink gerbera daisy motif. $10.00–12.00

White Coffeepots and Teapots with Cherries Ceramic. Japan. White coffeepots and teapots have a pebbled finish and are ornamented with bas-relief cherries with leaves. $12.00–14.00

"Chippendale" Teapots Ceramic. Japan. 1950s. Elegant, Chippendale-styled teapots have a green or yellow or blue all-over pattern and gold base and lids. $10.00–12.00

Pebbled Teapots Porcelain. White, bulbuous teapots have a pebbled surface and a rounded cap in place of the spout. $10.00–14.00

Round Teapots Porcelain. Spherical teapots with handles nearly on the top have rounded caps in place of spouts. These are available in a variety of colors, with a variety of hand-painted decorative motifs on the sides, and in a large as well as a smaller size. $10.00–18.00

Small Teapots and Coffeepots Ceramic. Japan. 1940s— 1950s. A variety of small (3½") teapots and coffeepots come in white ceramic with a wide range of hand-painted floral motifs. $10.00–14.00

Light Bulbs Ceramic. Japan. 1950s. White lightbulbs of uneven size have bright yellow sockets. $10.00–12.00

White Alarm Clocks Ceramic. Japan. 1950s. White alarm clocks stand on feet and have red numbers, dials, and dots on feet. $10.00–12.00

Star and Moon Ceramic. Japan. 1950s. A yellow star is teamed with a new moon. $10.00–12.00

Sewing Machines Ceramic. Japan. 1940s—1950s. White sewing machines with gold trim have a pink and green floral motif hand-painted on the sides. $10.00–12.00

Old Fashioned Gramophone Player Ceramic. Japan. 1940s—1950s. Bright pink speakers rise from brown bases. $10.00–12.00

Guitars with Flowers Ceramic. Japan. 1950s. Brown guitars lie at an angle on a trio of pink flowers. $10.00–12.00

Violins Porcelain and wire. White porcelain violins with lavender flower motifs have gold wire strings and frets. $10.00–12.00

Yellow, Flowered Violins Ceramic. Japan. 1950s. Yellow, wood-textured violins have a scattering of tiny multicolored flowers on the front. $10.00–12.00

Violin and Mandolin Ceramic. Japan. 1950s. A green violin with a brown back is teamed with a yellow mandolin with a brown heart and brown and green back. $12.00–14.00

Grand Piano with Bench Ceramic. Sarsaparilla. 1980s. A black grand piano has a black stool with a white seat. $15.00–18.00

Small Violins Porcelain. Small (3″) violins have white fronts and brown backs. $10.00–12.00

Red Violins Ceramic. Japan. 1950s. Red violins have white necks and backs and plastic yellow strings. $12.00–14.00

Piano and Bench Ceramic. Japan. 1950s. A brown piano with white and black keyboard has a separate bench that tucks in under the keyboard. $12.00–16.00

Treble Staff and Notes Ceramic. Japan. The white base is made in the shape of a musical staff with a black treble clef. Two black quarter notes nest on the staff as shakers. $24.00–28.00

Violin and Lute Ceramic. Japan. 1940s. Brown-backed violin and lute have pastel-colored fronts. $12.00–16.00

Red Viola and Harp Ceramic. Japan. 1950s. A bright red viola with white neck and trim is paired with a red harp with real strings. $16.00–20.00

Violin and Case, Large Ceramic. U.S.A. 1950s. A brown violin goes with a brown case. $16.00–18.00

Violin and Case, Small. Ceramic. U.S.A. 1950s. A small, yellow violin is teamed with a pale blue carrying case. $16.00–18.00

Music Book Ceramic. Japan. 1955. Music books have the words "Music Book" inscribed on the spines along with the date "1955." They are opened to show six staffs filled with notes. $12.00–18.00

Juke Box Ceramic. Sarsaparilla. 1980s. A replica of a Wurlitzer jukebox, very realistic, comes in two stackable components. The shakers are the lower and upper halves of the jukebox. $14.00–18.00

Tabletop Jukebox Ceramic. Marilyn and Gary Pelzman. Vandor. 1980s. This two-part jukebox is a replica of the chrome restaurant-table models. The jukebox divides vertically to form two shaker halves. $16.00–20.00

Porcelain Pipes Porcelain. White pipes with rounded bowl and gracefully curling stems have gold trim and hand-painted flowers. $10.00–12.00

Brown Pipes Ceramic. Japan. 1950s. Wood-grained pipes have different shapes and come in various colors. The one with the lid and high stem is marked "pepper." The one with the rounded bowl and squat stem is marked "salt." These are available in yellow, orange, dark brown, and reddish brown. $10.00–12.00

Plastic Pipes Plastic. Plastic, wood-grained "corn-cob"-shaped pipes are beige with brown highlighting and golden tops and bottoms. $10.00–12.00

Bellows Camera Ceramic. Japan. 1940s. Black bellows camera is made up of two pieces: the camera body (one shaker) and the bellows (another shaker). $14.00–18.00

Black and White Cameras Ceramic. Japan. 1960s. Hand cameras with excellent detail are white (salt) and black (pepper). $16.00–20.00

Lusterware Binoculars Lusterware. White theater binoculars with gold trim have shakers in each eyepiece. $12.00–18.00

Table Lamps Ceramic. Japan. 1950s. Small white table lamps with gold trim are ornamented, on the shade part, with decals of a turn-of-the-century gentleman and lady and antique car. $10.00–14.00

Axe and Stump Ceramic. Japan. 1940s. An axe with a black head fits into a green stump. $10.00–14.00

Gold Frames Porcelain. Japan. 1950s. Square frames with circular cutouts are deeply textured and painted with 22 karat gold paint. The frames actually accommodate photographs. $10.00–14.00

White Pillows Porcelain. Japan. 1950s. White plump pillows have gold trim and scattered floral design. $10.00–14.00

Kitchen Sink and Stove Ceramic. U.S.A. 1950s. Yellow kitchen stove matches a kitchen sink in a four-cabinet base. $12.00–14.00

Sewing Machine on Base Ceramic. U.S.A. 1950s. A beautifully detailed black sewing machine sits on a brown base. The two components are individual shakers. $16.00–20.00

Coffee Grinders Ceramic. U.S.A. 1950s. Nicely detailed dark brown coffee grinders are identical except for the letters "S" or "P" on their fronts. $10.00–12.00

S and P Range Sets Ceramic. Range sets in a variety of Deco and Streamline shapes, marked with the letters "S" and "P," were given as standard issue with kitchen stoves. These include such shapes as matching rectangles with fluted faces and elongated "S" and "P" in black on a raised knob; rectangles with rounded outside corners and a simple, three-line ornament in the front below the letters; and rectangles with semicircular knobs in the center which, when placed side by side, form a complete circle. $18.00–28.00

Computers Ceramic. Japan. 1980s. Yellow computers with black boards have the words "Salt" and "Pepper" in computer print on the screens. $12.00–14.00

S and P Range Sets Ceramic. Range sets in a variety of Deco and Streamline shapes were given as standard issue with kitchen stoves. $18.00–28.00

Television Set Ceramic. Japan. 1960s. A two-part television set from the 1960s has a brown speaker-type stand and a screen component with a paper picture of a cowboy. $18.00–22.00

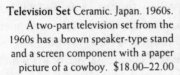

Television Set Ceramic. 1960s. A two-part television set from the 1960s has a black, speaker-type stand, and a white set with four black knobs and a paper picture of the Beatles in the screen. $18.00–22.00

Television Set and Record Player Ceramic. Japan. 1950s. A brown and white record player is accompanied by a very small screen television set. $10.00–14.00

Radios Ceramic. Vandor. 1980s. Replicas of the Deco Bakelite radios are done in black with red dials or blue with red dials. $16.00–18.00

Record Player and Stack of Records Ceramic. Vandor. 1980s. A pink, sea foam green, and red record player is teamed with a stack of black records. $18.00–20.00

Candles in Candlesticks Ceramic. Japan. 1950s. Red candles with yellow flames stand in green candlesticks. $10.00–12.00

White-and-Gold Candles Ceramic. Japan. 1960s. White candles and candlesticks have gold trim and gold flames. $10.00–12.00

Starry Candles Ceramic. Japan. 1960s. White candles in yellow and black candlesticks have red flames and a scattering of golden stars on the candles. $10.00–12.00

Black and White Oxfords Ceramic. Japan. 1940s—1950s. This pair of oxfords has white body with black toe, vamp, and heel. $10.00–14.00

Cowboy Boots Ceramic. Japan. 1940s—1950s. Yellow cowboy boots have embossed design highlighted in green. $10.00–12.00

Blond Cowboy Boots Ceramic. Japan. 1940s—1950s. Beige cowboy boots have black soles and embossed sunburst pattern. $10.00–12.00

Red Running Shoes Ceramic. Japan. 1950s. Red running shoes with white toes and soles have white diagonal stripes and yellow tongues. $10.00–14.00

Japanese Thong Slippers Porcelain. Japan. 1950s. Deep red Japanese slippers have yellow thongs. $10.00–14.00

Slipper Socks Ceramic. Japan. 1950s. Yellow slipper socks have green trim and pompoms. $10.00–14.00

His and Hers Underwear Ceramic. Japan. Man's white boxer shorts are teamed with a round white "fanny" with black lines tracing a pair of panties. $10.00–12.00

Collar and Bow Tie Ceramic. Japan. A white collar is teamed with a blue bow tie with dark blue dots. $10.00–12.00

Confederate Hats Ceramic. Japan. 1940s. Black confederate hats have yellow bands and yellow crossed-rifle logo in front. $10.00–12.00

Doctor's Bag and Lawyer's Briefcase Ceramic. Japan. 1940s—1950s. A deep orange doctor's bag goes with a pale tan briefcase. $10.00–12.00

Gloves with Card Motif Ceramic. Japan. Olive-green gloves (same hand) have, on the palm, a black club and a red heart card. $14.00–18.00

Fedoras Ceramic. Occupied Japan. 1940s. A brown fedora with a red band is teamed with a red fedora with a green band. $24.00–28.00

Civil War Hats Ceramic. Japan. Pale blue Civil War hats have Confederate insignias and are shaped like calvary or infantry headgear. $16.00–20.00

Pilgrim Hats Ceramic. Japan. White pilgrim hats have black bands with gold buckles. $12.00–14.00

Shriner Hats Ceramic. Matching red shriner hats have a gold insignia painted on the front. They are market "Temple Treasures, F.N. Kisstner, Chicago, 441307." $18.00–24.00

Fedora and Briefcase
Ceramic. Japan. 1940s–1950s.
A gray fedora is teamed with a
russet brown briefcase.
$10.00–14.00

Clothes on Hangers on Rack Ceramic.
Japan. 1950s. This three-piece set consists of a stand made in the shape of a
rack with two hooks. From each ceramic
hook hangs a dress or a suit jacket. The
racks come in a variety of colors.
$18.00–24.00

Shriner Hats Ceramic. One large and one small shriner hat
have embossed insignias on the front. The insignias are highlighted in golden paint. $18.00–24.00

Boots and Hat Ceramic. Japan. A pair of brown riding boots
goes with a black fedora. $12.00–18.00

Baby Shoes Ceramic. Japan. 1950s. Worn baby shoes are
glazed to appear bronzed. $12.00–16.00

Two-Story and Three-Story Houses on Tray Ceramic.
Noritake. Japan. This three-piece set consists of an octogonal
tray, pale green with orange rim, on which sit two shakers in
the shape of two houses. One is a two-story cottage, the other
has three stories. Both replicate the tray colors. $30.00–40.00

Log Cabins Ceramic. Japan. Small brown log cabins have blue
windows, green roofs, and red chimneys. $10.00–12.00

"God Bless Our Mortgaged Home" Homes Ceramic.
U.S.A. Beige "brick" cottages with shutters have either a pink
or a blue roof with the slogan "God bless our mortgaged
home" on the roof. $12.00–14.00

Orange-Roofed Cottages Ceramic. White cottages with
very pointy red "tile" roofs have green chimneys. They look
like fairy tale houses. $10.00–12.00

Tudor Cottages Ceramic. White cottages with brown Tudor timbering effects, have yellow "thatched" roofs and green lawns. $12.00–14.00

"Brick" Cottages Ceramic. Two-story "brick" cottages with yellow roofs have a crackled glaze finish. $10.00–12.00

Windmills Ceramic. Cute white windmills with yellow blades have a profusion of foliage and flowers clinging to the bottom and sides. $10.00–12.00

Delft Windmills Delftware and metal. Holland. Blue and white windmills, in a variety of shapes, have revolving metal blades. $16.00–12.00

Beehive Houses Ceramic. Occupied Japan. 1940s. White beehives, painted with a profusion of vines and flowers, have red roofs. To the top and the side of the house cling painted bees. $18.00–24.00

Beehive Houses Ceramic. Japan. Conical-roofed white beehives have red doors, a red and black bee, and a profusion of verdant foliage clinging to the sides of the house. $10.00–12.00

Tiny Gothic Houses Lusterware. Tiny gothic-style houses with blue roofs, gold sides, and black lines sit on a blue tray. $14.00–20.00

House and Windmill on Tray Lusterware. A tiny white cottage with a red roof and a beige windmill with yellow blades nestle in the circular sides of a blue tray with a keyhole-type handle in the middle. $14.00–20.00

Corset and Pantaloons Ceramic. Japan. 1950s. White corset and pantaloons are trimmed in pink. $14.00–18.00

Cottages Ceramic. Japan. White cottages with pink doors have yellow thatched roofs, green vine-effect, and three windows on the front. $10.00–12.00

Victorian "Painted Ladies" Ceramic. Otagiri. Japan. Detailed replicas of Victorian "painted ladies" are available with a matching sugar bowl and cookie jar. $11.00–14.00

English Cottage Ceramic. Ron Gordon Designs, Inc. A two-part English cottage is made of a white base (pepper) and thatched roof (salt). $12.00–14.00

Typewriter Heads Ceramic. Black typewriters sit on human bodies dressed in trousers (green or yellow) and shirts (white or blue). On the white sheets of paper coming out of the typewriters are cartoony human faces with large, Betty Boop eyes and big smiles. $20.00–24.00

Desk-Blotter Heads Ceramic. Japan. 1950s. White desk blotters with black handles sit on boy bodies in pink shirts and yellow or blue trousers. Faces have Betty Boop eyes. $16.00–20.00

Clock Heads Ceramic. Japan. 1950s. White clocks with Betty Boop eyes and smiling mouths sit on cross-legged boy bodies in blue overalls. $16.00–20.00

Cashbox Heads Ceramic. Japan. 1950s. Gray cashboxes with Betty Boop eyes sit on little boy bodies in yellow or pink shirts and blue or brown pants. $16.00–20.00

Adding Machine Heads Ceramic. Japan. 1950s. Girls in long pink dresses with dots hold pencil and paper and have as their heads either a pale green or pale gray adding machine. Baby-doll eyes look off to the sides. $16.00–20.00

Glue Heads Ceramic. Japan. 1950s. Sitting girl bodies in polka-dotted dresses (pink or gray) hold brushes and have, as their heads, tubes of glue that leak off to one side. $16.00–20.00

Telephone Heads Ceramic. Japan. 1950s. Standing girl bodies in long dresses (pink or blue) hold telephone books and have, as their heads, either a pink or a yellow telephone. The yellow phone has a winking face. $16.00–20.00

Ink Bottle Heads Ceramic. Japan. 1950s. Standing girl bodies in long, aproned dresses hold quill pen and paper. As their heads they have ink bottles in either pink or blue and smiling faces with baby-doll eyes. $16.00–20.00

Spoon and Fork Couples Ceramic. Japan. This enchanting set of spoon and fork couples was available in many color combinations: yellow, pink, blue, or black bodies. Always, the

Kingpin People Ceramic. Japan. 1950s. Red kingpins have white, heart-shaped faces and wear bow ties. On each is written either "Pin Salt" or "Pin Pepper." $18.00–20.00

Clothespin Couple Ceramic. Taiwan. Late 1960s. This one-piece shaker is a hinge-type clothespin each of whose sides is painted a different color. The white side has a lady's face in black. The black side has a gent's face in white. $12.00–16.00

utensils are dancing, holding one arm up, the other down. They have round eyes, dot mouths, and wear aprons. Their "legs" are tiny excrescences that sprout from the bottom of the handles and cling to a semispherical, generally black base. $20.00–24.00

Bus and Fire Engine People Ceramic. Japan. A blue bus has a smiling Betty boop face on its front. The red fire engine has a similar face. $14.00–20.00

Teapot and Coffeepot People Ceramic. Japan. A pink teapot girl goes with a pink coffeepot boy. She wears a red jumper over a yellow blouse. He wears checkered pants with a green cable-knit vest. $16.00–20.00

Creamer and Sugar Bowl People Ceramic. Japan. 1940s. White sugar bowl and pitcher with pink cheeks and Betty Boop eyes are the heads of little girl bodies with knock knees standing on green, grassy bases. Sugar bowl wears a white dress shading into pink; creamer wears a pale green dress and shows her undies. $16.00–20.00

Fork and Spoon Couple Ceramic. Japan. 1940s. This simple set of utensil people has black, crude bodies, pink faces with white, round eyes with black centers, button noses, and red "U" lips. Both wear aprons with embossed ties, and wave. $14.00–20.00

"I'm in the Pink" and "I'm So Blue" Creamer and Sugar Bowl Ceramic. U.S.A. 1950s. These clever, reversible shakers are made in the shape of a creamer and a sugar bowl. Both have two faces. The blue, frowning one is inscribed "I'm so blue," and the pink smiling one is inscribed "I'm in the pink." $12.00–14.00

Egg-Cup People Ceramic. Japan. Egg-cup people bodies have insertable shaker heads in the shape of eggs. Their cartoony features derive from Victorian fashion. $16.00–20.00

Teacup Heads Ceramic. Japan. 1950s. Conical white heads sprout from collar bases and wear teacups as hats. The lady's teacup is red with green saucer. The gentleman's teacup is yellow with black saucer. $14.00–20.00

Clothespin Couple Plastic. U.S.A. 1970s. The two sides of a clothespin each have a face. The white side has a woman's face in black; the black side has a man's face in white. This is a one-piece shaker. $12.00–16.00

Kingpin People Ceramic. Japan. 1950s. Red kingpins have white heart-shaped faces and wear bow ties. On each is written either "Pin Salt" or "Pin Pepper." $18.00–20.00

Fork and Spoon Couple Ceramic. Japan. 1950s. Pink fork and spoon are dressed in formal wear and hold their bodies in readiness for a slow foxtrot. She wears yellow gown, he wears tails and pale blue trousers. $14.00–20.00

ON THE ROAD

New Jersey Turnpike Tray with Cars Metal. This three-piece set consists of a silver tray fashioned in the shape of the entrance to the Holland Tunnel and embossed with the words, "New Jersey Turnpike." On it sit two silver old-fashioned jalopies, the shakers. $24.00–30.00

Ceramic Statute of Liberty and Empire State Building Ceramic. Japan. 1980s. White replicas of the Statute of Liberty and the Empire State Building have golden flame and top, respectively. $18.00–20.00

Metal Statue of Liberty and Empire State Building In Base Metal. 1930s. Finely detailed replicas of the Empire State and the Statue of Liberty stand in a base sculpted with three-dimensional high-rise buildings and the words "New York City." $50.00–70.00

New York Ocean Liner Metal and wood. U.S.A. 1930s. A black, wooden hull is capped with a silver-painted metal top into which fit silvery shaker smokestacks. $40.00–50.00

Metal Space Needle Silver-painted metal. Japan. 1960s. Replicas of the Seattle World's Fair space needle stand on a silver metal tray. $14.00–24.00

Nova Scotia Lighthouse Ceramic. Japan. Two parts of a white, octagonal lighthouse on a gray base are embossed with the words "Peggy's Cove, Nova Scotia—The Lighthouse." $14.00–18.00

Statue of Liberty and Empire State Building
Metal. Japan. 1930s or 1940s. Metal, detailed replicas of the Statue of Liberty and the Empire State building stand on a metal tray embossed with hand-colored flowers. $14.00–20.00

Space Needle, Seattle, Washington
Ceramic. Japan. 1960s. This ceramic pair of Space Needles is yellow with red and yellow domes and the words "Space Needle, Seattle, WA." on the bases. $14.00–18.00

Mount Rushmore Ceramic Shaker
Ceramic. 1940s. Two halves of the Mount Rushmore monument are rendered in bas-relief with the words "Mount Rushmore" and "Shrine of Democracy" embossed on each base. $14.00–18.00

Ocean Liner from South Park, Pittsburgh Metal. 1940s. An ocean liner with two removable stacks (the shakers) bears the label from South Park, Pittsburgh. $12.00–14.00

Mount Rushmore Metal Shakers Metal. 1930s. Two halves of the Mount Rushmore monument are in silver-colored metal. $14.00–18.00

Ozark Jugs Ceramic. Japan. Beige jugs are hand-painted with profiles of pipe-smoking Ma and Pa in black and blue. Corks fit into the spouts. $10.00–12.00

Brown Ozark Jugs Ceramic. Japan. Brown jugs are hand-painted with profiles of pipe-smoking Ma and Pa in red, white, yellow, and black. $10.00–12.00

Horseshoe and Four-Leaf Clover from Torrington, CT Ceramic. Japan. 1950s. An orange horseshoe and a green, four-leaf clover come from Torrington, Ct. The back of the horseshoe is embossed "Lucky 75th Anniversary, 1950." $14.00–18.00

Flying Saucers Ceramic. Coventry Ware Inc. 1950s. Green flying saucers have red windows, fins, and the letters "S" and "P." $15.00–20.00

White Flying Saucers Ceramic. 1950s. White flying saucers with a row of dots for windows have the words "Flying Saucers" in green "scary" letters on the side. $15.00–20.00

Martian and Rocket Ceramic. Enesco. A thumb-shaped, tan Martian in a white and blue bow tie holds a suitcase marked "To Mars." He is flanked by a silver rocket with green door and windows. $35.00–40.00

State Profiles Ceramic. Milford Pottery. Geographical silhouettes of the forty-eight states are embossed with the state's name across the side. $14.00–24.00

State Profiles with Emblem and Name Ceramic Very crude geographical silhouettes of the states have a floral emblem embossed on one side and the name of the capital engraved in the other side. $10.00–16.00

Halves of State Profiles Ceramic. 1960s. Crude geographical profiles of states are divided down the middle so that the two halves together make up the profile of the state. A map of the state decal appears on the face. On it is the name of the state, the capital, and a series of representative vignettes. $14.00–18.00

Ceramic State Profiles Ceramic. Japan. 1950s. White geographical profiles of the forty-eight states have a scattering of landmarks embossed on one side and the state's name in black. $10.00–14.00

Metal Arizona Metal. Japan. Parksmith, NYC. Importer. Metal, geographical profiles of Arizona have embossed and hand-colored images of various tourist attractions. On the base is embossed the name of the state. $18.00–24.00

Metal State Profiles Metal. Japan. Parksmith, NYC, Importer. Metal geographical profiles of the forty-eight states have embossed and hand-colored images of various tourist attractions. On the base is embossed the name of the state. $18.00–24.00

State Profiles and Symbol Ceramic. Geographical profiles of the forty-eight states are teamed with the state's emblem. On the state is embossed the name and its nickname. These are not Parkcraft, as can be seen by the fact that the bottom of the state is indented and takes a regular cork. $20.00–30.00

Suitcases, NYC Ceramic. Japan. Suitcases with yellow handles and red stitch marks have images of the Statue of Liberty and the Empire State Building. $12.00–14.00

Pocketbooks, NYC Ceramic. Japan. Pocketbooks have representations of either the Statue of Liberty or the Empire State Building. $12.00–14.00

Rectangular Embossed Souvenir Sets Ceramic. Hand-painted. Japan. 1940s. These handsome shakers represent, in two installments, a scenic view in bas-relief that is then hand-painted. On the base of each shaker is the site identification. Many sites are commemorated on these shakers, among them Aquarena, San Marcos, Texas; Mount Hood, Oregon; Grand Canyon National Park. $24.00–30.00

Alamo, Texas Ceramic. Japan. 1940s. Small, identical, white replicas of the Alamo are highlighted in terra-cotta paint and bear the name "Alamo" on the base. $12.00–14.00

Tower, San Antonio World's Fair, 1968 Ceramic. Japan. 1960s. Tall, white shakers of the 1968 World's Fair in San Antonio, Texas, are ornamented in gold and inscribed with the name of the event on the base. $14.00–18.00

Oregon Beaver State Ceramic. Japan. 1950s. One half of Oregon's Mount Hood is embossed on each of these rectangular shakers that are hand-painted. $24.00–30.00

New York World's Fair, 1964. Metal. Japan. 1964. A silver tray with "New York's World Fair 1964–1965" in gold, holds two silver globes. $18.00–24.00

Pot Metal Washington Monument Silver-painted pot metal. 1960s. Replicas of the Washington Monument obelisks sit on round bases. $14.00–20.00

Metal Washington Monuments on Tray Silver-colored and painted metal. Japan. 1950s. Replicas of the Washington Monument stand on a tray embossed with a design of the Capital Building and bordered with cherry blossoms painted red. $24.00–30.00

Metal Washington Monument and Capital Building on Tray Silver-colored and painted metal. Japan. 1950s. Replicas of the Washington Monument and the Capital Building stand on a tray embossed with the Capital Building against cumulus clouds and, in the foreground, cherry blossoms. $24.00–30.00

Washington, D.C. Snow Dome Shakers Plastic and water. Japan. 1960s. Plastic snow domes with images of the Washington Monument and the Capitol building are oblong in shape. $14.00–18.00

Idaho Spud Heads Ceramic. U.S.A. 1940s. Grinning, baby-doll-eyed potato heads in crown sit in pink bases. Each is inscribed "Idaho Spud" and "Pepper" or "Salt." $18.00–24.00

Pennsylvania Teddy Bears Ceramic. Japan. 1960s. Waving beige teddy bears sit on brown stumps marked "Pennsylvania." $10.00–14.00

Movieland Wax Museum Metal. A gold tray with the words "Movieland Wax Museum" has an image of a Rolls Royce and holds two small metal replicas of Rolls Royces. $35.00–40.00

Disneyland Castle Silver-colored metal. 1960s. Silver-colored Cinderella's castle from Disneyland splits down the middle at the entrance into two equal halves. $14.00–20.00

Nevada Slot Machines Ceramic. Red and white slot machines marked "Pepper" and "Salt" are inscribed "Reno, Nevada." $14.00–20.00

Famous Cities Series Ceramic. Parkcraft. Distributed by Heather House. Burlington IA. This eighteen-set series teams a book with a figurine representing the symbol associated with the city. The book has the name of the city and some landmark on the left, and some aspect of its economic or cultural life on the right-hand side. Among the sets are the following: Chicago and the Wrigley Building; Springfield, Illinois and a bust of Lincoln; Philadelphia and the Liberty Bell; Washington, D.C. and the Washington Monument; Hannibal, Missouri and Tom Sawyer; Havana, Cuba and the cigar; Rio de Janerio, Brazil, and a bag of sugar; Honolulu and a ukelele; Killarney, Ireland, and a green shamrock; Amsterdam and a wooden shoe; Toronto and a blue maple leaf; London and a crown; Agra, India, and the Taj Mahal; Tokyo and a pagoda; Paris and the Eiffel Tower; Venice and a gondola. $22.00–30.00

Parkcraft State Sets, 48-State Series Ceramic. Parkcraft. Taneycomo Ceramic Factory. Hollister, MO. 1957. This forty-eight set series consists of a geographical silhouette of the state, embossed with its name and symbol, and a sculptural figurine representing some object associated with the state. These are as follows, in alphabetical order by state: Alabama: cotton; Arizona: cactus; Arkansas: razorback; California: bathing beauty; Colorado: pack mule; Connecticut: graduation cap; Delaware: light corn; Florida: bathing beauty; Georgia: Confederate cap; Idaho: potato; Illinois: corn; Indiana: racer; Iowa: corn; Kansas: wheat; Kentucky: jug; Louisiana: cotton; Maine: lighthouse; Maryland: oyster; Massachusetts: bean pot; Michigan: car; Minnesota: canoe; Mississippi: cotton; Missouri: mule; Montana: six-shooter; Nebraska: corn; Nevada: ace of spades; New Hampshire: snowman; New Jersey: Miss America; New Mexico: pueblo; New York: Statue of Liberty; North Carolina: cigarettes; North Dakota: wheat; Ohio: tire; Oklahoma: oil well; Oregon: duck; Pennsylvania: coal; Rhode Island: rooster; South Carolina: lighthouse; South Dakota: pheasant; Tennessee: cotton; Texas: oil well; Utah: covered wagon; Vermont: maple syrup bucket; Virginia: ham; Washington: apple; West Virginia: coal; Wisconsin: cheese; Wyoming: bronco. $22.00–30.00 per set and up

Parkcraft State Sets, 50–State Series Ceramic. Parkcraft. Taneycomo Ceramic Factory. Hollister, MO. 1968. This fifty-set series consists of a geographical silhouette of the state, embossed with its name and symbol, and a sculptural figurine represented some object associated with the state. These are as follows, in alphabetical order by state: Alaska: igloo; Alabama: watermelon; Arizona: cactus; Arkansas: razorback; California: orange; Colorado: pack mule; Connecticut: mortarboard; Delaware: lighthouse; Florida: fish; Georgia: Confederate cap; Hawaii: hula dancer; Idaho: potato; Illinois: Lincoln; Indiana: racer; Iowa: corn; Kansas: wheat; Kentucky: jug; Louisiana: sugar sack; Maine: pine tree; Maryland: oyster; Massachusetts: bean pot; Michigan: car; Minnesota: canoe; Mississippi: steamboat; Missouri: mule; Montana: six-shooter; Nebraska: cowboy boots; Nevada: ace of spades; New Hampshire: snowman; New Jersey: Miss America; New Mexico: pueblo; New York: Statue of Liberty; North Carolina: cigarettes; North Dakota: oil well; Ohio: tire; Oklahoma: Indiana; Oregon: duck; Pennsylvania: Liberty Bell; Rhode Island: rooster; South Carolina: cotton; South Dakota: pheasant; Tennessee: bucket; Virginia: ham; Washington: apple; West Virginia: coal; Wisconsin: cheese; Wyoming: bronco. $22.00–30.00 per set and up

American Flags Ceramic. Parkcraft. Taneycomo Ceramic Factory. Hollister, MO. White trapezoidal shakers have American flags on one side. $10.00–24.00

Chicago Travel Building White-painted metal. 1930s. Replicas of the Chicago Travel Building from 1933 are painted white. $40.00–50.00

1939 World's Fair Trylon and Perisphere Plastic. Emeloid Company. Arlington, New Jersey. 1939–39. One-piece shaker consists of an oval base to which are attached a trylon and perisphere, the symbols of the 1939 World's Fair. These come in several color combinations. $24.00–36.00

Trylon and Perisphere Silverplate. William Rodgers. The symbol of the trylon and perisphere are attached to a base made up of two adjacent circles into which fit glass cylindrical shakers. $50.00–60.00

Trylon and Perisphere on Tray Ceramic. Japan. 1939. Ceramic versions of the trylon and perisphere are housed on a tray with a toast-shaped structure separating the two halves. The white shakers have, in brown, the words "Salt," and "Pepper," and "New York, N..Y.W.F." $30.00–40.00

Parkcraft Texas and Oil Well Ceramic. Parkcraft. Taneycomo Ceramic Factory. Hollister, MO. 1957. This geographic cutout of Texas is embossed with the state's name and emblem. The oil well is embossed and deep green. This set is one of the forty-eight issued by Parkcraft in 1957. $22.00–30.00

Niagara Falls Three-Piece Set Ceramic. Japan. 1950s. The base is fashioned to show one side of the falls meeting turbulent water. One the base nestles a red pleasure boat (one shaker). From the right side rises a detachable waterfall (another shaker). $24.00–30.00

Trylon and Perisphers in Pot Metal Silver-painted pot metal. Japan. 1939. The trylon and perisphere are rendered in pot metal painted shiny silver. $20.00–24.00

New York World's Fair Push-Button Shaker Plastic. 1939. One-piece, plastic shaker consists of an orange, Deco-style base with a central column containing two push buttons and flanked by two plastic, transparent cylinders. The words "New York World's Fair" are inscribed in black on the base and an image of the trylon and perisphere, together with the date "1939," appears on the push-button housing. $20.00–24.00

Mount Rushmore Ceramic. Japan. 1950s. Cylindrical shakers have round decals representing Mount Rushmore. $10.00–14.00

Niagara Falls Ceramic. Japan. 1950s. This basically rectangular, two-piece shaker represents, in bas-relief, the American and the Canadian sides of the Falls. Each shaker is one-sided. This set is beautifully hand-painted in pastel colors. $14.00–20.00

Niagara Falls Ceramic. Japan. 1960s. Urn-shaped white shakers with blue trim have round decals representing Niagara Falls. $12.00–14.00

Golden Gate Bridge Ceramic. Japan. The Golden Gate Bridge is represented in this horizontal, two-part shaker which comes apart in the middle of the central span. $25.00–30.00

Mt. St. Helen's Volcano Ceramic and volcanic ash. Zoeller. Washington. 1980. This nester is made out of volcanic ash and ceramic and represents the volcanic crater and the mountain top. When stacked atop each other, the shakers constitute a single, pre-eruption Mt. St. Helen's. $24.00–30.00

Plymouth Rock Ceramic. Japan. 1940s. Identical versions of Plymouth Rock have a crack running across one end and the date 1620 embossed on each. $12.00–14.00

Plymouth Rock and the Mayflower Ceramic. Japan. 1950s. A brown-hulled, white-sailed Mayflower goes with a pastel-colored Plymouth Rock with the date 1620 embossed on its side. $14.00–18.00

Santa' Workshop, North Pole, NY Ceramic. Japan. 1950s. Matching cottages with pink-gabled shake roofs, a water mill, and log construction sit on a green base inscribed "Santa's Workshop, North Pole, N.Y." $14.00–18.00

House of the Seven Gables Ceramic. Japan. 1950s. Black replicas, in miniature, of the House of the Seven Gables are from Salem, MA. $10.00–14.00

Little America, Wyoming Silver-painted metal. Japan. 1950s. The "Little America" house is divided into two uneven sections. The base of one is stamped "Little America," the other, "Wyoming." $14.00–18.00

Hershey Park Kisses Ceramic. Japan. 1970s. Large replicas of chocolate kisses are brown and have white "S" and "P" as well as "Hershey Park." $12.00–14.00

Television Set Snow Dome Shakers Plastic and water. Japan. 1950s—1960s. Pastel-colored plastic television sets have clear screens behind which are souvenir scenes and snow. The shakers are on either side of the screen. These

Mount Fuji Television Set Plastic and water. Japan. 1950s–1960s. Pink plastic television set is a snow dome. Behind the clear screen is the souvenir scene with snow. The actual shakers are on the size of the screen. $15.00–20.00

kinds of shakers were very popular as souvenirs and could be found for a number of cities and sights. $15.00–20.00

Snow Dome Shakers Plastic and water. Japan. 1950s–1960s. Snow domes in elongated or squat models have souvenir scenes from all over the country and even the world. The condiments are stored in the opaque rear half of the dome. $14.00–18.00

One-Piece Push-Button Shakers Plastic. U.S.A. 1950s. One-piece push-button shakers were made so that an opaque, inverted "T" base serves as the stage for figurines on either side. The holes were on the bottom of the "T" and spices were released by pushing the button. This style was very widely used as a vehicle for souvenirs and came in a kaleidoscopic range of colors. Some examples are Black chefs/Louisiana; Amish couple/Pennsylvania Dutch Country; alligators/ Florida; penguins/ Victoria, B.C. $12.00–18.00

Souvenir Toasters Plastic. U.S.A. 1950s. A white toaster on a black base has two slices of yellow toast that are the shakers. A souvenir image of a city landmark was stenciled on the toaster side. $12.00–18.00

Lusterware Car Condiment Set Lusterware. An old-fashioned Lusterware automobile in beautiful, pearlescent finish has a pepper shaker in the front hood, a mustard pot inserted into the roof, and a salt well in the trunk. A picture-postcard sticker with an image of Weymouth Bay is attached to the side. $35.00–40.00

Pink Cable Cars Ceramic. Japan. Small pink cable cars have blue people stuck to the sides. These come in various colors, including green, mustard, and metal. $10.00–12.00

Florida One-Piece Button Shaker
Plastic. U.S.A. 1950s. This one-piece push-button shaker dispenses salt and pepper from the base beneath the alligator figurines.
$12.00–18.00

Comical Green Cable Cars Ceramic. U.S.A 1940s. Wacky-looking, green cable cars with yellow bases and roofs are inscribed "San Francisco." $10.00–12.00

"Desire" Streetcars Ceramic. Japan. Streetcars in mustard yellow have the inscriptions "Desire" and "New Orleans." $10.00–12.00

"Salty" and "Peppy" Racing Cars Ceramic. A pink "Peppy" racing car is identical to the blue "Salty" model. $10.00–12.00

Gold Race Cars Ceramic. Japan. 1940s. Covered, old-fashioned race cars are painted in 22-karat-gold paint. $14.00–20.00

Gold Race Cars Ceramic. Japan. 1940s. Open, old-fashioned race cars are painted in 22-karat gold. $14.00–20.00

Stanley Steamer and Ford T Red clay. Black replicas of the Stanley Steamer 1909 and Ford T 1908 have red trim and gold wheels. $14.00–20.00

Roadsters Ceramic. Japan. 1960s. Replicas of early roadsters are light brown with dark brown detailing. One is inscribed "Pepper," the other "Salt." $12.00–14.00

Black Jalopies Ceramic. Japan. 1960s. Black-canopied jalopies have a pattern of pink flowers. $10.00–12.00

Car with Airstream Trailer Ceramic. Japan. 1940s. A ruby-colored sedan is followed by an identically colored airstream trailer. $14.00–18.00

Train Set, Four Pieces Ceramic. Japan. 1940s. A light-blue train set consists of four components, each of them a shaker. These are locomotive, coal car, tanker, and caboose. This set was available in other colors as well. $24.00–30.00

Locomotive Condiment Set Ceramic. Japan. 1940s. This large set consists of a 7″ base shaped as the locomotive, in white with green, red, and gray highlights. The twin smokestacks are the shakers, and the roof of the engine room is the lid for the mustard pot. $26.00–30.00

Black Locomotives with Pink Flowers Ceramic. Japan. 1950s. Black locomotives with very high smokestacks have a scattering of pink flowers. $12.00–14.00

Metal Locomotives Metal. U.S.A. Small, realistically detailed replicas of locomotives are made of metal. $12.00–14.00

Black Locomotive and Tender Ceramic. U.S.A. A heavy black locomotive with little detail is followed by a black tender. $10.00–14.00

White Locomotive and Tender Painted metal. U.S.A. 1950s. A metal locomotive and tender set is painted white with a floral design. $14.00–18.00

Black Locomotive and Tender Ceramic. Japan. 1940s. A black locomotive goes with a black and brown tender. $14.00–18.00

Brown Locomotives Ceramic. Japan. 1960s. Very realistically detailed replicas of old coal locomotives are brown and have the words "Salt" and "Pepper" inscribed on the sides. $10.00–14.00

"S & P Co" Trailer Truck Ceramic. This two-piece set consists of a green cab and a green trailer with the words "S & P Co" on the side. $14.00–18.00

Trailer Truck Ceramic. Japan. Late 1950s–early 1960s. A beautiful, reddish-pink cab on gray wheels hooks to a green and black trailer. $14.00–18.00

Ford Cars Painted metal. These replicas of the 1918 Ford are made of metal painted green, gold, black, and red. $18.00–22.00

Couple in Metal Car Ceramic and metal. Japan. The busts of an old-fashioned, cartoony couple sit on the bench of a black metal and wire automobile. She wears a yellow hat and pink bowl, he wears a blue bow tie and black hat. $20.00–24.00

Canine Couple in 1950s Convertible Ceramic. 1950s. A green 1950s convertible holds two removable Scotch terriers. The back trunk has a lid which hides access to the mustard pot. $24.00–34.00

Plastic Couple in Car Plastic. Japan. A white, old-fashioned couple in hats sits inside a black, old-fashioned jalopy with red wheels and golden grill. He wears a red hat, she wears a yellow one. The man and the woman are the shakers. $12.00–18.00

Black and White Jalopies Ceramic. "S.D.D. copyright 1931." Replicas of early car models come in black or white. $12.00–18.00

Wooden Jalopies Wood. 1930s. Wooden jalopies, complete with carved wheels, are hand-painted in black, yellow, white, and red. $15.00–20.00

Racing Cars with Movable Wheels Ceramic and metal. Pink, bullet-shaped racing cars with blond male drivers at the wheel have movable wire wheels. Labels on the hood carry the names of various automobiles, such at Mercedes Benz, Connaught, etc. 14.00–18.00

Car and Driver Condiment Set Ceramic and metal. Japan. This three-part condiment set sits on a metal base in the shape of an automobile chassis with wheels. The front hood of the car is a pepper shaker, the back, trunk part is the salt shaker, and the central shaker is the mustard pot to which the man is the top. $24.00–30.00

Bumper Cars Ceramic. Vandor. 1980s. Bumper cars have blue seats and yellow or red bodies. $15.00–17.00

Surfing Cow in Station Wagon Ceramic. Vandor. 1980s. This two-part shaker consists of a woody station wagon body (the bottom half) and a top from the driver's window, on which appears a black and white cow. On the top of the car is a surfboard. $17.00–20.00

Conestoga Wagons Ceramic. Japan. 1950s. Yellow Conestoga wagons have white tops. $10.00–12.00

Stylized Conestoga Wagons Ceramic. Japan. 1960s. Brown Conestoga wagons with very high tops are marked "S" or "P" and have white banners reading "Warren, Pa." A yellow patch appears on each near the top. $10.00–12.00

Conestoga Wagon and Oxen Ceramic. U.S.A. A white and tan Conestoga wagon is drawn by a pair of yellow oxen. $12.00–14.00

Conestoga Wagon and Pioneer Ceramic. U.S.A. 1940s. A white Conestoga wagon with black wheels is teamed with a settler in brown pants and yellow hat. $18.00–24.00

Wooden Conestoga Wagons Wood. Wooden Conestoga wagons with carved wheels are marked "Green Mts. Vermont." $12.00–14.00

Chuck Wagons Ceramic. U.S.A. 1940s. Brown chuck wagons have white, Conestoga-wagon-type tops. $10.00–14.00

Conestoga Wagon with Oxen Ceramic. U.S.A. 1940s. Red-wheeled, yellow-topped Conestoga wagon has the word "Colorado" inscribed on the side. A pair of brown and black oxen stand in front. $12.00–14.00

Stagecoach Ceramic. Japan. 1960s. Realistic replicas of a stagecoach are painted brown with dark brown highlights on the embossed detailing. $12.00–14.00

Yellow Stagecoach Ceramic. Japan. 1950s. Yellow stagecoach has black wheels and brown frames of doors and windows. $12.00–14.00

Airplanes Ceramic. Japan. Pale blue airplanes have black propellers on their noses. $10.00–12.00

Helicopter Ceramic. Sarsaparilla. 1980s. This stacker consists of a green helicopter body and lavender and black rotor that is detachable as a shaker. $15.00–18.00

Hot Air Balloon on Cloud Ceramic. Sarsaparilla. 1980s. A yellow hot-air balloon with a red heart motif nestles in a white cloud. $15.00–18.00

Zeppelin in Cloud Ceramic. Sarsaparilla. 1980s. A gray zeppelin nestles in a white cloud. $15.00–18.00

Metal Airplanes Metal. 1970s. Silver passenger planes stand on streamlined bases. $14.00–18.00

Metal Tricycle Metal and glass. Metal tricycle with a black seat and handles has, on the back footrest, a glass and metal pair of shakers. $16.00–24.00

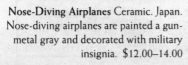

Nose-Diving Airplanes Ceramic. Japan. Nose-diving airplanes are painted a gunmetal gray and decorated with military insignia. $12.00–14.00

Ocean Liner with Twin Smokestacks Ceramic. U.S.A. 1950s. This beautiful nester consists of a black ocean liner base that includes green waves and, at the helm, the figurine of a tiny sailor holding a telescope to his eye. On top of the ocean liner sit two yellow and white cylindrical smokestacks, the shakers. $24.00–28.00

Pink Ocean Liner with Smokestacks Ceramic. Japan. 1950s. This nester comprises an ocean liner with a pink hull and yellow superstructure with two removable smokestacks in brown and black. $18.00–22.00

Plastic Ocean Liner Plastic. U.S.A. 1950s. This three-piece set consists of a red plastic hull and two glass smokestacks with red plastic caps which are the shakers. $14.00–20.00

Sidewinder Riverboats Ceramic. Japan. 1950s. Nicely detailed riverboats have a side paddlewheel. They are colored in shakes of olive, mustard, and brown. $10.00–14.00

Gondola Ceramic. Japan. 1950s. A red, blue, and yellow gondola is a three-piece set with the base as the boat, and the shakers as the two-part "cabin." $14.00–20.00

Couple on Boats Ceramic. Japan. 1940s. Orange and yellow ocean liners on a strip of blue have sitting on them out-of-scale figurines of a little boy and girl (one per shaker) holding a suitcase. $18.00–24.00

Galleons Ceramic. Japan. 1950s. White galleons with unfurled sails have brownish-gold highlights. $10.00–12.00

Three-Piece Ocean Liner Ceramic. Japan. 1940s. This delightful shaker consists of a hand-painted ocean liner to the bow of which is attached a sea captain peering through a telescope. The smokestacks are the shakers. $20.00–24.00

Aircraft Carrier and Plane Ceramic. A rather crudely made sepia-colored aircraft carrier has a yellow detachable airplane on its deck. $18.00–22.00

Sailboat and Lighthouse on Tray Ceramic. A tray in the shape of a blue ocean sets the base for an attached lighthouse of dark gray with a red roof. The detachable nesting sailboat has a green hull and a yellow sail. This is a beautifully executed two-piece set. $20.00–24.00

Sailboat and Lighthouse Ceramic. This three-piece set consists of a base mimicking blue water, a white sailboat, and a yellow lighthouse. $14.00–18.00

Three Sailboats on Tray Ceramic. This three-piece set consists of a tray with an attached sailboat that functions as a handle and two detachable sailboats. The tray has a blue wave design. The sailboats have an orange, green, and pink sail, respectively. $16.00–20.00

Sailboat Ceramic. Ron Gordon. 1980s. This three-piece set has a white base in the shape of the hull, and triangular sails in white, red, and yellow that make up the shakers. $12.00–14.00

Delft Galleons Delftware. Holland. White and blue galleons have fully unfurled sails and are presented in profile. $12.00–16.00

Greyhound Buses Metal 1930s. Scaled-down replicas of Greyhound Scenicruiser buses, complete with movable, rubber wheels, are painted blue, white, and gold. $36.00–50.00

GO-WITHS

Pear with Worm Ceramic. U.S.A. 1950s. A pink and yellow pear is teamed with a green worm that emerges from a dimple in the pear's bottom. $14.00–16.00

Bear with Garbage Pail Ceramic. Japan. 1950s. This 5″ bear has a gray body and rounded ears. It puts its paws around a white garbage can with black handles. $14.00–16.00

Bear with Beehive Ceramic. U.S.A. 1950s. A brown bear is flanked by a yellow conical beehive with a single bee sculpted on the side. $12.00–14.00

Mouse with Cheese Ceramic. U.S.A. 1950s. A gray mouse goes with a wedge of yellow cheese. $10.00–14.00

Duck with Buckets Ceramic. U.S.A. 1950s–1960s. This carrier features a yellow duck with black, hooklike wings from which are suspended two buckets, one marked "P," the other "S." $20.00–24.00

Rabbit with Carrot Ceramic. Japan. 1950s. A brown bunny rabbit with baby-doll eyes and gray tail is tamed with a pink carrot with green foliage. $14.00–20.00

White Mouse with Swiss Cheese Ceramic. Japan. 1950s. A pensive white mouse with large ears fits inside a gnawed-out wedge of Swiss cheese. $14.00–20.00

Chick and Egg Ceramic. Ron Gordon Designs, Inc. This three-piece set consists of an oval tray to which is attached a yellow chick. On the other end of the tray nestles an egg decorated in pastel stripes. The egg splits in half to become two shakers. The lower half contains the yolk. $14.00–18.00

Skunk and Cent Ceramic. U.S.A. 1950s–1960s. A black and white skunk goes with a red "one-cent" piece. $20.00–24.00

"Chunky" Mouse with Cheese Ceramic. Japan. A stylized gray mouse with a kingpin-shaped body, very large ears, and round eyes cups its arms. Into the little shelf that is thereby formed fits a piece of yellow cheese. The word "Chunky" is inscribed on one of the mouse's feet. $12.00–18.00

Schnauzer with Hat Ceramic. Japan. 1950s. A very glossy gray schnauzer pup fits inside the crown of a pink bonnet with a large patch on the brim. $18.00–22.00

Camel with Load Porcelain. China. A buff, sitting camel is teamed with a brown parcel. $18.00–22.00

Pig with Sausage Ceramic. U.S.A. A white, simplified pig with a pink tush and nose has as its partner a plump pink sausage. $14.00–18.00

Cow with Milk Can Ceramic. U.S.A. A buff-colored sitting cow with black horns and bell is accompanied by a white milk can. $14.00–18.00

Squirrel with Acorn Ceramic. U.S.A. A tan, cartoonish squirrel with pink head stands next to a giant acorn. $14.00–18.00

Mouse with Bowling Pin Ceramic. U.S.A. A beige, cartoonish mouse with oversize pink ears and human eyebrows reaches out for a white bowling pin with brown band. $14.00–18.00

Dog with Victrola Ceramic. U.S.A. A pale green dog sits next to an old-fashioned record player with an RCA-Victor-like speaker. $14.00–18.00

Donkey with Horseshoe Ceramic. U.S.A. A comical white donkey with brown ears and hooves sits on its haunches and points its muzzle into the air. Next to it sits a large horseshoe with brown nails. $14.00–18.00

Birdhouse with Bird Ceramic. Japan. 1950s. A little birdhouse on a branch is teamed with a blue and white bird with red head. $12.00–14.00

Binoculars and Case Ceramic. U.S.A. 1950s–1960s. Black binoculars lie next to a brown case. $16.00–20.00

Scarecrow and Crow Ceramic. Poinsettia Studios. CA. A pink and green scarecrow with a straw hat goes with a small, black crow. $18.00–24.00

Mother Bird with Nest and Nestlings on Log Tray Ceramic. Japan. 1960s. This three-part set consists of a white mother bird on a green base stretching out her blue wings, an orange nest with two nestlings, and a log-shaped tray with two depressions for holding the bird figurines. $18.00–24.00

Salmon and Creel Ceramic. Japan. 1960s. A brown creel goes with a pink salmon with blue fins. $14.00–18.00

Cat and Goldfish in a Bowl Ceramic. Menschik-Goldman, Inc. NY. 1960. A white, cartoonish kitten sits on a tabouret covered in yellow, red, and gray checks. On an identically styled tabouret sits a green glass dome covering a small pink goldfish. $25.00–34.00

Skunk with Blue Flower Ceramic. Poinsettia Studios. CA. A black skunk, blue flowers running along the white stripe of its tail, holds out its hands like a ledge. On them sits a blue flower, another shaker. $24.00–30.00

Cannon with Cannon Balls Ceramic. Japan. 1950s. A bulbous dark green cannon on wheel-less carriage is tamed with a pyramidal stack of cannon balls in gun-metal gray. $12.00–14.00

Cannon with Cannon Balls Ceramic. Japan. 1950s. A red cannon on wheels is teamed with a stack of five black cannon balls. $10.00–12.00

Frog and Toadstool Ceramic. Japan. 1950s. A small green frog looks up at a large brown mushroom. $10.00–12.00

Cigarette Pack and Lighter Ceramic. U.S.A. 1950s–1960s. A Camel cigarettelike soft pack with three protruding cigarettes is teamed with a gray Zip-style lighter. $20.00–24.00

"Gold Fold" Cigarette Pack and Matches Ceramic. Japan. A white and yellow pack of cigarettes with the words "Gold Fold Cigarettes" is teamed with a book of matches with the same logo and inscription. $16.00–20.00

Screwball (8 Ball and Screw) Ceramic. U.S.A. 1950s–1960s. A black 8 ball is teamed with a gray screw. $20.00–24.00

Thimble and Thread Ceramic. C.C. Co. U.S.A. 1950s–1960s. A thimble with a silver band goes with a spool of silver thread. $20.00–24.00

Watering Pot and Flower Porcelain. 1950s. A pale yellow watering can with a pink carnation on its side is teamed with a pink flower atop a columnar green stem attached to a flat, leaflike base. $20.00–24.00

Bible and Gavel Ceramic. U.S.A. 1950s—1960s. A black Bible is teamed with a beige judge's gavel. $20.00–24.00

Helmet and Shield Ceramic. U.S.A. 1950s—1960s. Salmon-colored helmet, nicely detailed, is teamed with a shield that lies on its back. $20.00–24.00

Shaving Brush and Mug Ceramic. Trevewood. Roseville, OH. A yellow shaving soap mug goes with a black shaving mug with white bristles. $20.00–24.00

Razor and Shaving Brush Ceramic. U.S.A. A yellow safety razor goes with a shaving brush with a white handle terminating in a red band and white bristles. $12.00–18.00

Hairbrush and Comb Ceramic. Sarsaparilla. 1980s. A pink ladies' hairbrush is teamed with a green comb. $12.00–15.00

Drunk with Lamp Post
Ceramic. U.S.A. 1950s. A formally attired drunk in a top hat holds a bottle in one hand and reaches from the top of a drooping lamp post with the other. The lamp post may be entirely black, entirely pink, or combine a black base with a red shaft and yellow lamp. $20.00–24.00

Saddle and Cowboy Boot Ceramic. U.S.A. 1950s–1960s. Tan saddle, complete with blanket and saddle stand, is teamed with a shiny, deep brown cowboy boot. $20.00–24.00

Revolvers Ceramic. U.S.A. 1950s–1960s. Shiny brown revolvers have dark brown detailing. $12.00–16.00

Cigar in Ashtray Ceramic. U.S.A. Brown cigar butt with white ash nestles in square yellow ashtray. This set has been reproduced by Sarsaparilla in the 1980s. $20.00–24.00

Toothpaste and Toothbrush Ceramic. U.S.A. 1950s. A yellow tube of toothpaste is teamed with a blue toothbrush. $20.00–24.00

Lock and Key Ceramic. U.S.A. 1950s–1960s. A yellow key goes with a gray lock labelled "Safe Lock." $20.00–24.00

Gun and Bullet Ceramic. U.S.A. 1950s–1960s. A brown gun with a black handle is paired with a small gray bullet. $20.00–24.00

MacArthur's Hat and Pipe Ceramic. U.S.A. 1950s. A deep rich brown MacArthur's hat is paired with his yellow cob pipe. $20.00–24.00

Mortarboard and Diploma Ceramic. U.S.A. 1950s–1960s. A black mortarboard accompanies a white diploma, rolled up and tied with a blue ribbon. $20.00–24.00

Dice Ceramic. U.S.A. 1950s–1960s. A pair of matching dice are white with black dots. These are also available in white with gold dots. $14.00–16.00

Dice and Cards Ceramic. Japan. 1950s–1960s. A pair of dice, stacked atop each other and balanced on a white "tee," is paired with three playing cards wrapped around the top of a "tee." $20.00–24.00

Black Dice Ceramic. U.S.A. 1950s–1960s. A pair of black dice has white dots. $12.00–20.00

Hot Water Bottle and Bare Feet
Ceramic. Japan. 1950s. White feet with red nails are matched with a brownish-orange hot water bottle. $12.00–16.00

Drip and Drop Ceramic. Japan. 1950s. A spherical Drop with a winking face is teamed with a tear-shaped Drip with a sour face. The set in pink has names embossed on the bottoms of the faces. The black ones have white features. $18.00–24.00

Moonshiner and Jug Ceramic. Japan. 1950s. A white-faced moonshiner in a big black hat slumps with a pig on his bare feet. Next to him is a large white and brown jug of moonshine. $20.00–24.00

Moonshiner with Jugs Nester/Carrier Ceramic. Japan. 1950s. A moonshiner with a long black beard, black hat, blue pants, and red shirt is attached to a green base with a brown stump. In one arm he cradles one jug, from the other hand, the other jug. Both are marked "Snake bite." $20.00–26.00

Mexican with Jugs Ceramic. Japan. 1950s. A sleeping Mexican in yellow pants and sombrero has a hyperbolic moustache, from each end of which are suspended enormous red and yellow jugs. $20.00–24.00

"There's One In Every Bar" Red clay. This unusual shaker set has a brown base from the back of which rises a tall "backdrop" depicting a bartender presiding over a bar. Into indentations in the bar fit two shaker figurines: a brown-suited drunk, and a hatted, brown ass. The inscription at the bottom reads "There's one in every bar." $24.00–30.00

Bourbon Street Drunk Ceramic. U.S.A. A formally attired drunk sits on the ground and reaches out his arms for the street-sign shaker that is capped with the arrow inscribed with "Bourbon St." $24.00–30.00

"Goodbye, Cruel World." Ceramic. Japan. 1950s. A yellow toilet bowl-cum-water tank holds a nester in the shape of a large-nosed man in yellow straw hat and black-and-white-striped shirt with one arm out of the toilet about to flush the water. The inscription read "Goodbye, Cruel World." $24.00–30.00

Jailbirds in Cage Ceramic and metal. Fitz and Floyd. Late 1970s. One yellow and one red jailbird in black and white uniforms and caps sit inside a white metal rounded cage. $24.00–30.00

Metal Tombstones Metal. U.S.A. Gray metal tombstones with a Colonial look to them are inscribed, "Here lies Salt" and "Here lies Pepper." $14.00–20.00

Salty O'Day and Pepper Tate Tombstones Ceramic. U.S.A. White tombstones from Tombstone, Arizona, are inscribed with the following legends: "Boot Hill/Here lies/ Salty O'Day/1861–1881 / Hoss Thief/A rope necktie/ an old oak tree/ and Salty wasn't/ what he used to be./ Tombstone" and "Boot Hill/ Here lies/ Pepper Tate/1860–1881 /Hanged by mistake/ he was right/ we was wrong/ but we strung him up/ and now he's gone./Arizona." $16.00–20.00

Eskimo with Igloo Ceramic. U.S.A. 1950s. A pink Eskimo is teamed with a white igloo that is nearly his size and cradles his back. $20.00–24.00

Eskimo with Igloo Ceramic. U.S.A. 1940s. A brown Eskimo is paired with a small, rounded igloo which reaches only to the man's shoulder. $20.00–24.00

Arab and Camel Ceramic. U.S.A. 1940s. An Arab in white robes is flanked by a sitting, brown camel. $20.00–24.00

Gnome with Toadstool Porcelain. A tiny white gnome with red cap and shoes and blue-dotted shirt sits holding his knees with his hands. His toadstool house has a brown roof with dark brown spots, a door, and windows. $20.00–24.00

Blonde with Bust Ceramic. U.S.A. 1950s. A pale blond with shoulder-length bob is detachable from her pink bosom. $19.00–22.00

Spinster Praying by Bed Ceramic. U.S.A. 1950s. A spinster in white nightgown and nightcap kneels next to a white bed. From beneath the footboard of the bed protrude two black, male feet. $20.00–24.00

His and Hers Yellow Polka-Dot Bikini Ceramic. U.S.A. Gorgeously proportioned torsoes display skimpy male and female versions of the yellow polka-dot-on-black bikini. The male torso is of a body builder; the female is definitely a bombshell. $20.00–24.00

Tire and Pump Ceramic. U.S.A. 1950s. A gray flat tire is teamed with a salmon-colored air pump. $14.00–22.00

Angel on Swan Ceramic. Japan. 1950s. An adorable, naked cherub nestles in the pink wings of a pastel-tinted swan. $20.00–24.00

Pot-Bellied Stove and Coal Hod Ceramic. Japan. 1950s. Gray pot-bellied stove has fine detailing in dark gray. The yellow hod is heaped with shiny, black coal. $14.00–20.00

Pot-Bellied Stove and Rocker on Tray Ceramic. U.S.A. A brown and gold pot-bellied stove sits alongside a rocker, inscribed "S" on a brown rectangular tray. $14.00–20.00

Pump and Bucket Ceramic. U.S.A. Clunky ceramic pump in pale brown has barely legible pump features, looking more like a nondescript post. The yellow bucket is an equally sorry specimen. $6.00–8.00

Outhouse and "Kat-A-Log" Ceramic. U.S.A. A brown outhouse is matched with a pale green cube purporting to be a "Kat-A-Log." $10.00–14.00

Female Legs in High Heels Ceramic. U.S.A. Female legs in thigh-high pink nylon stockings wear gold high-heeled shoes. $12.00–18.00

Feet Ceramic. Japan. 1950s. A pair of white feet with painted red toenails is truncated at the ankle. $14.00–20.00

Feet in Sandals Ceramic. Japan. 1950s. White feet with pink toenails are shod in blue Grecian sandals. $12.00–16.00

Record Player Ceramic. Japan. 1950s. A green record player with a gray turntable has a removable red arm which is one of the shakers. $20.00–24.00

Football and Helmet Ceramic. Japan. 1950s. A white football helmet with black and red details is matched with a very shiny, podlike football. $10.00–12.00

Stork and Baby Ceramic. U.S.A. 1950s. A white stork, whose legs are attached to a gray chimney, has a bundled baby slung to its beak. This hanger set has been reproduced by Sarsaparilla in the 1980s. $14.00–20.00

Glum and Glee Ceramic. U.S.A. 1940s. Black Glum in top hat carries an umbrella and has his name inscribed in gold on his hat. White, fat Glee lies on his back, kicking up a leg. He wears a white clown costume trimmed in gold and his name is inscribed on his conical hat. $20.00–24.00

Bowling Ball and Pin Ceramic. U.S.A. The black shiny ball has as its mate a large yellow pin with a double red stripe running around its middle. $10.00–12.00

Baseball Mitt and Ball Ceramic. U.S.A. 1960s. A tan baseball mitt cradles a white ball. $14.00–16.00

Golf Bag and Ball Ceramic. U.S.A. 1950s. A white golf ball accompanies a brown golf bag with four clubs protruding from the top. $14.00–16.00

Briefcase and Hat Ceramic. U.S.A. A brown briefcase is teamed with a white man's hat. $12.00–14.00

Typewriter and Ink Bottle Ceramic. U.S.A. 1950s. A brown manual typewriter has as its mate a blue bottle of ink with a dark blue stopper. $14.00–18.00

Ink Bottle and Desk Blotter Ceramic. U.S.A. A white ink bottle with a yellow top is ornamented with green vines and red roses. The desk blotter has a red handle, a brown top, and a white bottom, the latter being decorated with the same vine and rose pattern which enlivens the bottle. $14.00–18.00

Pen and Pencil Ceramic. U.S.A. 1980s. A yellow pencil stub with a black lead is teamed with a yellow pen with a golden nib. $14.00–18.00

Bucket and Scrub Brush Ceramic. U.S.A. 1950s. A brown scrub brush goes with a green bucket. $12.00–14.00

Paint Bucket and Brush Ceramic. Japan. 1940s. A brown paint bucket filled with yellow paint has a yellow brush with a brown handle. $10.00–14.00

Pot and Hot Plate Ceramic. U.S.A. 1950s. A white Dutch oven (or casserole pot) is teamed with a brown hot plate. $14.00–18.00

Frying Pan with Egg Ceramic. U.S.A. 1950s. A brown frying pan accommodates a removable egg, sunny side up. $14.00–18.00

Devil on Cards Ceramic. A column composed of three figure cards is surmounted by grinning red devil. These shakers are extremely valuable for their Royal Bayreuth devil figure. $120.00–150.00

Sewing Machine and Mannequin Ceramic. Japan. A white sewing machine with yellow spool and gray details is the match for a white mannequin in the form of an hourglass female figure with flounces along its bottom, a black bow, and yellow guide lines across hips, waist, and bust is marked "Lifton's exclusive U.S. pat. made in Japan." $16.00–20.00

Fireplace and Rocker Ceramic. Japan. A red "brick" fireplace, complete with burning fire, is flanked by a brown rocking chair. $12.00–14.00

Little Red Schoolhouse and School Desk Ceramic. Japan. A little red schoolhouse has as its mate an old-fashioned school desk that is completely yellow. $12.00–14.00

Fire Engine and Fireman's Hat Ceramic. Sarsaparilla. 1980s. A red fire engine with black wheels goes with a gray fireman's hat with the number "1" embossed on the front. $12.00–14.00

Gavel and Law Books Ceramic. Sarsaparilla. 1980s. A stack of law books is teamed with a brown gavel. $12.00–14.00

Piano and Accordion Ceramic. U.S.A. A brown piano, marked "P," is teamed with a brown accordion marked "S." $12.00–14.00

Guitar and French Horn Ceramic. U.S.A. A brown French horn, marked "P," is teamed with a brown guitar marked "S." $12.00–14.00

S and P Ceramic. U.S.A. 1950s. A capital idea: capital letters "S" and "P" hold corresponding condiment. These sets come in a variety of typical 1950s colors: pale salmon, smoky clue, and seafoam green. $14.00–20.00

Bacon and Egg Ceramic. U.S.A. 1950s. A pink and brown rasher of bacon goes with a sunny-side-up egg. $12.00–14.00

Bodice and Pantaloons Ceramic. U.S.A. A white, hourglass-figure bodice with pink trim is teamed with a wasp-waisted pair of lady's pantaloons with pink trim. $14.00–20.00

Lipstick and Perfume Bottle Ceramic. U.S.A. 1950s. A red lipstick protrudes from a white lipstick case that is banded in black. The white perfume bottle has red ornamentation and a black cap. $14.00–20.00

Tire and Nail Ceramic. U.S.A. 1950s. A gray, flat tire is teamed with a large light gray nail that stands on its head. $14.00–20.00

Hitchhiker and Bag Ceramic. U.S.A. 1950s. A pale hitchhiker in brown pants, beige shirt, and blue tie sticks out a red thumb. Next to him sits a brown tote bag. $14.00–20.00

Pipe and Slipper Ceramic. U.S.A. 1950s. A tan man's slipper is teamed with a tan pipe with a black mouthpiece. $10.00–14.00

Hammer and Thumb Ceramic. U.S.A. 1950s. A bruised thumb is shown with a red hammer with a black head. $12.00–16.00

Lock and Key Ceramic. U.S.A. 1960s. A green padlock marked "Safe Lock" goes with a yellow key. $12.00–14.00

Typewriter and Ink Ceramic. U.S.A. 1950s. A black manual typewriter goes with a black ink bottle. $12.00–14.00

Eater and Hat Ceramic. U.S.A. 1950s. A bust of a bald man with a black handlebar moustache wears a bib and holds

Bug and Bug Sprayer Ceramic. U.S.A. 1950s. A white bug strayer with a floral motif is teamed with a dead white fly. $16.00–18.00

spoon and fork. Next to the man is a tall white hat with a golden band. $18.00–24.00

King and Queen of Diamonds Ceramic. Japan. Two diamonds set on pedestal bases have the images of the Queen of diamonds or the King of Diamonds on their sides. A pattern of red or black diamonds ornaments the sides. $18.00–24.00

Parkcraft Month Series Ceramic. Parkcraft. This twelve-month series is comprised of a cylindrical shaker with the name of the month of it, and an object commonly associated with that month, as for example: January and snowman; February and heart; March and shamrock with Irish pipe; April with blue Easter egg; May with basket of flowers; June with wedding cake; July with red firecracker; August with bather; September with schoolbooks; October with pumpkin; November with pilgrim hat; December with present. $24.00–30.00

Days of the Week Series Ceramic. Parkcraft. This seven-set series is comprised of paired objects associated with each day of the week. Monday (wash day) has a bar of soap and a washtub. Tuesday (ironing day) has an iron and a basket of laundry. Wednesday (mending day) has a spool of thread and a sewing basket. Thursday (visiting day) has a door and a lady. Friday (cleaning day) has a broom and dustpan. Saturday (baking day) has a long of bread and a plate with two bread slices. Sunday (church day) has a bible and organ. $24.00–30.00

Kissing Couple Ceramic. The profiles of two faces interlock to form a single block. The man's side may be red or blue, the woman's white or green. $18.00–24.00

Pick and Shovel Ceramic. Japan. A silver-headed, yellow-handled pick goes with a shovel in the same color distribution. $12.00–14.00

Martini Glass and Aspirin Ceramic. U.S.A. 1960s. An aqua martini glass, complete with a slice of lemon, goes with a huge, white aspirin tablet. $16.00–20.00

Stop and Caution Signs Ceramic. Octagonal signs bear the following inscriptions: On red, "Stop. Too much pepper ruins good cooking;" and on yellow, "Caution. Don't use too much salt." $12.00–16.00

False Teeth Ceramic. U.S.A. 1950s. A set of false teeth may either be stacked on top of each other or laid side by side. $14.00–18.00

Two Front Teeth Ceramic. Sarsaparilla. 1980s. A pair of huge incisors (the shakers) sits in a lower jaw of baby teeth in this three-piece set. $14.00–16.00

Green Thumb and Flower Ceramic. U.S.A. 1950s. A pink hand with a green thumb is flanked by a pink flower with a yellow center. $14.00–18.00

Green Thumb and Trowel Ceramic. Japan. 1980s. A white hand with a giant green thumb is paired with a yellow trowel. $12.00–15.00

Violin and Case Ceramic. U.S.A. 1950s. A brown violin is teamed with a tortoise-shell-colored case. $14.00–18.00

Rocket and Moon Ceramic. U.S.A. 1960s. A gray rocket is teamed with a yellow moon crescent with a cartoony, human face. $15.00–20.00

Moon and Star Ceramic. Vandor. 1980s. A silver crescent on a white cloud is flanked by a golden star on a white cloud. Both have human faces. $18.00–20.00

Football and Megaphone Ceramic. Japan. 1980s. A yellow megaphone with an "S" inside a banner shape is teamed with a brown football. $12.00–15.00

Iron with Stand Ceramic. Sarsaparilla. 1980s. A black iron goes with a brown stand. $12.00–14.00

Corvette with Hot Dog Stand Ceramic. Sarsaparilla. 1980s. A red (1960) Corvette is paired with a hot dog stand. $15.00–18.00

Thunderbird with Hot Dog Stand Ceramic. Sarsaparilla. 1980s. A pink 1957 Thunderbird is paired with a hot dog stand. $15.00–18.00

Fat Lady and Refrigerator Ceramic. Clay Art. 1980s. A fat lady in rollers and a pink bathrobe is paired with an opened refrigerator. $15.00–18.00

Nude in Keyhole Ceramic. U.S.A. 1960s. A white, headless and armless nude with red nipples fits into a green keyhole. $15.00–20.00

Bird in Hand Ceramic. Sarsaparilla. 1980s. A pink lady's hand with red nails holds a detachable little bird. $15.00–18.00

Chicken with Chicken Soup Ceramic. Vandor. 1980s. A bowl of chicken soup is teamed with a white chicken dressed in a yellow dress and holding a blue spoon. $18.00–20.00

Easy Chair with Ottoman Ceramic. U.S.A. 1950s. A brown easy chair is teamed with a brown ottoman. A white, swirling design appears on both. $15.00–20.00

Rolling Pin with Scoop Ceramic. Japan. 1950s. A white rolling pin and scoop have a red and green scroll and floral design. $10.00–12.00

Salt and Pepper Books Ceramic. U.S.A. 1950s. White books decorated along their spines with flowers and roosters are inscribed "Salt" or "Pepper." $10.00–12.00

Car with Airstream Trailer Ceramic. U.S.A. 1950s. A yellow car with a green roof goes with a yellow Airstream-type trailer. $18.00–24.00

Camel and Pyramid Ceramic. U.S.A. 1950s. Beige camel is flanked by a beige and brown pyramid. $18.00–24.00

Birthday Cake with Package Ceramic. Birthday cake, frosted in brown, is accompanied by a blue-ribboned package. $16.00–18.00

Oil Lamp and Book Ceramic. Old-fashioned oil lamp goes with an open book. $12.00–15.00

Wagon and Star Ceramic. "Hitch your wagon to a star" duo features a wagon and star in white with blue trim. $9.00–14.00

Sailboat and Lighthouse Ceramic. Sailboat and lighthouse sit on a base fashioned to look like waves in motion. $16.00–18.00

Heart and Arrow Ceramic. A broken, divided heart has arrow running through it. Versions exist in pale blue or red and white. $8.00–12.00

Apple and Worm Ceramic. A worm emerges from the side of green or yellow apple. $10.00–13.00

Spinning Wheel and Stool Ceramic. Brown spinning wheel and stool are trimmed in black. $6.00–8.00

Spinning Wheel and Stool Ceramic. Spinning wheel and stool are featured in multiple colors. $6.00–8.00

Coffeepot on Stove Ceramic. Graniteware-look coffeepot rests on top of black and white stove. $7.00–9.00

Stove and Coal Scuttle Ceramic. A coal scuttle rests beside a pot-bellied stove. $5.00–6.00

Fish on Scale Ceramic. Japan. 1940s—1950s. A gray fish rests on an old-fashioned scale whose arrow points halfway between fifteen and twenty pounds. $16.00–18.00

Six-Shooter and Conestoga Wagon Ceramic. U.S.A. 1950s. A dark green six-shooter goes with a Conestoga wagon in the same color. $14.00–18.00

NESTERS, NODDERS,
CARRIERS, HUGGERS...

NESTERS

Mouse in Swiss Cheese Ceramic. Japan. 1950s. A gray mouse in a red hat with a black brim sits atop a wedge of yellow Swiss cheese. There is an indentation in the cheese to accommodate one of the mouse's feet $14.00–18.00

Mouse in Gouda Cheese Ceramic. Japan. 1950s. A white mouse in a black top hat sits atop a wheel of yellow Gouda cheese. There is an indentation in the cheese to accommodate one of the mouse's feet. $14.00–18.00

Viking Mouse in Red Gouda Cheese Ceramic. Japan. 1950s. A brown mouse in a silver Viking's helmet sits atop a wheel of red-rinded Gouda cheese. There is an indentation in the cheese to accommodate one of the mouse's feet. $14.00–18.00

Small Mouse in Wedge of Cheese Ceramic. Japan. 1950s. A small gray mouse fits into the gnawed-out tip of a wedge of Swiss cheese. $14.00–18.00

Mouse with Two Pieces of Cheese Ceramic. Japan. 1950s. A yellow sitting mouse with pink ears holds in its two curved arms two pieces of green Swiss cheese. $14.00–18.00

White Mouse with Piece of Cheese Ceramic. Japan. 1950s. A white mouse with pink ears and blue eyes holds a sleeping, smiling piece of Swiss cheese. $14.00–18.00

Kangaroo Mother and Joey Nester Ceramic. Japan. 1950s. A comical mother and joey set is pale beige with brown high-

Mouse in Swiss Cheese Ceramic. Japan. 1960s. A gray mouse sits inside a hole in a wedge of Swiss cheese. $14.00–18.00

lights. The large ears are pink, as are the cheeks. Both characters have human eyebrows. The joey sits in the mother's pouch. $14.00–18.00

Kangaroo Mother and Joey Nester Ceramic. Japan. White mother kangaroo has a round, bowllike pouch in which nestles the white joey. $20.00–24.00

Kangaroo Mother and Joey Twins Nester Ceramic. Japan. This three-piece set consists of a mother kangaroo with a bowllike pouch in which sit identical joeys, which are the shakers. The three are golden yellow with brown highlights and baby-doll eyes. $20.00–24.00

Beige Kangaroo Mother and Joey Nester Ceramic. Japan. 1950s. A beige kangaroo mother and joey have dark brown shading and realistic features. $20.00–24.00

Brown Nesting Hippopotamus Ceramic. Japan. 1950s. Brown hippopotamus with tan faces stack up on top of each other so that the lower one lies down and the upper one rests its forepaws on the lower one's back. $12.00–14.00

Horse in Trough Ceramic. Japan. 1950s. A golden palomino with a black mane and tail lies on its back in an oval brown "trough." $16.00–20.00

Cat on Cushion Ceramic. U.S.A. 1950s. A beige cat nestles on a yellow pillow. $14.00–18.00

Bear Holding Salmon Ceramic. Japan. 1950s. A brown bear holds a blue salmon in each arm. $14.00–18.00

Bear Holding White Salmon Ceramic. Japan. 1950s. A matte-finish brown bear with a comical face cradles a white and blue salmon in each arm. $14.00–18.00

Bear Holding Beehive Ceramic. Japan. 1950s. Brown bear holds a yellow, smiling beehive in his hands. $14.00–18.00

Cow Holding Milk Can Ceramic. Japan. 1960s. A green cow with pink cheeks and ears and blue eyes holds a smiling, sleeping white milk can. $14.00–18.00

Robin in Nest Ceramic. Japan. 1960s. This four-piece nester consists of a base that is shaped like a nest, a robin that lifts up, and two eggs within the nest that are the actual shakers. $16.00–20.00

Dog Head, Dog Body on Cushion Ceramic. Japan. Late 1940s–early 1950s. A white, sitting dog with blue spots perches on a plaid pillow. The dog has plastic bug-eyes. The dog's head is one shaker, the body with cushion is another shaker. $12.00–14.00

Dog with Smiling Bone Ceramic. Japan. 1960s. A pale, tan dog with giant blue eyes holds a white smiling and sleeping bone. $14.00–16.00

Frog with Mushroom Ceramic. Japan. 1950s. A green, smiling frog with a heart-shaped pink cheek holds a smiling brown mushroom with red dots. $14.00–16.00

White Frogs Ceramic. Fitz & Floyd. Japan. 1970s. A small white frog sits atop a large white frog. $20.00–24.00

Round White Frogs Ceramic. Fitz & Floyd. Japan. 1970s. A round white frog sits atop another round white frog. Both have large pink bug-eyes. $18.00–14.00

Sleeping Mexican Ceramic. Japan. 1940s–1950s. A sitting Mexican peasant in red trousers, blue shirt, and yellow sombrero sleeps. One shaker consists of everything from the waist up, the other shaker of everything from the waist down. $12.00–14.00

Monkey with Pineapples Ceramic. Japan. 1950s–1960s. A brown monkey cradles in its arms a pair of yellow pineapples. $14.00–16.00

Monkey with Banana Bunches Ceramic. Japan. 1950s–1960s. A brown monkey cradles in its arms a pair of banana bunches. $14.00–16.00

Squirrel with Acorns Ceramic. Japan. 1950s–1960s. A brown squirrel cradles in its arms a pair of deep brown acorns. $14.00–16.00

Cow Head on Cow Torso Ceramic. U.S.A. 1950s. A black and white cow head balances on a black and white cow torso. $14.00–18.00

Chef in Toque Ceramic. Japan. 1970s. A white chef with a cartoony face, red bow tie, black shoes, and yellow utensils balances a white toque on his head. $14.00–18.00

Fisherman in Rowboat Ceramic. U.S.A. Sticker: Elbee Art, Cleveland, Ohio. A sleeping fisherman in yellow with black boots nestles in a beige rowboat. $20.00–24.00

Stagecoach on Carriage Ceramic. U.S.A. 1950s. A white upper section of a stagecoach nestles on the brown carriage section. $18.00–24.00

Television Set Ceramic. U.S.A. 1960s. A 1960s television set has a speaker as its lower section and the screen as its upper section. These were available in a variety of colors with a range of images on paper, glued to the screen, from the Beatles to Westerns. $15.00–18.00

Hurricane Lamp Ceramic. U.S.A. 1950s. Hurricane lamp in white with floral and gold ornamentation is made up of two parts: the base and the glass. $12.00–16.00

Pennsylvania Dutch Couple in Barrel Porcelain. The heads of a four-eyed man and a cross-eyed woman are inserted into a vase shaped like a barrel and colored white with red trim. $40.00–55.00

Mexican Couple in Rectangular Base Porcelain. Japan. 1930s–1940s. A Mexican couple, both in sombreros, is inserted into a yellow, rectangular base hand-painted with a Mexican

Bellhop with Suitcases Ceramic. Occupied Japan. 1945–1952. A small white bellhop has a red cap, orange hair, a little-boy face, and a bright blue jacket. In each hand he carries a yellow suitcase. $24.00–28.00

rural scene. Between the couple's busts is a yellow sombrero which functions as the lid to the mustard pot. $40.00–60.00

Indian Couple in Rectangular Base Porcelain. Japan. 1930s–1940s. The heads of a pale-faced Indian couple, presumably of a chief and a squaw (she wears braids and one feather, he wears a headdress) are inserted into a rectangular base hand-painted with a vignette depicting a bow, two flying arrows, and a couple furiously paddling a canoe. $40.00–60.00

Couple with Nodding Heads Porcelain. Japan. 1930s–1940s. A hand-painted couple's bodies constitute the base, the heads are the shakers. The girl wears a pink, flouncy dress, and carries a yellow handbag. The boy wears brown trousers, green jacket, and black cap. She has strawberry blond hair. This set is rare. $60.00–100.00

Pig Couple with Nodding Heads Porcelain. Japan. 1930s–1940s. A brightly colored, striding pig couple is made so that the bodies are the base, while the heads are the shakers. Pigs are yellow with large, pink ears. She wears a white skirt and yellow top, he wears orange jacket and tan trousers. $60.00–100.00

Elephant Base with Clown and Dog Porcelain. A gray elephant in a red blanket trimmed in black and a green headdress is the base for a white clown and a white dog in a green jacket. $60.00–100.00

Mother Cat with Kitten Porcelain. Japan. 1930s. The cats' black bodies are the base. The mother cat's head and the kitten's head are the shakers. $50.00–80.00

Irish Couple in Heart Base Porcelain. 1930s–1940s. An Irish boy and girl are inserted into a heart-shaped base, hand-paint-

Boys in a Canoe Ceramic. Japan. 1940s. Boys in plaid shirts hold paddles and nestle in a pink canoe. The details on this lovely set are hand-painted. $24.00–30.00

ed with a rose design and inscribed "Wild Irish Rose." At the tip of the heart is a red, heart-shaped lid for the mustard pot. $60.00–100.00

Black Woman With Watermelon Slice Porcelain. 1930s–1940s. An old Black woman with gray hair sits cross-legged. Her head is one shaker, the watermelon slice in her arms is another. When the watermelon is removed it reveals a bare bosom. $60.00–80.00

Young Black Woman With Watermelon Slice Porcelain. 1930s–1940s. A Black woman in a white shirt and golden wrist and ankle bracelets holds a slide of watermelon in arms. The head is one shaker, the watermelon wedge is another. $50.00–80.00

Camel with Monkeys Porcelain. Japan. 1930s–1940s. A yellow, sitting camel with an orange ornamented blanket provides the base. Into the humps are inserted small, dressed monkeys in hats. $50.00–60.00

Kangaroo and Joey Heads in Bodies Porcelain. Japan. 1930s–1940s. The heads of a mother kangaroo and her joey are inserted into a base made to look like the kangaroo mother's body with a large pouch. $50.00–70.00

Indian Couple in a Pot Porcelain. Japan. 1930s–1940s. A yellow pot with a brown, geometric pattern is the base for two Indian head nodders, a brave and a squaw. $50.00–70.00

Indian Couple in Drum Porcelain. Japan. 1950s. A white drum, embossed with Indian motifs (such as axe, teepee, arrows, bow, canoe), is the base for the heads of an Indian couple. $50.00–70.00

Thai Couple with Nodding Heads Porcelain. A Thai lady and gentleman, in black and orange robes, respectively, have heads which balance on springs attached to the bodies. $25.00–40.00

Brown and White Bears Ceramic. 1940s. Sitting dark brown and white bears in a flowered base. $36.00–40.00

Medium Brown Bears Ceramic. 1950s. Medium brown sitting bears, one with yellow trim on ears and feet, the other with pink trim, sit on base with raised Patent TT. $36.00–40.00

Bears on Canada Map Base Ceramic. 1950s. Medium brown sitting bears rest on a base with pink flowers on one side, a map of Canada showing the provinces on the other. $40.00–44.00

Running Bears Ceramic. Patent TT on set. Running bears in brown or gray are set on a plain base. $40.00–44.00

Sideways-Looking Bears Ceramic. Standing brown bears look sideways. $40.00–42.00

Fat Sitting Bears Ceramic. Fat little bears in light brown color are sitting on the base. $35.00–38.00

Cats Ceramic. One green and one orange cat sit on base. $36.00–40.00

Running Deer Ceramic. 1950s. Light brown running deer with "Pat T" incised on the nodders are inserted into a white base with flower and "Salt" and "Pepper" in cursive. $45.00–50.00

Reclining Deer Ceramic. 1950s. One brown deer and one yellow-tan deer are lying down and facing each other. Patent TT is incised on the base, raised on the nodders. Base is ornamented with flowers. $45.00–50.00

Reclining Deer Ceramic. 1940s–1950s. Lying deer in medium brown and white face in the same directions with PAT on base and nodders. The base is ornamented with flowers. $40.00–45.00

Lying Deer on Irish Cottage Base Ceramic. 1950s. One brown and white and one yellow-tan deer lie down on an Irish cottage base with "An tSeapain Tir a Dheanta" in red letters, Patent TT on both. $50.00–55.00

Lying Deer Ceramic. ANCO. Japan. Large medium brown and white lying deer sit in a flowered base with a "Yosemite" stick-

Yellow Bird Hangers Ceramic. Japan. 1940s. Yellow and blue birds hook swirling tails around the arms of a T-shaped branch that rises from a white base. This design was quite popular, and was made with a variety of birds in a range of colors. $14.00–20.00

er and red and gold triangular label reading "ANCO. Made in Japan." PAT TT is incised on the nodders. $50.00–55.00

Pheasants Ceramic. 1950s. Orange winged and tailed pheasants with blue backs and heads perch on a base that is ornamented with flowers and "Salt" and "Pepper" written in script. Patent TT is on the nodders and incised on the base. $34.00–40.00

Backward-Looking Pheasants Ceramic. 1950s. Orange winged and tailed pheasants with blue backs and heads have orange beaks and face backward. $34.00–40.00

Pheasants and Hunter Ceramic. 1950s. The base depicts a hunter in a red jacket aiming a gun. The reverse side features hills and trees. One yellow bird has a dark green head, back, and wings with red beak. The other is pale yellow with pinkish-lavender wings and back and red beak. $40.00–45.00

Greenish Pheasants Ceramic. 1950s. Brightly colored pheasants in green, brown, dark green, and fuchsia have a flowered base. Base is marked PAT and nodders are incised PAT T. $34.00–40.00

Rattlesnake Ceramic. Vandor. 1988. Head and tail shakers rock back and forth when touched. $30.00–34.00

Mary and Lamb Ceramic. Ruth van Telligen Bendel. Mary hugs a gray, spotted lamb. $24.00–30.00

Yellow Ducks Ceramic. Ruth van Tellingen Bendel. Two yellow ducks, with black highlights, hug. $20.00–24.00

Dutch Boy and Girl Ceramic. Ruth van Tellingen Bendel. White Dutch boy and girl hug. She has blue highlights and yellow shoes. He has red highlights and yellow shoes. $18.00–24.00

Sailor and Mermaid Ceramic. Ruth van Tellingen Bendel. A white sailor in black shoes hugs a beige mermaid with brown hair. $26.00–30.00

Love Bugs Ceramic. Ruth van Tellingen Bendel. Cute green love bugs with white faces hug. $18.00–24.00

Bunnies Ceramic. Ruth van Tellingen Bendel. White and salmon or white and pink bunnies with smiling faces hug. $18.00–24.00

CARRIERS

Cat Carrier Ceramic. Japan. Early 1950s. Dark brown glazed cat with light brown paws, ears, and tail and gold collar arches her back on which a pair of salt and pepper shakers balance. $16.00–20.00

Cow Carrier Ceramic. Japan. 1940s. Dark brown and black-glazed cow in a crouch position carries "S" and "P" embossed buckets on her back. $20.00–24.00

Cow Carrier Ceramic. Japan. Late 1940s. White and black spotted cow balances a huge pair of milk-can shakers across her back. $12.00–16.00

Cow Family Carrier Ceramic. Japan. 1940s. Purple cow family consists of pink-nosed "Mama" sitting up on her haunches, balancing the yellow-horned, blue-trousered youngsters (salt and pepper shakers) on her horns. $20.00–24.00

Deer and Bunnies Carrier Ceramic. Japan. 1940s. Black deer with red tongue and hooves, blue eyes, pink ears, and gold horns supports two long-eared bunnies (salt and pepper shakers) on either side of its flanks. $24.00–30.00

Doe Carrier Ceramic. Japan. 1940s. Dark-brown-glazed doe with pink ears and lips and gold hooves strikes a stiff-legged pose while balancing salt-and-pepper urns from hooks on her back. The shakers are marked "S" and "P." $16.00–20.00

Donkey Carrier Ceramic. Japan. Early 1950s. White donkey with "Mohawk" black mane, black-rimmed eyes and nostrils, red mouth and ears, carries a pair of buckets on either side of its neck (salt and pepper shakers) and two bundles of straw (oil and vinegar cruets) on either side of its belly. $24.00–30.00

Boy Pulling Cart with Terriers Ceramic. Occupied Japan. 1945–1952. A boy in black shorts and green jacket pulls a cart that holds a yellow and a black terrier. This is a wonderful nodder set. $24.00–30.00

Donkey Carrier Ceramic. Japan. Early 1950s. White donkey with black-tipped mane, ears, and nose grins a pink grin as he slings a pair of white salt and pepper shaker buckets across his back. His collar is yellow with black dots and his hooves are pink. $20.00–24.00

Donkey with Wagon Carrier Ceramic. Japan. Early 1950s. White donkey with gray spots and yellow-lined ears struggles to haul a brown wood-grain wagon crammed with black-banded, brown barrels: a black-handled creamer, a round sugar bowl, and a pair of salt and pepper shakers. He tucks his head low and his body all but disappears beneath the wagon. $30.00–36.00

Donkey with Conestoga Wagon Carrier Ceramic. Japan. Early 1950s. White donkey with black markings and pink-lined ears pulls a Conestoga wagon whose top is cleverly sectioned into a pair of salt and pepper shakers flanking a central mustard "pot." The "canvas" top is white and sits astride a yellow wagon body. The donkey has a slightly porcine face. $24.00–30.00

Donkey with Chicks Carrier Glazed clay. Mexico. Early 1950s. Brown-glazed donkey with splayed feet, cubical head, and upright ears holds two brown baskets across his back. In each flower-decorated basket snuggles a brown chick with yellow beak and wings. $20.00–24.00

Braying Donkey Carrier Ceramic. Japan. Early 1950s. White braying donkey with orange and black markings wears a floral collar in shades of blue and pink and shoulders a pair of yellow buckets marked "S" and "P." $16.00–20.00

Donkey Carrier Ceramic. Japan. Early 1950s. A white, stubborn-looking donkey with orange and black markings lays back his ears and plants his feet firmly. A beige bucket hangs on either side of his back, bearing the initials "S" and "P." The donkey has pronounced bags under his eyes and a yellow harness studded with black balls. $16.00–20.00

Prospector Donkey Carrier Ceramic. Japan. Early 1950s. Beige, smiling donkey wears blue hat and black bridle. He tips one ear rakishly to the side, and carries a pick and shovel (salt and pepper shakers) on his back. $16.00–20.00

Cowboy Nodder Ceramic. Japan. 1950s. The cowboy's body is the base. One hand and the head are the shakers. This is a very unusual set. $30.00–35.00

Prospector Donkey Carrier Ceramic. Japan. Early 1950s. Brown donkey with white nose and fetlocks smiles a graceful pink smile. He wears a small black hat and carries prospecting tools on his back. $16.00–20.00

Donkey Carrier Ceramic. Japan. Early 1950s. Brown donkey with white fetlocks and black hooves and tail carries a pair of green, straw-covered jugs across his back. His ears are swept back to resemble an Indian headdress. $16.00–20.00

Donkey Carrier Ceramic. Japan. Early 1940s. White donkey with floppy ears and blue hooves carries a pair of white baskets. The baskets are decorated with a pattern of red zig-zags and black bands and contain, respectively, red apples and black grapes. $12.00–16.00

Donkey Carrier Glazed red clay. Japan. Late 1940s. Black-glazed donkey with asymmetrically positioned ears (one up, one down) carries a pair of jugs. Donkey's forehead and the tops of the jugs have touches of gold highlight. $12.00–16.00

Donkey Carrier Ceramic. Japan. Early 1950s. White and gray donkey carries white pots containing something resembling cauliflower. The pots are decorated with a red squiggle and black band. $12.00–16.00

Pink Elephant Carrier Ceramic. Japan. 1940s. Plump pink elephant with upturned trunk and swept back, rosy ears with a yellow ruffle around his neck, carrying salt and pepper shaker "baskets" on one side and a vinegar and oil cruet on the other. $30.00–36.00

Poodle Carrier Ceramic. Japan. Early 1950s. Bright yellow poodle with white belly and black and white face balances two poodle pups (salt and pepper shakers) on her collar. $16.00–20.00

Poodle Carrier Ceramic. Japan. 1940s. White French poodle with pink nose carries a pair of yellow wicker urns across its back. The urns are marked "S" and "P." $16.00–20.00

Poodle Carrier Ceramic. Japan. 1940s. Black-glazed French poodle with red ears and nose in "show-dog" stance balances a pair of black jugs embossed "S" and "P." $16.00–20.00

Purple Cow Carrier Ceramic. Japan. 1940s. This three-piece shaker set consists of an upright purple cow in white skirt and orange snout balancing a pair of calves on each yellow horn. The purple calves grin mindlessly in their pale blue shorts. $20.00–24.00

Rooster Carrier Ceramic. Japan. 1940s. Dark-brown glazed rooster with red comb, black and white feathers and eyes holds a salt-and-pepper valise on either side of his wings. $16.00–20.00

Monkeys Hanging from Tree Ceramic. Japan. 1950s. Brown monkeys hang from a tree with two branches. $12.00–14.00

Monkey Hanging from Palm Tree Ceramic. Japan. 1940s. An orange palm tree with Deco-style green frogs stands on a brown base. The Capuchin monkey hangs from one leaf by one arm. $24.00–28.00

Two Monkeys Hanging from Palm Tree Ceramic. Vandor. 1980s. Two monkeys hang from a central palm tree stand. $15.00–20.00

Banana Bunches Hanging from Banana Tree Ceramic. Japan. 1950s–1960s. This three-piece set has a matte finish. Two bunches of bananas hang from the arms of a banana tree that rises from a brown base. $14.00–18.00

Bears Hanging from a Tree Ceramic. Japan. 1950s–1960s. Brown bears hang from two branches of a tree rising from a base textured to look like forest floor with a stack of acorns. $14.00–18.00

Lanterns Hanging from a Pole Ceramic. Japan. 1940s–early 1950s. Reddish-brown squirrels hang from a tree trunk with a sign marked "S" and "P." $14.00–18.00

Squirrels Hanging from a Tree Ceramic. Japan. 1950s–early 1960s. Reddish-brown squirrels hang from a tree trunk with a sign marked "S" and "P." $14.00–18.00

Monkeys Hanging from Tree Ceramic. Japan. 1950s. Brown monkeys hang from the branches of what appears to be an apple tree. $12.00–14.00

Brown Squirrels Ceramic. Japan. 1950s–1960s. Matching brown squirrels has white striations along their tails. These are 6½" long. $14.00–18.00

Chickens Hanging from an Apple Tree Ceramic. Japan. 1930s–early 1940s. Orange, featherless chickens hang from the branches of an apple tree that is studded with pink apples. At the base of the tree sit two yellow chicks. $14.00–20.00

Chicken in a Basket Ceramic. Taiwan. 1970s. A white chicken with a red polka-dotted comb nestles in a white "wicker" basket. $14.00–18.00

Chicken in Green Basket Ceramic. U.S.A. 1950s. A white chicken nestles in a green "grass" clump. $14.00–18.00

Chicken in Yellow Basket Ceramic. Trevewood. U.S.A. 1950s–1960s. A brown chicken nestles in a yellow "wicker" basket. $14.00–18.00

Rooster Head in Rooster Body Ceramic. U.S.A. 1950s. A crested, brown rooster head nestles on a rooster body, whose long tail loops back to form a handle. $14.00–18.00

Egg Ceramic. U.S.A. 1970s. A white egg decorated with orange and yellow flowers comes apart in the middle. $12.00–14.00

Bluebird in Yellow Nest Ceramic. Japan. 1950s. A blue bird nestles in a yellow "nest." $14.00–18.00

Bluebird Twins in Brown Nest Ceramic. Japan. 1950s. Bluebird twins with open beaks joined at the sides nestle in a brown nest. $14.00–18.00

Salmon on Landscape Base
Porcelain. Japan. 1930s–1940s.
This nodder set consists of blue-gray salmon inserted into a rectangular base that is hand-painted with a landscape motif. $30.00–40.00

Fish Hanging from Seaweed on Scallop Shell Ceramic. Japan. 1930s–1940s. A pink fish hangs by its tail from a circle of green seaweed rising from a gray scallop shell. The scallop shell opens with the top serving as the lid for a mustard pot. $20.00–30.00

Melon Hanging from Vine Ceramic. Japan. 1930s–1940s. A green and yellow, very shiny melon, hangs from a brown vine which is itself a shaker. $14.00–18.00

Girl with Hatboxes Ceramic. Japan. 1930s–1940s. A blonde in a blue cap, red blouse, white skirt, and blue shoes, is attached to a white rectangular base. From her hands hang two hatboxes. One is yellow, the other, green. $20.00–24.00

Dutch Girl with Flower Baskets Ceramic. Japan. 1930s. A Dutch girl in a blue bonnet and skirt and pale blue bodice, holds a yoke across her shoulders. From each end of the yoke is suspended a basket of flowers. $16.00–24.00

Dutch Girl with Water Buckets Ceramic. Japan. 1930s. A Dutch girl in a white bonnet and apron, red blouse, and pale blue skirt holds a yoke across her shoulders. From each end of the yoke a bucket is suspended. $16.00–24.00

TALLBOYS

Green Chickens Ceramic. Japan. Green chickens with embossed bodies and red combs are 6½ tall. $14.00–18.00

Black Cats with White Cheeks Ceramic. Japan. Black cats with white feet and round, white cheeks are 6½" tall. $16.00–24.00

Indian Couple in a Pot Porcelain. Japan. 1930s–1940s. This nodder set consists of a pot, either in yellow or white, with a brown, geometric pattern, into which are inserted the heads of a brave and a squaw. $50.00–70.00

Deer Ceramic. Japan. Beige deer with blue baby-doll eyes and pink ears are 6½" tall. $14.00–18.00

Spotted Dogs Ceramic. Japan. Sitting, white-spotted dogs with brown and yellow spots, are 6½" tall. $14.00–18.00

Grinning Dogs Ceramic. Japan. Sitting, beige dogs with large grins and baby-doll eyes are 6½" tall. $14.00–18.00

Wooden Gentlemen Wood. Spindle-shaped, wooden gentlemen without arms wear top hats and frock coats. "Salty" is in gray, "Peppy" is in white. $14.00–18.00

Laughing Cats Ceramic. NAPCO. Japan. Sitting, long-necked cats with blue hats and blue and white dotted bow ties are over 8½" tall. $18.00–24.00

Siamese Cats Ceramic. Japan. White, stylized Siamese cats with green eyes and blue dots are 8½" tall. $14.00–18.00

Poodle Couple Ceramic. Japan. White poodles with smiling faces, baby-doll eyes, and pointed noses are 8½" tall. Girl has fluffly black clumps of ceramic fur, boy, in yellow hat, has brown fur. $15.00–20.00

Black Porter Ceramic. Japan. 1930s–1950s. Baggage shakers hang from the porter's hands. $90.00–110.00

HUGGERS

Dog and Garbage Can Ceramic. Japan. 1950s. A forlorn yellow dog with big blue eyes hugs a gray garbage can. $12.00–16.00

Dog Body with Dog Head Ceramic. Japan. Late 1940s–early 1950s. A white and black bulldog with big blue eyes hugs a gray garbage can. $12.00–16.00

Bear Holding Salmon Ceramic. Japan. 1950s. A brown beer holds a blue salmon in each arm. $14.00–18.00

Cat Body with Cat Head Ceramic. Japan. Late 1940s–early 1950s. A white and black cat has a body shaker and a head shaker that together make a sleeping cat. $12.00–14.00

Cat with Ball of Yarn Ceramic. Japan. 1960s. A smiling, yellow cat with big eyes hugs a pink ball of yarn. $16.00–18.00

Cat and Garbage Can Ceramic. Japan. 1950s. A smiling, yellow cat with giant blue eyes hugs an orange and gray garbage can. $12.00–16.00

Monkey with Coconut Ceramic. Japan. 1950s. A yellow monkey with blue eyes hugs a brown coconut. $12.00–16.00

Monkey with Coconut Ceramic. Japan. 1950s. A brown monkey with black eyes hugs a brown coconut. $12.00–16.00

Horse with Hay Ceramic. Japan. 1950s. A smiling brown blue-eyed horse hugs a bale of yellow hay. $12.00–16.00

Bear with Beehive Ceramic. Japan. 1950s. A white bear with giant blue eyes hugs a yellow beehive with a bee embossed on its side. $12.00–16.00

Squirrel with Acorn Ceramic. Japan. 1950s. A brown squirrel with big, black eyes hugs a beige and brown acorn. $12.00–16.00

Cuddling Pigs Ceramic. Fits and Floyd. Japan. 1970s. White pigs snuggle up with each other. One lies on the shelf and the other sits up and curls its paws around the sleeper. $18.00–22.00

Toad Hugs Mushroom Ceramic. Japan. 1960s. A green toad hugs a brown mushroom. $14.00–18.00

NODDERS

Dutch Boy and Girl on Floral Base Porcelain. Japan. 1930s–1940s. A small Dutch girl and boy are inserted in a rectangular base decorated with pink roses. $40.00–45.00

Orange Fish on Floral Base Porcelain. Japan. 1930s–1940s. Orange and blue fish are inserted into a rectangular base decorated with pink roses. $30.00–40.00

Salmon on Floral Base Porcelain. Japan. 1930s–1940s. Blue-gray salmon are inserted into a rectangular base decorated with pink roses. $30.00–40.00

Bears on Floral Base Porcelain. Japan. 1930s–1940s. Small brown bears are inserted into a rectangular base with pink roses. $30.00–40.00

Fawns on Floral Base Porcelain. Japan. 1930s–1940s. Small gray fawns are inserted into a rectangular base with pink roses. $30.00–40.00

Fawns on Landscape Base Porcelain. Japan. 1930s–1940s. Small brown fawns are inserted into a rectangular base hand-painted with a landscape of hillocks, grass, and trees. $30.00–40.00

Ducks on Floral Base Porcelain. Japan. 1930s–1940s. Orange and gray ducks are inserted into a rectangular base with pink roses $30.00–40.00

Chickens on Floral Base Porcelain. Japan. 1930s–1940s. Yellow rooster and hen are inserted into a white rectangular base hand-painted with a rose motif. $30.00–40.00

Blue Chickens on Floral Base Porcelain. Japan. 1930s–1940s. White chickens with blue tail feathers and orange wings are inserted into a rectangular base with a double, curved top, hand-painted with roses and golden lines. $30.00–40.00

Pelicans on Floral Base Porcelain. Japan. 1930s–1940s. Pelicans with long beaks are inserted into a rectangular base with a double, curved top, hand-painted with roses and golden lines. $30.00–40.00

Flamingos on Floral Base Porcelain. Japan. 1930s–1940s. Pink flamingos are inserted into a rectangular base with a double, curved top, hand-painted with roses and golden lines. $30.00–40.00

Alligators on Floral Base Porcelain. Japan. 1930s–1940s. Beige alligators are inserted into a rectangular base hand-painted with roses, bluebells, asters, and peonies. $30.00–40.00

Monkeys on Floral Base Porcelain. Japan. 1930s–1940s. Little "See No Evil," "Hear No Evil" monkeys are inserted into a rectangular base hand-painted with a blue rose and blue flower. $30.00–40.00

Turkeys on Floral Base Porcelain. Japan. 1930s–1940s. Yellow turkeys, one male and one female, have gray tails and are inserted into a rectangular base with an embossed and hand-painted floral base. $30.00–40.00

Ducks on Large Floral Base Porcelain. Japan. 1930s–1940s. Yellow orange and gray ducks are inserted into a double-curved base with a design of pink roses and golden lines and the words "Salt" and "Pepper." $30.00–40.00

Pheasants on Large Floral Base Porcelain. Japan. 1930s–1940s. White, pink, and blue pheasants are inserted into a double-curved base with a design of pink roses and golden lines and the words "Salt" and "Pepper." $30.00–40.00

Kittens on Floral Base Porcelain. Japan. 1930s–1940s. One orange and one gray kitten are inserted into a rectangular base hand-painted with a rose motif. $30.00–40.00

Cat Heads on Floral Base Porcelain. Japan. 1930s–1940s. One blue-green and one orange cat wearing ribbons are inserted into a rectangular, double-curved top base with hand-painted rose motif and golden lines. $30.00–40.00

Skulls on Floral Base Porcelain. Japan. 1930s–1940s. White skulls with rhinestone eyes and golden jaws are inserted into rectangular bases hand-painted with a rose motif and embossed with the lower jaw just beneath the point at which the heads rest. $30.00–40.00

White Skulls on Patterned Base Porcelain. Japan. 1930s–1940s. White skulls with rhinestone eyes and golden jaws are inserted in rectangular bases hand-painted with a cir-

Monkey on a Swing Ceramic. Japan. 1930s. This hanger set consists of a U-shaped base made to resemble two tree trunks. Between them hangs a swing with a clown monkey. $35.00–40.00

cular design and embossed with the lower jaw just beneath the point at which the heads rest. $30.00–40.00

Gray Skulls on Floral Base Porcelain. Japan. 1930s–1940s. Gray skulls are inserted into a white rectangular base hand-painted with a gray floral motif. The bases have a bas-relief of the lower jaws rising to meet the heads. $35.00–45.00

Sailboats on Floral Base Porcelain. Japan. 1930s–1940s. Brown sailboats with blue or yellow sails are inserted into a double-curved, rectangular base hand-painted with roses and golden lines. $35.00–45.00

Matador and Bull in Rectangular Base Porcelain. Japan. 1930s–1940s. The bust of a matador and the head of a bull are inserted into a rectangular base hand-painted with a landscape in the forefront of which dances a Spanish couple. Between the shakers rises a gray hat which is the lid to the mustard pot. $60.00–80.00

Irishman and Rabbit on Rectangular Base Porcelain. Japan. 1930s–1940s. An Irishman in black frock coat, yellow breeches, and blue scarf, and a golden-brown rabbit are inserted into a rectangular base handpainted with a landscape depicting a lake and identified as "Upper Lake Killarney." $60.00–80.00

Steeplechasers on Rectangular Base Porcelain. Japan. 1930s–1940s. Red-jacketed riders on gray, leaping horses are inserted into a rectangular base hand-painted with a rural scene. Between the horses there is a lid which covers the mustard pot inserted into the base. $40.00–60.00

Pennsylvania Dutch Couple in Rectangular Base Porcelain. Japan. A cross-looking Pennsylvania Dutch couple (he has four eyes, she is cross-eyed) are inserted into a rectangular base shaped like a board and inscribed, in Gothic script, "We get too soon old and too late smart." $40.00–60.00

LONGFELLOWS

Brown Foxes Ceramic. Japan. 1950s–1960s. Matching brown foxes have deep brown backs and white underbellies. $14.00–18.00

Brown Squirrels Ceramic. Japan. 1950s–1960s. Matching brown squirrels have white striations along their tails. $14.00–18.00

Dachshunds in Coats Ceramic. Japan. 1950s–1960s. Brown dachshunds with red, upturned noses, wear black-and-white plaid sweaters marked "S" and "P." $14.00–18.00

Brown Dachshunds Ceramic. Japan. 1950s–1960s. Pale brown dachshunds have deep brown stripes running down their backs. $14.00–18.00

Gray and Marmalade Siamese Cats Ceramic. Japan. 1950s–1960s. One gray and one marmalade Siamese cat stretch out. $14.00–18.00

White Skunks Ceramic. Japan. 1950s–1960s. White skunks have black V on their heads. $14.00–18.00

MINIATURES

Dill's Tobacco Tin and Pipe Ceramic. Japan. 1950s. A brown tobacco tin marked "Dill's Tobacco" is teamed with a squat, yellow pipe with black stem. $10.00–12.00

Perfume Bottle and Pomade Jar Ceramic. Arcadia Ceramics, Inc. Arcadia, CA. 1950s–1960s. A brown, faceted perfume bottle with a pink sprayer bulb is teamed with a pink, footed, pomade jar. Both have gold trim. $12.00–14.00

Mirror and Hairbrush Set Ceramic. Arcadia Ceramics, Inc. Arcadia, AC. 1950s–1960s. White, scalloped, standing mirror goes with a golden hairbrush into which a golden comb is inserted. $14.00–18.00

Candlesticks Ceramic. Arcadia Ceramics, Inc. Arcadia, CA. 1950s–1960s. A pair of golden candlesticks holds blue candles. $12.00–18.00

Horoscope Books Ceramic. Arcadia Ceramics, Inc. Arcadia, CA. 1950s–1960s. A pair of books are opened to reveal, on the left-hand side, the sign of the zodiac corresponding to a particular time, and on the right-hand side, the horoscope. These were available for each sign of the zodiac. $14.00–18.00

Valentine Card and Heart-Shaped Candy Box Ceramic. Arcadia Ceramics, Inc. Arcadia, CA. 1950s–1960s. A red, heart-shaped box of chocolates goes with a Valentine card that reads "Be My Valentine." $14.00–18.00

Pot-Bellied Stove and Coal Hod
Ceramic. Japan. 1940s. A gray pot-bellied stove stands next to a brown coal hod heaped high with black coal. $14.00–20.00

Box of Chocolate and Flowers Ceramic. Arcadia Ceramics, Inc. Arcadia, CA. 1950s–1960s. White, gardenia-looking flower in a green leaf is paired with a pink box with black-and-gold chocolates. $14.00–18.00

Chocolate Candies in Paper Wrap Ceramic. Arcadia Ceramics, Inc. Arcadia, CA. 1950s–1960s. One rectangular gold "chocolate" and one round "swirled" chocolate truffle sit in real paper fluted wrappers. $14.00–18.00

Purse and Pocket Watch Ceramic. Arcadia Ceramics, Inc. Arcadia, CA. 1950s–1960s. A red coin purse with a gold clasp goes with a gold and white pocket watch. $12.00–14.00

Diary and Love Letters Ceramic. Arcadia Ceramics, Inc. Arcadia, CA. 1950s-1960s. A pink diary with a gold clasp and the word "Diary" written across the cover is accompanied by a stack of letters wrapped in a pink ribbon. $14.00–18.00

Gift and Congratulations Book Ceramic. Arcadia Ceramics, Inc. Arcadia, CA. 1950s–1960s. A white book with scalloped pages and the word "Congratulations" on the front (the "C" is extraordinarily large and red), goes with a rectangular package nicely tied with a pink ribbon. $12.00–14.00

Marriage License and Ring Ceramic. Arcadia Ceramics, Inc. Arcadia, CA. 1950s–1960s. A rolled-up wedding license, sufficiently unrolled to reveal the word "License" and several lines of text, is paired with a black ring box, opened to reveal, in its snowy-white interior, a golden ring with a "diamond." $14.00–20.00

Suitcases Ceramic. Arcadia Ceramics, Inc. Arcadia, CA. 1950s–1960s. Matching white rectangular suitcases have silver corners and handles. $14.00–20.00

Bathtub and Kettle Ceramic. Arcadia Ceramics, Inc. Arcadia, CA. 1950s–1960s. An old-fashioned, oval white bathtub that is "filled" with water, goes with a round, speckled kettle with a gold handle. $12,00–16.00

Bride's Cookbooks Ceramic. Arcadia Ceramics, Inc. Arcadia, CA. 1950s–1960s. A pair of white cookbooks with a blue forget-me-not floral motif are inscribed either "This Way to His" with a picture of a red heart, or "Bride's Cook Book." $14.00–18.00

Mailbox and Package Ceramic. Arcadia Ceramics, Inc. Arcadia, CA. 1950s–1960s. A golden mailbox on a wooden stump is teamed with a rectangular white package bound with golden twine. $14.00–18.00

Garden Gate and Garden Hat Ceramic. Arcadia Ceramics, Inc. Arcadia, CA. 1950s–1960s. A crenelated wooden gate is set into an arching arbor brimming with green foliage and pink flowers. The garden hat is a large, floppy affair with pink bows and blue flowers. $14.00–24.00

School Bell and McGuffey Reader Ceramic. Arcadia Ceramics, Inc. Arcadia, CA. 1950s–1960s. A golden, wooden-handled school bell comes with a miniature copy of the McGuffey reader. $14.00–20.00

Laundry Tub and Soap Ceramic. Arcadia Ceramics, Inc. Arcadia, CA. 1950s–1960s. A white, oval tub with a green and yellow dot towel draped across one edge, holds a detachable bar of green soap which is nearly the size of the tub. $12.00–18.00

Ink Bottle and Blot
Ceramic. U.S.A. 1950s.
A gray ink bottle stands
next to a shiny blot of
ink. $14.00–20.00

Wringer Washer and Laundry Basket Ceramic. U.S.A. 1940s. An old-fashioned wringer washer with a red wringer is teamed with a yellow, straw laundry basket heaped high with laundry. $24.00–28.00

Washtub and Scrub Board Ceramic. Arcadia Ceramics, Inc. Arcadia, CA. 1950s–1960s. A gray washtub with white suds is flanked by a gray scrub board. $24.00–28.00

Book and Hurricane Lamp Ceramic. Arcadia Ceramics, Inc. Arcadia, CA. 1950s–1960s. A black book with gold pages goes with a white hurricane lamp with a gold and pink base. $14.00–18.00

Dust Pan and Whisk Broom Ceramic. Arcadia Ceramics, Inc. Arcadia, CA. 1950s–1960s. A green dust pan goes with a yellow whisk broom. Both have gold ornamentation. $12.00–16.00

Dust Pan and Broom Ceramic. U.S.A. 1940s. A brown-handled, yellow broom goes with a yellow dust pan. $12.00–14.00

Washtub and Ironing Board Ceramic. Arcadia Ceramics, Inc. Arcadia, CA. 1950s–1960s. A brown, wooden washtub, complete with washboard, goes with a golden ironing board draped with a white shirt. $20.00–24.00

Sewing Machine and Dress Form Ceramic. Arcadia Ceramics, Inc. Arcadia, CA. 1950s–1960s. A gray sewing machine, complete with thread spool, has a piece of pink fabric in place under the needle mechanism. The fabric appears to be a woman's top. The mannequin wears a white skirt and a gray top. $14.00–20.00

Pancakes and Syrup Ceramic. Arcadia Ceramics, Inc. Arcadia, CA. 1950s–1960s. A short stack of pancakes on a blue plate goes with a black-capped syrup dispenser. $14.00–20.00

Thimble and Spool of Thread Ceramic. Arcadia Ceramics, Inc. Arcadia, CA. 1950s–1960s. A golden thimble accompanies a spool of golden thread. $20.00–12.00

Key and Keyhole Ceramic. Arcadia Ceramics, Inc. Arcadia, CA. 1950s–1960s. A gray, old fashioned key is teamed with a rather ordinary yellow keyhole, which, however, lacks a hole. $10.00–12.00

Outhouses Ceramics. Arcadia Ceramics, Inc. Arcadia, CA. 1950s–1960s. Brown outhouses with half-moons on doors have one unusual detail: one of the outhouses has an antenna attached to it. The antenna is fashioned from an unfolded paper clip. $14.00–18.00

Pump and Bucket Ceramic. Arcadia Ceramics, Inc. Arcadia, CA. 1950s–1960s. Brown indoor water pump with a golden handle is teamed with a green, wood-grained bucket with a ladle. $14.00–18.00

Barbecue and Picnic Table Ceramic. Arcadia Ceramics, Inc. Arcadia, CA. 1950s–1960s. A river-rock-like barbecue is teamed with a green picnic table covered with a white cloth. $14.00–18.00

Picnic Basket and Thermos Ceramic. Arcadia Ceramics, Inc. Arcadia, CA. 1950s–1960s. A yellow "wicker" basket, partially opened, goes with a blue thermos with silver top. $14.00–18.00

Coffeepot and Coffee Grinder Ceramic. Arcadia Ceramics, Inc. Arcadia, CA. 1950s–1960s. A brown coffee grinder of the old-fashioned variety is teamed with gray, speckled coffeepot. $12.00–16.00

Coffee Grinder and Butter Churn Ceramic. Arcadia Ceramics, Inc. Arcadia, CA. 1950s–1960s. Brown coffee grinder goes with a taller butter churn, both ornamented in gold. $12.00–16.00

Waffle Iron and Pancake Stack Ceramic. Arcadia Ceramics, Inc. Arcadia, CA. 1950s–1960s. A stack of pancakes on a white plate sits next to a silver waffle iron, opened to reveal a waffle in the making. $14.00–18.00

Eggs and Sausage Ceramic. Arcadia Ceramics, Inc. Arcadia, CA. 1950s–1960s. A blue plate with two sunny-side-up eggs on one side accommodates two brown sausages as a separate piece. $12.00–16.00

Pancakes and Syrup Ceramic. Arcadia Ceramics, Inc. Arcadia, CA. 1950s–1960s. A stack of pancakes on a white plate framed by a gold spoon and fork is teamed with a yellow-capped syrup bottle. $14.00–20.00

Coffeepot with Coffee Cup and Saucer Ceramic. Arcadia Ceramics, Inc. Arcadia, CA. 1950s–1960s. A black coffeepot (round type) with gold handle sits next to a white cup-and-saucer combination. $14.00–20.00

Ice Cream Maker and Plate of Ice Cream Ceramic. Arcadia Ceramics, Inc. Arcadia, CA. 1950s–1960s. An old-fashioned ice-cream maker goes with a plate of strawberry ice cream with cherry on top and gold fork. $18.00–24.00

Cake and Slice Ceramic. Arcadia Ceramics, Inc. Arcadia, CA. 1950s–1960s. A layer cake on a white, fluted plate with a golden cake cutter is teamed with a slice of cake on a white plate and golden fork. The cake comes in various flavors: lemon, chocolate, strawberry. $14.00–20.00

Birthday Cake and Slice Ceramic. Arcadia Ceramics, Inc. Arcadia, CA. 1950s–1960s. The birthday cake is decorated with tiny roses and the words "Happy Birthday." The slice on the white plate is flanked by a golden fork. $14.00–20.00

Pie with Rolling Pin Ceramic. Arcadia Ceramics, Inc. Arcadia, CA. 1950s–1960s. A golden pie with crust is shown with a white rolling pin. $12.00–14.00

Coffee with Donut Ceramic. Arcadia Ceramics, Inc. Arcadia, CA. 1950s–1960s. The white coffee mug, brim-

Camera and Photo Album Ceramic. Arcadia Ceramics, Inc. Arcadia, CA. 1940s–1950s. A pink, bellows-type camera stands in front of an opened photograph album with gold-tipped pages. The photographs parody old-fashioned portraits. $14.00–20.00

ming with coffee, is decorated with red flowers and the words "Coffee Time." The donut is highly glazed. $12.00–14.00

Bread Rolls in Tin and Rolling Pin Ceramic. Arcadia Ceramics, Inc. Arcadia, CA. 1950s–1960s. A tin filled with a dozen golden buns is accompanied by a rolling pin. $12.00–14.00

Gingerbread Man and Rolling Pin Ceramic. Arcadia Ceramics, Inc. Arcadia, CA. 1950s–1960s. A brown gingerbread man with white eyes and black mouth is teamed with a small rolling pin with brown handles. $12.00–14.00

Pumpkin and Gourd Ceramic. Arcadia Ceramics, Inc. Arcadia, CA. 1950s–1960s. An orange pumpkin with green stem is flanked by a gourd with a bluish bottom. $12.00–16.00

Toaster and Toast Ceramic. Arcadia Ceramics, Inc. Arcadia, CA. 1950s–1960s. A silver toaster with a slice of white bread sticking from the top goes with a plate holding bread. $12.00–16.00

Chicken and Roaster Ceramic. Arcadia Ceramics, Inc. Arcadia, CA. 1950s–1960s. A speckled, gray roaster is teamed with a golden, baked chicken on a golden platter. $14.00–20.00

Ice Cream Soda and Straw Dispenser Ceramic. Arcadia Ceramics, Inc. Arcadia, CA. 1950s–1960s. A pink ice cream soda in a silver holder is teamed with a silver straw dispenser bursting with yellow straws. $14.00–20.00

Pie a la Mode Ceramic. Japan. 1940s. A slice of pie is served with a scoop of chocolate ice cream in a shallow plate. $12.00–14.00

Coca Cola Bottle and Hot Dog Ceramic. Japan. A wonderful replica of a Coca Cola Bottle is teamed with a hot dog in a bun. $30.00–40.00

Coffee and Pie a la Mode Ceramic. Arcadia Ceramics, Inc. Arcadia, CA. 1950s–1960s. A brimming white cup of black coffee goes with a slice of pie topped with a dollop of vanilla ice cream. $14.00–20.00

Loaf of Bread with Butter Ceramic. Arcadia Ceramics, Inc. Arcadia, CA. 1950s–1960s. A loaf of white, freshly baked bread with a knife in the process of detaching two slices off one end goes with a butter dish with a slab of yellow butter. $14.00–18.00

Ice Box and Stove Ceramic. Arcadia Ceramics, Inc. Arcadia, CA. 1950s–1960s. An old-fashioned wooden ice box stands next to a black, old-fashioned stove on curvaceous legs. Gold trim enlivens the duo. $24.00–30.00

Grandfather Clock and Wingback Chair Ceramic. Arcadia Ceramics, Inc. Arcadia, CA. 1950s–1960s. A stately brown grandfather clock indicating five o'clock has a golden pendulum. The white wingback chair on brown feet has a white cushion on the seat. The wingback chair also appears in a print finish and in skirted models. $24.00–28.00

Water Pump and Bucket Ceramic. U.S.A. 1950s. A gray water pump goes with a brown bucket. $16.00–20.00

Office Table and Pedestal Chair Ceramic. Arcadia Ceramics, Inc. Arcadia, CA. 1950s–1960s. Standard-issue office table is flanked by a pedestal, revolving office chair to which a green wastepaper basket is permanently attached. $20.00–28.00

Castle and Crown Ceramic. Arcadia Ceramics, Inc. Arcadia, CA. 1940s. A pink castle with many turrets and with crennelated walls is accompanied by a golden and red velvet crown. $14.00–18.00

Old-Time Car and Gas Pump Ceramic. Arcadia Ceramics, Inc. Arcadia, CA. 1940s–1950s. The gray old-timer car is trimmed with gold. The red gas pump stands on a white base. It has a gold pump and a white sign that is inscribed "gas." $18.00–20.00

Lipstick and Perfume Bottle
Ceramic. Arcadia Ceramics, Inc.
Arcadia, CA. 1940s–1950s.
White, Deco-style perfume bottle is teamed with a red lipstick in a white case. $14.00–20.00

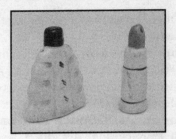

Telephone and Typewriter Ceramic. Arcadia Ceramics, Inc. Arcadia, CA. 1950s–1960s. A black dial telephone has an actual cord connecting the earpiece to the set. The typewriter, a manual, is green with a white sheet of paper inserted in the roller. $18.00–24.00

Mailbox and Garbage Can Ceramic. Arcadia Ceramics, Inc. Arcadia CA. 1950s–1960s. A silvery mailbox on a brown pedestal base goes with a silver garbage can. $14.00–20.00

Sherlock Holmes Hat and Book Ceramic. Arcadia Ceramics, Inc. Arcadia, CA 1950s–1960s. A gray, speckled Sherlock Holmes hat with white and black meerschaum pipe attached to it is teamed with a pinkish book to which adheres a golden magnifying glass. $24.00–28.00

Paint Can and Paint Brush Ceramic. U.S.A. A black-handled paintbrush with shiny black paint on the brush is teamed with a white can to the side of which is affixed the golden label reading "Hershey 50th Anniversary." $20.00–24.00

Red and Blue Couple Ceramic. Arcadia Ceramics, Inc. Arcadia, CA. 1950s–1960s. Simplified figurines depict a boy-faced man in blue suit, red tie, and blue hat, and a girlish lady in a red cloche and long dress. $14.00–20.00

Coat Rack and Umbrella Stand Ceramic. Arcadia Ceramics, Inc. Arcadia, CA. 1950s–1960s. A yellow coat rack holds a hat, scarf and coat. The yellow and gold umbrella stand is jammed with walking sticks and umbrellas. $18.00–24.00

Semaphores Ceramic. Arcadia Ceramics, Inc. Arcadia, CA. 1950s–1960s. Shiny, gun-metal semaphores each have a "banner" sticking out of the side. One is red, the other white. $10.00–14.00

Stop Sign and Car Ceramic. Arcadia Ceramics, Inc. Arcadia, CA. 1950s–1960s. A round red stop sign on a white, columnar base looms over a small brown jalopy. $14.00–20.00

Bum on Park Bench and Lamp Post Ceramic. Arcadia Ceramics, Inc. Arcadia, CA. 1950s–1960s. A white park bench holds a sleeping bum in brown. The white, Deco-style lamp post is topped with a pearlized globe and attached to a green garbage container. $18.00–24.00

Fireman's Hat and Hydrant Ceramic. Arcadia Ceramics, Inc. Arcadia, CA. 1950s–1960s. A gray fireman's hat goes with a red fire hydrant, at the base of which is coiled a gray water hose terminating in a golden nozzle. $12.00–18.00

Haystack and Log with Axe Ceramic. Arcadia Ceramics, Inc. Arcadia, CA. 1950s–1960s. A bundle of hay or wheat is tied just beneath the top. The log, yellow and tipped in green, has attached to it a black-headed axe. $10.00–14.00

Barn and Haywagon Ceramic. Arcadia Ceramics, Inc. Arcadia, CA. 1950s–1960s. A wagon piled high with hay into which a golden pitchfork is impaled, goes with a red barn with a black roof and golden vents. $14.00–20.00

Scarecrow and Corn Stalks Ceramic. Arcadia Ceramics, Inc. Arcadia, CA 1950s–1960s. A scarecrow in black stretches out its arms. The corn stalks are bound close to the top, and there is an orange pumpkin at the base of the stalks. $14.00–20.00

Fish and Creel Ceramic. Arcadia Ceramics, Inc. Arcadia, CA. 1950s–1960s. A bright yellow fish with curly fins and lips gasping for air sits next to a fishing creel. $12.00–14.00

Slippers and Coin Purse Ceramic. Arcadia Ceramics, Inc. Arcadia, CA. 1940s–1950s. A pair of brown, shiny slippers is teamed with a brown coin purse trimmed in gold. $14.00–20.00

Thermos and Lunch Box Ceramic. Arcadia Ceramics, Inc. Arcadia, CA. 1940s–1950s. The green thermos bottle has a silver cup. The lunch box has a green bottom and a black top. $14.00–20.00

Two Fish and Creel Ceramic. Arcadia Ceramics, Inc. Arcadia, CA 1950s–1960s. A stack of three gray fish lies alongside a yellow fishing creel. $14.00–20.00

Cowboy Boots Ceramic. Arcadia Ceramics, Inc. Arcadia, CA. 1950s–1960s. Brown cowboy boots have handsome golden spurs. $14.00–18.00

Cowboy Hat and Gun-In-Holster Ceramic. Arcadia Ceramics, Inc. Arcadia, CA 1950s–1960s. A brown holster holds a white-handled gun. The Stetson is white with a golden band. $12.00–18.00

Anvil and Forge Ceramic. Arcadia Ceramics, Inc. Arcadia, CA. 1950s–1960s. A black forge, its mouth filled with coal and pincers, goes with a silver anvil resting on a brown base to which a mighty hammer adheres. $14.00–20.00

Guitar and Accordion Ceramic. Arcadia Ceramics, Inc. Arcadia, CA. 1950s–1960s. A light brown accordion goes with a brown guitar. $14.00–20.00

Roller Skates Ceramic. Arcadia Ceramics, Inc. Arcadia, CA. 1950s–1960s. White roller shakes with great detailing have golden wheels. $14.00–20.00

Ice Skates and Sled Ceramic. Arcadia Ceramics, Inc. Arcadia, CA. 1950s–1960s. White ice skates with golden blades are attached to each other. The brown sled has golden runners. $14.00–20.00

Bowling Ball and Pin Ceramic. Arcadia Ceramics, Inc. Arcadia, CA. 1950s–1960s. A black bowling ball is teamed with a white bowling pin with a red top. $10.00–14.00

Baseball Mitt and Cap with Bat Ceramic. Arcadia Ceramics, Inc. Arcadia, CA. 1950s–1960s. A brown mitt holds a baseball. The green baseball cap rests on the yellow bat. $14.00–20.00

Cards Ceramic. Arcadia Ceramics, Inc. Arcadia, CA. 1950s–1960s. Two halves of a deck of cards confront each other. On one is the Ace of Hearts, on the other, the Two of Clubs. Gold enlivens the sides. $10.00–14.00

Sailboat and Lighthouse Ceramic. Arcadia Ceramics, Inc. Arcadia, CA. 1950s. A white sailboat with all its sails unfurled goes with a brown and white lighthouse on a rocky base. $14.00–18.00

Treasure Chest and Map Ceramic. Arcadia Ceramics, Inc. Arcadia, CA. 1950s–1960s. A green treasure chest is flanked by a treasure map that is partially unrolled to reveal the contours of an island on a sea of red lines. $14.00–20.00

Pot and Rainbow Ceramic. Arcadia Ceramics, Inc. Arcadia, CA. 1950s–1960s. A brown pot is accompanied by a rainbow arc. $10.00–14.00

Stagecoach and Saloon Ceramic. Arcadia Ceramics, Inc. Arcadia, CA. 1950s–1960s. A pink stagecoach goes with a yellowish Wild-West-style saloon front inscribed with the word "Saloon." $20.00–24.00

Barroom Door and Spittoon Ceramic. Japan. 1940s. A butterscotch-colored spittoon stands next to a swinging-type barroom door. $12.00–14.00

Windmill and Wooden Clogs Ceramic. Arcadia Ceramics, Inc. Arcadia, CA. 1950s–1960s. Yellow wooden clogs, ornamented with a tulip motif on the instep, stand next to a brown windmill with golden blades. $12.00–18.00

Locomotive and Coal Car Ceramic. Arcadia Ceramics, Inc. Arcadia, CA. 1950s–1960s. A pink locomotive with golden pistons is followed by a coal car brimming with black coal. $12.00–16.00

Telephone and Telephone Book Ceramic. Arcadia Ceramics, Inc. Arcadia, CA. 1940s–1950s. The brown old-fashioned crank-style telephone goes with a gray telephone book with yellow pages. $14.00–20.00

Lobster and Oyster Ceramic. Arcadia Ceramics, Inc. Arcadia, CA. 1950s–1960s. A red lobster with black bug-eyes, skulks next to a black oyster, opened to reveal its lovely, nacreous interior and a plump pearl. $24.00–28.00

Crab and Lobster Ceramic. Japan. 1940s. A red crab hoists itself up on its legs, while a pink lobster curls itself on its tail. The lobster has a scattering of red dots on its carapace. $20.00–24.00

Donkey with Grape Wagon Ceramic. Arcadia Ceramics, Inc. Arcadia, CA. 1950s–1960s. A gray donkey with a red harness sits down stubbornly in front of a green, two-wheeled cart overflowing with purple grapes. $14.00–20.00

Bumblebee with Flower Ceramic. Arcadia Ceramics, Inc. Arcadia, CA. 1950s–1960s. A yellow, gold-striped bumble-bee peeks at a yellow, gerbera daisy on a green stem. $12.00–18.00

Bunny with Easter Egg Ceramic. Arcadia Ceramics, Inc. Arcadia, CA. 1950s–1960s. A pink-eared bunny sits up on its round bottom next to a blue egg decorated with white scalloping around its middle. $12.00–14.00

Dog and Dog Food Ceramic. Arcadia Ceramics, Inc. Arcadia, CA. 1950s–1960s. Fluffy white dog wags tail as he sniffs a yellow bowl of brown dog food. $14.00–18.00

Mouse and Mouse Trap Ceramic. Arcadia Ceramics, Inc. Arcadia, CA. 1950s–1960s. Little gray mouse contemplates a gray mousetrap baited with a piece of white cheese. $12.00–14.00

Worm on Hook and Oyster Ceramic. Arcadia Ceramics, Inc. Arcadia, CA. 1950s–1960s. A green worm wriggles on a golden hook. The gray oyster is opened to its pink interior to reveal a perfect pearl. $14.00–18.00

Fish in Rowboat, Sailor in Water Ceramic. Arcadia Ceramics, Inc. Arcadia, CA. 1950s–1960s. A smiling, yellow fish sits in a white rowboat, ignoring the gasping, yellow-haired sailor whose head protrudes from a blue patch of water. $12.00–18.00

Beach Umbrella and Body under Sand Ceramic. Arcadia Ceramics, Inc. Arcadia, CA. 1950s–1960s. A bather's body appears from beneath a mound of white sand, in which are also sticking a golden bucket and shovel. The blue and white beach umbrella has a drape attached, from beneath which a pair of feet appears. $20.00–24.00

Giraffes. Ceramic. Japan. 1940s. Large-eared yellow giraffes stand on splayed feet and curl back their graceful necks. Their bodies bear an even brown spotting. $12.00–14.00

Elephants Ceramic. Japan. 1940s. Realistic gray elephants throw back their trunks and flap back their pink ears. $12.00–14.00

Zebras Ceramic. Japan. 1950s. Cartoonish zebras with pink ears, doe eyes, and pink muzzles, have a black zig-zag pattern. $12.00–14.00

Blue and White Bears Ceramic. Japan. 1950s. Sitting bears with hands on their laps have small, semicircular ears. One bear is white with gold paws and ears, the other is blue with black paws and ears. $12.00–14.00

Owls Ceramic. Japan. Yellow owls on perches have brown heads and are less than 2″ tall. $10.00–12.00

Deer Ceramic. Japan. 1950s. Cartoonish deer in a lovely shade of brown have very long, delicate ears. One sits up, the other lies down. $12.00–14.00

Donkeys Ceramic. Japan. 1950s. Gray donkeys have pink muzzles and ears. One sits, the other prances. $12.00–14.00

Squirrels Ceramic. Japan. 1950s. Squirrels reminiscent of Chip and Dale ponder an acorn in the hands of one of the little rodents. They have extravagant, curly tails and pointy ears. $12.00–14.00

Rooster and Hen Ceramic. Japan. 1940s. A very cocky rooster with a white body, blue and green wings, black, circular tail, and brown head, is matched with a less arrogant hen in the same color scheme. Both have round bodies and simplified profiles. $12.00–14.00

Birds on Flower Bases Ceramic. Japan. 1940s. Legless birds with pastel bodies and navy blue wings dip low into bases made to resemble a brown branch filled with clusters of pink generic flowers. $12.00–14.00

Raccoons Ceramic. Japan. 1940s. Identical gray raccoons with cartoonish, serious faces that include well-articulated human eyebrows, sit up and point their ringed tails. $12.00–14.00

Christmas Card and Package Ceramic. Arcadia Ceramics, Inc. Arcadia, CA. 1940s–1950s. The Christmas card is illustrated with a pine tree and snowflake design. The present pictured here may be part of another set. Originally, the Arcadia miniatures were packaged in clear dome bubble packs that made them charming gifts for all occasions. $14.00–20.00

Rosemead Raccoons Ceramic. Rosemead/Pottery. Beautifully detailed, realistic brown raccoons have black eye patches and ringed tails. One sits up and waves its paws on either side of its plump head. The other simply squats down. $22.00–26.00

Terrier Musicians Ceramic. Japan. 1940s. White terriers are engaged in playing musical instruments. One sits up and works a green accordion. The other pounds on a yellow drum. $12.00–14.00

Dressed Raccoons Ceramic. Japan. Beige raccoons in yellow hats, red shirts, and blue pants sit, spread-legged, and grin inanely. $12.00–14.00

Rub-A-Dub, Three Men in a Tub Ceramic. Arcadia Ceramics, Inc. Arcadia, CA. A tub, to which a man is attached, holds two removable men: one, in yellow, is marked "S;" the other, in red, is marked "P." $14.00–20.00

Dutch Boy and Girl Ceramic. Japan. 1940s. A yellow-jacketed, white-bodied boy in a red cap looks down in disgust. The girl, in red scarf and skirt, green shawl, and yellow clogs, also holds her arms akimbo and looks displeased. $12.00–14.00

Pixies Ceramic. Japan. 1940s. Large-eared pixies in red caps and green jumpsuits have baby-doll eyes with spidery eyelashes. One seems to be practicing the splits, the other folds its legs one atop the other. $12.00–14.00

Kitten with Pan of Milk Ceramic. Arcadia Ceramics, Inc. Arcadia, CA. 1950s–1960s. A gray angora kitten licks its paw. By its side is a golden saucepan filled with milk. $12.00–18.00

Snake Charmer with Cobra Basket Ceramic. Arcadia Ceramics, Inc. Arcadia, CA. 1950s–1960s. A white-clad snake charmer plays his golden flute. The lid of the round straw basket rises to reveal the black eyes of the cobra. $20.00–24.00

Aladdin and his Magic Lamp Ceramic. Arcadia Ceramics, Inc. Arcadia, CA. 1950s–1960s. Aladdin, in white robes, sits cross-legged on a seemingly flying carpet. Next to him is a very large, very gold magic lamp. $20.–24.00

Sir George and the Dragon Ceramic. Arcadia Ceramics, Inc. Arcadia, CA. 1950s–1960s. A knight in gray armor holds red shield. The green dragon opens its red mouth. $14.00–20.00

Monks Plastic. Hong Kong. Two, tiny, rotund monks in brown habits, clasp their hands in prayer. $10.00–12.00

Nuns Plastic. Hong Kong. Two, tiny, rotund nuns in pink habits clasp prayer books. $10.00–12.00

Organ and Holy Bible Ceramic. Arcadia Ceramics, Inc. Arcadia, CA. 1950s–1960s. A black organ with golden organ pipes is flanked by a black Holy Bible. $20.00–24.00

Teddy Bear and Jack in the Box Ceramic. Arcadia Ceramics, Inc. Arcadia, CA. 1950s–1960s. A yellow teddy bear with black paws and winning smile is flanked by a pink-faced jack-in-the-box wobbling at the end of a golden spring that has sprung from a gray box. $20.00–24.00

Baby Bottle and Booties Ceramic. Arcadia Ceramics, Inc. Arcadia, CA. 1950s–1960s. A pair of baby booties, in blue or pink, goes with a white baby bottle and golden nipple. $18.00–24.00

Rocking Horse and Drum Ceramic. Arcadia Ceramics, Inc. Arcadia, CA. 1950s–1960s. A pale blue rocking horse with a golden saddle, mane, tail, and hooves, goes with a celadon blue drum with golden trim. $18.00–24.00

Cradle and Spinning Wheel Ceramic. Arcadia Ceramics, Inc. Arcadia, CA. 1950s–1960s. A wooden cradle with an argyle blanket and white pillow is teamed with a spinning wheel whose spindle is awash with fluffy white wool. $14.00–12.00

Mortarboard and Diploma
Ceramic. Arcadia Ceramics, Inc.
Arcadia, CA. 1940s–1950s. The
black mortarboard is teamed up
with a white diploma tied with a
pale blue ribbon. $14.00–20.00

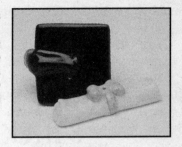

TWA Shakers Plastic U.S.A. These cylindrical shakers are white with aqua "TWA" and aqua with pale blue "TWA." $10.00–12.00

Northwest Airlines Shakers Cardboard. U.S.A. cylindrical shakers bear the old Northwest Airlines logo on a blue (salt) or red (pepper) ground. $14.00–20.00

Pipe and Slippers Ceramic. Arcadia Ceramics, Inc. Arcadia, CA. 1950s–1960s. Pink men's slippers are teamed with a white and black pipe with gold trim. $14.00–20.00

Shaving Brush and Shaving Mug Ceramic. Arcadia Ceramics, Inc. Arcadia, CA. 1950s–1960s. A gray, speckled shaving mug is spilling over with foam. The shaving brush has a black and white handle and a blob of foam on the bristles. $14.00–20.00

Safe and Safe-Cracking Tools Ceramic. Arcadia Ceramics, Inc. Arcadia, CA. 1950s–1960s. A green safe is teamed with a pink bag bursting with golden safe-cracking tools. $14.00–20.00

NON-CERAMIC
SHAKERS

WOOD

Wooden Couple Wood. Japan. 1940s–1950s. The busts represent a man in black bowler and suit wearing a red bow tie. She wears a white dress with a red collar, a pink hat, and has a heart-shaped mouth. Both have large, white, crossed eyes. $14.00–16.00

Cat Sailor Couple Squakers Wood. Japan. 1950s. Cartoon cats wear blue sailor suits. One cat has red cap, the other has a white one. $14.00–16.00

Mouse Chefs Wood. Japan. 1950s. Hand-painted mouse faces on spindle-shaped shakers have large, black eyes. "Peppy" wears red toque, "Salty" wears white toque. $12.00–14.00

Cats in Tophats Squaker Wood. Japan. 1950s. Hand-painted cat faces have large eyes. "Salty" wears white top hat, "Peppy" wears red top hat. $12.00–14.00

Spindle "Peppy and Salty" Wood. Japan. 1960s. Tall shakers in a spindle shape represent a girl "Peppy" in white hat and coat, and man "Peppy" in gray top hat and coat. $14.00–18.00

"Salty and Peppy" Chefs Wood. Japan. 1960s. "Salty" has small eyes, white toque, and red base. "Peppy" has red toque and white base, large eyes, and a grinder in the top. $12.00–14.00

Salt and Pepper Chefs Wood. Japan. 1930s. Small chef heads come in a variety of facial styles and toque heights. These range in size from ½" to 6". $8.00–20.00

Ethnic Figurines Wood. Japan. 1930s. A variety of wooden ethnic types was available. These ranged from Mexicans to Japanese and Chinese and Native Americans. All were hand-painted. $10.00–18.00

Household Objects Wood. Japan. 1930s–1940s. A variety of household objects was available in wood. These might be hand-painted. Items included sofa and armchair, iron cooking pots, rolling pins, sleds, dice, etc. $8.00–18.00

Pigs Wood. Japan. 1960s. Spherical pigs with elongated snouts have four spindle legs and wooden or leather ears. One is large, the other small. These come in many shades of brown. $10.00–12.00

Painted Pigs Wood. Japan. 1960s. Pigs are made up of two components: a large cylinder for the body and a smaller one for the head. Their snouts are hand-painted as are the "bib" and suit collar on the bodies. $12.00–14.00

Soldier Wood and metal. Japan. 1950s. This painted wood figurine consists of a cylindrical torso, painted to resemble a uniform and topped by a long, metallic neck, and a head with cap, which is a second shaker. The soldier has a red nose and a big black moustache. $12.00–14.00

Poultrymaid with Eggs Wood and metal. A pear-shaped dairymaid with a ball head has, as her arms, two wire loops, into which fit two wooden eggs. $14.00–18.00

Confederate and Yankee Soldiers Wood. Identical figurines of soldiers presenting arms are marked "South" (gray uniform) and "North" (blue uniform). $16.00–18.00

Round Couple Holding Hands Wood. Japan. 1960s. Small shakers have round bodies on flat base and round heads. They hold out their hands to each other. One wears red jacket, white pants, and yellow hat. The other wears blue jacket, black pants, and red hat. $12.00–14.00

Longhorn Heads in Holders Wood. 1950s. Longhorn steer heads with long white horns and protruding ears fit into cylindrical holders painted black and inscribed "Salty" or "Peppy." Salty's head is black, Peppy's head is red. $12.00–14.00

Steer Heads on Fence Wood. Enesco. Japan. Hand-painted wooden steer heads with long white horns hang from a wood-

Steer Heads on Fence Wood. Japan. 1956. Identical, dark wooden heads of longhorned steer hang on pale, wooden fence which also holds napkins. $14.00–18.00

en fence which serves as a napkin holder. Salt is black, Pepper is red. $14.00–18.00

Penguin Wood and metal. A tall penguin made of a deeply grained wood has a long body with leather flippers and a metallic neck. Into the neck fits the wooden head, which is another shaker. $10.00–12.00

Cat Wood and metal. Japan. The brown, bottle-shaped body has two flat legs attached to the side and ends in a conical metal neck. The head, with leather ears, fits into the neck. $10.00–12.00

Owls on Perch Wood. Japan. 1950s. This three-piece set consists of a perch to the crossbar of which are attached two owls with bodies hand-painted in feather pattern. $12.00–14.00

Carriage and Team of Horses Wood. A beautifully detailed carriage with an attached driver and team of black horses holds two containers marked "P" and "S." The white and red containers can be seen through the cutouts on the carriage sides. $14.00–20.00

Conestoga Wagon with Team of Horses Wood. A beautifully painted Conestoga wagon complete with driver and team of horses holds two shakers which make up the "covered" part of the wagon. $14.00–20.00

Brewery Delivery Wagon with Team of Horses Wood. A beautifully detailed and hand-painted brewery delivery wagon is equipped with a driver and team of horses. The two barrels in the back are the shakers. $14.00–20.00

Jigsaw Shakers Wood. 1940s–1950s. Jigsaw shakers were made in numerous shapes and were generally hand-painted

Magnet Cats with Rolling Eyes
Wood. Black, spindle-shaped cats have leather ears, plastic wiskers, and plastic, rolling eyes. Around their necks they have a bit of golden ribbon to which is attached a golden jingle bell. In the gold they are inscribed "S" (tall cat) and "P" (short cat). A magnet on each cat flank holds the shakers together. These came in plain wood or black. $12.00–14.00

with the anatomical features of the animals and a place name. Jigsaw shakers may be found in the following shapes: cowboy boots, skunks, fish, rabbits, dogs, ducks, cats, squirrels, bears. $10.00–12.00

Wooden Ducks Wood. Japan. 1950s. Realistically carved wooden ducks have no painted detail. $14.00–16.00

Television Sets Wood. Japan. 1950s. Wooden television sets have hand-painted knobs, screens, and speakers and a decal TV image. $12.00–14.00

Candles with Flames Wood. Candle bases have some bark attached to resemble dripping wax, and hand-painted red flames. $10.00–12.00

Creamer and Sugar Bowl Wood. Japan. 1950s. Wooden creamer and sugar bowl have no ornamentation. $10.00–12.00

Totem Poles Wood. Japan. 1940s. Small "thunderbird" design totem poles are hand-painted. $10.00–12.00

Humpty Dumpty Wood. Japan. 1940s. Hand-painted wooden eggs sit on bases with a red brick design. $10.00–12.00

Walnut Birds Wood and pipe cleaners. U.S.A. Birds are made of two stacked walnuts ornamented with red pipe cleaners and set on circular, wooden bases. $8.00–10.00

Axe in Stump Wood and metal. A metal, red and silver axe is lodged in a birch-type stump, which has pepper holes on one side, and salt holes on the other. $10.00–12.00

Cylinders with Deer Wood. Japan. 1960s. Cylinders with some bark remaining have carved out of the side a bas-relief image of a fawn. $12.00–16.00

Girls with Jingle Bell Earrings Wood. Japan. 1950s. Conical shakers have spherical heads with jingle bells attached to each protruding ear. The yellow or green costumes are enameled. $12.00–14.00

Peppy and Salty Penguins Wood. Spindle-shaped penguins wear top hats and have yellow beaks. They are hand-painted. $12.00–14.00

Windmills Wood. Cylindrical, dark wooden mills have lighter-colored, movable sails. $10.00–12.00

Vikings Wood. Denmark. Wooden Viking heads are very simplified and reduced to an egg-shaped helmet with horns atop a cylindrical "face." $10.00–12.00

Clocks Wood. Clock bodies are cross-cut from branch. The bark remains and the face of each clock is inscribed with numbers and the words "Time for Pepper" and "Time for Salt." $8.00–10.00

Picnic Table Wood. 1950s. A replica of a picnic table has inserted into the table two cylinders, each in a different shade of wood. $10.00–12.00

Lampost Wood. Small lamposts have signs reading "Salt" or "Pepper" and hand-painted lamps with a bird motif. $10.00

Black Lampost Wood. Large lamposts are painted black and have yellow signs with the words "Salt" and "Pepper." The lamps themselves are painted yellow with a floral motif. $10.00

Walnuts on Stumps Wood. 1950s. Two stumps, with bark partially removed, are capped by a walnut each. On the stripped side are the words "You're nuts if you don't use Salt" and "You're nuts if you don't use Pepper." $10.00

Stumps with Inscriptions Wood. Two halves of a stump with bark still intact are inscribed on the inside, "No use huntin' possum if ya ain't got no pepper" and "Dang. Fish won't taste no good with no salt." When placed together along their flat sides, the two halves form a whole. $10.00–12.00

Pot-Bellied Stove Wood. Nicely carved pot-bellied stoves with black stovepipes are marked "S" and "P." $10.00–12.00

Stove with Pots Wood. A brown, painted stove with a door and two drawers holds two pots, which are the shakers. The red coffeepot is marked "P" and the black saucepan is marked "S." $12.00–14.00

Barrels Wood. 1950s. Wooden barrels are either plain or painted. $8.00

Liquor Bottles Wood and metal. Gallon-sized liquor bottles are capped with metal and marked "XXX." $8.00–10.00

Peace Pipes Wood. 1950s. The stems of the pipes are branches with bark intact. The bows are hand-painted with profiles of Indian chiefs. $12.00–14.00

Flying Saucers Wood. Japan. Flying saucers are inscribed with the words "Salt" and "Pepper." $8.00–12.00

Spinning Wheel Wood. A spinning wheel with a turning wheel has two holes in the base of the "bench" into which the shakers are inserted. $10.00–12.00

Bench with Shakers Wood. Japan. 1940s. Wooden benches with two holes in the seat hold shakers. Souvenir decals were usually affixed to the back of the bench. $12.00–16.00

METAL

"Black and Whites" Pot metal. Japan. Mid-1930s–early 1950s. The cast, pot metal shakers were made in three sizes: miniatures, medium, and large. The shakers in a set were identical except for color, the black always being the pepper shaker and the white, the salt shaker. All are ornamented in hand-painted Pennsylvania Dutch designs consisting of small floral motifs in red and green. The range of objects represented by the black and whites seemed infinite. Household objects included various kinds of stoves, from pot-bellied to Franklin to cooking stoves; irons, pots, milk cans, coffeepots, teapots, coffee grinders, dustpans, sweepers, carpet sweepers, hourglasses, telephones, wishing wells, sewing machines, sugar scoops, covered wagons, candlesticks, pumps, rockers, shoeshine sets, clogs, trolleys, jalopies, rocking horses, cradles, grandfather alarm clocks, cannons, washing machines of all sorts, and even cats. The miniatures are hard to find and consequently more expensive than the mediums or the larges. $14.00–18.00 for the medium; $16.00–20.00 for the large

Amish Folk Pot metal and cast iron. 1930s–1940s. This series of shakers represents Amish folk in black with red shirts or blouses occupied in various activities or at rest. There are

Black and White Pot-Bellied Stoves Pot metal. Japan. Mid 1930s–early 1950s. The cast, pot metal shakers were hand-painted in Pennsylvania Dutch designs. The black is pepper, the white is salt. These are available in three sizes. $14.00–20.00

mixed-gender couples of various sizes sitting on cast-iron benches, Amish boy and girl, squat adult couples, Amish woman milking a cow, or Amish man in a black surrey with a brown horse, Amish man on horseback, Amish boy pushing a wheelbarrow. The smaller, less complicated ones are less expensive. $16.00–24.00

Old Folks on Rockers Painted pot metal. 1930s–1940s. Old men or old women in predominantly black clothing constitute one shaker, and the rocking chair constitutes the other shaker. $16.00–24.00

Metal Objects with Bronze Paint Metal with bronze paint. 1930s–1970s. A variety of objects is represented in the metal shakers finished with bronze paint. These are very nicely detailed, so they look quite realistic. Among the shapes you will find are cowboy boots with spurs, pineapples, jalopies, roadsters, locomotives with tenders, totem poles. $12.00–18.00

Metal Objects with Brass Paint Metal with brass paint. 1930s–1970s. These finely detailed metal shakers are made in a variety of forms, including cowboy boots, totem poles, trains, animals, musical instruments. $14.00–18.00

Painted Metal Mailboxes Painted metal. 1930s. Matching rural mailboxes are painted gray with red flag and embossed "U.S. Mail." $10.00–12.00

Painted Metal Doghouse Painted metal. 1930s. "Pep" and "Salty" are embossed above the door of the doghouses. The houses are beige with reddish-brown roofs and a bas-relief dog emerges from the door. $12.00–14.00

Painted Metal Spin-Dry Washer Painted metal. 1950s. White replicas of spin-dry washers have blue stripes and black feet. $20.00–24.00

Old Lady on Rocker Painted pot metal. 1930s–1940s. The old lady, in red and black, sits on a blue rocker. The lady is one shaker, the rocker another. $16.00–24.00

Silver-Colored Metal Squirrels on Branch Silver-colored metal. 1930s. Realistic-looking, silver-colored squirrels nestle on a tray crafted to resemble a branch. $18.00–28.00

Painted Metal Tombstones Painted metal. 1940s. Old-style tombstones, reminiscent of old New England gravestones, are painted gray. They are embossed "Here lies Salt" and "Here lies Pepper." $10.00–14.00

Metal Miniature Cars and Carriages Metal. 1940s. Finely detailed miniature replicas of old-time cars and carriages are painted with a silver or bronze finish and metallic paint. $10.00–14.00

Painted Steins, Coffeepots, and Teapots Hand-painted metal. Japan. 1940s. A variety of pouring vessels from beer steins to coffeepots are painted a basic white or black and then decorated with some sort of floral or human motif. $10.00–12.00

Light Bulbs Glass and metal. Japan. 1970. Light bulbs come in a variety of colors with metal screw-on caps. $10.00–14.00

Coffeepots with Burner Glass and metal. U.S.A. 1950s. A metal coffee warmer with red coils holds two glass coffeepots. $16.00–24.00

Silver-Colored Metal Animal Sets Silver-colored metal. 1930s–1970s. These silver-colored sets are beautifully detailed, realistic replicas of various birds, such as pheasants, peacocks, partridges, or sparrows, either without bases or perched on some branchy, leafy pedestals. The bestiary of animals in this genre includes bears, cats, squirrels, pigs, turtles, penguins, fish, owls, ducks, dogs, and horses. $18.00–28.00

Silver-Colored Coffeepots on Tray Souvenir Sets Silver-colored metal. 1930s–1970s. Matching, silver-colored teapots of various "traditional" designs sit on oblong trays. The flat side of each pot bears a sticker identifying some tourist attraction. $10.00–16.00

Metal and Glass Fruit Hanger Sets Silver- or gold-colored metal and colored glass. U.S.A. 1940s. Gold- or silver-colored metal stands are shaped like vines sprouting from a circular base. From the branching "arms" are suspended various glass fruits with metal caps in the shape of stems. Strawberries, grapes, and raspberries were among some of the designs of these popular shakers. $15.00–20.00

Painter's Palette with Plastic Shakers Metal and plastic. U.S.A. 1950s. A black metal palette on golden "feet" has "blobs" of paint scattered around the perimeter and a hole to accommodate toothpicks. The shakers are plastic pots in a swirled design. $20.00–24.00

Metal Lantern Hangers Metal and glass. U.S.A. 1950s. Metal stand is shaped like a plant rising from a base. From each arm hangs a metal lantern with a glass interior. $15.00–20.00

Metal and Plastic Scales Hanger Metal and plastic. U.S.A. 1950s. Metal stand in the shape of a scale has a plastic bucket hanging from each arm. The upper half of the bucket is a transparent bulb. $14.00–18.00

Metal Scale Hanger Metal. Japan. 1950s. A realistic replica of an old-fashioned postage scale has two brass-colored weights balancing on each pan. $18.00–24.00

Metal and Plastic Candelabrum Metal and plastic. U.S.A. 1950s. A gold-colored and black candelabrum has a pink plastic candle shaker in each arm. $15.00–20.00

Metal and Glass Flower Cart Painted metal and glass. This four-piece set consists of a black and "brass" flower cart ornamented with pink and green rose garlands. In the center of the cart is a black bucket for toothpicks. On either side of this stand fluted glass shakers. $18.00–20.00

Glass and Metal Ice Cream Cones in Holder Metal, glass, and plastic. U.S.A. 1950s. Glass cones with plastic "ice cream" are inserted into spiral, metal holders attached to a circular base. $18.00–20.00

Metal and Lucite "Tree" Lucite and metal. U.S.A. 1950s. A Lucite stand resembling a 1950s free-standing room divider holds, on each shelf, a silver metal shaker. $40.00–45.00

Cast-Iron Shriners Painted cast iron. U.S.A. 1950s. Matching Shriners in red fezzes wear either a black or white suit. $50.00–60.00

Silver-Colored Cocktail Shakers Silver-colored metal. U.S.A. 1950s. Cocktail shakers are silver colored. $18.00–24.00

Silver-Colored Ducks Silver-colored metal. Occupied Japan. 1945–1952. Ducks wearing caps are painted silver. $16.00–20.00

Chrome Ocean Liner Chrome. 1930s. U.S.A. Streamlined ocean liner has removable shaker smokestacks with red caps. $30.00–34.00

Chrome-Plated Spheres Chrome-plated metal. Chase Brass and Copper Company. Waterbury, CT. 1930s. One large and one small sphere sit on circular bases. $30.00–40.00

Chrome-Plated Cubes Chrome-plated metal. 1930s. Chrome-plated cubes sit on white, bakelite bases and have a Saturn and comet design on the top. $30.00–35.00

Brass Bellhop Carrier Brass and glass. U.S.A. 1930s. A brass bellhop that looks like a robot holds two cylindrical carriers into which glass shakers are inserted. $20.00–30.00

Tea Wagon Painted metal and glass. A black and brass painted tea wagon holds glass shakers. $14.00–18.00

Umbrella Stand Painted metal and glass. A brass, black, and silver-painted metal umbrella stand holds two glass shakers. $14.00–20.00

Paint Tubes Silver and gold-painted metal. U.S.A. 1970s. Silver and gold-painted paint tubes have silver caps. $24.00–28.00

Plastic

Red Toilets Plastic. U.S.A. 1950s. Red toilets have openable lids. $10.00–14.00

Mirror Hat Stand With Hats Plastic. U.S.A. 1950s. A white, mirrored hat stand has a yellow boater and a black bowler hanging from each side. $16.00–24.00

Coat Rack with Umbrellas Plastic. U.S.A. 1950s. The coat rack is anchored to a base on which stand two pairs of shoes. Two umbrellas—the shakers—hang from the rack. $14.00–18.00

Coat Rack with Hats Plastic. U.S.A. 1950s. A yellow boater and black bowler—the shakers—hang from the two-tone coat rack. $14.00–18.00

Windmill, Mechanical Plastic. U.S.A. 1950s. A windmill stands on a base that is the lid for a sugar bowl. Shakers are in the roof. By turning the blades in one direction or another, one makes either the salt or the pepper shaker emerge. $20.00–24.00

Flower Pot with Roses Plastic. U.S.A. 1950s. A white flower pot serves as a sugar bowl. Two detachable roses are the shakers. $14.00–18.00

Arbor with Roses Plastic. U.S.A. 1950s. A white arbor consisting of a double row of picket fencing holds napkins. White flower pots hold a yellow and red rose, which are the shakers. $16.00–20.00

Champagne Bucket with Champagne Bottles Plastic. U.S.A. 1950s. A silver-colored champagne bucket holds two removable champagne bottles. $12.00–18.00

Roller Skates Plastic. U.S.A. 1950s. Roller skates on movable wheels are either blue or red. $12.00–14.00

Golf Balls on Green Nester Plastic. U.S.A. 1950s. White golf balls balance on beige tees that are inserted into a green base with an "18th hole" marker serving as a holder. $16.00–20.00

Guitar on Stand Plastic. U.S.A. 1950s. A guitar leans against a music stand. The guitar was available in plain colors or sparkling finish. $12.00–14.00

Wringer Washer Plastic. U.S.A. 1950s. A wringer washer is made so that the tub part is a sugar bowl and the wringers are the shakers. A small lever releases the wringer. $15.00–20.00

Mixer with Bowl Plastic. U.S.A. 1950s. A Mixmaster-type mixer is attached to a base. The beaters are the shakers. The bowl is the sugar bowl. $15.00–20.00

Christmas Piano Mechanical Plastic. U.S.A. 1950s. A red, green, and white upright piano has Christmas carols on the music stand. The top are the shakers which emerge when the keys are depressed. $20.00–24.00

Television Set, Mechanical Plastic. U.S.A. 1950s. A brown, console-type television set on spindly, late 1950s legs, has knobs. When these are turned, the shakers in the speaker pop up. $15.00–20.00

Cash Register, Mechanical Plastic. U.S.A. 1950s. A cash register with two keys and the signs "No Sale" and "$" releases the drawer shakers when the keys are depressed. $15.00–20.00

Old-Fashioned Telephone, Mechanical Plastic. U.S.A. 1950s. A crank-type telephone has two speakers (the shakers) which are released when the crank is turned. $14.00–18.00

Fireplace with Andirons Plastic. U.S.A. 1950s. A white fireplace with brown flagstones and a red fire holds, as golden andirons, salt-and-pepper shakers. $14.00–18.00

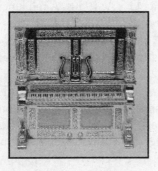

Piano, **Mechanical** Plastic. U.S.A. 1950s. An upright piano with gold trim has a keyboard which, when depressed, projects the shakers upward from the top of the piano. $20.00–24.00

Lawnmower, **Mechanical** Plastic. U.S.A. 1950s. A two-tone lawnmower with wheels and flippable handle has two cylinders (the shakers) which move up and down as the mower is moved across the dining room table. $15.00–24.00

Tricycle Metal and plastic. U.S.A. 1940s. A golden-metal tricycle with movable wheels and handlebars has plastic shakers in the back. $15.00–20.00

Birdcage with Canisters Plastic. U.S.A. 1950s. A yellow and white, carousel-type birdcage has a white and yellow pair of rectangular shakers marked "S" and "P." $12.00–14.00

Jalopy with Passengers Plastic. U.S.A. 1950s. An old-style jalopy with red wheels has a driving couple in yellow or red hats. The drivers are the shakers. $14.00–18.00

Slot Machines Plastic. U.S.A. 1950s. Silver-colored slot machines are embossed "Jackpot Pepper" and "Jackpot Salt." $10.00–12.00

Two-In-One Shaker Plastic. E.J. Springmeier Co. Cincinnati, OH. The Shake-a-Matic Two-in-One Shaker is a cylinder with two contiguous compartments and opaque plastic top and bottom. $10.00–14.00

Oyster Shell with Two Pearls Plastic. U.S.A. 1950s. A pearlescent shell opens to reveal two pearl shakers within. $15.00–24.00

Goose with Golden Eggs Plastic. U.S.A. 1950s. A golden-beaked goose opens up to reveal two golden egg shakers in the interior. The goose was available in white or beige. $12.00–14.00

Lunchbox with Thermos Plastic. U.S.A. 1950s. A red lunchbox holds two shaker thermos bottles. $10.00–14.00

Sewing Machine, Mechanical Plastic. U.S.A. 1950s. A console sewing machine with a flip-top has shaker drawers. $16.00–24.00

Small Kitchen Appliances Plastic. U.S.A. 1950s. Beautiful, silver-toned replicas of famous small kitchen appliances reproduced all the details of the originals. Available were irons, electric coffee makers, flip-top electric coffee makers, copper bottom Revere pans, lids, and Waring blenders. $12.00–16.00

Rotisseries with Chickens Plastic. U.S.A. 1950s. A realistic rotisseries oven with "chrome"-like sides has a see-through door. Inside are two chickens: one golden, the other "raw," which are the shakers. The full complement of dials is represented. $24.00–30.00

"Revere" Pans Plastic. U.S.A. 1950s. Copper-bottomed Revere pans are reproduced in this set. Sets packed in their original boxes command higher prices. $12.00–16.00

Musical Notes on Treble Staff Hangers Plastic. U.S.A. 1950s. A red and a yellow musical note hang on a metal staff with a plastic treble cleff, the whole affair being attached to a plastic base. $16.00–24.00

Pop-Up Toaster, Mechanical Plastic. U.S.A. 1950s. Two slices of toast pop out of the toaster when the side is depressed. $15.00–24.00

Water Pump and Bucket, Mechanical Plastic. U.S.A. 1950s. A water pump on a base holds a sugar-bowl bucket beneath the faucet. When the pump is depressed, the divided top of the pump rises as two individual shakers. $16.00–24.00

Ice Boxes Plastic. U.S.A. 1950s. Wood-grained iceboxes have metal-like hinges. $10.00–14.00

Bowling Ball and Bowling Pins Plastic. U.S.A. 1950s. A black bowling ball is attached to a diamond-shaped base. The bowling ball opens to reveal a sugar bowl. On either side stand white shaker bowling pins. $15.00–20.00

Rosebud Vases Plastic. U.S.A. 1950s. White swirly vases hold a rosebud. Each shaker is marked either "S" or "P." $12.00–16.00

Butler and Maid Wind-Ups Plastic. Hong Kong. 1970s. Wind-up butler and maid, in black, dispense salt and pepper from their heads. $20.00–24.00

Santa Claus Wind-Ups Plastic. Hong Kong. 1970s. Wind-up Santas dispense salt and pepper from their heads. $10.00–24.00

Kitchen Witches Plastic. U.S.A. 1960s. Kitchen witches come in yellow capes with either blue or red dresses. $10.00–12.00

Silver-Tone Cupid Hanger Plastic. Hong Kong. 1950s. Silver-toned Cupid figurine carries a yoke across his back.

From either end of the yoke is suspended a silver bucket holding salt or pepper. $14.00–16.00

Peanut Tree Hanger Plastic. Japan. 1950s. A transparent plastic "tree" with tinted leaves and birds holds, from two branches, yellow peanuts with metallic-tinted caps. $15.00–20.00

Umbrella Stand Plastic and metal. U.S.A. 1940s. A black metal umbrella stand has two circular holders through which are slipped plastic umbrellas with "S" and "P" handles. $14.00–20.00

Mantelpiece Clocks Plastic. U.S.A. 1950s. Replicas of fancy china mantelpiece clocks have mauve detailing. They are also available in a gold tone. $12.00–14.00

Pocket Watches Plastic. U.S.A. 1950s. Deceptive replicas of silver pocketwatches have Roman numerals. $15.00–20.00

Sunnyside-up Eggs Plastic. Japan 1950s. Whites are the base to two yellow shaker yolks. $14.00–18.00

Oranges on Palm Tree Stand Plastic. Japan. 1950s. A double-trunked palm tree rises from a green plastic tray on which sit, at either end, perfectly round oranges. $24.00–30.00

Lanterns Plastic. U.S.A. 1950s. Clear lanterns in metal-colored plastic holders have either black or white tops and handles. $12.00–16.00

Orange Tree on Stand with Fruit Baskets Plastic. U.S.A. 1950s. This shaker and napkin set is an entire scenario. A green orange tree with oranges stands on a base, flanked by a white picket fence and backed by a frame which holds napkins. A white ladder leans against the tree. On either side stand white and orange fruit baskets. $16.00–24.00

Ice Cream Sodas Plastic. U.S.A. 1950s. Chocolate and strawberry ice cream sodas have yellow straws. $14.00–20.00

Fruit Bowl Plastic. U.S.A. 1950s. A beige bowl (sugar bowl) has a lid molded into various fruit shapes. The pineapple and the grapefruit are removable as shakers. $14.00–20.00

Onion People on Vegetable Cart Plastic. U.S.A. 1960s. One pink and one white onion person wearing a black top hat nestle amid smaller plastic vegetables attached to a plastic cart. $14.00–20.00

Television Set Snow Dome Shakers Plastic and water. Japan. 1950s–1960s. Pastel-colored plastic television sets have clear screens behind which is a souvenir scene and snow. The shakers are on either side of the screen. These kinds of shakers were very popular as souvenirs and could be found for a number of cities and sights. $15.00–20.00

Snow Dome Shakers Plastic and water. Japan. 1950s–1960s. Snow domes in elongated or squat models have souvenir scenes from all over the country and even the world. The condiments are stored in the opaque rear half of the dome. $14.00–18.00

Humpty Dumpty Plastic. U.S.A. Red Humpty Dumpty kicks his legs to the side and clings to his head. One closes his eyes, the other opens them wide. $12.00–18.00

Tomato and Pepper Plastic. U.S.A. 1950s. Red pepper and red tomato both have green stems. $10.00–12.00

Dutch Couple Plastic. U.S.A. Dutch couple wears red, white, and yellow clothing. $10.00–12.00

Monkeys Hanging From Tree Hanger Plastic. U.S.A. 1960s. Brown monkeys with red grins hang from a beige tree rooted in a green, grass-textured base. $10.00–12.00

Ocean Liners Plastic. U.S.A. 1950s. Ocean liners have removable shaker smokestacks. These were available in a variety of colors. $10.00–14.00

One-Piece Push-Button Shakers Plastic. U.S.A. 1950s. One-piece, push-button shakers were made so that an opaque, inverted "T" base serves as the stage for figurines on either side. The holes were on the bottom of the "T" and spices were released by pushing the button. This style was very widely used as a vehicle for souvenirs and came in a kaleidoscopic range of colors. Some examples were Black chefs/Louisiana; Amish couple/Pennsylvania Dutch Country; alligators/ Florida; penguins/Victoria, B.C. $12.00–18.00

Watering Cans Plastic and aluminum. U.S.A. 1950s. Watering cans have transparent, plastic sides and aluminum tops and bottoms. $10.00–14.00

Camel with Shaker Humps Plastic. U.S.A. 1950s. A smug-looking, sitting camel has two shakers emerging from its hump. The set was available in many color combinations. $14.00–24.00

Croquet Set Hangers Plastic. Japan. 1950s. Tiny croquet salt-and-pepper mallets hang from a plastic stand. The balls are marbles, and the wickets are steak markers for "rare," "medium," and "well done" meat. $16.00–24.00

Cats Plastic. U.S.A. 1950s. Sitting, mewing cats are marked "Salt" and "Pepper." $10.00–14.00

Parakeets on Branch Stand Plastic. U.S.A. 1950s. Yellow parakeets are shakers that are inserted into a white and black speckled plastic branch with leaves. $14.00–20.00

Silver-Tone Binoculars Plastic. U.S.A. 1950s. Silver-toned binoculars have white "lens" lids. $12.00–14.00

Light Bulbs Glass and metal. Japan. 1970. Light bulbs come in a variety of colors with metal screw-on caps. $10.00–14.00

Coffeepots with Burner Glass and metal. U.S.A. 1950s. A metal coffee warmer with red coils holds two glass coffeepots. $16.00–24.00

Book Rack Plastic. Japan. 1950s. A set of books sits on a tray. The two end books are shakers, the row of five intermediate books with initials on the spines that spell "SUGAR" constitute the sugar bowl. $15.00–20.00

Dream Home Plastic. U.S.A. 1950s. A red and white "colonial" front door with curving white railing forms the napkin holder. Potted conical trees at the door are the shakers. $24.00–30.00

BAKELITE

Washington Monument/Obelisks Bakelite. U.S.A. 1920s. Heavy yellow marbleized Bakelite shakers in the shape of the Washington Monument bear a golden "P" and "S" on one of their faces. $24.00–30.00

Mortar and Pestle Bakelite and wood. U.S.A. 1920s. A yellow and black Bakelite pair of pestles nestles in a wooden mortar. $24.00–30.00

Streamlined Wedges Bakelite. 1920s. Two streamlined, wedge-shaped shakers in heavy, marblelized Bakelite have round caps and nestle against each other along their long side. Salt is a deep amber color, while pepper is dark brown. Also available in dark green with black tops. $20.00–24.00

Bullet-Nosed Ribbed Cubes Bakelite 1920s–1930s. Resting on ribbed, quadrangular bases, these shakers are topped by bullet-nosed caps which continue the ribbing. The base and top come in different shades, with the top usually black and the bottom ranging from dark green to amber. $20.00–24.00

Barrel-Shaped Shakers on Footed Tray Bakelite and metal. 1930s. A pair of barrel-shaped shakers in amber-colored, marbleized Bakelite is banded in metal across the middle and topped with metal caps. Both rest on a rectangular Bakelite tray supported by four tiny legs. $20.00–24.00

Spheres Bakelite. 1930s. A pair of perfect spheres is surmounted by a short, circular chunk. These heavy Bakelite shakers are found in matching or contrasting colors ranging from all red to red with amber caps, or amber with gold metal caps. $20.00–24.00

Mechanical Glass Shakers on Plastic Base Bakelite and glass. 1940s. A Deco-styled plastic base consisting of a stepped-up horizontal base with a perpendicular rectangular element holds a pair of glass, bullet-shaped shakers. If the black button between the shakers is depressed, salt and pepper are released from the bottom. $16.00–20.00

Tapering Cylinders Bakelite. 1920s–early 1930s. These tapering cylinders simulate a telescoping effect in three sections that rise from a gently tapering base to culminate in a three-step series of circles of diminishing circumference. The shakers are made of heavy, sometimes marbleized, Bakelite in a variety of colors that range from red to amber, pale green, and olive green. $24.00–30.00

Shot-Gun Shells Plastic and metal. 1940s. A pair of plastic, cylindrical shakers is set into metal shotgun-shaped bases. These shakers come in red and blue. $12.00–16.00

Two-Piece Streamlined Mechanical Bakelite. 1930s. This oval two-piece mechanical consists of a tall, oval base into which are inserted snugly fitted shakers. Black button signals "Pepper," while white button marks "Salt." These elegant shakers are made of high-grade Bakelite and have been seen in a variety of colors, including creamy white, seafoam green, and red. $10.00–16.00

Carrier with Boxy Shakers Bakelite. 1930s–early 1940s. A ribbed tray with a carrying handle issuing from the middle holds two matching mechanical shakers in the shape of a ribbed box with a plain base and top from the middle of which protrudes a square pushbutton embossed with a large "S" or "P." The condiment is released when the button is depressed. These shakers come in gray or taupe or pale green marbelized Bakelite. $10.00–14.00

Hexagonal Columns with Dome Tops Bakelite. 1930s–early 1940s. Hexagonal columns with semispherical tops rest on black bases. These lovely shakers come in a variety of colors that include bright yellow, seafoam green, and red. $10.00–14.00

Rounded Hexagonal Columns with Dome Tops Bakelite. 1930s–early 1940s. These hexagonal columns have rounded facets two-thirds up the sides of which rise attached semicircular rods. From the tops protrude hemispheres punctured by condiment holes. These shakers can be found in seafoam green, yellow, red, and brown. $10.00–14.00

Mechanical Cylinders Bakelite. 1930s–early 1940s. Heavy, marbelized Bakelite cylinders rest on small bases and in their rounded tops have round protruding buttons embossed with the letters "S" or "P." When depressed, the buttons activate a

One-Piece Mechanical: Twin Peaks Bakelite. 1930s. A twin pair of tapering cylinders joined by a narrow band rests atop a squat ziggurat and is surmounted by another, though steeper, ziggurat. The terminal pieces are usually in a shade that contrasts with the body. Combinations of red and white and white and white have been seen. The mechanism is activated by pressing buttons concealed in the base. $16.00–25.00

Bombs Bakelite. 1930s–early 1940s. Bulb-headed, bomb-shaped shakers have three tailfins which run two-thirds up the sides. Fashioned of lightweight Bakelite in a variety of colors that range from gold, orange, and red to baby blue, these shakers may also be found with travel stickers attached to the sides. $24.00–30.00

release mechanism which dispenses salt or pepper from the bottom of the shaker. Available in gray, pale green, pink or red. $10.00–16.00

Ridged Bullets Bakelite. U.S.A. 1920s–1930s. Bullet-shaped, ridged shakers have black tops and kelly-green bottoms. $30.00–40.00

Telescoping Cylinder Bakelite. U.S.A. 1920s–1930s. Three-tiered cylinders, with each tier increasing in size (from bottom to top), come in black bottom with orange lid or orange bottom and red lid. $30.00–40.00

Horizontally Ridged Cylinder Bakelite. U.S.A. 1920s–1930s. Horizontally ridged cylinders have four ridges, a base wider than the cylinder, and a top narrower than the cylinder. The body comes in a marbleized tan, the top is black. $30.00–40.00

Vertically Fluted Cylinders Bakelite. U.S.A. 1920s–1930s. Vertically fluted cylinders taper toward the top. Solid green shaker has red lid, marbleized green shaker has yellow lid. $30.00–40.00

Triangular Solids Bakelite. U.S.A. 1920s–1950s. When put together, these triangular shakers form a cube. They are a beautiful golden, marbleized color. Pepper lid is black, salt lid is yellow. $30.00–40.00

Domed Columns Bakelite. U.S.A. 1920s–1930s. These quintessentially Deco-inspired shakers have ridged, hexagonal bases; smooth, hexagonal shafts; and three-tiered dome caps. Bases and shafts are red, domes are seafoam green. $30.00–40.00

Condiment Set Bakelite. U.S.A. 1920s–1930s. This butterscotch-colored condiment set consists of an oval tray that steps back three tiers to a flat surface that has indentations for the shakers and the sugar bowl. A metal handle arches from one side of the base to the other. The shakers are cylindrical, tapering from the bottom to the top along a series of setbacks. Salt terminates in a smooth top, pepper ends in a cone. The sugar bowl is rectangular and tapers outward from the base. $50.00–70.00

Penguins Bakelite. U.S.A. 1920s–1930s. Streamlined, sitting penguins have spoutlike beaks. Bottoms halves are black, top halves are white. $35.00–45.00

Push-Button Semi-Ovals Bakelite. U.S.A. 1920s–1940s. Pale-yellow shakers are streamlined and, when placed together on their flat side, form an oval. Each has a series of seven ridges similar to accordion pleats on the side closest to the smooth face. A black or white push button, located on the top, is activated to dispense the condiment. $25.00–30.00

Elongated Teardrop in Bakelite Holder Bakelite and glass. U.S.A. 1920s–1940s. Traditional, elongated teardrop-shaped glass shakers with ornamented faces are capped with ivory-colored dome caps made of Bakelite. The carrier, a fluted basket with a "piano-leg" handle, is also of ivory Bakelite. $25.00–30.00

One-Piece Push Button Bakelite and Glass. U.S.A. 1920s–1940s. A red Bakelite stand with an elongated, hexagonal "footprint" and a central column with a long black and a long white "button" on top holds glass bottles that are inserted into the stand bottom up. The stand is red Bakelite, and the condiment is dispensed by means of the push-button mechanism. $35.00–40.00

Cylinders with Push-Button Mechanism Bakelite. 1930s. Streamlined Moderne-inspired cylinders with rounded tops

Arch on Base Bakelite. 1930s. A short, thin arch is supported on two substantial bases with quadrilateral "footprints" that fit into a rectangular base. This handsome shaker is found in a variety of colors, usually with a black base. $25.00–30.00

have slightly protruding buttons on their tops. The initials "S" and "P" appear in raised letters on the button tops. These shakers come in a variety of colors, fashioned of beautiful, heavy, marbleized Bakelite. $35.00–45.00

Tapering Hexagonal Columns Bakelite. 1930s. Tapering hexagonal columns rise from round bases and terminate in a pyramidal top. At their bottoms they have short fins rising to midpoint on the column shaft. These have been seen in olive green, pale green, and butterscotch yellow. $30.00–35.00

Spheres with Push Buttons Bakelite. 1930s. Small spheres have push buttons protruding from the tops. The spheres come in identical colors, while the push buttons contrast. Olive green marbleized Bakelite spheres have one green and one black top. $35.00–30.00

Glass and Bakelite Spheres Glass and Bakelite. 1930s. Lower semispheres of brushed glass have upper semispheres in Bakelite in a pale green color. $30.00–35.00

Long Bullets Bakelite. 1930s. Long, bullet-shaped shakers have small caps with a ridged band. These come in many colors, usually with contrasting caps. $20.00–25.00

Semi-Cylinders Bakelite. 1930s. When placed together along their flat sides, these two shakers make up a cylinder. Each half has a protruding cap with five holes. The pepper cap comes in a color contrasting with the dominant color of the pair. $25.00–30.00

LUCITE

Lucite Block with Rose Lucite. Clear Lucite block resting on rectangular base has a red rose embedded in the center between the routed-out cylinders for salt and pepper. $12.00–16.00

Trylon and Perisphere Bakelite. Late 1930s. The trylon and perisphere emblems of the 1939 World's Fair ("World of Tomorrow") rests on a teardrop-shaped base. This shaker is found in a variety of color combinations and is highly desirable. $40.00–50.00

Double Domes on Tray Bakelite. 1930s. Elongated double domes nestle tightly into the circular holes of an oval white base. A semicircular strip of Bakelite joins the tops of the shakers and is anchored, at each side, by a plug-like cap. The condiment holes are formed by two sets of triple lines on each shaker. This set is found in blue with white base and trim, as well as in red. $25.00–35.00

Lucite Block Lucite. A plain block of Lucite holds two cylindrical columns bisected at three vertical points by horizontal planes. $12.00–16.00

Red Spheres on Base Bakelite. 1930s. Bright red spheres are affixed to a black, rectangular base. $20.00–24.00

Lucite Columns Lucite. Cylinders of clear Lucite are intersected by five square planes at regular intervals. $24.00–30.00

Lucite Block with Colored Cylinders Lucite. A rectangular block of clear Lucite is anchored to a black, rectangular base. The salt and pepper cylinders, routed out of the block of Lucite, are tinted red or black and clearly visible. $20.00–24.00

Elongated Bullet Bakelite. 1930s. Elongated bullet shapes rise in three gradually tapering tiers from a wide base. The cap is ziggurat-shaped. This design is available in the entire range of Bakelite colors, including marbelized patterns. $24.00–30.00

Squat Bullets Bakelite and plastic. Squat bullets with Bakelite tops and bottoms and plastic bodies come in a range of colors, including red and blue. $24.00–30.00

Lucite Block Lucite. Plain, rectangular, Lucite block is taller than it is wide and reveals two frosted cylindrical openings along its height. $20.00–24.00

Double Deco Mechanical Columns Carvanite. U.S.A. 1930s. This single-piece shaker consists of two tapered cylinders rising from a rectangular, double-stepped base. The cylinders are connected along their height by a three-tiered, Bakelite membrane. They are capped with tops in the shape of a cross, stepping up in increasing narrow steps to a flat top. The tops are depressed to activate the release mechanims that dispense the salt and pepper. This beautiful shaker can be found in a variety of colors, either in solids or with the base and top in a color contrasting with the body. $30.00–40.00

Lucite Stars Lucite. Three-dimensional star-shaped shakers have multiple facets. $24.00–30.00

Lucite Earrings Lucite. Dangling earrings are fashioned from a block of transparent Lucite into which two channels have been carved to hold salt and pepper, and a kelly-green "border" piece of Lucite at the top. These are from Helene Guarnaccia collection. $35.00–50.00

Red Lucite Cubes Lucite. Bright red Lucite cubes rest on bases that are slightly larger than the body of the shaker. $20.00–25.00

Push-Button Tops Bakelite. 1930s. Cylindrical shakers rest on double-stepped back, circular bases. Two-thirds up the sides of the shats, the shakers begin a three-step set back. The push-button mechanism is inserted into the very top. The letters "S" and "P" are inscribed on the buttons. This shape was available in a wide range of colors. $25.00–30.00

CHALKWARE

Sumo Wrestlers Chalkware. U.S.A. 1920s–1950s. Pale pink Sumo wrestlers with baby faces and topknots sit naked on chairs. $10.00–12.00

Pig Heads Chalkware. U.S.A. 1920s. Round white pig's heads wear little red hats and have red snouts. $14.00–20.00

Tanks Chalkware. U.S.A. 1920s–1950s. Olive-drab-colored tanks are crudely detailed. $10.00–12.00

Radio Sets Chalkware. U.S.A. 1920s–1950s. Brown "Deco" radio sets have two black knobs. $10.00–14.00

Suitcases Chalkware. U.S.A. 1920s–1950s. Orange suitcases with double black bands are festooned with multicolored labels. $10.00–14.00

Liberty Bell Chalkware. U.S.A. 1920s–1950s. White replicas of the Liberty Bell are topped by red, white, and blue crowns. The word "Liberty" appears directly above the crack. $10.00–14.00

Log Cabins Chalkware. U.S.A. 1920s–1950s. Brown log cabins with textured roofs and sides have bright red chimney rising from off center. $8.00–12.00

Gold Miners Chalkware. U.S.A. 1920s–1950s. Gold miners in black boots crouch low, holding goldpanning pan in their hands. One wears blue jacket, the other, brown, but both are in orange hats. $10.00–14.00

Sheaves of Wheat Chalkware. U.S.A. 1920s–1950s. Identical sheaves of wheat, tied just before the ears of grain, are colored bright yellow. $6.00–10.00

Little Orphan Annie and Sandy the Dog Chalkware. U.S.A. Late 1930s–early 1940s. Dressed in yellow with matching, curly hair, Little Orphan Annie is in a kneeling position. Her brown dog Sandy has a yellow snout and paws. $40.00–50.00

Hula Dancers Chalkware. U.S.A. 1940s. Identical yellow hula dancers with upraised arms have long, black, flowing hair. $10.00–12.00

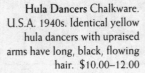

Log Cabin with Green Roof Chalkware. U.S.A. 1920s–1950s. Brown log cabins with green roofs have red chimneys on the side opposite the window. $8.00–12.00

Indian Braves Chalkware. U.S.A. 1920s–1950s. The naked torso of one brown Indian brave emerges from a bright yellow wrap. The other brave is shrouded to mid-chest. Both are sitting. $8.00–10.00

Teepees Chalkware. U.S.A. 1920s–1950s. White teepees with characteristic hieroglyphs have red and blue markings. Tent flaps are red for pepper, and blue for salt. $8.00–12.00

Tom-Tom Drums Chalkware. U.S.A. 1920s–1950s. Matching pair of tom-tom drums are beige with white "skin" tops marked with black lines. $8.00–12.00

Conestoga Wagons Chalkware. U.S.A. 1920s–1950s. Brown Conestoga wagons with white tops sit on green bases textured to resemble grass. $8.00–12.00

Barrel Cactus in Pot Chalkware. U.S.A. 1920s–1950s. Dark green barrel cacti emerge from plain yellow pots. $6.00–8.00

Acorns with Oak Leaves Chalkware. U.S.A. 1920s–1950s. Brown acorns sit on caps to the sides of which yellow oak leaves are attached. $6.00–8.00

Devil Chalkware, U.S.A. 1940s. Red devils with black, pointed ears and "V"-shaped eyebrows sit in red capes. $10.00–12.00

Kilroy Chalkware. U.S.A. 1940s. Out of the tops of brown barrels emerge identical heads of Kilroy, who clutches the rim with both hands. $25.00–30.00

Banana Bunches Chalkware. U.S.A. 1920s–1950s. Vertical bunches of yellow bananas have black stems and bases and are three and a half bananas high. $6.00–8.00

Black Seguaro Cacti Chalkware. U.S.A. 1920s–1950s. Black Seguaro cacti with gold highlights stand on bases. On one is inscribed "Prewitt," on the other "New Mexico." $6.00–8.00

T-Bone Steaks Chalkware. U.S.A. 1920s–1950s. Red T-bone steaks have white fat. $6.00–10.00

Corn Cobs Chalkware. U.S.A. 1920s–1950s. Yellow ears of corn sit on their green, leafy bases. $6.00–10.00

Idaho Potatoes Chalkware. U.S.A. 1920s–1950s. Bright brown potatoes have dimpled surfaces. $6.00–10.00

Rolls of Toilet Paper Chalkware. U.S.A. 1920s–1950s. White rolls of toilet paper, shading to yellow on the top, are inscribed with the motto "For toilet use only—the Wipewell Co." $8.00–12.00

His and Hers Outhouses Chalkware. U.S.A. 1920s–1950s. Brown, wood-grained outhouses have different colored roofs. "Hers" has black roof, "His" has red roof. $6.00–10.00

Bowls of Fruit Chalkware. U.S.A. 1920s–1950s. Blue and white bowls are heaped with red and yellow fruit. $6.00–10.00

Swiss Cheese Chalkware. U.S.A. 1920s–1950s. Wedges of white Swiss cheese have typical holes. $6.00–10.00

Blue Jays Chalkware. U.S.A. 1920s–1950s. Solid blue blue jays have solemn expressions. $8.00–12.00

Rooster and Hen Chalkware. U.S.A. 1920s–1950s. Burnt-orange rooster with yellow beak and red comb scolds fat hen. $8.00–12.00

Turtle Doves Chalkware. U.S.A. 1920s–1950s. White turtle doves with orange beaks perch atop conical bases. Salt has orange base, Pepper has brown base. $8.00–12.00

White Rooster and Hen Chalkware. U.S.A. 1920s–1950s. White chicken and rooster in identical poses (heads in line with the body) have bright yellow beaks and red combs. $8.00–12.00

Bears with Beehives Chalkware. U.S.A. 1920s–1950s. Black baby bears clamber up the sides of a silver hive, at the top of which a yellow bee sits in wait. $10.00–14.00

Musical Bear Chalkware. U.S.A. 1920s–1950s. Little brown bears play musical instruments. One strums a guitar, the other pulls on an accordion. $10.00–14.00

Bears on Tree Stumps Chalkware. U.S.A. 1920s–1950s. One brown bear and one black bear embrace tree stumps. $10.00–14.00

Sitting Bears Chalkware. U.S.A. 1920s–1950s. Little brown bears sit cross-legged. $10.00–14.00

Begging Monkeys Chalkware. U.S.A. 1920s–1950s. Little brown monkeys in blue caps hold silver cups in their hands and grin from ear to ear. $10.00–14.00

Silver Cannon Chalkware, U.S.A. 1940s. The silver cannon reflects the military theme in shakers prevalent during the war years. $15.00–18.00

Owls Chalkware. U.S.A. 1920s–1950s. White owls with huge heads stare from tremendous eyes ringed with orange, black, and white. $8.00–12.00

Pelicans Chalkware. U.S.A. 1920s–1950s. Stylized pelicans, one orange and one yellow, look out of black beady eyes. $8.00–12.00

Teapot and Coffeepot Chalkware. U.S.A. 1920s–1950s. Cream-colored teapot is teamed with coffeepot. Both have repeating circle borders. $6.00–10.00

Angry Hydrant and Sad Dog Chalkware. U.S.A. 1920s–1950s. A frowning red hydrant is accompanied by a despairing brown hound dog who rests his elbows on the ground and covers his eyes with his paws. $10.00–14.00

Begging Scotties Chalkware. U.S.A. 1920s–1950s. A white and a black Scottie dog sit up and beg. $10.00–14.00

Green Hydrants with Black Pups Chalkware. U.S.A. 1920s–1950s. A white Yorkie-type dog raises a hind paw on a red fire hydrant. $10.00–14.00

White Dog with Fire Hydrant Chalkware. U.S.A. 1920s–1950s. A white Yorkie-type dog raises a hind paw on a red fire hydrant. $10.00–14.00

Puppies in Shoes Chalkware. U.S.A. 1920s–1950s. Tan puppies emerge from the tops of tan, lace-up shoes. $10.00–14.00

Bunny Couple Chalkware. U.S.A. 1920s–1950s. Tan, floppy-eared bunnies flirt. He wears a red beret, she wears white wreath. $10.00–14.00

Cat in Hat Chalkware. U.S.A. 1920s–1950s. White pussy cat pops out of black top hat. $10.00–14.00

Dog Meeting Own Tail Around Tree Stump Chalkware. U.S.A. 1940s. A dog is wrapped around a tree stump smelling its own tail. On the stump is written, "I thought I knew all the dogs in town." One figurine is yellow, the other is red. $20.00–24.00

Rattlesnake Chalkware. U.S.A. 1940s. Realistic-looking rattlesnakes are coiled around a green stump. $14.00–18.00

Rocking Horses Chalkware. U.S.A. 1920s–1950s. White rocking horses have either red mane and green rocker or green mane and red rocker. $10.00–14.00

Braying Donkey Chalkware. U.S.A. 1920s–1950s. Gray sitting donkeys have orange faces and bray, exposing white teeth. $10.00–14.00

Wooly Lambs Chalkware. U.S.A. 1920s–1950s. Identical white wooly lambs have black eyes. $10.00–14.00

Horses Chalkware. U.S.A. 1920s–1950s. Tan horses stand on grass bases. $10.00–14.00

Flowered Pigs Chalkware. U.S.A. 1920s–1950s. Pink pigs have red and green flowers on their backs. $10.00–14.00

Yellow Elephants Chalkware. U.S.A. 1920s–1950s. Small yellow elephants with black feet throw up their trunks. $10.00–14.00

Skunks Chalkware. U.S.A. 1920s–1950s. Black and white skunks stand on brown bases. $10.00–14.00

Squirrels with Stumps Chalkware. U.S.A. 1920s–1950s. Orange, realistic squirrels embrace tree stumps. $10.00–14.00

Buffalo Chalkware. U.S.A. 1920s–1950s. Dark brown buffalo have massive bodies and lowered heads. $10.00–14.00

Snakes on Rocks Chalkware. U.S.A. 1920s–1950s. A snake is coiled atop a cylindrical rock. Salt has black snake on yellow rock, pepper has brown snake on green rock. $10.00–14.00

Squirrels Chalkware. U.S.A. 1920s–1950s. Dark brown squirrels in "begging" position stand on brown base. $10.00–14.00

Bunnies Chalkware. U.S.A. 1920s–1950s. White bunnies with pink whiskers and ears sit on their haunches. $10.00–14.00

Dick Tracy and Junior Chalkware. U.S.A. Late 1930s–early 1940s. A yellow-raincoated and hatted Dick Tracy is flanked by an orange suited and crouching Junior. $40.00–50.00

Snuffy Smith and Barney Google Chalkware. U.S.A. Late 1930s–early 1940s. Barney Google and Snuffy Smith from Billy DeBeck's cartoon strip are shown in their characteristic costume. $40.00–50.00

Moon Mullins and Kayo Chalkware. U.S.A. 1940s. Cartoon strip characters Moon Mullins and Kayo are faithfully rendered. $40.00–50.00

Cap'n Midnite and Joyce Chalkware. U.S.A. 1940s. Joyce, in a yellow dress, is teamed with Cap'n Midnite in brown. $40.00–50.00

Panda and Brown Bear Chalkware. U.S.A. 1920s–1950s. A brown bear is teamed with a black and white panda bear. Both sit and hold out their paws. $25.00–30.00

Bears with Tree Stump Chalkware. U.S.A. 1920s–1950s. This three-piece set consists of a base textured to resemble a leafy forest floor, from the middle of which rises a brown stump. On either side of the stump sits a small black bear. $30.00–40.00

Polar Bears Chalkware. U.S.A. 1920s–1950s. White polar bears with black paws and ear tips sit with arms outstretched. $25.00–30.00

Squirrels Chalkware. U.S.A. 1920s–1950s. Bright brown squirrels stand on all fours and look curiously to the side. $20.00–24.00

Crouching Cats Chalkware. U.S.A. 1930s. Crouching cats with erect tails and "Sphinx" expressions and pose have large, green eyes and Art-Deco-inspired eyebrows. $36.00–40.00

Pig Heads Chalkware. U.S.A. 1920s–1950s. Fat-faced, puffy-cheeked white pig heads rise from white collars. Salt wears blue cap, pepper wears yellow cap. $30.00–35.00

Horse Heads Chalkware. U.S.A. 1920s–1950s. Deep brown, finely crafted horse heads with necks have black flowing manes. $25.00–30.00

Rooster and Hen Chalkware. U.S.A. 1920s–1950s. Small set depicts a rooster with white bosom, brown wings, and prominent red comb with open beak. Hen is smaller and rounder. $20.00–24.00

Geese Preening Chalkware. U.S.A. 1920s–1950s. Beige geese twist their necks and bury their beaks under their left wings to preen. Both stand on bases that are colored green in the case of salt, and brown in the case of pepper.

White Siamese Cat Chalkware. U.S.A. 1920s–1950s. White Siamese cat with black tail, ears, and collar sits with tail curled around back legs. $20.00–24.00

Boxer Dog Chalkware. U.S.A. 1920s–1950s. White sitting boxer has one brown eye, one brown ear, and brown paws. $20.00–24.00

Jiggs and Maggie Chalkware. U.S.A. Late 1930s–early 1940s. Mason Jiggs and his washerwoman wife Maggie from George McManus's **Bringing Up Father**, are shown in their rich, old age. Both are sitting. Maggie holds a white rolling pin on her lap and is ready for action. $40.00–50.00

Freshwater Trout Chalkware. U.S.A. 1930s. Two clusters of red-lipped, silvery-finned trout rise up from their tails. $28.00–30.00

Billy Can't and Billy Can
Chalkware. U.S.A. 1940s. Little, fat Billy sits on the chamber pot with diametrically opposite results. Frowning face and green pot is inscribed "Billy Can't." Smiling face and orange pot is inscribed "Billy can." $35.00–40.00

Yorkshire Terrier Chalkware. U.S.A. 1920s–1950s. Brown Yorkshire terrier has red tongue. $20.00–24.00

Turtle Couple Chalkware. U.S.A. 1920s–1950s. Mr. Turtle grins, wearing a yellow jacket, white trousers, and black shoes. Mrs. Turtle, in pink skirt and yellow-trimmed top, purses her lips. Both are sitting. $24.00–30.00

Mouse with Cheese Chalkware. U.S.A. 1920s–1950s. Gray mouse sits next to a piece of white Swiss cheese. $24.00–30.00

Buffalo Chalkware. U.S.A. 1920s–1950s. Brown buffalo with gray horns are lying down. $20.00–24.00

Captain and Mate Chalkware. U.S.A. 1920s–1950s. Crouching figures of sea captain holding pair of binoculars and red-capped first mate. Both are in blue. $35.00–40.00

Rocking Horse Chalkware. U.S.A. 1920s–1950s. Rocking horses whose legs are of one piece with the base have red or yellow highlights. Pepper is black, and salt is white. $25.00–30.00

Sinking Battleship Chalkware. U.S.A. 1940s. A sinking gray battleship disappears into blue waves painted atop a rectangular base. Salt is inscribed, "U.S.S. Arizona, Dec. 7, 1941" and pepper is inscribed, "Remember Pearl Harbor." $40.00–60.00

Green Tanks Chalkware. U.S.A. 1940s. Green tanks are on black bases. $40.00–60.00

White Angora Cats Chalkware. U.S.A. 1940s. Fluffly white angoras are depicted in sitting position. $20.00–24.00

Calico Cats Chalkware. U.S.A. 1940s. Sitting white calico cats have red stitch marks, blue ribbon, ears, and mouth, and pink and green design. $20.00–24.00

Jack-In-The-Box Chalkware. U.S.A. 1940s. A white-faced clown on an accordion body erupts out of an opened box. Pepper has blue-gray accordion and hatband with red bow and box. Salt has red accordion body, hatband, and box, and blue-gray bow and cuffs. $20.00–24.00

Black Chef and Mammy Chalkware. U.S.A. Early 1930s. Fat, squat Mammy and Chef show off their broad girth. He wears red pants under a white shirt and apron. She is in a red dress with a white apron, and has a red bandanna on her head. $36.00–40.00

Black Boy and Girl Eating Watermelon Chalkware. U.S.A. 1930s. A Black boy and girl each hold up a slice of watermelon to their chins. Both are depicted from the elbows up. She wears a red dress and red bow. He is in black. $50.00–56.00

Pigs Chalkware. U.S.A. 1940s. Identical yellow pigs with black dots extend red tongues from their smiling mouths. $20.00–24.00

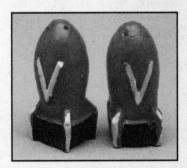

"Victory" Bombs Chalkware. U.S.A. 1940s. V for "victory" bombs in patriotic colors evoke the World War II era. $20.00–24.00

The ⊙NFIDENT ⊙LLECTOR™
KNOWS THE FACTS
Each volume packed with valuable information that no collector can afford to be without

THE OVERSTREET COMIC BOOK PRICE GUIDE, 24th Edition
by Robert M. Overstreet   77854-8/$15.00 US/$17.50 Can

THE OVERSTREET COMIC BOOK GRADING GUIDE, 1st Edition
by Robert M. Overstreet and Gary M. Carter   76910-7/$12.00 US/$15.00 Can

• • •

FINE ART
Indentification and Price Guide, 2nd Edition
by Susan Theran   76924-7/$20.00 US/ $24.00 Can

BOTTLES
Identification and Price Guide, 1st Edition
by Michael Polak   77218-3/$15.00 US/$18.00 Can

ORIGINAL COMIC ART
Identification and Price Guide, 1st Edition
by Jerry Weist   76965-4/$15.00 US/$18.00 Can

COLLECTIBLE MAGAZINES
Identification and Price Guide, 1st Edition
by David K. Henkel   76926-3/$15.00 US/$17.50 Can

COSTUME JEWELRY
Identification and Price Guide, 2nd Edition
by Harrice Simons Miller   77078-4/$15.00 US/$18.00 Can